THE ENCYCLOPAEDIA OF ASSOCIATION FOOTBALL

Other Encylopaedias published by Robert Hale and Company

The Encyclopaedia of
ASSOCIATION FOOTBALL

Compiled by
MAURICE GOLESWORTHY

Foreword by
SIR STANLEY ROUS, C.B.E.

TENTH EDITION

LONDON
ROBERT HALE & COMPANY
63 Old Brompton Road, S.W.7

First edition November 1956

Second edition January 1957

Third edition February 1958
Reprinted June 1958

Fourth edition November 1959

Fifth edition October 1961

Sixth edition (*completely re-written and reset*) 1963

Seventh edition October 1965

Eighth edition November 1967

Ninth edition November 1969

Tenth edition November 1970

ISBN 0 7091 1874 0

PRINTED IN GREAT BRITAIN BY
BRISTOL TYPESETTING CO. LTD.
BARTON MANOR - ST. PHILIPS
BRISTOL

FOREWORD

by

SIR STANLEY ROUS, C.B.E.
President of F.I.F.A.

For more than a century, Association Football has been played and has prospered in an organised regulated manner. It was formed and moulded in the first place by the British and they have had a distinctive part to play in its history and evolution. The credit for the development of what has now become a truly international sport is due to many men—to the brilliant players who, over the years, have excited the emotions of the public and drawn them to the artistry of the game; to the referees who have married justice and discipline and common sense on the field of play; to the teachers who have enlightened the young at home and spread the word abroad; to the legislators who have kept football basically a simple game and brought to it a spirit of service without thought of personal reward.

Thus the game, organised in many stirring competitions like the F.A. Cup and the Football League, has a history bristling with facts and achievements, of individuals and clubs and countries which, over such a long time, assumes massive proportions. The first obvious merit of *The Encyclopædia of Association Football* is that it collects this great mass into one compact volume, invaluable for settling quickly and accurately the manifold arguments and discussions which a great game continually throws up!

But as President of F.I.F.A., I am particularly happy to note that since the book was first published in 1956, a great deal more space has been given to records and information concerning the game abroad. One often feels that the days of exploration are long gone, that there is little new to be learned about the world, that football among many other things is established finally in all corners of the earth.

Yet the fact is that there has never been a more exciting time in football as an international game. In recent years, dozens of new countries have been formed, in Africa and Asia. All have clamoured for membership of F.I.F.A. and a place in the international football sun formerly so firmly held by the " older " nations of Europe and

South America. All these new countries need help. They need financial help. They need coaching assistance. They have to be helped organise their game in every possible sense. And they have to be helped play the game in the very best spirit and to take their place in the international brotherhood of football nations above and beyond and apart from any political considerations. This is the present great challenge to F.I.F.A. and it is a responsibility which excites me very much as I travel around the world and see these new nations find their football feet, as it were.

The spread of international television has brought the great occasions of Europe and South America home to our own public. The ever-increasing interest in the World Cup, and the great new European competitions, have added a new dimension to spectating. The spread of fast jet travel has allowed journalists to range ever further to record these things, and the " Encyclopædia " has kept pace with all this in recognising that Santos and Benfica and Milan are no longer remote from Manchester and Birmingham.

I find this volume very useful as a quick, reliable reference book, and I suggest that it should be on every football-lover's library shelf. I commend it to you with pleasure.

INTRODUCTION

In YEARS gone by I often felt the need for a standard reference book of Soccer records for although one's shelves might be crammed with football books it was difficult to find the answer to a particular query at a particular time. Various interesting facts and records had become buried within the pages of so many previous publications amidst a mass of information.

To the best of my knowledge there had never been a book on Association Football which contained all the facts and records of the game arranged for easy reference in alphabetical order.

My experience as a sports writer, newspaper librarian and also as a respondent of readers' questions for a national sports magazine convinced me that the lack of such a reference book was a serious omission, and so, in 1956, I produced the first edition of *The Encyclopaedia of Association Football* with the hope that this would fill that gap on the sportsman's bookshelf.

The grand reception given to this publication surpassed even my expectations and its success has been a great source of satisfaction to me as well as an encouragement to maintain and, I hope, improve the standard of each edition.

The years since the appearance of the first edition have been particularly busy ones in the football world with more changes than in the previous 30 or 40 years.

Apart from changes on the domestic front the greatest development has been in the outlook of the average football fan. No longer is he (or she) interested only in the progress of the game at home for the fast increase in the number of international competitions has broadened the soccer horizon until today names like Real Madrid, Di Stefano, Eusebio, Santos, Pele, Juventus, and Benfica, mean as much among British fans as Arsenal, Tottenham Hotspur, Celtic, Rangers, Bobby Charlton or Dennis Law.

Therefore, since the sixth edition more attention has been paid to football abroad, although as yet, I am still restricting the number of special sections on foreign countries to those that have met the home countries in international matches.

The results of these Internationals are given under each of the foreign countries, but the records of the four home countries which compete in the International Championship are given under the heading Internationals, sub-sections England, Scotland, Ireland and Wales.

Overseas football is not the only aspect of the game that has received greater attention in the compilation of this book, for the latest editions have included more references to Scottish football, more about the foundation of many of the clubs, a longer list of players with the greatest number of first-class appearances or goals to their credit, and at the end of the statistics of each Football League and Scottish League club I have added their record victory and record defeat.

A word here about this last item may save some arguments later. Please note that only games in the Football League, Scottish League, F.A. Cup (Proper), Football League Cup, Scottish F.A. Cup, and the old Southern League (before 1920) have been considered. And for these records 9-3 is, for example, considered a bigger win or defeat than 8-2, 10-2 before 9-0, etc., etc.

The division of the various sections under appropriate headings continues to be something of a problem, but I have done my utmost to overcome this difficulty with liberal cross-references, and just to make sure that no fact is lost you will find that an index has been added which contains all the players, other personalities and clubs mentioned throughout.

In compiling this book the aim for quick and easy reference has been constantly at the back of my mind and I hope that you will find it both interesting and useful.

MAURICE GOLESWORTHY.

Dellwood,
Kenn,
Nr. Exeter, Devon.
August, 1970

ILLUSTRATIONS

ACKNOWLEDGEMENTS

This book is published with special thanks to The Football Association and The Football League for their valuable assistance and for allowing me to include information from their official histories (*The History of The Football Association* and *The Story of The Football League*).

In addition I would like to thank the officials of all other Associations, Leagues and clubs, both at home and abroad, as well as such friends as Roger Macdonald, Morley Farror and Peter King, who provided valuable information.

M.G.

The photographs facing page 49 (top), page 97 (top) and page 112 are reproduced by courtesy of the Football Association. The photographs of Billy Gillespie and Colin Stein are by courtesy of the *Morning Telegraph*, Sheffield, and the *Evening Times*, Glasgow, respectively.

A

ABANDONED

On Nov. 26, 1898, a First Division game between Sheffield Wednesday and Aston Villa was abandoned because of bad light after 79½ min. play. Sheffield Wednesday were leading 3—1. The remaining 10½ min. were played on Mar. 13, 1899, during which time Sheffield Wednesday scored a further goal. The final result was officially recorded as 4—1.

Today, according to the rules of the Football League and most other Leagues, a match which is not completed must be replayed IN FULL, or the score at the time of abandonment taken as the final result. The choice—in the case of the Football League—rests entirely with the League Management Committee.

The Football League ordered the result to stand after Barrow v. Gillingham, Division IV game, Oct. 9, 1961, abandoned 15 min. before time, owing to bad light. The game had started late after Gillingham had missed a train and chartered a plane to fly up. The result at time of abandonment was Barrow 7, Gillingham 0.

In Feb. 1904 a Second Round F.A. Cup tie at Tottenham had to be abandoned at half-time when Aston Villa were leading 1—0 because the crowd invaded the pitch and it was found impossible to clear them off. The F.A. ordered the tie to be re-played at Villa Park but Tottenham won 1—0.

The First Division game between Middlesbrough and Oldham Athletic, on April 3, 1915, was abandoned after 55 min. when Oldham's left-back, W. Cook, refused to leave the field when ordered off by the referee.

Middlesbrough were leading 4—1 and the Football League ordered the result to stand. Cook was suspended for 12 months. Oldham missed the League Championship by two points that season.

The F.A. Cup Semi-final between Sheffield United and Liverpool, at Fallowfield, Manchester, in 1899, was abandoned at half-time because the crowd had encroached on to the pitch. Prior to the interval the game had been interrupted while police forced the crowd back beyond the touchlines.

The Scotland v. Austria International at Hampden Park, May 8, 1963, was abandoned 9 min. before full-time after persistent fouling and two players sent off.

ABERDEEN F.C.

Founded 1903. Joined Scottish League, Division II, 1904, Division I, 1905. Honours: Champions, Division A, 1954-5. Runners-up (I), 1910-11, 1936-7. Scottish Cup: Winners, 1947, 1970. Finalists, 1937, 1953, 1954, 1959, 1967. Record attendance: 46,061 v. Hearts, Scottish Cup, 4th Round, Mar. 13, 1954. Address: Pittodrie Stadium, Aberdeen (Tel. 21428). Nickname: Dons. Colours: Scarlet shirts, white shorts. Record League goalscorer: B. Yorston, 38 goals, Division I, 1929-30. Record victory: 13—0 v. Peterhead, Feb. 9, 1923. Record defeat: 9—2 v. Dundee, April 17, 1909.

ADMISSION CHARGES
FOOTBALL LEAGUE

1919-20: Minimum charge raised from 6d. to 1s.

1942-3: Minimum charge raised from 1s. to 1s. 3d. (1s. 6d. in the League South).

1951-2: Minimum charge raised from 1s. 3d. to 1s. 6d.

Subsequent increases: 1952-3, 1s. 6d.; 1955-6, 2s.; 1960-61, 2s. 6d.; 1965-6, 4s.; 1968-9, 5s.; 1970-71, 6s.

AGE
Oldest (Football League)

The oldest player ever to appear in the Football League is N. McBain. At the age of 52 years 4 months, he played in goal for New Brighton v.

Hartlepools United, Mar. 15, 1947.

R. Suter is the oldest Englishman ever to appear in the Football League. Born in July, 1878, he last played in goal for Halifax Town v. Darlington, April 24, 1929. He was 50 years 9 months old.

G. Shenton was 36 years old when he made his Football League debut for Port Vale v. Barnsley, Division II, Nov. 17, 1928.

A. Cunningham was 38 years 2 days old when he made his Football League debut for Newcastle United v. Leicester City, Division I, Feb. 2, 1929.

Oldest (F.A. Cup)

W. Meredith is the oldest player ever to appear in the F.A. Cup competition proper. He was 49 years 8 months when he played for Manchester City v. Newcastle United, semi-finals, Mar. 29, 1924.

Oldest (Internationals)

The oldest player to make his debut in the International Championship is L. Compton. He was 38 years 2 months when he played centre-half for England v. Wales, Nov. 15, 1950.

The oldest player to appear in the International Championship is W. Meredith. He was nearly 46 when he played for Wales v. England, Mar. 15, 1920.

Youngest Player (Football League)

The youngest player ever to appear in the Football League is A. Geldard, for Bradford v. Millwall, Division II, Sept. 16, 1929. He was 15 years 156 days old. C. C. Buchanan is often mentioned as the youngest Football League debutant. He made his League debut for Wolverhampton Wanderers v. West Bromwich Albion, Sept. 26, 1942, at the age of 14. However, this distinction cannot be recognised as it occurred during the war.

Next to Geldard is K. Roberts, 15 years 158 days when making his League debut for Wrexham v. Bradford, Division III(N), Sept. 1, 1951.

The youngest ever to appear in Division I is D. Forster, who kept goal for Sunderland v. Leicester City, Aug. 22, 1964, 15 years 185 days.

R. Parry played in Division I for Bolton Wanderers v. Wolverhampton Wanderers, Oct. 13, 1951, when 15 years 207 days old.

R. Stockhill was 15 years 280 days when making his League debut in Division III(N) for York City, at Wigan, Aug. 31, 1929.

The youngest goal scorer in the Football League is R. Dix, 15 years 180 days, for Bristol Rovers v. Norwich City, Division III(S), Mar. 3, 1928. He had made his League debut 7 days earlier v. Charlton Athletic.

Youngest Player (F.A. Cup)

A. Jeffrey appeared for Doncaster Rovers v. Aston Villa on his 16th birthday, F.A. Cup, 4th Round, Jan. 29, 1955.

The youngest to appear in the Final—H. Kendall, 17 years 345 days, for Preston North End v. West Ham United, May 2, 1964

Youngest Player (Scottish League)

A. Edwards, aged 16 years and 5 days, is the youngest player to appear in First Division of the Scottish League—Dunfermline v. Hibernian, Mar. 19, 1962. Here again there may be argument for goalkeeper, R. Simpson, played for Queen's Park at the age of 14 during the war.

Youngest (Internationals)

The youngest players ever to appear in the International Championship are:

England—D. Edwards, Manchester United, 18 years 6 months, left-half v. Scotland, April 2, 1955. A. Brown, Sheffield United, 18 years 10 months, centre-forward, v. Wales, Feb. 29, 1904.

Ireland—W. K. Gibson, Cliftonville, 17 years, v. Wales, Feb. 24, 1894. N. Kernoghan, Belfast Celtic, 17 years, 3 months, outside-right, v. Wales, Mar. 11, 1936. J. Nicholson, Manchester United, 17 years, 8 months, inside-left, v. Scotland, Nov. 9, 1960.

Scotland—D. Law, Huddersfield Town, 18 years 7 months, v. Wales, Oct. 18, 1958

Wales—J. Charles, Leeds United, 18 years 3 months, centre half-back, v. Ireland, Mar. 8, 1950.

The youngest internationals among foreign countries include: G. Dorval,

15, outside-right for Brazil, v. Argentine, 1957. A. R. Nascimento (Pele), 16 years 9 months, inside-left for Brazil v. Argentine, July 1957. F. Brichant, 16, Belgium v. England (Amateurs), Feb. 24, 1914. A. Bickel (Grasshoppers), 16, Switzerland, 1935.

Youngest (Inter-League)

N. Kernoghan, Belfast Celtic, was the youngest player ever to play in an inter-League match. He appeared for the Irish League v. The Football League, Sept. 25, 1935, aged 16 years 9 months.

AIRDRIEONIANS F.C.

Founded 1878. Promoted to Scottish League, Division I, 1903. Honours: Runners-up, Division I, 1922-3, 1923-4, 1924-5, 1925-6. Champions, Division II, 1902-3. (B) 1954-5. Runners-up, 1965-6. Scottish Cup: Winners, 1924. Record attendance: 26,500 v. Hearts, Scottish Cup, 4th Round, Mar. 9, 1952. Address: Broomfield Park, Airdrie (Tel. Airdrie 2067). Colours: White, with red diamond, red shorts. Record goal-scorer in Division I: H. G. Yarnall, 45 goals, 1916-17. Record victory: 11—1 v. Falkirk, Division A, 1950-51. Record defeat 11—1 v. Hibernian (H.), Division I, 1959-60.

ALBANIA

The Albanian F.A. was formed in 1932 but for many years they remained comparatively isolated from the international scene and it was not until 1965 that Albania met any of the home countries. Then they were grouped with Ireland in the World Cup Qualifying Competition. Results: Ireland 4, Albania 1, at Belfast, May 7, 1965. Albania 1, Ireland 1, at Tirana, Nov. 24, 1965.

ALDERSHOT F.C.

Founded 1927. Joined Football League, Division III(S), 1932. Best in Division III(S), 10th, 1938-9. Record attendance: 19,183 v. Carlisle United, F.A. Cup, 4th Round (replay), Jan. 28, 1970. Address: Recreation Ground, Aldershot (Tel. 20211). Nickname: Shots or Soldiers. Colours: Red shirts with blue numbers, red shorts. Record League goal-scorer: R. Howfield, 23 goals, Division IV, 1961-2. Record victory: 8—1 v.

Gateshead, Division IV, 1958-9. Record defeat: 9—0 v. Bristol City, Division III(S), Dec. 28, 1946.

AMATEUR FOOTBALL ALLIANCE

With the rapid increase in professionalism throughout the country in the early years of this century many of the old amateur clubs felt that they were not getting the same consideration and attention from the Football Association. This feeling grew until, in 1907, the true amateurs of the "old school" decided that the time had come for them to break away from the F.A. to form an amateur association of their own.

Accordingly, a meeting was called at the Holborn Restaurant at which the following resolution was adopted: "It is essential for the good of the game of Association football as played by amateurs that an Amateur Football Association be formed."

Clubs represented at this meeting included Cambridge University, Clapham Rovers, Corinthians, Old Carthusians, Old Etonians, Old Westminsters and the Swifts.

Many other amateur clubs, big and small, decided to accept the new Association as their governing body in preference to the F.A. The "split" continued until 1914 when representatives of both Associations got together and the amateurs decided once again to recognise the F.A. as being the governing body of the game in England.

The Amateur Football Association, however, still continued with some measure of independence.

Eventually, in May, 1934, the title was changed to the AMATEUR FOOT-BALL ALLIANCE, and representation was secured on the International Selection Committee of the F.A. and the Amateur Cup Committee.

The amateurs introduced a Senior Cup competition of their own in 1907 with a trophy presented by the Corinthians. This should not be confused with the much older Amateur Cup Competition instituted by the F.A.

Today, as always, the members of the A.F.A. are mainly composed of clubs from London Insurance and Banking offices, Government Departments, Public Schools, Old Boys' clubs, Hospitals, Southern Amateur League clubs, and, of course, Oxford and Cambridge Universities, numbering in all some 350 to 400 clubs, competing in something like 40 League and Cup competitions.

AMATEUR FOOTBALL (GENERAL)

Here in chronological order are the oldest of the principal amateur clubs in this country:

Sheffield 1856, Henley Town 1862, Hallam 1862, Civil Service (Chiswick) 1863, Hitchin Town 1865, Maidenhead United 1869, Southall 1871, Old Wykehamist 1875, Bournemouth 1875, Old Foresters 1876, Polytechnic 1876, Guildford 1877, Harwich and Parkeston 1877, Harlow Town 1879, Barking 1880, Ilford 1881, Liverpool Ramblers 1882, Guy's Hospital 1882, Hoddesdon Town 1883, Warminster Town 1883, Sandown 1883, Finchley 1884, Hounslow Town 1884, Bishop Auckland 1884, St. Mary's Hospital 1884.

AMATEURS (F.A. Cup)

Only three amateurs have gained F.A. Cup winners medals this century:

S. B. Ashworth, left-half, Manchester City, 1904; H. P. Hardman, outside-left, Everton, 1906; Rev. K. R. G. Hunt, right-half, Wolverhampton Wanderers, 1908.

In the same period the following amateurs have appeared in an F.A. Cup Final on the losing side:

C. B. Fry, r.b.; A. Turner, o.r., and J. Turner, o.l., Southampton, 1902. D. Davies, g., Bolton Wanderers, 1904. H. P. Hardman, o.l., Everton, 1907 (also a winners medal 1906). J. F. Mitchell, g., Preston North End, 1922. Dr. V. E. Milne, c.h., Aston Villa, 1924. A. Turner, c.f., Charlton Athletic, 1946. F. P. Kippax, o.l., Burnley, 1947. W. J. Slater, i.l., Blackpool, 1951.

AMATEURS (FOOTBALL LEAGUE)

The greatest number of amateurs to appear in a Football League team since normal football was resumed in 1946 is three—B. Joy, K. O'Flanagan and A. Gudmundsson for Arsenal v. Stoke City, Oct. 19, 1946.

Amateurs have almost disappeared from the Football League since World War II and, comparatively speaking, the number of amateurs who have appeared regularly in this competition since World War I is small. An attempt has been made below to list the principal amateurs who have played more than a dozen games in the Football League in peace-time since the competition re-commenced in 1919.

J. C. Burns, l.h., 263 appearances, Queen's Park Rangers, Brentford, 1927-36; W. V. Gibbins, c.f. or i.f., 176, West Ham United, Brentford, Bristol Rovers, Southampton, 1923-34; G. H. Armitage, c.h.b., 165, Charlton Athletic, 1923-30; W. I. Bryant, c.h.b., 131, Millwall, 1925-31; J. F. Mitchell, g., 120, Preston North End, Manchester City, 1920-26; Dr. V. E. Milne, c.h.b., 133, Aston Villa, 1924-9 (had previously played as a professional with Aberdeen and Aston Villa); H. L. Coates, i.l., 101, Southampton, 1928-34; B. H. Baker, g., 95, Everton, Chelsea, Oldham Athletic, 1920-29; M. Woosnam, c.h.b., 89, Manchester City, 1919-25; B. Joy, c.h.b., 87, Fulham, Arsenal, 1933-47; M. J. Pinner, g., 89, Aston Villa, Sheffield Wednesday, Queen's Park Rangers, Manchester United, Chelsea, Swansea Town, Leyton Orient, 1959-63; W. J. Slater, r.h.b., 81, Blackpool, Brentford, Wolverhampton Wanderers, 1949-54; J. R. Roxburgh, f., 80, Leicester City, Aston Villa, Sheffield United, 1920-27; G. J. Bromilow, c.f., 79, Southport, 1955-8; Dr. J. A. Paterson, o.r., 70, Arsenal, 1920-26; A. E. Knight, f.b., 69, Portsmouth, 1919-22; W. H. Fitchford, f., 69, Port Vale, 1919-23; C. T. Mortimore, c.f., 66, Aldershot, 1949-53; J. E. Beswick, h.b., 58, Stoke City, 1921-7; R. Boreham, i.r., 51, Arsenal, 1921-4; M. Edelston, i.r., 51, Brentford, Reading, 1937-47; H. J. McIlvenny, c.f., 43, Bradford, 1946-50; P. Thompson, c.f., 42, Wrexham, 1955-7; A. H. Gibbons, c.f., 39, Tottenham Hotspur, 1937-9; F. P. Kippax, o.l., 31, Burnley, Liverpool, 1946-9; G. P. Keizer, g., 29, Arsenal, Charlton Athletic, 1930-32; N. Middlehoe, h.b., 28, Chelsea, 1919-23; M. Costello, c.f., 28, Aldershot, 1956-7; C. W. Harbidge, h.b., 25, Reading, Charton Athletic, 1920-22; J. Brennan, h.b., 23, Manchester City, 1919-22; W. Holmes, c.f., 23, Doncaster Rovers, Blackburn Rovers,

14

1950-53; H. P. Evans, r.h.b., 23, Cardiff City, 1920-22; G. H. Smithies, c.f., 21, Preston North End, Birmingham, 1929-31; A Roxburgh, f., 19, Leicester City 1920-22; W. W. Parr, o.r., 18, Blackpool, 1935-9; S. C. P. O'Connell, i.l., 16, Chelsea, 1954-6; W. Steffen, l.b., 15, Chelsea, 1946-7; J. Surtees, f., 14, Durham City, 1921-3; Rev. H. Davies, f., 14, Wrexham, 1924-8; Dr. K. O'Flanagan, o.r., 14, Arsenal, 1946-7; J. Nicholls, i.r., 13, Newport County, Cardiff City, 1923-5.

A few of the above players subsequently turned professional, but for the most part, such men have been ignored when compiling this list, and in any case, the number of appearances given are amateur only.

The record for the longest period a player appeared as an amateur before turning professional with the same Football League club is held by R. Hawkes. He played for Luton Town, usually as a left-half, for 10 seasons before signing professional forms at the start of season 1911-12.

H. S. Stapley, an amateur centre-forward, was Glossop's principal goal-scorer in Division II for four seasons 1908-12. This is a Football League record for the greatest number of consecutive seasons that an amateur has headed a club's scoring list. During those four seasons Stapley scored 67 goals in 135 appearances.

The only amateurs to head their side's scoring list in the Football League for any season since World War I are W. V. Gibbins, 18 goals for West Ham United, Division I, 1930-31; C. F. Mortimore, 15 goals for Aldershot, Division III(S), 1949-50; G. Bromilow, 22 goals for Southport, Division III(N), 1955-6, and 8 in 1956-7.

The first amateur club to seek admission to the Football League were the Argonauts. Formed in 1928, they immediately applied for membership of Division III(S). They came third in a poll of six clubs. Only two being elected. The Argonauts tried again in 1929 when again they were third. In the 1930 election—their last attempt —they polled no votes. In the hope that they would gain admission to the League they had provisionally booked Wembley Stadium as their home ground.

AMATEURS (INTERNATIONALS)

The last amateur to appear in an English international XI with professionals was B. Joy who played centre-half v. Scotland, Oct. 14, 1944. Being a war-time game this is not included among the full internationals.

In a full peace-time International Championship game the last amateur to appear for England was A. G. Bower of the Corinthians. He made the last of his five appearances for England at right-back v. Wales, Feb. 12, 1927. Bower captained England in that game.

APPEARANCES (League)
Consecutive

The record for the number of consecutive appearances in the Football League is held by H. Bell, Tranmere Rovers' centre-half. From the opening of the 1946-7 season Bell did not miss a match until he was dropped for the visit of Gateshead, Aug. 30, 1955—a total of 401 consecutive Division III(N) appearances. Altogether, Bell's appearances totalled 459 for he also played in 26 F.A. Cup, 22 Liverpool Senior Cup, and 10 Cheshire Bowl games.

In the Argentine goalkeeper J. Saldumnere made 412 consecutive appearances for Racing Mar-del-Plata before he broke a leg. This run was spread over 18 years.

Returning to the Football League the runner-up to Bell is R. Powell who made 284 consecutive League appearances in goal for Chesterfield, 1952-8. Plymouth Argyle full-back, P. Jones, made 279 consecutive League appearances from April, 1947 to Nov. 7, 1953, when he was forced to drop out of the side with an ankle injury.

J. Trollope made 368 consecutive appearances for Swindon Town, Apr. 3, 1961 to Aug. 24, 1968 inclusive. 324 Football League, 25 F.A. Cup, and 19 Football League Cup.

R. Middleton made 277 consecutive Football League appearances with Chesterfield and Derby County, although if one includes war-time Football League (N) 1945-6 season's appearances then Middleton's run totalled 319, for it began in that season. Then followed 210 consecutive peace-time League games for Chesterfield before he was transferred to Derby County in June 1951. There he added another 67 consecutive appearances before being dropped from their side on Jan. 17, 1953.

R. McKinlay, Nottingham Forest, centre-half made 265 consecutive Football League appearances from April 1959 to October 1965.

A. Ingham, Queen's Park Rangers, full-back, 249 consecutive appearances, 1956-61.

E. Ditchburn, made 247 consecutive Football League appearances in goal for Tottenham Hotspur from April 1948 until Mar. 1954.

General

A. McNamara appeared in all four divisions of the Football League inside a period of 12 months. He made his last appearance for Everton (Division I), Oct. 12, 1957, and his debut for Bury (Division III) Sept. 27, 1958. Between these dates he played for Liverpool (Division II) and for Crewe Alexandra (Division IV).

Outside-left, R. Clarke, appeared in three divisions of the Football League in three successive matches. He was playing for Cardiff City in Division III(S) in 1946-7. Near the end of the season he was transferred to Manchester City in time to make one appearance in Division II before his new club was promoted to Division I.

During 1961 goalkeeper, C. Brodie, appeared in Division IV, I and III in three consecutive Football League appearances. He made his last League appearance for Aldershot in Division IV, Feb. 4, 1961, subsequently transferred to Wolverhampton Wanderers where he made one Division I appearance before the end of the season. His next appearance was with Northampton Town in Division III, Sept. 30, 1961.

Most Appearances

Here is a list of players with 500 or more peacetime Football League and/or Scottish League games to their credit:

J. Dickinson	Portsmouth	l.h.	1946-65	764‡
R. Sproson	Port Vale	h.b.	1950-70	750†‡
S. Matthews	Stoke City, Blackpool	o.r.	1932-65	701
I. Allchurch	Swansea Town (twice), Newcastle United, Cardiff City	i.f	1949-68	692(2)
W. Meredith	Manchester City, Manchester United	o.r.	1894-1924	670
R. Allen	Port Vale, West Bromwich Albion, Crystal Palace	f.	1946-65	637
J. Shaw	Sheffield United	c.h.	1948-66	629‡
P. Broadbent	Brentford, Wolverhampton Wanderers, Shrewsbury Town, Aston Villa, Stockport County	i.f.	1950-70	628(1)†
R. Ferrier	Motherwell	o.l.	1918-37	626‡
A. G. Rowley	West Bromwich Albion, Fulham, Leicester City, Shrewsbury Town	c.f.	1946-65	619
D. Blakey	Chesterfield	c.h.	1948-67	613‡
E Hine	Barnsley (twice, Leicester City, Huddersfield Town, Manchester United	i.r.	1921-38	612
J. W. Spence	Manchester United, Bradford City, Chesterfield	o.r.	1919-38	611
J. Brownsword	Hull City, Scunthorpe United	l.b.	1946-65	610
R. McKinlay	Nottingham Forest	c.h.	1951-70	614(3)†‡
J. Scoular	Portsmouth, Newcastle United, Bradford	w.h.	1946-64	602
R. C. Simpson	Queen's Park, Third Lanark, Newcastle United, Hibernian, Celtic		1946-70	602

R. F. Kelly	Burnley, Sunderland, Huddersfield Town, Preston North End, Carlisle United	i.r.	1913-36	601
A. Iremonger	Notts County, Lincoln City	g.	1905-27	600
S. Bloomer	Derby County, Middlesbrough	i.r.	1892-1914	600
J. Atyeo	Portsmouth, Bristol City	c.f.	1951-66	599
J. Haynes	Fulham	i.f.	1952-70	598‡
H. Bell	Tranmere Rovers	c.h.	1946-61	595‡
S. Milburn	Chesterfield, Leicester City, Rochdale	r.b.	1946-65	591
R. Ashman	Norwich City	l.b.	1946-64	590‡
A. McNair	Celtic	r.b.	1904-25	588‡
E. Lowe	Aston Villa, Fulham, Notts County	l.h.	1946-65	587
W. McGarry	Port Vale, Huddersfield Town, Bournemouth	w.h.	1946-63	586
W. Milne	Swansea Town	l.b.	1919-37	585‡
S. Bartram	Charlton Athletic	g.	1934-56	583‡
E. J. Langley	Leeds United, Brighton, Fulham, Queen's Park Rangers	l.b.	1952-67	583
G. Farm	Hibernian, Blackpool, Queen of the South	g.	1947-64	581
W. Fotheringham	Airdrie, Dundee, Morton, St. Mirren, Queen of South	g.	1919-37	580
R. Clayton	Blackburn Rovers	r.h.	1950-69	578‡
W. Robb	Birmingham, Rangers, Hibernian, Aldershot	g.	1913-37	571
C. C. Holton	Arsenal, Watford (twice), Northampton Town, Crystal Palace, Charlton Athletic, Leyton Orient	c.f.	1947-68	571
W. Cresswell	South Shields, Sunderland, Everton	l.b.	1919-36	569
J. W. Smith	South Shields, Portsmouth, Bournemouth, Clapton, Orient	i.f.	1919-37	569
T. Eglington	Everton, Tranmere Rovers	o.l.	1946-61	566
R. Evans	Celtic, Chelsea, Newport County, Morton, Third Lanark, Raith Rovers	c.h.b.	1947-68	564
W. A. Foulkes	Manchester United	c.h.	1952-70	563(4)‡
R. G. Williamson	Middlesbrough	g.	1902-23	561‡
R. Bentley	Newcastle United, Chelsea Fulham, Queen's Park Rangers	r.b or c.f.	1946-63	559
J. W. McCue	Stoke City, Oldham Athletic	l.b.	1946-62	558
A. Sherwood	Cardiff City, Newport County	l.b.	1946-61	558
T. D. Burden	Chester, Leeds United, Bristol City	w.h. or i.f.	1946-61	557
M. Downie	Kilmarnock, Bradford, Lincoln, Bradford City, Doncaster Rovers	g.	1946-64	557
M. Owen	Swindon Town	c.f. or c.h.	1946-63	554‡
T. Paine	Southampton	o.l. or r.	1956-70	554†‡
D. Blanchflower	Barnsley, Aston Villa, Tottenham Hotspur	r.h.	1949-64	553
S. Hardy	Chesterfield, Liverpool, Aston Villa, Nottingham Forest	g.	1903-25	552
A. Hodgkinson	Sheffield United	g.	1954-70	552†‡
W. McStay	Ayr United, Celtic, Hearts	f.b.	1912-30	550
J. McIlroy	Burnley, Stoke City, Oldham Athletic	i.f.	1950-68	547(4)

P. Gallagher	Celtic, Falkirk	i.r.	1911-32	546
J. Armfield	Blackpool	r.b.	1955-70	542†‡
H. Gallacher	Airdrieonians, Newcastle United, Chelsea, Derby County, Notts County, Grimsby Town, Gateshead	c.f.	1921-39	541
J. D. S. Gordon	Portsmouth (twice), Birmingham City	i.f.	1951-67	541
F. Tunstall	Sheffield United, Halifax Town	o.l.	1946-63	535
T. Fowler	Northampton Town, Aldershot	o.l.	1920-36	540
D. H. Harris	Newport County, Portsmouth	h.b.	1954-70	533†
J. Charlton	Leeds United	c.h.b.	1952-70	531†‡
J. Dawson	Burnley	g.	1906-29	530‡
A. Black	Leicester City	f.b.	1919-35	530‡
E. F. Brook	Barnsley, Manchester City	o.l.	1925-39	529
R. Flowers	Wolverhampton W a n d e r e r s, Northampton Town	l.h.b.	1952-69	528
J. McNichol	Brighton, Chelsea, Crystal Palace	i.f.	1949-63	528
R. Crompton	Blackburn Rovers	f.b.	1896-1920	528‡
J. Iley	Sheffield United, Tottenham Hotspur, Newcastle United, Peterborough United	w.h.b.	1954-70	526†
R. A. Parry	Bolton Wanderers, Blackpool, Bury	i.f.	1952-70	526(6)†
A. Sturgess	Stoke, Sheffield United, Norwich City	f.b.	1902-25	525
L. Allchurch	Swansea Town, Sheffield United, Stockport County	o.r.	1953-69	525
G. Harrison	Leicester Fosse, Everton, Preston North End, Blackpool	o.l.	1910-32	524
L. Weare	Newport County	g.	1955-70	524‡
W. Smith	Huddersfield Town, Rochdale	o.l.	1914-35	523
J. Rutherford	Newcastle United, Arsenal, Clapton Orient	o.r.	1901-27	522
J. L. Simpson	Lincoln City, Gillingham	g.	1957-70	522†
R. Robinson	Middlesbrough, Barrow	c.h.	1946-63	522
E. Hopkinson	Oldham Athletic, Bolton Wanderers	g.	1951-70	522
A. Ingham	Leeds United, Queen's Park Rangers	f.b.	1947-63	522
R. S. Marshall	Sunderland, Manchester City	i.f.	1920-38	521
A. Biggs	Bristol Rovers (twice), Preston N.E., Walsall, Swansea Town	c.f.	1953-69	520(1)
J. Sewell	Notts County, Sheffield Wednesday, Aston Villa, Hull City	i.f.	1946-61	520
Joe Smith	Bolton Wanderers, Stockport County	i.f.	1908-27	520
A. Archibald	Raith Rovers, Glasgow Rangers	o.r.	1916-34	519
P. Dobing	Blackburn Rovers, Manchester City, Stoke City	c.f.	1956-70	518(1)†
G. Mee	Blackpool, Derby County, Burnley, Mansfield, Accrington Stanley, Rochdale	o.l.	1920-39	517
J. McLaren	Bradford City, Leicester City, Watford	g.	1922-39	517
K. Furphy	Darlington, Workington, Watford	h.b.	1953-69	516(6)
James Oakes	Port Vale, Charlton Athletic	l.b.	1923-39	515
E. Burgin	Sheffield United, Doncaster Rovers, Leeds United, Rochdale	g.	1949-66	514
G. Stevenson	Motherwell	i.l.	1923-39	513‡

18

K. Coote	Brentford	f.b.	1949-64	513‡
A. Davidson	Hull City	r.b.	1952-68	511‡
E. A. Stuart	Wolverhampton Wanderers, Stoke City, Tranmere Rovers, Stockport County	c.h.b.	1952-68	511
R. Wylie	Notts County, Aston Villa, Birmingham City	h.b.	1951-70	510
J. W. Ruffell	West Ham United, Aldershot	o.l.	1921-39	510
E. Wilson	Brighton and Hove Albion	o.l.	1922-36	509‡
A. D. Holden	Bolton Wanderers, Preston North End	o.l.	1951-65	508
B. C. Trautmann	Manchester City	g.	1949-64	508‡
F. Womack	Birmingham, Torquay United	f.b.	1908-30	507
N. Bullock	Bury	c.h. or c.f.	1920-35	506‡
C. M. Buchan	Leyton, Sunderland, Arsenal	i.f.	1910-28	506§
W. P. Gray	Leyton Orient, Chelsea, Burnley, Nottingham Forest, Millwall	i.f.	1947-65	505
J. Melia	Liverpool, Wolverhampton Wanderers, Southampton, Aldershot	i.f.	1955-70	505†
C. Jones	Swansea Town, Tottenham Hotspur, Fulham	o.l. or o.r.	1952-70	504(6)
S. Anderson	Sunderland, Newcastle United Middlesbrough	r.h.	1952-66	504
G. Wall	Barnsley, Manchester United, Oldham Athletic, Hamilton Academicals	o.l.	1903-23	503
A. Jones	Wrexham	f.b.	1923-36	503‡
J. Mathieson	Raith Rovers, Middlesbrough, Brentford, Queen of South	g.	1923-39	502
A. Wilson	Sheffield Wednesday	i.r. or c.f.	1900-19	502‡
J. T. Brittleton	Stockport County, Sheffield Wednesday, Stoke	h.b.	1902-25	501
M. Hooper	Darlington, Sheffield Wednesday	o.r.	1921-38	500

Figures in brackets indicate appearances as substitute.
† Still adding to this total in 1970-71.
§ Includes 24 appearances in the old Southern League, then the principal League competition outside of the Football League.
‡ This is to emphasise the fact that these appearances were made for a single club. See also the succeeding item.

Most Appearances for a Single Club

Included in the preceding list and indicated so ‡ are a number of players whose total of appearances was made with a single club. Those names are not repeated here. However, that list also includes other players who can claim the distinction of making over 500 appearances for a single club although the figures given include appearances with more than one club. Those players and their totals for the one club are:

J. Brownsword	Scunthorpe United	l.b.	1950-65	600
J. Atyeo	Bristol City	c.f.	1951-66	597
A. Iremonger	Notts County	g.	1905-26	564
T. Fowler	Northampton Town	o.l.	1946-61	521
W. Smith	Huddersfield Town	o.l.	1914-34	520
E. Hopkinson	Bolton Wanderers	g.	1952-70	519
A. Ingham	Queen's Park Rangers	f.b.	1950-63	519
J. L. Simpson	Gillingham	g.	1957-70	517*
A. Archibald	Glasgow Rangers	o.r.	1917-34	513

| J. W. Ruffell | West Ham United | l.b. | 1921-38 | 508 |
| J. W. McCue | Stoke City | o.l. | 1946-60 | 502 |

The following have made between 450 and 500 appearances for a single club:

J. Charlton	Leeds United	c.h.b.	1952-69	499*
L. Weare	Newport County	g.	1955-69	496*
J. Hewie	Charlton Athletic	f.b.	1951-66	495
A. Mitchell	Exeter City	w.h.	1952-66	495
R. H. Morton	Luton Town	w.h.	1948-64	494
D. Meiklejohn	Glasgow Rangers	r.h.	1919-36	493
W. Liddell	Liverpool	c.f.	1946-61	492
D. Gray	Glasgow Rangers	r.b.	1925-39	490
S. Burton	Swindon Town	g.	1946-62	490
W. A. Wright	Wolverhampton Wanderers	c.h.b.	1946-59	490
R. Wilcox	Newport County	c.h.	1946-61	489
R. Charlton	Manchester United	c.f.	1956-70	488*
H. Bamford	Bristol Rovers	r.b.	1946-58	487
F. Womack	Birmingham	f.b.	1908-28	487
G. Merrick	Birmingham City	g.	1946-60	486
G. B. Edwards	Bolton Wanderers	h.b.	1950-65	483
A. Finney	Bolton Wanderers	l.b.	1922-37	483
K. Harvey	Exeter City	c.h.b.	1952-69	483
G. W. Curtis	Coventry City	c.h.b.	1956-70	483(2)
J. W. Spence	Manchester United	o.r.	1919-33	481
B. Jackson	York City	c.h.b.	1958-70	481
W. Walker	Aston Villa	i.l.	1919-34	480
P. P. Harris	Portsmouth	o.r.	1946-60	479
J. Parry	Derby County	c.h.	1949-66	478
R. McGrory	Stoke City	r.b.	1921-35	478
S. Bloomer	Derby County	c.f.	1892-1906, 1910-14	475
G. Barrowcliffe	Derby County	r.b.	1951-66	475
E. Lowe	Fulham	l.h.	1950-63	474
R. W. H. Powell	Chesterfield	g.	1952-66	471
S. Black	Plymouth Argyle	o.l.	1924-38	470
J. Callender	Gateshead	r.h.b.	1946-58	470
J. Pitt	Bristol Rovers	r.h.	1946-58	469
R. Flowers	Wolverhampton Wanderers	w.h.	1952-67	467
E. T. Vizard	Bolton Wanderers	o.l.	1910-31	467
E. Sagar	Everton	g.	1929-53	465
R. Murray	Stockport County	f.b.	1952-63	465
J. H. Brown	Sheffield Wednesday	g.	1922-37	465
J. Burkitt	Nottingham Forest	l.h.	1946-62	464
G. Hair	Leeds United	f.b.	1950-65	462
V. Watson	West Ham United	c.f.	1920-35	462
G. Farm	Blackpool	g.	1947-60	462
J. B. McAlpine	Queen's Park	i.l.	1919-34	460
J. Rowland	Newport County	w.h.b.	1958-69	460
D. T. Williams	Rotherham United	w.h..	1946-62	460
G. Bradford	Bristol Rovers	c.f.	1949-64	459
G. Petherbridge	Bristol Rovers	o.r.	1946-62	459
J. Pennington	West Bromwich Albion	l.b.	1903-22	455
W. Amos	Bury	o.l.	1923-35	453
A. Finney	Sheffield Wednesday	o.r.	1950-66	453
P. Broadbent	Wolverhampton Wanderers	i.f.	1951-65	453
R. A. Spiers	Reading	h.b.	1955-70	453
R. Warren	Bristol Rovers	c.h.	1935-56	452
N. Lofthouse	Bolton Wanderers	c.f.	1946-61	452
E. F. Brook	Manchester City	o.l.	1927-39	451
A. Anderson	Southend United	l.b.	1950-63	451
B. Turner	Bury	h.b.	1957-70	451(3)

Joe Smith	Bolton Wanderers	i.l.	1908-27	450
W. Edwards	Leeds United	r.h.	1924-39	450
K. Jobling	Grimsby Town	h.b.	1953-69	450

* Still adding to this total in 1970-71.

Figures in brackets indicate appearances as substitute.

APPEARANCES (Internationals)

Consecutive

R. D. Blanchflower, Aston Villa and Tottenham Hotspur, holds the record for the highest number of consecutive appearances in the International Championship.

Beginning with the game against Wales, at Swansea, Mar. 19, 1952, he played in every one of Ireland's International Championship games to the end of 1962. An uninterrupted run of 33 consecutive games.

Prior to this run Blanchflower had appeared in four International Championship matches while with Barnsley and Aston Villa.

The English record in the International Championship was set up by W. A. Wright, Wolverhampton Wanderers, with a run of 25 games beginning with that against Scotland at Wembley, April 14, 1951, and ending with that against Scotland on the same ground, April 11, 1959.

In all internationals for England Wright set up a world record with a run of 70 consecutive appearances beginning with the game against France, Oct. 3, 1951, and ending with that against U.S.A., May 28, 1959.

Most

In the list of players that follows the total of international appearances does not necessarily mean the total number of caps received. It should be remembered that at the present time only one cap is awarded *each* season for appearances in the International Championship between the home countries.

War-time and Victory Internationals are not included as they do not rank as full internationals. A list of players with most appearances in those games is given under WAR-TIME FOOTBALL.

England (30 or more appearances)	†I.C.	O.	T.	Total
R. Charlton (Manchester United)	32	74	—	106
W. Wright (Wolverhampton Wanderers)	38	67	—	105
R. Moore (West Ham United)	23	61	—	84
T. Finney (Preston North End)	29	47	1(2)d	77
R. Wilson (Huddersfield Town, Everton)	15	48	—	63
G. Banks (Leicester City)	19	43	—	62
J. Greaves (Chelsea, Tottenham Hotspur)	14	43	—	57
S. Matthews (Stoke City, Blackpool)	24	32e	1a	57
J. Haynes (Fulham)	16	40	—	56
R. Flowers (Wolverhampton Wanderers)	15	34	—	49
J. Dickinson (Portsmouth)	17	31	—	48
A. Ball (Blackpool, Everton)	11	34	—	45
J. Armfield (Blackpool)	13	30	—	43
R. Crompton (Blackburn Rovers)	34	8	—	42
M. Peters (West Ham United, Tottenham Hotspur)	11	31	—	42
G. Hurst (West Ham United)	12	29	—	41
G. Cohen (Fulham)	11	26	—	37
B. Douglas (Blackburn Rovers)	11	25	—	36
R. Clayton (Blackburn Rovers)	13	22	—	35
J. Charlton (Leeds United)	9	26	—	35
R. Hunt (Liverpool)	7	27	—	34
R. W. Byrne (Manchester United)	12	21	—	33
N. Lofthouse (Bolton Wanderers)	13	20	—	33
R. Springett (Sheffield Wednesday)	10	23	—	33
A. Ramsey (Southampton, Tottenham)	10	22	—	32

A. Mullery (Tottenham Hotspur)	8	23	—	31
E. Hapgood (Arsenal)	13	17	—	30

a. Includes one cap for Canadian Tour 1950 although no " Test " matches were played.

d. New Zealand Tour 1961.

e. Includes two games for Great Britain v. Rest of Europe.

†I.C.—International Championship. O.—Other countries. T.—Commonwealth Tours. Figure in brackets is actual number of " Test " matches played. Total.— The total includes Commonwealth Tours only if a cap was awarded. Usually one cap only is awarded for such Tours irrespective of the number of appearances in " Tests ".

Scotland (30 or more appearances)

G. Young (Rangers)	29	24	1	53
R. Evans (Celtic)	21	27	1	49
D. Law (Huddersfield Town, Manchester City, Turin, Manchester United)	22	20	—	42
E. Caldow (Rangers)	18	22	—	40
L. Reilly (Hibernian)	20	18	1	39
J. Greig (Rangers)	18	20	—	38
J. Baxter (Rangers, Sunderland)	17	17	—	34
W. Steel (Morton, Derby County, Dundee)	17	14‡	1	32
R. Collins (Celtic, Everton, Leeds United)	12	19	—	31
A. Morton (Queen's Park, Rangers)	30	1	—	31
W. Liddell (Liverpool)	18	12*	—	30

Ireland (30 or more appearances)

R. D. Blanchflower (Barnsley, Aston Villa, Tottenham Hotspur)	37	20‡	—	57
W. Bingham (Sunderland, Luton Town, Everton)	34	22	—	56
J. McIlroy (Burnley)	36	20‡	—	56
T. Neill (Arsenal)	24	20	—	44
A. McMichael (Newcastle United)	28	12	—	40
A. Elder (Burnley, Stoke City)	23	16	—	39
P. McParland (Aston Villa, Wolverhampton Wanderers)	20	14	—	34
J. Nicholson (Manchester United, Huddersfield Town)	21	13	—	34
M. Harvey (Sunderland)	15	17	—	32
E. Scott (Liverpool, Belfast Celtic)	31	—	—	31
R. Peacock (Glasgow Celtic, Coleraine)	18	13‡	—	31
O. Stanfield (Distillery)	30	—	—	30
W. Cunningham (St. Mirren, Leicester City, Dunfermline)	20	10	—	30
D. Dougan (Blackburn Rovers, Aston Villa, Leicester City, Wolverhampton Wanderers)	17	13	—	30

Wales (30 or more appearances)

I. Allchurch (Swansea Town, Newcastle United, Cardiff City)	37	31§	—	68
C. Jones (Swansea Town, Tottenham Hotspur)	31	28§	—	59
W. Meredith (Manchester City, Manchester United)	48	—	—	48
S. G. Williams (West Bromwich Albion, Southampton)	23	20	—	43
A. J. Kelsey (Arsenal)	23	19‡	—	42

A. Sherwood (Cardiff City, Newport County)	30	11§	—	41
W. J. Charles (Swansea Town, Leeds United, Juventus, Cardiff City)	19	20‡	—	39
T. Ford (Swansea Town, Aston Villa, Sunderland, Cardiff City)	26	12§	—	38
M. Hopkins (Tottenham Hotspur)	16	18	—	34
W. Hennessey, (Birmingham City, Nottingham Forest, Derby County)	18	16	—	34
R. Paul (Swansea Town, Manchester City)	23	10§	—	33
F. Keenor (Cardiff City, Crewe Alexandra)	32	—	—	32
T. R. Vernon (Blackburn Rovers, Everton, Stoke City)	18	14	—	32
M. England (Blackburn Rovers, Tottenham Hotspur)	17	15	—	32
R. Rees (Coventry City, West Bromwich Albion, Nottingham Forest)	14	17	—	31
R. Burgess (Tottenham Hotspur)	22	9§	—	31
M. Charles (Swansea Town, Arsenal, Cardiff City)	14	17	—	31
W. Lewis (Bangor, Crewe Alexandra, Chester)	30	—	—	30
T. C. Medwin (Swansea Town, Tottenham Hotspur)	16	14	—	30

* Includes two games for Great Britain v. Rest of Europe.
§ Includes one game v. Rest of United Kingdom.
§ Includes one game v, Rest of United Kingdom.
Above figures are correct to close season 1970.
In both amateur and full internationals, V. Woodward made a total of 67 appearances for England. He also played in three "Test" matches against South Africa.

Foreign Countries

International appearance figures for many of the foreign players are difficult to establish because the status of several so-called international games is rather doubtful. This is particularly the case among South American countries where "Internationals" are so numerous and where closer investigation reveals that a large percentage of these games could not possibly rate the title of full international.

This being the case the compiler regrets that a few of the figures quoted below can only be regarded as approximate but this list can still be treated as a useful guide to the world's leading players. It is based on records available to July, 1970.

Argentine: A. Roma (Boca Juniors) 49.

Austria: G. Hanappi (S.C. Wacker, S.C. Rapid) 96, K. Koller (1st Vienna) 83, E. Ocwirk (F.K. Austria, Sampdoria) 61.

Belgium: J. Jurion (Anderlecht) 77,

V. Mees (Royal Antwerp) 68, B. Voorhoof (F. K. Lierse) 61.

Brazil: D. Santos (Portuguesa de Desportos, Palmeiras) 101, Gilmar (Corinthians, Santos) 100, Pele (Santos) 96, N. Santos (Botafogo) 73.

Chile; L. Sander 94.

Czechoslovakia: L. Novak (Dukla) 75, F. Planicka (S.K. Slavia) 74.

Denmark: B. Hansen (Frem) 51.

Eire: C. Hurley (Millwall, Sunderland) 40, J. Carey (Manchester United) 29. (Carey also played in 7 games for Ireland). C. Martin (Glentoran, Leeds United, Aston Villa) 29. (Martin also played 6 games for Ireland). N. Cantwell (West Ham, Manchester United) 35.

Finland: S. Mynti (VIFK) 61.

France: R. Marché (R.C. Paris) 63, R. Jonquet (Rheims) 58.

Germany (East): G. Schroeter (Dynamo Berlin) 39.

Germany (West): P. Janes (Fortuna) 71, U. Seeler (Hamburger SV) 69, E. Lehner (Schwaben Augsburg) 65.

Holland : P. Van Heel (Feyenoord) 64.

Hungary : J. Bozsik (Honved) 100, G. Grosics (Honved, Tatabanya) 89, F. Puskas (Honved) 84 (Puskas added to this total with 3 appearances for Spain after joining Real Madrid).

Italy : U. Caligaris (Juventus) 59, G. Meazza (Inter-Milan) 53, Rosetta (Juventus) 52, G. Facchetti (Inter-nazionale) 52.

Luxembourg : Kettel 67.

Mexico : A. Carbajal (Leon) 79.

Norway : T. Svennsen (Sandefjord) 104, Thorensen (Larvik) 64, H. B. Karlson (Larvik Turn) 60, A. Bakker (Asker) 54.

Portugal : M. Coluna (Benfica) 73, J. Augusto (Benfica) 62, Eusebio (Benfica) 53.

Russia : L. Yashin (Dynamo) 84, A. Shesternev (Moscow Army) 76.

Spain : R. Zamora 47 (Espanol, C.F. Barcelona, Real Madrid).

Sweden : O. Bergmark (Orebro and Roma) 88, K. Svensson (Halsingborg) 73.

Switzerland : S. Minelli (Servette, Grasshoppers) 79, A. Bickel (Grass-hoppers) 71, M. Ableggen (Grass-hoppers) 68, R. Ramseyer (Grass-hoppers) 58, C. Antenen (Lausanne) 57.

Turkey : K. Lefter (Fenerbahce) 46.

Uruguay : P. Rocha (Penarol) 74.

Yugoslavia : B. Zebec (Partizan) 65, Bobek (Partizan) 63, V. Beara (Red Star Belgrade Hadjuk-Split) 60.

General

S. Davies played for Wales in six different positions : right-half (two), left-half (one), outside-right (two), in-side-right (three), centre-forward (six), and inside-left (four). Total 18 appear-ances.

T. Pearson (Newcastle United), a Scot, played for England v. Scotland in a war-time Red Cross international match at Newcastle, Dec. 1939. Pear-son was called in at the last minute to replace E. Brook (Manchester City) who had been injured in an accident.

S. Mortensen made his international debut (war-time) against his own country. It was at Wembley, Sept. 25, 1943. England were playing Wales. Mortensen was reserve for England, but when the injured Wales left-half, I. Powell, was unable to resume after the interval, it was agreed that Mort-ensen should take his place.

J. Reynolds of West Bromwich Albion and Aston Villa, appeared for England and for Ireland in the 1890s. Reynolds was born at Blackburn.

R. E. Evans (Aston Villa and Sheffield United) played for Wales against England, and for England against Wales, in the early 1900s. He also played for both countries against Scotland and Ireland. Evans was by birth an English player.

L. Kubala, one of the finest inside-forwards of the post-war era, has appeared in internationals for three different countries. Born in Hungary he was first capped for that country, but subsequently appeared with Czechoslovakia and with Spain.

A. Di Stefano has also played for three countries : his native Argentine, Colombia and Spain.

Another player to appear for three countries is J. Kennaway who was a Glasgow Celtic goalkeeper in the 1930s. Prior to joining Celtic he had played for Canada v. U.S.A. in 1928, U.S.A. v. Canada in 1930, and while with Celtic he made two appearances for Scotland.

Many players have appeared in in-ternationals for two different coun-tries and here we mention only a few of them.

H. Maschio, Argentine inside-for-ward was capped for his country in the 1950s and subsequently made appearances for Italy. Others include Lojacono, Montuori, Martino and Sivori, and pre-war—Demaria, Guaita, Monti, and Orsi.

G. Altafini, led the Brazilian attack on a number of occasions when he was with Palmeiras, and, after transferring to A.C. Milan in 1958, he appeared for Italy.

J. Schiaffino, another brilliant in-side-forward, appeared in many inter-nationals for his native country, Uru-guay, before being transferred from Penarol to A.C. Milan and subse-quently playing for Italy.

J. Santamaria was born in Monte-video and while with Penarol F.C. he appeared in many internationals for Uruguay. In 1957 he was transferred to Real Madrid and subsequently made a number of appearances for Spain.

Other Uruguayans to appear for

their own country and for Italy are Ghiggia (1950s) and Faccio (1930s).

I. Beck, Yugoslavian centre-forward of the 1930s made 15 appearances for his country before becoming a naturalised Frenchman and playing in five internationals for France.

Another French international who had previously played for the country of his birth was goalkeeper R. Hiden who moved from Wiener A.C. to Racing Club de Paris in the 1930s.

F. Puskas, the brilliant Hungarian inside-forward made 84 appearances for his country before quitting at the time of the revolution in 1956. After that he made four appearances for Spain.

The first player to appear in an England representative side while not attached to an English club was C. Rutter, right-back of Cardiff City. He played for England " B " v. Holland at Amsterdam, Mar. 26, 1952.

The first professional to appear for England while on the books of a club outside the Football League was J. Baker, Hibernian, who was in the England Under 23 side v. Poland, Sept. 24, 1958. He subsequently appeared in five Full Internationals for England while still with Hibernian.

ARBROATH F.C.
Founded 1878. Joined Scottish League, Division II, 1902. Honours: Runners-up, Division II, 1934-5, 1958-9, 1967-8. Record attendance: 13,510 v. Rangers, Scottish Cup, 3rd Round, Feb. 23, 1952. Address: Gayfield Park, Arbroath. (Tel. 2157). Colours: Maroon shirts, white shorts. Record goalscorer in Division I, A. Brand, 22 goals, 1936-7. Record victory: 36—0 v. Bon Accord, Scottish Cup, 1st Round, Sept. 5, 1885. Record defeat: 8—0 v. Dundee and East Fife, 1945-6, v. Kilmarnock 1948-9.

ARGENTINE
Football was introduced into the Argentine by Britishers in the 1860s, when they were, for the most part, engaged in the building of the railways in that country.

The Buenos Aires F.C. was formed by these British residents in 1865 and is, therefore, the oldest football club in the Argentine.

Despite the fact that it was the British who sowed the seed it is really the Italians who must take most credit for the development of the game in the Argentine and today it is one of the foremost soccer loving nations in the world. Italians immigrated to the Argentine in large numbers around the time of World War I.

The Argentinian Football Association was founded as early as 1895 when the British influence was still at its strongest and Sir Thomas Lipton kept interest alive when he presented a cup in 1902 to be competed for annually between the Argentine and Uruguay.

However, it was much later, in the decade before World War II that Argentinian football really became world class. In 1928 the Argentine reached the final of the Olympic Games soccer tournament to draw with Uruguay, 1—1, before losing the replay 2—0. In 1930 they were defeated by the same opponents in the final of the World Cup, but from then on the reputation of the Argentinian footballer as a soccer artist quickly built up to one of such renown that by the time the second World War had come to an end these South Americans were in great demand abroad.

Their early elimination from the final tournaments of the World Cup in 1958 and again in 1962 was followed by violent demonstrations against the Argentine F.A., and noone will ever forget the fantastic scene at Wembley in the 1966 tournament when the Argentine were eliminated with a 1—0 defeat by England. The game was held up for seven minutes while their captain, A Rattin, refused to leave the field after being ordered off by the referee.

The address of the national association is Associación del Futbol Argentino, Viamonte 1366/76, Buenos Aires. Colours: blue and white striped shirts, blue shorts.

May 9, 1951	England 2, Argentine 1; Wembley
May 13, 1951	Eire 0, Argentine 1; Dublin
May 17, 1953	Argentine 0, England 0; Buenos Aires
	(Abandoned after 23 min, pitch waterlogged)

June 11, 1958	Ireland 1, Argentine 3; Sweden†
June 2, 1962	England 3, Argentine 1; Chile†
June 6, 1964	Argentine 1, England 0; Rio de Janeiro
July 23, 1966	England 1, Argentine 0; Wembley†

† World Cup

ARSENAL F.C.

Founded 1886 as Royal Arsenal, Woolwich. Joined Football League, Division II, 1893. Honours: Champions, Division I, 1930-31, 1932-3, 1933-4, 1934-5, 1937-8, 1947-8, 1952-3. Runners-up, 1925-6, 1931-2. Runners-up, Division II, 1903-4. F.A. Cup: Winners, 1930, 1936, 1950. Finalists, 1927, 1932, 1952. League Cup, Runners-up, 1968, 1969. Fairs Cup: Winners, 1970. Record attendance: 73,295 v. Sunderland, Division I, Mar. 9, 1935. Address: Arsenal Stadium, Highbury, N.5 (Tel. 01-226 5841). Nickname: Gunners. Colours: Red shirts, white collars and sleeves, white shorts. Record League goalscorer: E. Drake, 43 goals, Division I, 1934-35. Record victory: 12—0 v. Loughborough Town, Division II, Mar. 12, 1900. Record defeat: 8—0 v. Loughborough Town, Division II, Dec. 12, 1896.

ASTON VILLA F.C.

Founded 1874. One of the original members of the Football League 1888. Honours: Champions, Division I, 1893-4, 1895-6, 1896-7, 1898-9, 1899-1900, 1909-10. Runners-up, 1888-9, 1902-3, 1907-8, 1910-11, 1912-13, 1913-14, 1930-31, 1932-33. Champions, Division II, 1937-8, 1959-60. F.A. Cup: Winners 1887, 1895, 1897, 1905, 1913, 1920 and 1957. Seven F.A. Cup victories is a record. Finalists, 1892, 1924. In season 1896-7 Aston Villa achieved the "double" in winning both the F.A. Cup and League Championship. League Cup: Winners, 1961. Finalists, 1963. Record attendance: 76,588 v. Derby County, F.A. Cup, 6th Round, Mar. 2, 1946. Address: Villa Park, Birmingham 6. (Tel. 021-327 6604). Nickname: Villans. Colours: Claret shirts, light blue collars and cuffs, white shorts with claret stripe. Record League goal-scorer: T. Waring, 49 goals, Division I, 1930-31. Record victory: 13—0 v. Wednesbury Old Athletic, F.A. Cup, 1st Round, Oct. 30, 1886. Record defeat:

8—1 v. Blackburn Rovers, F.A. Cup, 3rd Round, 1888-9.

ATTENDANCES
F.A. Amateur Cup

An attendance of 100,000 has been recorded at five F.A. Amateur Cup finals at Wembley—in 1951 (Pegasus v. Bishop Auckland), 1952 (Walthamstow Avenue v. Leyton), 1953 (Pegasus v. Harwich and Parkeston), 1954 (Bishop Auckland v. Crook Town), and 1955 (Bishop Auckland v. Hendon).

F.A. Cup

For attendances at Final ties see complete list under FOOTBALL ASSOCIATION CHALLENGE CUP.

The record for the Cup Final is 126,047, at Wembley, April 28, 1923, when Bolton Wanderers defeated West Ham United 2—0. This is the official figure. However, several thousands more broke into the ground. Various estimates of the actual number have been given. It is generally considered that in all something like 200,000 spectators gained admission.

The smallest attendance at an F.A. Cup tie in the competition proper was a few hundred who were admitted free to the Norwich City v. Bradford City, 3rd Round (second replay), at Lincoln, in 1915. Officially the game was played behind closed doors so as not to interfere with the production of armaments at nearby factories.

Football League

Aggregate of attendances at all Football League games in each season:

1946-47	35,604,606
1947-48	40,259,130
1948-49	41,271,424
1949-50	40,517,865
1950-51	39,584,987
1951-52	39,015,866
1952-53	37,149,966
1953-54	36,174,590
1954-55	34,133,103
1955-56	33,150,809
1956-57	32,744,405
1957-58	33,562,208
1958-59	33,610,985

26

1959-60	32,538,611
1960-61	28,619,754
1961-62	27,979,902
1962-63	28,885,852
1963-64	28,535,022
1964-65	27,641,168
1965-66	27,206,960
1966-67	28,902,596
1967-68	30,107,298
1968-69	29,382,172
1969-70	29,600,972

Record attendance for each division at a single game:

Division I: Manchester United v. Arsenal, at Maine Road, Jan. 17, 1948, 83,260.

Division II: Aston Villa v. Coventry City, Oct. 30, 1937, 68,029.

Division III(S): Notts County v. Nottingham Forest, at Meadow Lane, April 22, 1950, 46,000.

Division III(N): Hull City v. Rotherham United, at Boothferry Park, Dec. 25, 1948, 49,655.

Division III: Hull City v. Millwall, Dec. 27, 1965, 40,231.

Division IV: Crystal Palace v. Millwall, Mar. 31, 1961, 37,774.

The smallest attendance recorded at a Football League game is 13. This number paid to see a Division II match between Stockport County and Leicester City at Old Trafford, Manchester, May 7, 1921, when Stockport County's ground was under suspension.

Football League Cup
Record attendance at a Final tie: 98,189 in 1969.

Friendlies
The record attendance at a friendly game between Football League clubs is 44,840, Newcastle United v. Liverpool, Feb. 14, 1948.

The record attendance at a friendly game played in England between a Football League club and any other club was at Stamford Bridge when Chelsea drew 3—3 with Moscow Dynamo in Nov. 1945. The attendance can only be estimated as several thousands broke into the ground after the gates had been closed. It is recorded as 82,000 but was probably nearer 90,000.

The record for a friendly game in Scotland is 91,708, Celtic v. Tottenham Hotspur, Hampden Park, Aug. 5, 1967.

Internationals
British record: 149,547. Scotland v. England, Hampden Park, Glasgow, April 17, 1937.

World Record. 199,850, Brazil v. Uruguay, World Cup Final, Rio de Janeiro, July 16, 1950. This is a world record for any football match.

Mid-Week
The British record for a mid-week match is 133,570. This was the attendance at the replayed Scottish Cup Final between Glasgow Rangers and Morton at Hampden Park, Glasgow, April 21, 1948.

The record in England is 100,000 at Wembley Stadium. This was first established at the England v. Argentine international match on May 9, 1951, and has since been equalled on a number of occasions.

The Football League mid-week record is 72,077, Everton v. Manchester United, Division I, Sept. 4, 1957.

The F.A. Cup mid-week record is 80,407, Derby County v. Birmingham City, Maine Road, Manchester, semi-finals (replay), Mar. 28, 1946.

Provincial
The record for a game in England outside London is 84,569 at Maine Road, Manchester, Mar. 3, 1934, when Manchester City defeated Stoke City 1—0 in the 6th Round of the F.A. Cup.

Scottish Cup
The record attendance for a Scottish Cup Final is 146,433, Celtic v. Aberdeen, Hampden Park, Glasgow, April 24, 1937.

For any game other than an international or a Cup Final the British attendance record is also a Scottish Cup match: 143,570, Glasgow Rangers v. Hibernian, semi-final tie, Mar. 27, 1948.

Scottish League
Record attendance: 118,567, Rangers v. Celtic, Ibrox Stadium, Glasgow, Jan. 2, 1939.

Scottish League Cup

Record attendance: 107,609, Final tie, Hampden Park, Oct. 23, 1965.

AUSTRALIA

Organised football in Australia dates from the early 1880s and the Anglo-Australian Association was formed as long ago as 1884, but for more than 50 years soccer was a very poor relation to the Rugby League game so popular in New South Wales and Queensland or the Australian Rules game which is the number one sport in South Australia, Victoria, Tasmania and Western Australia.

The word "soccer" is included in the title of the senior governing body, The Australian Soccer Football Association, to differentiate between Association Football and the local (Australian rules) game.

The recent boom has brought with it headaches for the authorities. In 1960 the A.S.F.A. was banned for three years from F.I.F.A. for poaching players from Austria. Then, in 1961, feeling against the governing body of Australian soccer grew to such proportions that in November of that year a rival organisation, the Australian Federation of Soccer Clubs, was formed and claimed recognition as the leading soccer authority. It quickly gained support and is now the official governing body.

Whereas soccer in Australia was a strictly amateur game before the last war, most of the leading clubs now employ part-time professionals and the wages offered together with jobs outside the game have attracted many professionals from Britain.

Australia entered for the World Cup for the first time in 1965 but were eliminated with two defeats by North Korea. In 1969 they were eliminated by Israel.

The first visit of a representative F.A. team to Australia was made in the summer of 1925 when the side was undefeated in 25 matches. A second tour by an F.A. team was made in 1937. This time they lost twice in 10 games. In the third F.A. tour, 1951, 20 matches were played and the F.A. emerged undefeated.

Address of the governing body—Australian Soccer Federation, Room 413, 155 King Street, Sydney, N.S.W.

Results of Tests and internationals:

Date	Australia	England/Scotland	Venue
July 27, 1925	Australia 0,	England 5;	Brisbane
July 4, 1925	Australia 1,	England 2;	Sydney
July 11, 1925	Australia 2,	England 8;	Maitland
July 18, 1925	Australia 0,	England 5;	Sydney
July 25, 1925	Australia 0,	England 2;	Melbourne
July 10, 1937	Australia 5,	England 4;	Sydney
July 17, 1937	Australia 0,	England 4;	Brisbane
July 20, 1937	Australia 4,	England 3;	Newcastle
May 26, 1951	Australia 1,	England 4;	Sydney
June 30, 1951	Australia 0,	England 17;	Sydney†
July 7, 1951	Australia 1,	England 4;	Brisbane
July 14, 1951	Australia 1,	England 6;	Sydney
July 21, 1951	Australia 0,	England 5;	Newcastle
May 28, 1967	Australia 0,	Scotland 1;	Sydney
May 30, 1967	Australia 1,	Scotland 2;	Adelaide
June 3, 1967	Australia 0,	Scotland 2;	Melbourne

† 17—0 is England's highest score in international matches—a world record win.

AUSTRIA

For the greater part of the last 40 years Austria has been rated among the leading football nations of the world. But like most countries they have had their ups and downs in the international field. The early 1930s was one of their better periods when the famous "Wunderteam" beat Scotland 5—0, Germany 6—0, and lost by only the odd goals of seven to a powerful England side at Stamford Bridge.

The second half of the 1950s was one of Austria's down-hill periods and this decline prompted them not to

28

enter for the 1962 World Cup, and although they have since recovered they have still not been restored to their former glory, and failed to qualify for the World Cup in 1966 and 1970.

The British introduced soccer to Vienna in the 1880s and helped form one of the first clubs to play the game in that country, the Cricketers, in 1889.

The first English club to visit Austria was Oxford University in 1899, followed by Southampton in 1901.

The Austrians figured in the earliest international match to be played on the continent of Europe, beating Hungary 5—0 in 1902, and A.C. Wiener (formed 1896) was the first club to defeat an English professional side touring abroad when they beat Sunderland 2—1 in Vienna in 1909.

However, little progress was made in the game in Austria until after the formation of their F.A. in 1926. To-day, they control over 1,500 clubs with a membership of over 200,000.

The address of the governing body is: Oesterreichischer Fussball-Bund, Postfach 161, Vienna 1061. Colours: White shirts, black shorts.

Results of international matches:

June 6, 1908	Austria 1, England 6; Vienna
June 8, 1908	Austria 1, England 11; Vienna
June 1, 1909	Austria 1, England 8; Vienna
May 14, 1930	Austria 0, England 0; Vienna
May 16, 1931	Austria 5, Scotland 0; Vienna
Dec. 7, 1932	England 4, Austria 3; Chelsea
Nov. 29, 1933	Scotland 2, Austria 2; Glasgow
May 6, 1936	Austria 2, England 1; Vienna
May 9, 1937	Austria 1, Scotland 1; Vienna
Dec. 13, 1950	Scotland 0, Austria 1; Glasgow
May 27, 1951	Austria 4, Scotland 0; Vienna
Nov. 28, 1951	England 2, Austria 2; Wembley
May 7, 1952	Austria 6, Eire 0; Vienna
May 25, 1952	Austria 2, England 3; Vienna
Mar. 25, 1953	Eire 4, Austria 0; Dublin
May 9, 1954	Austria 2, Wales 0; Vienna
June 16, 1954	Austria 1, Scotland 0; Zurich*
May 19, 1955	Austria 1, Scotland 4; Vienna
Nov. 23, 1955	Wales 1, Austria 2; Wrexham
May 2, 1956	Scotland 1, Austria 1; Glasgow
May 14, 1958	Austria 3, Eire 1; Vienna
June 15, 1958	England 2, Austria 2; Sweden*
May 29, 1960	Austria 4, Scotland 1; Vienna
May 27, 1961	Austria 3, England 1; Vienna
Apr. 4, 1962	England 3, Austria 1; Wembley
Apr. 8, 1962	Eire 2, Austria 3; Dublin
May 8, 1963	Scotland 4, Austria 1; Glasgow†
Sept. 25, 1963	Austria 0, Eire 0; Vienna
Oct. 13, 1963	Eire 3, Austria 2; Dublin
Oct. 20, 1965	England 2, Austria 3; Wembley
May 22, 1966	Austria 1, Eire 0; Vienna
May 27, 1967	Austria 0, England 1; Vienna
Nov. 6, 1968	Scotland 2, Austria 1; Glasgow*
Nov. 10, 1968	Eire 2, Austria 2; Dublin
Nov. 5, 1969	Austria 2, Scotland 0; Vienna*

† Abandoned after 81 minutes   * World Cup

AWAY POINTS

The record for each division is:

				W.	D.	L.	
Division I	33 points	Arsenal		14	5	2	1930-31
	33 "	Tottenham Hotspur		16	1	4	1960-61
Division II	30 "	Tottenham Hotspur		13	4	4	1919-20
		Leeds United		12	6	3	1963-64

Division III(S)	32 points	Nottingham Forest	14	4	5	1950-51
Division III(N)	37 „	Doncaster Rovers	18	1	2	1946-47
Division III	29 „	Bury	12	5	6	1960-61
	29 „	Portsmouth	12	5	6	1961-62
	29 „	Hull City	12	5	11	1965-66
Division IV	32 „	Walsall	14	4	5	1959-60
Scottish League:						
Division I	37 „	Glasgow Rangers	16	5	0	1920-21

No points

Throughout the history of the Football League only five clubs have gone through a season without gaining a single away point:

Division II: Northwich Victoria, 1893-4; Crewe Alexandra, 1894-5; Loughborough Town, 1899-1900; Doncaster Rovers, 1904-5. Division III(N): Nelson, 1930-31.

AWAY WINS

Doncaster Rovers 18 away wins in Division III(N) in season 1946-7 is a Football League record.

Tottenham Hotspur's eight consecutive away wins in 1960-61 is a Football League record. Their total of 16 away wins that season is a First Division record.

Huddersfield Town were not defeated away from home between Nov. 15, 1924 and Nov. 14, 1925. During that time they played 18 Division I games, winning 12 and drawing six.

On Jan. 30, 1937, there was not one away win in all the 35 F.A. Cup and Football League matches played.

The most away wins in any division of the Football League on a single day is eight: Division III, Sept. 27, 1958; Division II, Sept. 12, 1959, and Nov. 25, 1967.

Record Away Wins

Division I	Cardiff City 1, Wolverhampton Wanderers 9; Sept. 3, 1955
	Newcastle United 1, Sunderland 9; Dec. 5, 1908
Division II	Burslem Port Vale 0, Sheffield United 10; Dec. 10, 1892
Division III (South)	Northampton Town 0, Walsall 8; Feb. 2, 1947
Division III (North)	Accrington Stanley 0, Barnsley 9; Feb. 3, 1934
Division III	Halifax Town 0, Fulham 8; Sept. 16, 1969
Division IV	Stockport County 0, Peterborough United 6; Feb. 4, 1961

SCOTTISH LEAGUE:

Division I	Airdrieonians 1, Hibernian 11; Oct. 24, 1959
	Partick Thistle 2, Hibernian 10; Dec. 19, 1959
Division B	Alloa Athletic 0, Dundee 10; Mar. 8, 1947
F.A. Cup (Proper)	Clapton 0, Nottingham Forest 14; Round 1, 1890-91
Scottish Cup	Coldstream 1, Raith Rovers 10; 2nd Round, Feb. 13, 1954

AYR UNITED F.C.

Founded 1910. First promoted to Scottish League, Division I, 1913. Honours: Champions, Division II, 1911-12, 1912-13, 1927-8, 1936-7, 1958-9, 1965-6. Runners-up, 1968-9. Record attendance: 24,617 v. Celtic, Scottish Cup, 2nd Round, Feb. 3, 1934. Address: Somerset Park, Ayr.

(Tel. 63435). Nickname: Honest Men. Colours: White shirts, black shorts. Record League goal-scorer: T. McGibbon, 35 goals, Division I, 1933-4. Record Victory: 11—2 v. Clackmannan, Scottish Cup, 1st Round, Jan. 17, 1931. Record defeat: 9—0 v. Rangers, Scottish League, Division I. Nov. 16, 1929, and v. Hearts, Division I, Feb. 28, 1931.

B

BALL, THE

According to the Laws of Football, the ball must be spherical with an outer casing of leather or other approved materials. The circumference shall not be more than 28 in., nor less than 27 in., while the weight at the start of the game must not be more than 16 oz., nor less than 14 oz.

The law further stipulates that no material shall be used in the manufacture of the ball which might prove dangerous to the players.

As regards the use of coloured balls, these must be available for all games during the months of Nov., Dec., Jan. and Feb.

The ball selected at the start of a match, coloured or otherwise, must be used throughout the game. It can only be changed if defective, and then must be replaced by a ball of the same type and colour.

Bursting Ball

The first time the ball burst in a Cup Final at Wembley was in 1946 during the Derby County v. Charlton Athletic tie. Oddly enough, the chances of the ball bursting in a Cup Final were discussed in a B.B.C. broadcast shortly before this particular game, and the referee, Mr. E. D. Smith, of Cumberland, remarked that it was a million to one chance.

The ball also burst when Derby County met Charlton Athletic in a Football League match only five days after the Wembley meeting.

The ball also burst thirty minutes after the start of the following year's Cup Final—Charlton Athletic v. Burnley, 1947.

BARNSLEY F.C.

Founded 1887 as Barnsley St. Peter's. Joined Football League, Division II, 1898. Honours: Champions, Division III(N), 1933-4, 1938-9, 1954-5. Runners-up, Division III, 1967-8. Best in Division II, 3rd 1914-15, 1921-2. F.A. Cup: Winners, 1912. Finalists, 1910. Record attendance: 40,255 v. Stoke City, F.A. Cup 5th Round, Feb. 15, 1936. Address: Oakwell Ground, Barnsley. (Tel. 4113). Nickname: Tykes. Colours: Red shirts, white shorts. Record League goal-scorer: C. McCormack, 33 goals, Division II, 1950-51. Record victory: 9—0 v. Loughborough Town, Jan. 28, 1899, and v. Accrington Stanley (at Accrington), Division III(N), Feb. 3, 1934. Record defeat: 9—0 v. Notts County, Division II, Nov. 19, 1927.

BARROW F.C.

Founded 1901. Joined Football League, Division III(N), 1921. Best in Division III(N), 5th, 1931-2. Record attendance: 16,874 v. Swansea Town, F.A. Cup, 3rd Round, Jan. 9, 1954. Address: Holker Street Ground, Barrow-in-Furness (Tel. 20346). Colours: Royal blue shirts and shorts. Record League goal-scorer: J. Shankly, 39 goals, Division III(N), 1933-4. Record victory: 12—1 v. Gateshead Division III(N), May 5, 1934. Record defeat: 10—1 v. Hartlepools United, Division IV, April 4, 1959.

BELGIUM

A strange situation existed in Belgium for many years inasmuch as the F.A. were reluctant to recognise professionalism yet most of the leading clubs employed part-time professionals referred to as "Independent Footballers" because they did not sign contracts with their particular clubs.

That state of affairs was brought to

an end in 1962, however, and there has been a strengthening of the game in this country.

The Belgian F.A. was formed in 1895. It became the Royal F.A. in 1920, the prefix "Royal" being granted by King Albert I. Today there are over 2,000 clubs affiliated.

The Belgians have appeared in four World Cup final tournaments, 1930, 1934, 1938, 1954 and 1970, but they were beaten in every game except that against England at Basle in the 1954 finals when they drew 4—4 after extra time, and against El Salvador in Mexico in 1970 when they won 3—0.

The address of the governing body is Union Royale Belge des Sociétés de Football Association, 14, Rue Guimard, Bruxelles 4. Colours: Red shirts with tri-coloured (Black-Yellow-Red) collars and cuffs, black shorts.

Results of international matches:

May 21, 1921	Belgium 0, England 2; Brussels
Mar. 19, 1923	England 6, Belgium 1; Highbury
Nov. 1, 1923	Belgium 2, England 2; Antwerp
Dec. 8, 1924	England 4, Belgium 0; West Bromwich
May 24, 1926	Belgium 3, England 5; Antwerp
May 11, 1927	Belgium 1, England 9; Brussels
Feb. 12, 1928	Belgium 2, Eire 4; Liege
May 19, 1928	Belgium 1, England 3; Antwerp
April 30, 1929	Eire 4, Belgium 0; Dublin
May 11, 1929	Belgium 1, England 5; Brussels
May 11, 1930	Belgium 1, Eire 3; Brussels
May 16, 1931	Belgium 1, England 4; Brussels
Feb. 25, 1934*	Eire 4, Belgium 4; Dublin
May 9, 1936	Belgium 3, England 2; Brussels
Jan. 19, 1946†	England 2, Belgium 0; Wembley
Jan. 23, 1946†	Scotland 2, Belgium 2; Hampden
May 18, 1947	Belgium 2, Scotland 1; Brussels
Sept. 21, 1947	Belgium 2, England 5; Brussels
April 28, 1948	Scotland 2, Belgium 0; Hampden
April 24, 1949	Eire 0, Belgium 2; Dublin
May 22, 1949	Belgium 3, Wales 1; Liege
Nov. 23, 1949	Wales 5, Belgium 1; Cardiff
May 10, 1950	Belgium 5, Eire 1; Brussels
May 18, 1950	Belgium 1, England 4; Brussels
May 20, 1951	Belgium 0, Scotland 5; Brussels
Nov. 26, 1952	England 5, Belgium 0; Wembley
June 17, 1954*	England 4, Belgium 4‡; Basle
Oct. 21, 1964	England 2, Belgium 2; Wembley
Mar. 24, 1964	Eire 0, Belgium 2; Dublin
May 25, 1966	Belgium 2, Eire 3; Liege
Feb. 25, 1970	Belgium 1, England 3; Brussels

* World Cup

† Victory Internationals

‡ After extra time

England's scorers in the 9—1 victory in 1927 were Dean 3, Brown 2, Rigby 2, Page and Hulme.

BENEFITS

Only three players have received benefits with three different Football League clubs. Goalkeeper J. McLaren received benefits with Bradford City, Leicester City and Watford between 1922 and 1939. Outside-right T. Urwin received benefits with Middlesbrough, Newcastle United and Sunderland between 1915 and 1935. Full-back S. Milburn had benefits with Chesterfield, Leicester City and Rochdale between 1946 and 1965.

APPEARANCES (LEAGUE). Two players who made more than 700 peacetime Football League appearances: Sir Stanley Matthews (*left*) and Jimmy Dickinson.

ARSENAL F.C. This group (the 1932 team) includes six players who helped the club win the Championship four times in five years: back row. (*left to right*) Parker, Jones, Moss, Roberts, John, Black; front row, H. Chapman (manager), Hulme, Jack, Lambert, James, Bastin, T. Whittaker (trainer).

DOUBLE, THE. (*Above*) Preston North End—Old Invincibles—who won both F.A. Cup and League in 1888–89: back row, Mills-Roberts, Graham, Sudell, Homes, Russell, Tomlinson, Hanbury, Howarth, Drummond; front row, Thompson, Dewhurst, Goodall, Ross, Gordon. (*Below*) Tottenham Hotspur, 1960–61, the first side to complete the Double this century: back row, Brown, Baker, Henry, Blanchflower, Norman, Mackay; front row, Jones, White, Smith (R.), Allen, Dyson.

Regulations

Football League clubs may, with the consent of the Management Committee, permit a Testimonial match to be arranged on behalf of any player who has completed 10 years or more in the service of a club.

BETTING

As long ago as 1892 the F.A. introduced a rule which prevented any club official or players from making bets on matches. At the same time it ruled that each club was made responsible for taking measures to prevent betting by spectators at football matches.

That rule, in a modified form, stood until 1957, when, at the annual meeting of the F.A. Council, it was decided to lift the ban which prevented officials and players from betting on authorised football pools. This was indeed a momentous decision when one considers the strong line which the F.A. has taken against football pools in the past.

It is interesting to note that an Act which was passed in 1920 to make ready-money betting illegal was first introduced into Parliament at the request of the F.A. in 1913.

During season 1935-6 the Football League made an effort to stop the football pools by scrapping the fixture lists and embarking upon a system whereby fixtures were arranged only from week to week, and clubs informed of their matches only in time to make necessary arrangements. Even then everyone was sworn to secrecy so that the pools promoters would be prevented from preparing coupons in time for distribution.

The system had to be abandoned after only a few weeks because it was found that the necessary information was still leaking out to the pools promoters. And in any case attendances showed an alarming drop and clubs were irritated by the many inconveniences the new system created.

In May, 1959, the Football League were successful in obtaining a judgment in the Chancery Division to the effect that their fixture lists are copyright. This meant that the pools would only be able to use their fixtures after agreement with the League who would thereby derive some financial benefit from the pools.

The Football League subsequently received something like £250,000 a year from the Pools for use of fixture lists until, in 1964, a new agreement guaranteed the Football League and Scottish League a total minimum of £500,000 a year.

In 1965 the F.A. and the Scottish F.A. agreed with the Pool Promoters Association to receive £60,000 and £15,000 respectively for use of their Cup fixtures.

Prior to this there had often been talk of the game in this country obtaining financial benefit from the pools. But the controlling bodies of the game had refused to be associated with the pools in this way.

As recently as 1949 the Football Association reiterated its uncompromising attitude towards betting in a statement to the Royal Commission on Lotteries, Betting and Gaming.

The F.A. said it was confident that betting had " no influence whatsoever upon results of any matches played under its jurisdiction " but was always mindful that if betting were to gain a hold on the game the present position might well be seriously undermined.

According to a statement made at that time to the Commission by Sir Stanley Rous (then Secretary of the F.A.) there had only been one case of a player receiving money from a bookmaker to share among the teams if a certain match was " fixed ".

Mr. J. Lamb (President of the Scottish F.A.) stated that many years ago two players were permanently suspended (presumably in Scotland) after being found guilty of accepting a bribe.

Subsequently, however, in Dec. 1960, the F.A. relaxed its betting ban by announcing that in future clubs would be permitted to run their own pools competitions to raise money and in 1963 they went as far as to approve a scheme for establishing their own Football Pool but this was shelved.

J. Pennington, the captain of West Bromwich Albion, was once involved in a case of attempted bribery. He was offered a sum of £55 (to be shared among his team mates) if they either lost or drew their game with Everton on Nov. 29, 1913. Pennington persuaded the briber to put his offer in writing, and then reported the facts to his club. The police were informed and were present after the game when the man was arrested as he handed over the money, for, as it happened, the match was drawn. The man was sentenced to five months' imprisonment.

There were rumours of bribery and corruption in football in 1960 but although evidence was placed in the hands of the Director of Public Prosecutions this was apparently inconclusive for no further action was taken.

However, in 1963, a national Sunday newspaper published fresh evidence of this kind and following their disclosures the police carried out an extensive investigation. The result was that 10 players and former players, including internationals, received jail sentences and were subsequently suspended from football.

See also under SUSPENSION.

BIRMINGHAM CITY F.C.

Founded 1875 as Small Heath Alliance. In 1888 they changed their name to Small Heath F.C. Ltd. and were the first football club to become a limited liability company. The name Birmingham was adopted in 1905, and " City " was added to this in 1945. They were among the original members of the Football League, Division II, 1892. Honours: Champions, Division II, 1892-3, 1920-21, 1947-8, 1954-5. Runners-up, 1893-4, 1900-1, 1902-3. Best in Division I, 6th, 1955-6. F.L. Cup: Winners, 1963. F.A. Cup: Finalists, 1931, 1956. Fairs Cup: Runners-up, 1960, 1961. Record attendance: 66,844 v. Everton, F.A. Cup, 5th Round, Feb. 11, 1939. Address: St. Andrew's, Birmingham 9. (Tel. 021-772 0101). Nickname: Blues. Colours: Royal blue shirts and shorts. Record League goalscorer: J. Bradford, 29 goals, Division I, 1927-8. Record victory: 12—0 v. Walsall Town Swifts, Division II, Dec. 17, 1892, and v. Doncaster Rovers, Division II, April 11, 1903. Record defeat: 9—1 v. Sheffield Wednesday, Division I, Dec. 13, 1930.

BLACKBURN ROVERS F.C.

Founded 1874. One of the original members of the Football League in 1888. Honours: Champions, Division I, 1911-12, 1913-14. Champions, Division II, 1938-9. Runners-up, 1957-8. F.A. Cup: Winners 1884, 1885, 1886, 1890, 1891, 1928. Finalists, 1882, 1960. Record attendance: 61,783 v. Bolton Wanderers, F.A. Cup, 6th Round, Mar. 2, 1929. Address: Ewood Park, Blackburn (Tel. 55432). Nickname: Blue and Whites. Colours: Blue and white halves, white shorts. Record League goal-scorer: E. Harper, 43 goals, Division I, 1925-6. Record victory: 11—0 v. Rossendale United, F.A. Cup, 1884-5. Record defeat: 8—0 v. Arsenal, Division I, Feb. 25, 1933.

BLACKPOOL F.C.

Founded 1887. Amalgamated with South Shore F.C. 1899. Became members of Football League, Division II, 1896. Not re-elected, 1899. Regained admission to Division II, 1900. Honours: Champions, Division II, 1929-30. Runners-up, 1936-7, 1969-70. Runners-up Division I, 1955-6. F.A. Cup Winners, 1953. Finalists, 1948, 1951. Record Attendance: 39,118 v. Manchester United, Division I, April 19, 1952. Address: Bloomfield Road, Blackpool (Tel. 46118). Nickname: Tangerines or Seasiders. Colours: Tangerine shirts, white shorts. Record League goal-scorer: J. Hampson, 45 goals, Division II, 1929-30. Record victory: 8—4 v. Charlton Athletic, Division I, 1952-3. Record defeat: 10—1 v. Huddersfield Town, Division I, Dec. 13, 1930.

BOLTON WANDERERS F.C.

Founded in 1874 as Christ Church F.C. Changed to present title in 1877. One of the original members of the Football League in 1888. Honours: Champions, Division II, 1908-9. Runners-up, 1899-1900, 1904-5, 1910-11, 1934-5. Best in Division I, 3rd, 1891-2, 1920-21, 1924-5. F.A. Cup: Winners, 1923, 1926, 1929, 1958. Finalists, 1894, 1904, 1953. Record attendance: 69,912 v. Manchester City, F.A. Cup, 5th Round, Feb. 18, 1933. Address: Burnden Park, Bolton (Tel. 21101). Nickname: Trotters. Colours: All white. Record League

34

goal-scorer: J. ("Joe") Smith, 38 goals, Division I, 1920-21. Record victory: 13—0 v. Sheffield United, F.A. Cup, 2nd Round, Feb. 1, 1890. Record defeat: 7—0 v. Manchester City, Division I, Mar. 21, 1936.

BOURNEMOUTH AND BOSCOMBE ATHLETIC F.C.

Founded 1890 as Boscombe St. John's. Re-formed 1899 as Boscombe F.C. Joined Football League, Division III(S) in 1923 and adopted present title. Honours: Runners-up, Division III(S,) 1947-8. Record attendance: 28,799 v. Manchester United, F.A. Cup, 6th Round, Mar. 2, 1957. Address: Dean Court, Bournemouth (Tel. Bournemouth 35381). Nickname: Cherries. Colours: Red shirts with red and white trimmings, white shorts. Record League goal-scorer: R. Eyre, 32 goals, Division III(S), 1928-9. Record victory: 10—0 v. Northampton Town, Division III(S), Sept. 2, 1939. Record defeat: 7—0 v. Torquay United, Division III(S), Mar. 8, 1930, and v. Southampton, Division III(S), Oct. 5, 1957.

BRADFORD CITY F.C.

Founded 1903. Elected to Football League Division II, 1903. Honours: F.A. Cup, winners, 1911. Champions, Division II, 1907-8. Champions, Division III(N), 1928-29. Best in Division I, 5th, 1910-11. Record attendance: 39,146 v. Burnley, F.A. Cup, 4th Round, Mar. 11, 1911 (the oldest Football League club ground record). Address: Valley Parade, Bradford (Tel. 26565). Nickname: Bantams. Colours: Claret and amber striped shirts, black shorts. Record League goal-scorer: D. Layne, 34 goals, Division IV, 1961-2. Record victory: 11—1 v. Rotherham United, Division III(N), Aug. 25, 1928. Record defeat:

9—1 v. Colchester United, Division IV, Dec. 30, 1961. In a war-time game, Dec. 26, 1944, Bradford City also lost 9—1 to Leeds United.

BRAZIL

The only country to have appeared in all nine World Cup tournaments, Brazil are truly the masters of soccer.

A glance through the list of results at the end of this section will show that Brazil have suffered only one defeat in fourteen games with the home countries and that was the first meeting with England in 1956 when the home team's superiority was more marked than the result suggests.

It was two years after this defeat that Brazil first reached the peak by winning the World Cup in Sweden. They repeated the performance four years later in Chile but failed in 1966 when, with too many old players, they were outmanoeuvred and outclassed.

This set-back was only temporary, however, for in Mexico in 1970 the Brazilians came back better than ever to win the trophy for a third time and so make it their own property. In this tournament they gave some magical displays of exciting, skilful, attacking football, and when they demolished the defensive minded Italians 4—1 in the Final there were many who hoped that the inspiration of the Brazilians might serve to revolutionise the duller football played in so many other countries.

The oldest club in Brazil, Flamengo, was formed in 1895 or some eleven years after the game is said to have been introduced to that country by British sailors. It was the Royal Navy which added another fillip to the Brazilian game when a team from H.M.S. *Amethyst* met Fluminese F.C. in 1906. At least it was only a matter of weeks after this that a League was formed in Rio.

May 9, 1956	England 4, Brazil 2; Wembley
June 11, 1958	England 0, Brazil 0; Sweden†
June 19, 1958	Wales 0, Brazil 1; Sweden†
May 13, 1959	Brazil 2, England 0; Rio
May 12, 1962	Brazil 3, Wales 1; Rio
May 17, 1962	Brazil 3, Wales 1; San Paulo
June 11, 1962	Brazil 3, England 1; Chile†
May 8, 1963	England 1, Brazil 1; Wembley

May 30, 1964	Brazil 5, England 1; Rio
May 14, 1966	Brazil 3, Wales 1; Rio
May 18, 1966	Brazil "B" 1, Wales 0; Belo Horizonte§
June 25, 1966	Scotland 1, Brazil 1; Hampden Park
June 12, 1969	Brazil 2, England 1; Rio
June 7, 1970	Brazil 1, England 0; Guadalajara†

§ Accorded full international rating by Wales F.A.

† World Cup

The Brazilian F.A. was founded in 1914 and it now has a membership of nearly 5,000 clubs. The address of the governing body is: Confereraçao Brasileira de Desportos, Caixa Postal 1078, Rua da Alfandega 70, Rio de Janeiro. Colours: Yellow shirts, blue shorts, white stockings.

BRENTFORD F.C.

Founded 1888. Elected to Football League, Division III, on its formation in 1920. Honours: Champions, Division II, 1934-5. Champions, Division III(S), 1932-3. Runners-up, 1929-30, 1957-8. Best in Division I, 5th, 1935-6. Champions, Division IV, 1962-63. Record attendance: 39,626 v. Preston North End, F.A. Cup, 6th Round, Mar. 5, 1938. Address: Griffin Park, Brentford (Tel. 01-560 2021). Nickname: Bees. Colours: Red and white striped shirts, black shorts. Record League goal-scorer: J. Holliday, 36 goals, Division III(S), 1932-3. Record victory: 9—0 v. Wrexham, Division III, Oct. 15, 1963. Record defeat: 7—0 v. Swansea Town, Division III(S), Nov. 8, 1924.

BRIGHTON AND HOVE ALBION F.C.

Founded 1900 as Brighton and Hove Rangers. A club known as Brighton United had been formed two years earlier but had to disband because of lack of support. Brighton and Hove Rangers became Brighton and Hove Albion in 1901. Joined Football League, Division III, on its formation in 1920. Honours: Champions, Division III(S), 1957-8, Runners-up Division III(S), 1953-4, 1955-6. Champions, Division IV, 1964-5. Address: Goldstone Ground, Hove (Tel. Hove 739535). Record attendance: 36,747

v. Fulham, Division II, Dec. 27, 1958. Nickname: Shrimps. Colours: white shirts with blue trim, white shorts with blue stripe. Record League goal-scorer: H. Vallance, 30 goals, Division III(S), 1929-30. Record victory: 10—1 v. Wisbech, F.A. Cup, 1st Round, Nov. 13, 1965. Record defeat: 9—0 v. Middlesbrough, Division II, Aug. 23, 1958.

BRISTOL CITY F.C.

Founded 1894 as Bristol South End. Changed to present title, 1897. Joined Football League, Division II, 1901. Honours: Runners-up, Division I, 1906-7. Champions, Division II, 1905-6. Champions, Division III(S), 1922-3, 1926-7, 1954-5. Runners-up, 1937-8. Runners-up, Division III, 1964-5. F.A. Cup: Finalists, 1909. Record attendance: 43,335 v. Preston North End, F.A. Cup, 5th Round, Feb. 16, 1935. Address: Ashton Gate, Bristol (Tel. 664093). Nickname: Robins. Colours: All red. Record League goal-scorer: D. Clark, 36 goals, Division III(S), 1946-7. Record victory: 11—0 v. Chichester, F.A. 1st Round, Nov. 5, 1960. Record defeat: 9—0 v. Coventry City, Division III(S), April 28, 1934.

BRISTOL ROVERS F.C.

Founded 1883 as Black Arabs F.C. Changed to Eastville Rovers 1884. Changed to Bristol Eastville Rovers, 1897, and to Bristol Rovers, 1898. Among the original members of Football League, Division III, 1920. Honours: Champions, Division III(S), 1952-53. Record attendance: 38,472 v. Preston North End, F.A. Cup, 4th Round, Jan. 30, 1960. Address: Eastville Stadium, Bristol 5 (Tel. 558620). Nickname: Pirates. Colours: Royal blue shirts, white shorts. Record

League goal-scorer: G. Bradford, 33 goals, Division III(S), 1952-53. Record victory: 7—0 v. Swansea Town, Division II, Oct. 2, 1954; v. Brighton and Hove Albion, Division III(S), Nov. 29, 1952 and v. Shrewsbury Town, Division III, Mar. 21, 1964. Record defeat: 12—0 v. Luton Town, Division III(S), April 13, 1936.

BROADCASTING

See also TELEVISION.

The first football match to be broadcast in England was the Football League, Division I, match between Arsenal and Sheffield United at Highbury, Jan. 22, 1927. Ever since there has been almost continuous arguments about the advisability of allowing important football matches to be broadcast. At different times, both the F.A. and the Football League have banned broadcasting.

The first Cup Final to be broadcast was Cardiff City v. Arsenal on April 23, 1927. The 1928 Final tie between Blackburn Rovers and Huddersfield Town was also broadcast but in 1929 there was a dispute between the F.A. and the B.B.C. over the broadcasting fee, and the F.A. refused to allow the broadcast to be made. The B.B.C. however, succeeded in providing a running commentary of sorts by setting up a broadcasting point near to the ground and engaging about half a dozen commentators to leave the stadium at regular intervals to broadcast a description of the play up to the moment of their departure. With one commentator following another at intervals of something like 15 min., the B.B.C. was able to provide a complete non-stop description of the game.

Agreement was reached for the 1930 Final, but, following renewed opposition—particularly from the smaller League clubs who complained bitterly that broadcasts adversely affected attendances at their matches —the Football League decided at its annual meeting of June 1, 1931, that no League matches would be broadcast.

Thereafter, the F.A. imposed a ban on the broadcasting of all games under its jurisdiction with the exception of the Cup Final.

The F.A. subsequently permitted the broadcasting of international matches, but the League did not relent until 1937 when it permitted the B.B.C. to broadcast certain matches on overseas wavelengths.

In 1938 more matches were added to the list of those which might be broadcast, but, in most cases, broadcasting was only allowed during the second half of the game.

More broadcasts were permitted during, and immediately after, the war, but, in June 1951, the Football League dealt a major blow to radio listeners when it re-introduced a complete ban on the broadcasting of any of its games.

It was not long, however, before the League relented to the extent of allowing broadcasts of matches providing that no prior announcement was made as to the match chosen. That is how the situation stands now.

BROKEN TIME PAYMENTS

For many years the four British Associations have made a determined stand against payment for broken time to amateurs. They insisted as early as 1881 that players should only receive payment for actual expenses, and, of course, the F.A. emphasised this point after professionalism had been legalised in 1885—amateurs only receive payment for actual expenses and any wages lost through taking part in any match.

It was because of disagreement with other Football Associations over the question of broken time payments to amateurs that the British Associations withdrew from membership of F.I.F.A. in Feb. 1928.

They did, of course, rejoin F.I.F.A. in 1948, but while many countries now draw only a very slender line between their amateurs and professionals, the British Associations still abide by the strictest definition of the word "amateur"

BROTHERS

See FAMILIES (Brothers).

BULGARIA

Bulgaria first entered the international football field in 1924 but it was not until after World War II that they improved enough to make any real impression in world football. A steady improvement culminated in them reaching the final tournament of the World Cup competition, at their fourth attempt, in Chile, in 1962.

Since then the Bulgarians have qualified for the World Cup Finals in 1966 and 1970, but a 1—1 draw with Morocco in Mexico produced their only point in these two tournaments.

They have been more successful in the Olympics, reaching the Final in 1968 before losing 4—1 to Hungary.

The game was first played in Bulgaria in 1894, the first club was formed in 1909, the governing body in 1923 and a national league competition in 1925.

Football clubs as such were disbanded by the new Communist regime in 1946 and the principal teams are all from sports clubs which run football sections. The leading side in the country, Red Banner (formerly CDNA) is fielded by the Central House of the People's Army, and was formed in 1948.

In 1970 there are about 9,000 teams, all amateurs (the leading players are all provided with jobs outside the game), competing in four zonal and 14 regional groups throughout the country.

Address of the governing body: Bulgarian Football Federation, Stade (V.-Levsky), Sofia. Colours: All white.

June 7, 1962: England 0, Bulgaria 0; Chile†

Dec. 11, 1968: England 1, Bulgaria 1; Wembley.

† World Cup

BURNLEY F.C.

Founded in 1881 as Burnley Rovers and dropped the title "Rovers" in 1882. One of the original members of the Football League, 1888. Honours: Champions, Division I, 1920-21, 1959-60. Runners-up, 1919-20, 1961-2. Champions Division II, 1897-8. Runners-up, 1912-13, 1946-7. F.A. Cup: Winners, 1914. Finalists, 1947, 1962. Record attendance: 54,775 v. Huddersfield Town, F.A. Cup, 3rd Round, Feb. 23, 1924. Address: Turf Moor, Burnley (Tel. 27777). Nickname: Clarets. Colours: Claret with blue collars and cuffs, white shorts. Record League goal-scorer: G. W. Beel, 35 goals, Division I, 1927-8. Record victory: 9—0 v. Darwen, Division I, Jan. 9, 1892; v. Crystal Palace, F.A. Cup, 2nd Round (Replay), 1908-9; v. New Brighton, F.A. Cup, 4th Round, Jan. 26, 1957. Record defeat: 10—0 v. Aston Villa, Division I, Aug. 29, 1925, and v Sheffield United, Division I, Jan. 19, 1929.

BURY F.C.

Founded 1885. Joined Football League, Division II, 1894. Honours: Champions, Division II, 1894-5. Runners-up, 1923-4. Best in Division I, 4th, 1925-6. Champions Division III, 1960-61. Runners-up, 1967-8. F.A. Cup: Winners, 1900, 1903. Record attendance 35,000 v. Bolton Wanderers, F.A. Cup, 3rd Round, Jan. 9, 1960. Address: Gigg Lane, Bury (Tel. 061-764 4881). Nickname: Shakers. Colours: White shirts, dark blue shorts with white stripe. Record league goal-scorer: N. Bullock, 31 goals, Division I, 1925-6. Record victory: 12—1 v. Stockton, F.A. Cup, 1st Round (Replay), 1896-7. Record defeat: 10—0 v. Blackburn Rovers, F.A. Cup, 1887-8.

C

CAMBRIDGE UNITED F.C.

Founded 1920. Originally known as Abbey United. Elected to Football League, Division IV 1970. Record attendance: 14,000 v. Chelsea, Friendly, May 1, 1970. Colours: white shirts with black and amber trim, white shorts. Address: Abbey Stadium, Newmarket Road, Cambridge. (Tel. Teversham 2170).

CANADA

While football has been played in Canada since about 1880 when it was introduced by Scottish migrants, it is only in the last one or two decades that any significant progress has been made in the development of the game in this part of the world.

The large increase in the number of European emigrants to Canada after World War II brought a greater enthusiasm for Soccer, the main interest being centred around Toronto and Montreal but many clubs springing up in all parts of the country.

A National Soccer League has been formed and despite the difficulties created by the great distances involved a national championship has been in existence for more than 50 years.

The last decade has seen the introduction of professional football to Canada and an Eastern Professional League was formed in 1961 by Toronto Italia, Hamilton Steelers, Toronto City and Montreal Cantalia.

This organisation collapsed in 1967 when the leading clubs either joined the predominantly American professional Leagues or the Canadian National League.

Many famous Football League professionals have taken summer engagements in Canadian football in recent years including, S. Matthews, D. Blanchflower, T. Macedo, J. Mudie, and J. Haynes.

The first Association to be formed in Canada was the Western Association of Ontario in 1880. Eight years later a Canadian team toured Britain, playing 23 games, including one against Scotland in which the visitors were defeated 4—0, and one against the Swifts in which the visitors were beaten 1—0. This latter game was played against an England XI at the of Wales.

A second tour by a Canadian team took place in 1891 when a match was played against an England XI at the Oval. Canada lost 6—1.

Since then, no fully representative international matches or "Tests" have been played between any of the home Associations and Canada. However, representative F.A. teams toured Canada in 1926 (played and won 18 games), 1931 (played and won 17 games), and 1950 (played 11 games, won 10, drew one). In the 1950 tour one of the 11 games was played in the United States against the U.S. World Cup XI. A twelfth game was played, Blues v. Whites at Winnipeg, in aid of the Winnipeg Flood Disaster, but, in this game, each side was a combination of F.A. and Canadian players.

The F.A. of Canada was formed in May 1912 and has been represented on the Council of the English F.A. since 1929.

Address of the governing body: F.A. of Canada, P.O. Box 44, Station "F", Winnipeg 2, Manitoba. Colours: Blue shirts with maple leaf crest, white shorts.

CARDIFF CITY F.C.

Founded 1899 as River Side F.C. Turned to professional football as Cardiff City, 1910. Joined Football League, Division II, 1920. Honours: Runners-up, Division I, 1923-4. Runners-up, Division II, 1920-21, 1951-2, 1959-60. Champions, Division III(S), 1946-7. F.A. Cup: Winners 1927. Record attendance: 61,566, Wales v. England, Oct. 14, 1961. Colours: Royal blue shirts with white

trimmings, white shorts. Address:
Ninian Park, Cardiff (Tel. 28501).
Nickname: Bluebirds. Record League
goal-scorer: S. Richards, 31 goals,
Division III(S), 1946-47. Record vic-
tory: 9—2 v. Thames, Division III(S),
Feb. 6, 1932. Record defeat: 11—2 v.
Sheffield United, Div. I, Jan. 1, 1926.

CARLISLE UNITED F.C.

Founded 1903 by the amalgamation
of Carlisle Red Rose and Shaddon-
gate United. Joined Football League,
Division III(N), 1928. Honours:
Champions, Division III, 1964-5.
Runners-up, Division IV, 1963-4.
Record attendance: 27,500 v. Bir-
mingham City, F.A. Cup, 3rd Round,
Jan. 5, 1957 and v. Middlesbrough,
F.A. Cup, 5th Round, Feb. 7, 1970.
Address: Brunton Park, Carlisle
(Tel. 26237). Nickname: Cumbrians.
Colours: Royal blue shirts, white
shorts. Record League goal-scorer:
J. McConnell, 42 goals, Division
III(N), 1928-29. Record Victory:
8—0 v. Hartlepools United, Division
III(N), Sept. 1, 1928. Record defeat:
11—1 v. Hull City, Division III(N),
Jan. 14, 1939.

CASUALTIES

See also DISASTERS, INJURIES.

Fatal

R. W. Benson, Arsenal full-back, retired from the field when playing
against Reading, Feb. 19, 1916, and
died soon afterwards. Benson had not
played for nearly 10 months. Death
was due to a burst blood vessel.

D. Jones, Welsh international full-
back, who played for Bolton Wanderers and Manchester City at the
end of the 19th century, cut his knee
while in training with the latter club;
lock-jaw set in and he died.

S. Raleigh, Gillingham centre-forward, died from concussion sustained
in a match with Brighton and Hove
Albion, Dec. 1, 1934.

J. Thomson, Glasgow Celtic goalkeeper, died after fracturing his skull
in a game with Glasgow Rangers,
Sept. 5, 1931.

J. Thorpe, Sunderland goalkeeper,
died a few days after a game against
Chelsea on Feb. 1, 1936. His death
was due to diabetes but a coroner's
jury found that the illness had been
accelerated by the game.

S. Wynne, Bury full-back, collapsed
when taking a free-kick against
Sheffield United at Bramall Lane,
April 30, 1927, and died in the dress-
ing-room. Death was primarily due to
pneumonia.

Serious Injuries

D. Dooley, Sheffield Wednesday
centre-forward fractured a leg in a
game against Preston North End,
Feb. 14, 1953. Gangrene set in and his
leg was amputated.

L. Ritson, Leyton Orient full-back,
fractured a leg in a game against
Northampton Town, Sept. 11, 1948.
He recovered, but in 1950 it was discovered that a bone had become dis-
eased and the limb was amputated.

CELTIC F.C.

Founded 1887 by a number of the
Catholics of the East End of Glasgow
with the object of raising funds for the
maintenance of the " Dinner Tables "
of needy children in the Missions of
St. Mary's, Sacred Heart, and St.
Michael's. One of the original members
of the Scottish League, 1890.
Honours: Champions, Scottish
League, Division 1, 1892-3, 1893-4,
1895-6, 1897-8, 1904-5, 1905-6, 1906-
7, 1907-8, 1908-9, 1909-10, 1913-14,
1914-15, 1915-16, 1916-17, 1918-19,
1921-2, 1925-6, 1935-6, 1937-8, 1953-
4, 1965-6, 1966-7, 1967-8, 1968-9,
1969-70. Runners-up, 1891-2, 1894-5,
1899-1900, 1900-1, 1901-2, 1911-12,
1912-13, 1917-18, 1919-20, 1920-21,
1927-8, 1928-9, 1930-31, 1934-5,
1938-9, 1954-5. Scottish Cup: Winners, 1892, 1899, 1900, 1904, 1907,
1908, 1911, 1912, 1914, 1923, 1925,
1927, 1931, 1933, 1937, 1951, 1954,
1965, 1967, 1969. Finalists, 1889,
1893, 1894, 1901, 1902, 1909 (cup
withheld by Scottish F.A. after a riot),
1926, 1928, 1955, 1956, 1961, 1963,
1966, 1970. European Cup: Winners,
1967. Finalists, 1970. Record attendance: 92,000 v. Rangers, Division I,
Jan. 1, 1938. Address: Parkhead,
Glasgow (Tel. Glasgow Bridgeton
2710). Colours: Green and white
hooped shirts, white shorts. Record
League goal-scorer: J. McCrory, 50
goals, Division I, 1935-6. Record victory: 11—0 v. Dundee, Division I,
Oct. 26, 1895. Record defeat: 8—0
v. Motherwell, Division I, 1936-7.

CHANNEL ISLANDS

The first native of the Channel Islands to become a professional in the Football League was E. Hurel who joined Everton as an inside-forward in April 1936. Hurel came from Jersey and was discovered in St. Helier by D. Murray, a former Everton player, who was coaching there.

Since then several Channel Islanders have figured in the Football League. They include L. Duquemin, Tottenham Hotspur centre-forward 1947-57; R. P. Degruchy, Nottingham Forest, Grimsby Town, Chesterfield, full-back, 1953-59; R. Le Flem, forward with Nottingham Forest, Wolves, Middlesbrough and Leyton Orient, 1960-67; R. Farmer, Nottingham Forest, Coventry City, Notts. County, wing-half, 1953-69; W. Whare, Nottingham Forest, full-back, 1948-60, and W. Spurdle, Manchester City and Oldham Athletic wing-half, 1948-64.

CHARLTON ATHLETIC F.C.

Founded 1905. Turned professional, 1920. Elected to Division III(S) 1921. Honours: Champions, Division III(S), 1928-9, 1934-5. Runners-up, Division II, 1935-6. Runners-up, Division I, 1936-7. F.A. Cup: Winners, 1947. Finalists, 1946. Record attendance: 75,031 v. Aston Villa, F.A. Cup, 5th Round, Feb. 12, 1938. Address: The Valley, Floyd Road, Charlton, S.E.7 (Tel. 01-858 3711). Nickname: Haddicks. Colours: All red. Record League goal-scorer: R. Allen, 32 goals, Division III(S), 1934-5. Record victory: 8—1 v. Middlesbrough, Division I, Sept. 12, 1953. Record defeat: 11—1 v. Aston Villa, Division II, Nov. 14, 1959.

CHELSEA F.C.

Founded 1905. Elected in the same year to the Football League, Division II after application for membership of the Southern League had been turned down. Honours: Champions, Division I, 1954-5. Runners-up, Division II, 1906-7, 1911-12, 1929-30, 1962-63. F.A. Cup: Winners, 1970. Finalists, 1915, 1967. F.L. Cup: Winners, 1965. Record attendance: 82,905 v. Arsenal, Division I, Oct. 12, 1935. Address: Stamford Bridge, London, S.W.6 (Tel. 01-385 5545). Colours:

Royal blue shirts and shorts. Record League goal-scorer: J. Greaves, 41 goals, Division I, 1960-61. Record victory, 9—1 v. Worksop, F.A. Cup, 1st Round, Jan. 11, 1908. Record defeat: 8—1 v. Wolverhampton Wanderers, Division I, Sept. 26, 1953.

CHESTER F.C.

Founded 1884. Elected to Football League, Division III(N), 1931. Honours: Runners-up, Division III(N), 1935-6. Record attendance: 20,500 v. Chelsea, F.A. Cup, 3rd Round (replay), Jan. 16, 1952. Address: Sealand Road Stadium, Chester (Tel. 21048). Colours: Sky blue shirts and shorts. Record League goal-scorer: R. Yates, 36 goals, Division III(N), 1946-47. Record victory: 12—0 v. York City, Division III(N), Feb. 1, 1936. Record defeat: 11—2 v. Oldham Athletic, Division III(N), Jan. 19, 1952.

CHESTERFIELD F.C.

Founded 1866. Re-formed 1871. Became a limited company in 1899 and elected to Football League, Division II in the same year. Re-organised as Chesterfield Town in 1904. Left the Football League 1909. In 1918 in another re-shuffle, Chesterfield Corporation took control and the club became the first to play municipal football. Continued in the Midland League until the Football League formed Division III(N) in 1921. Honours: Champions, Division III(N), 1930-31, 1935-6. Runners-up, Division 3-4. Champions, Division IV, 1969-70. Best in Division II, 4th, 1946-7. Record attendance: 30,968 v. Newcastle United, Division II, April 7, 1939. Address: Recreation Ground, Chesterfield (Tel. 2318). Nickname: Blues. Colours: Royal blue shirts, white shorts. Record League goal-scorer: J. Cookson, 44 goals, Division III(N), 1925-6. Record victory: 10—0 v. Glossop North End, Division II, Jan. 17, 1903. Record defeat: 9—1 v. Port Vale, Division II, Sept. 24, 1932.

CHILE

Rather overshadowed by other South American countries, Uruguay Brazil and Argentina, Chile has never been reckoned a powerful footballing nation, but they have victories to their credit over several European countries, most of them in home matches.

In Chile the home side has the advantage of being acclimatised to the special conditions of playing football at nearly 2,000 ft. above sea level.

As World Cup hosts in 1962 Chile was automatically seeded to the final tournament, and they won through to the semi-finals and to third place in the competition with victories over Switzerland (3—1), Italy (2—0),

Russia (2—1) and Yugoslavia (1—0). However, the best they could do in 1966 was a draw with North Korea.

The governing body of football in Chile was established in 1895 and is the second oldest in South America. It now controls about 3,000 clubs.

Address of F.A.: Federacion de Football de Chile, Heurfanos 1535, Casilla 3733, Santiago. Colours: Red shirts, blue shorts, white stockings.

Results of international matches:

June 25, 1950	Chile 0, England 2; Brazil†	
May 24, 1953	Chile 1, England 2; Santiago	
Mar. 30, 1960	Eire 2, Chile 0; Dublin	
May 23, 1966	Chile 2, Wales 0; Santiago	

† World Cup

CLYDE F.C.

Founded 1877. Joined Scottish League, Division I, 1906-7. Honours: Champions, Scottish League, Division II, 1904-5, 1951-2, 1956-7, 1961-2. Runners-up, 1963-4. Best in Division I, 3rd, 1908-9, 1911-12, 1966-7. Scottish Cup: Winners, 1939, 1955, 1958. Finalists, 1910, 1912, 1949. Record attendance: 52,000 v. Rangers, Division I, Nov. 21, 1908. Address: Shawfield Stadium, Glasgow C.5. (Tel. 041-788 6329). Nickname: Bully Wees. Colours: White shirts with red collar, black shorts. Record League goal-scorer in Division I, W. Boyd, 32 goals, 1932-3. Record victory: 11—1 v. Cowdenbeath, Division B, Oct. 6, 1951. Record defeat: 11—0 v. Rangers, Scottish Cup, 4th Round, 1880-81.

COLCHESTER UNITED F.C.

Became a professional club in 1937. Elected to Football League, Division III(S), 1950. Honours: Runners-up, Division IV, 1961-2. Record attendance: 19,072 v. Reading, F.A. Cup, 1st Round, Nov. 27, 1948. Address: Layer Road, Colchester (Tel. 74042). Colours: Royal blue with white trim, royal blue shorts with white stripe. Record League goal-scorer: R. R. Hunt, 37 goals, Division IV, 1961-2. Record victory: 9—1 v. Bradford City (H), Division IV, Dec. 30, 1961. Record defeat: 7—0 v. Leyton Orient, Division III(S), Jan. 5,

1952; 7—0 v. Reading, Division III(S), Sept. 18, 1957.

COLOMBIA

Colombia first hit the football headlines around 1950 when they tempted many leading players, mostly Argentinians, but including such British stars as Neil Franklin, Bobby Neil, Charlie Mitten and Roy Paul, to join their principal clubs—Independente and Millionarios. Colombia were not members of F.I.F.A. at that time and, therefore, had no need to comply with transfer regulations.

Result of international: May 20, 1970. Colombia 0, England 4, Bogota.

COLOURED PLAYERS

Several coloured players have appeared in Football League matches. These include:

T. Balogun, centre-forward with Queen's Park Rangers, 1956-7.

T. Best, centre-forward with Chester, Cardiff City, Queen's Park Rangers, 1948-9.

R. Brown, centre-half or centre-forward with Stoke City, Watford, 1947-58.

J. Charles, half-back with West Ham United, 1962-.

L. Delapenha, inside or outside-right with Portsmouth, Middlesbrough, Mansfield Town, 1948-61.

P. Foley, outside-right, Workington, Scunthorpe United, 1965-68.

G. Francis, outside-right, Leeds United, York City, 1957-64.

A. Johanneson, outside-left, Leeds United, 1960-

J. Leslie, inside-forward with Plymouth Argyle, 1921-35.

S. Mokone, outside-right with Coventry City, Cardiff City, Barnsley, 1956-62.

J. Parris, outside-right or left with Bradford, Luton Town, Northampton Town, Bournemouth and Boscombe Athletic, 1928-39. (Parris is the only coloured player to appear in the International Championship. He was capped for Wales against Ireland in Dec. 1931.)

E. Onyeali, centre-forward, Tranmere Rovers, 1960-61.

S. Stacey, Wrexham. Ipswich Town, 1966-69.

D. Tull, forward with Northampton Town (then in the Southern League), Tottenham Hotspur, 1908-14.

CORINTHIANS A.F.C.

Although this club is no longer in existence (it was amalgamated with the Casuals in 1939), it remains the most famous amateur club in the history of English football.

It was formed in 1882 by N. L. Jackson, then honorary assistant-secretary of the Football Association. He was distressed by England's poor international record against Scotland and considered it would benefit the England international team if a number of leading players could be given the opportunity of playing together more often in the same club side.

It was an unwritten law of the club that only public school and university men should be admitted as members. There were very few exceptions to this rule.

The Corinthians also made a rule never to enter for competitions, and, with the exception of charity matches (the Sheriff of London Shield), this rule was adhered to until 1922-3 season when the club first entered for the F.A. Cup.

No club did more than the Corinthians in developing the passing game in England during the 1880s. The advantages of this style, as opposed to the individual dribbling game, were soon apparent when the Corinthians defeated Blackburn Rovers, 8—1, at Blackburn, in Dec., 1884, when the Rovers were recognised as the best team in the country and were holders of the F.A. Cup.

Other outstanding victories of the Corinthians against professional opponents included a 5—0 win over Preston North End, then F.A. Cup holders and League Champions, at Richmond, Nov. 8, 1889; 10—3 v, Bury, F.A. Cup holders, 1904; 2—1 v. Aston Villa, League champions, 1900.

If the Corinthians had chosen to enter for the F.A. Cup in those earlier days they might well have won it. But when they entered the competition in 1922-3, through a lack of fixtures, the professional game had reached such a high standard that the amateurs were not able to make much of an impression.

Probably their best game in the F.A. Cup competition was against Newcastle United in the 4th Round in 1926-7. They led the powerful Newcastle team (League Champions in that season) by 1—0 until 15 minutes from the end when the professionals equalised and went on to score two more goals.

The Corinthians had been the first English soccer club to play outside Europe when they made a tour of South Africa in 1897.

More players have been drawn from the Corinthians to play for England in full internationals than from any other amateur club. On two occasions the whole England team was composed of Corinthians (see INTERNATIONALS, Club Records).

During the 1880s and 1890s the Corinthians included such great internationals as N. C. Bailey (with 19 full England international appearances to his credit), E. C. Bambridge (18), R. E. Foster (5), G. O. Smith (20), and W. Arnott (14 for Scotland).

Even in the 1920s when teams for full internationals were drawn almost entirely from the professional ranks a number of Corinthians could not be denied a place in these games. Such men were B. Howard Baker (2 full, 10 amateur caps), A. G. Bower (6 full, 13 amateur), F. H. Ewer (2 full, 14 amateur), A. E. Knight (1 full, 28 amateur), F. N. S. Creek (1 full, 5 amateur), A. G. Doggart (1 full, 4 amateur), B. Joy (1 full, 12 amateur).

As already stated the Corinthians finally amalgamated with the Casuals in 1939 and now the Corinthian-Casuals A.F.C. competes in the Isthmian League.

CORNER KICK

See also LAWS OF THE GAME.

The corner kick was adopted by the F.A. in 1872 (the Sheffield Rules had included the corner kick since 1868), and in the early days these kicks were usually taken by the wing halves. It was not until the late 1890s that the wing forwards began to take corners.

In 1924 the law was altered so that a goal could be scored direct from a corner kick, following a proposal of the Scottish F.A. This alteration brought some confusion in its first season as some thought that it was permissible for the player taking the corner to dribble the ball in from the flag. The F.A. decided against this and before the next season began the wording of the law was altered to make the position clear.

There is thought to have been only one Football League game without a corner kick. That was a Division I match between Newcastle United and Portsmouth, Dec. 5, 1931. Result 0—0.

COVENTRY CITY F.C.

Founded 1883 by factory workers and known as Singers F.C. Re-organised 1908. Elected to Football League, Division II, 1919. Honours: Champions Division II, 1966-67. Champions, Division III(S), 1935-6. Runners-up 1933-4. Champions, Division III, 1963-4. Runners-up, Division IV, 1958-9. Record attendance: 51,455 v. Wolverhampton W., Division II, Apr. 29, 1967. Address: Highfield Rd., Coventry (Tel. 57171). Nickname: Sky-blues. Colours: Sky blue shirts and shorts. Record League goal-scorer: C. Bourton, 49 goals, Division III(S), 1931-2. Record victory: 9—0 v. Bristol City (H), Division III (S), April 28, 1934. Record defeat: 10—2 v. Norwich City (A), Division III(S), Mar. 15, 1930.

COWDENBEATH F.C.

Founded 1881. Re-organised 1905. Promoted to Scottish League Division I 1924. Honours: Champions, Division II, 1938-39. Runners-up 1969-70. Record attendance: 25,586 v.

Rangers, Scottish League Cup, Q.F. (2nd leg, Sept. 21, 1949. Address: Central Park, Cowdenbeath (Tel. 3205). Colours: Royal blue shirts, white shorts with red stripe. Record goal-scorer in Division I: W. Devlin, 40 goals, 1925-6. Record victory: 12—0 v. Johnstone, Scottish cup, 1st Round, Jan. 21, 1928. Record defeat: 10—1 v. St. Bernards, Division II, 1934-5.

CREWE ALEXANDRA F.C.

Founded 1876. One of the original members of the Football League, Division II, 1892. Adopted professionalism 1893. Failed to gain re-election to Division II, 1896. Became member of newly-formed Division III(N), 1921. Best in Division II, 10th, 1892-3. Best in Division III(N), 6th, 1921-2, 1922-3, 1931-2, 1935-6. Record attendance: 20,000 v. Tottenham Hotspur, F.A. Cup, 4th Round, Jan. 30, 1960. Address: Gresty Road, Crewe (Tel. 3014). Nickname: Railwaymen. Colours: All red. Record League goal-scorer: J. T. Harkin, 34 goals. Division IV, 1964-5. Record victory: 8—0 v. Rotherham United (H.), Division III(N), Oct. 1, 1932. Record defeat: 13—2 v. Tottenham Hotspur (A.), F.A. Cup, 4th Round (replay), Feb. 3, 1960.

CRICKETERS

In League football today there are several players who have also made their mark in first-class cricket. Following is a list of men who have made international appearances in both sports:

J. Arnold, former Oxford City, Southampton and Fulham outside-left and Hampshire batsman. Capped at football for England v. Scotland, 1933. Capped at cricket for England v. New Zealand (at Lords), 1931.

D. C. S. Compton, Arsenal outside-left and Middlesex batsman. Played in 11 war-time soccer internationals for England as well as one " Victory " international v. Scotland. He made the first of his 78 Test appearances in 1937 against New Zealand at the Oval.

A. Ducat, Arsenal, Aston Villa and Fulham wing-half and Surrey batsman. Capped at football for England v. Scotland, Wales and Ireland, 1919,

v. Scotland and Wales 1920, and v. Ireland, 1921. Capped at cricket v. Australia (at Leeds), 1921.

R. E. Foster, Oxford University inside-left and Worcestershire batsman. Capped at football for England v. Wales, 1900, v. Scotland, Wales, Ireland and Germany, 1901, and v. Wales, 1902. Foster played in 8 Test matches: 3 v. South Africa, 1907, and 5 v. Australia in the winter of 1903-4.

C. B. Fry, Corinthians right-back and Sussex and Hampshire batsman. Capped at football for England v. Ireland, 1901. Played in 26 Test matches, 18 of them against Australia, 8 against South Africa, 1895-1912.

L. H. Gay, Old Brightonians goalkeeper and Cambridge University wicket-keeper. Capped for England v. Scotland, 1893, and v. Scotland and Wales, 1894. Played in one Test against the Australians at Sydney in 1894-5.

W. Gunn, Notts County outside-left and Nottinghamshire batsman. Capped for England v. Scotland and Wales, 1884. Played in 11 Test matches, all of them against Australia, 1886-99.

H. T. W. Hardinge, Sheffield United inside-forward and Kent batsman. Capped for England v. Scotland, 1910. Capped at cricket v. Australia (at Leeds), 1921.

E. Hendren, outside-right with Manchester City, Coventry City and Brentford. Middlesex batsman. Played for England at football in "Victory" international v. Wales, 1920. Played for England at cricket in 51 Tests.

Hon. A. Lyttelton, Old Etonians forward and Middlesex batsman. Capped for England v. Scotland, 1877. Played in 4 Tests against Australia, 1880-84.

H. Makepeace, Everton wing-half and Lancashire batsman. Capped for England v. Scotland, 1906, 1910 and 1912, v. Wales, 1912. Played in 4 Tests in Australia, 1920-21.

C. A. Milton, Arsenal outside-left and Gloucestershire all-rounder. Capped for England v. Austria in 1951 and appeared in 6 Tests in 1958 and 1959.

J. Sharp, Everton outside-right and Lancashire batsman. Played for England v. Ireland, 1903, v. Scotland, 1905, and in 3 Tests v. Australia, 1909.

W. Watson, Huddersfield Town and Sunderland wing-forward or winghalf, and left-handed batsman for Yorkshire and Leicestershire. Appeared for England in "Victory" international v. Wales, 1946. Capped v. Ireland and Italy, 1950, v. Wales and Yugoslavia, 1951. Played the first of 23 Tests for England in 1951 against South Africa.

CROSSBAR

The crossbar over the goalmouth was first introduced into Football Association rules in 1875. Before that a tape was used although the word "bar," was mentioned in other rules as far back as 1863.

The Sheffield Association made bars obligatory some time before 1875. But it was not until the international conference—held in Manchester in 1882 —that crossbars became generally compulsory.

See also LAWS OF THE GAME, Law 1, Part 6, and Law 10.

CRYSTAL PALACE F.C.

Founded 1905. Immediately joined Southern League. One of the original members of the Football League, Third Division, 1920. Honours: Runners-up, Division II, 1968-9. Champions, Division III(S), 1920-21. Runners-up, 1928-9, 1930-31, 1938-9. Runners-up, Division III, 1963-4. Runners-up, Division IV, 1960-61. Record attendance: 49,498 v. Chelsea, Division I, Dec. 27, 1969. Address: Selhurst Park, London, S.E.25. (Tel. 01-653 2223). Nickname: Glaziers. Colours: Claret shirts with thin light blue stripes, white shorts. Record League goalscorer: P. Simpson, 46 goals, Division III(S), 1930-31. Record victory: 9—0 v. Barrow, Division IV, Oct. 10, 1959. Record defeat: 11—4 v. Manchester City, F.A. Cup, 5th Round, Feb. 20, 1926.

CUP MEDALS

See also FOOTBALL ASSOCIATION CHALLENGE CUP, FOOTBALL ASSOCIATION AMATEUR CHALLENGE CUP, SCOTTISH CUP, WELSH CUP, TROPHIES.

J. Delaney created a unique record by gaining Scottish, English, N. Ireland and Eire Cup medals—Celtic 1937, Manchester United 1948, Derry City 1954, and Cork Athletic 1956.

J. Welford is often referred to as another player with a similar record, but the fact is that he gained only English and Scottish medals.

Only two players have gained winners' medals in both the F.A. Cup and the F.A. Amateur Cup. T. Morren was Middlesbrough's centre-half when they won the Amateur Cup in 1895 and Sheffield United's centre-half when they won the F.A. Cup in 1899. Morren again appeared in the F.A. Cup Final when Sheffield United were beaten in 1901. And R. Chatt was inside-right for Aston Villa when they won the Cup in 1895. Subsequently reinstated as an amateur, he received a winners' medal in the F.A. Amateur Cup with Stockton in 1899.

Three other players have appeared in both the F.A. Cup final and the F.A. Amateur Cup final:

S. B. Ashworth: Oxford City, Amateur finalists, 1903. Manchester City, F.A. Cup winners, 1904.

Rev. K. R. G. Hunt: Wolverhampton Wanderers, F.A. Cup winners, 1908. Oxford City, Amateur Cup finalists, 1913.

R. Topham: Casuals, Amateur Cup finalists, 1894. Wolverhampton Wanderers, F.A. Cup winners, 1893.

Members of Charlton Athletic's team which was defeated 4—1 by Derby County in the 1946 Cup Final each received two medals from the F.A. Gold was scarce at the time and as losers they were presented with bronze medals. The gold medals came later.

For players who have gained both English and Scottish Cup medals see under F.A. CUP (Scotland).

F. Gento gained eight European Cup medals with Real Madrid, including six winners' medals.

CYPRUS

The Cypriots are enthusiastic about soccer, but with a population of only a little over half a million it is hardly surprising that they have been unable to make much impression at International level.

They withdrew from the 1958 World Cup and have failed to win any subsequent games in this competition.

Address: Cyprus F.A. (KOP), P.O. Box 1471, Nicosia. Colours: Blue shirts, white shorts.

Results of internationals: Dec. 11, 1968, Cyprus 0, Scotland 5, Nicosia; May 17, 1969, Scotland 8, Cyprus 0, Glasgow. Both World Cup games.

CZECHOSLOVAKIA

Soccer was played in Prague before the formation of the Republic of Czechoslovakia when Bohemia was part of Austria-Hungary. Clubs like SK Slavia and A.C. Sparta were playing the game in the 1880s and 1890s and Slavia, now known as Dynamo, were formed as early as 1882.

The Bohemian F.A. was formed in 1902 and with the visit of British coaches to Prague in the years before World War I the game developed quickly.

In 1920 the Republic of Czechoslovakia came into being and in that same year their international side reached the final of the Olympic Games but disgraced themselves by walking off the field when losing 2—0 to Belgium after one of their number had been sent off by the referee.

The new Czechoslovakian F.A. was formed in 1922 and since then they have always been among the better European footballing nations.

Czechoslovakia reached the final of the World Cup in 1934 when they were beaten 2—1 by Italy after extra time.

They were finalists again in 1962 when a side noted for its strong defence surprised the critics by winning through to meet Brazil. In that final the man who had previously been the star of their defence, goalkeeper V. Schroif, did not maintain his brilliant form and partly because of this they were beaten 3—1.

Czechoslovakia failed to qualify in 1966, and, after reaching Mexico in 1970, their all-amateur side did not collect a single point.

Address of the governing body which now controls about 5,000 clubs is Section Tchécoslovaque de Football, Na Porici 12, Prague 1. Colours: White shirts, white shorts, red, white and blue stockings.

A match against Bohemia is included in these results of international matches:

June 13, 1908	Bohemia 0, England 4; Prague
May 16, 1934	Czechoslovakia 2, England 1; Prague
May 22, 1937	Czechoslovakia 1, Scotland 3; Prague
Dec. 1, 1937	England 5, Czechoslovakia 4; Tottenham
Dec. 8, 1937	Scotland 5, Czechoslovakia 0; Ibrox Park
May 18, 1938	Czechoslovakia 2, Eire 2; Prague
May 1, 1957	Wales 1, Czechoslovakia 0; Wrexham*
May 26, 1957	Czechoslovakia 2, Wales 0; Prague*
June 8, 1958	Ireland 1, Czechoslovakia 0; Sweden*
June 17, 1958	Ireland 2, Czechoslovakia 1; Sweden*
May 10, 1959	Czechoslovakia 4, Eire 0; Prague†
April 5, 1959	Eire 2, Czechoslovakia 0; Dublin†
May 14, 1961	Czechoslovakia 4, Scotland 0; Bratislava*
Sept. 26, 1961	Scotland 3, Czechoslovakia 2; Hampden*
Oct. 8, 1961	Eire 1, Czechoslovakia 3; Dublin*
Oct. 29, 1961	Czechoslovakia 7, Eire 1; Prague*
Nov. 29, 1961	Scotland 2, Czechoslovakia 4; Brussels*
May 29, 1963	Czechoslovakia 2, England 4; Bratislava
Nov. 2, 1966	England 0, Czechoslovakia 0; Wembley
May 21, 1967	Eire 0, Czechoslovakia 2; Dublin†
Nov. 22, 1967	Czechoslovakia 1, Eire 2; Prague†
May 4, 1969	Eire 1, Czechoslovakia 2; Dublin*
Oct. 7, 1969	Czechoslovakia 3, Eire 0; Prague*
June 11, 1970	England 1, Czechoslovakia 0; Guadalajara*

* World Cup † Nations Cup

D

DARLINGTON F.C.

Founded 1883. Adopted professionalism, 1908. One of the original members of the Football League, Division III(N), 1921. Honours: Champions, Division III(N), 1924-5. Runners-up, 1921-2. Runners-up Division IV, 1965-6. Best in Division II, 15th, 1925-6. Record attendance: 21,864 v. Bolton Wanderers, Football League Cup, 3rd Round, Nov. 14, 1960. Address: Feethams Ground, Darlington (Tel. 5097). Nickname: Quakers. Colours: White shirts with three black rings, black shorts. Record League goal-scorer: D. Brown, 39 goals, Division III(N), 1924-25. Record victory: 9—2 v. Lincoln City, Division III(N), Jan. 7, 1928. Record defeat: 10—0 v. Doncaster Rovers, Division IV, Jan. 25, 1964.

DEATHS

See CASUALTIES (Fatal); DISASTERS.

DEBUTS

For youngest and oldest players see AGE. For goal-scoring debuts see GOAL-SCORING (Debuts).

S. Milton had an unhappy Football League debut as goalkeeper for Halifax Town against Stockport County, Jan. 6, 1934. He conceded 13 goals. An unenviable record.

D. Murray conceded 11 goals when making his Football League debut in goal for Crewe Alexandra v. Lincoln City, Division III(N), Sept. 29, 1951.

DEFEATS

See also under DEFENSIVE RECORDS (Goals) and WITHOUT A WIN.

Manchester United lost their first 12 games of season 1930-31. The club's first victory was against Birmingham (2—0) at Old Trafford, Nov. 1, 1930. This is the worst start to the season any club has ever made in the Football League.

In season 1931-2 Rochdale lost 17 games in succession in Division III(N). On Nov. 7, 1931, they defeated New Brighton, 3—2, then failed to gain another point until drawing 1—1 with the same opponents on Mar. 9, 1932.

Nelson lost every one of their away games in Division III(N) during season 1930-31, the only club to do so in a season of at least 21 away games. After drawing, 1—1, with Halifax Town, Mar. 29, 1930, they played 24 away games without gaining a point.

Only two clubs have ever had 10 or more goals scored against them in more than one Football League game in a single season—Darwen and Rotherham. Darwen suffered three 0—10 defeats in Division II, 1898-9, v. Manchester City, Feb. 18, 1899, v. Walsall, Mar. 3, 1899, v. Loughborough Town, April 1, 1899. All were away matches. Rotherham had two big defeats in Division III(N) during 1928-9: 1—11 v. Bradford City, away, Aug. 25, 1928, 1—10 v. South Shields away, Mar. 16, 1929.

In the Scottish League, Division II, season 1937-8, Brechin City suffered three 10—0 defeats: v. Airdrieonians, v. Albion Rovers, and v. Cowdenbeath.

Other double-figure scores are mentioned under GOAL-SCORING (Teams and General).

Most Defeats in a Season

Football League:

Division I: 30 defeats in 42 games, Leeds United, 1946-7; Blackburn Rovers, 1965-6.

Division II: 31 defeats in 42 games, Tranmere Rovers, 1938-9.

Division III(S): 29 defeats in 42 games, Merthyr Town, 1924-5.

Division III(N): 33 defeats in 40 games, Rochdale, 1931-2.

Division III: 31 defeats in 46

EUROPEAN CHAMPION CLUBS CUP. (*Above*) Celtic, 1966–67, the first British club to win the competition. (*Below*) Manchester United, winners 1967–68, pose with the European Cup.

FOOTBALL ASSOCIATION CHALLENGE CUPS. (*Above*) left to right: F.A. Challenge Cup, International Trophy and F.A. Amateur Cup. (*Below*) Football Association Challenge Cup Match at Kennington Oval, 1890–91, Blackburn Rovers *v*. Notts County.

games, Newport County, 1961-2.

Division IV: 31 defeats in 46 games, Bradford, 1968-69.

Scottish League:

Division I: 31 defeats in 42 games, St. Mirren, 1920-21.

Division II: 30 defeats in 38 games, Lochgelly United, 1923-4. 30 defeats in 36 games, Brechin City, 1962-3.

DEFENSIVE RECORDS
Goals

Here are the best defensive records for a single season of at least 42 games in the Football League:

DIVISION I

		Goals	Games
Liverpool	1968-69	24	42
Leeds United	1968-69	26	42

DIVISION II

Manchester United	1924-25	23	42
Birmingham City	1947-48	24	42

DIVISION III(S)

Southampton	1921-22	21	42
Plymouth Argyle	1921-22	24	42

DIVISION III(N)

Port Vale	1953-54	21	46
Rochdale	1923-24	26	42

DIVISION III

Watford	1968-69	34	46

DIVISION IV

Gillingham	1963-64	30	46

SCOTTISH LEAGUE

(a complete season of 30 or more games).

DIVISION I

Celtic	1913-14	14	38
	1916-17	17	38
	1921-22	20	42
Rangers	1923-24	22	38

DIVISION II

Morton	1966-67	20	38

The worst defensive records for a single season in the Football League are as follows:

DIVISION I

		Goals	Games
Blackpool	1930-31	125	42
Ipswich Town	1963-64	121	42

DIVISION II

Darwen	1898-99	141	34
Newport County	1946-47	133	42

DIVISION III(S)

Merthyr Town	1929-30	135	42
Walsall	1952-53	118	46

DIVISION III(N)

Nelson	1927-28	136	42
Rochdale	1931-32	135	40

DIVISION III

Accrington Stanley	1959-60	123	46

DIVISION IV

Hartlepools United	1959-60	109	46

SCOTTISH LEAGUE
DIVISION I

Leith Athletic	1931-32	137	38

DIVISION II

Edinburgh City	1931-32	146	38

Preston North End won the F.A. Cup without conceding a goal in 1888-9. The club's tally for five Cup-ties was 11—0. In the same season they also won the League Championship without losing a game. Their goals tally in the League was 74—15.

Bury also accomplished this Cup feat in 1902-3 when their tally for five ties was 12—0.

The highest number of consecutive F.A. Cup ties without conceding a single goal is 12 by Bradford City in seasons 1910-11 and 1911-12. The run came to an end after three goal-less draws with Barnsley in the 4th Round of 1911-12. In the third replay Bradford City were knocked out 2—3.

Queen's Park (Glasgow) were formed in 1867 and did not have a goal scored against them by a Scottish club until Jan. 16, 1875. Vale of Leven broke the 7-year record.

Since the offside rule was changed in 1925 the record number of games in any one season that a club has prevented their opponents from scoring in Football League games is 30 by Port Vale in Division III(N) in 1953-4.

In Division III(S) in 1925-6, Millwall did not have a goal scored against them in 11 consecutive matches.

Huddersfield Town completed all their Football League matches in Division I, 1924-5, without conceding more than two goals in any one match. Tranmere Rovers did the same in Division III(N), 1937-8.

Cardiff City completed season 1928-9 with the best defensive record in the First Division (59 goals conceded). Nevertheless they were relegated.

Undefeated

See also HOME WINS, AWAY WINS.

The record for the longest run without defeat in the Football League is held by Leeds United. After losing 5—1 at Burnley, Oct. 19, 1968, they enjoyed a run of 34 Division I games without a defeat before losing 3—2 at Everton, Aug. 30, 1969.

Liverpool won the championship of Division II, 1893-4, winning 22 of their 28 games, and drawing 6. They followed this by winning their " Test Match " for promotion, then drew their first two games of season 1894-5 in Division I before going down to Aston Villa. A total of 31 games without defeat.

The longest run without defeat in the Football League in a single season was made by Burnley. They were undefeated in 30 matches played between Sept. 4, 1920 (when they lost 0—2, away to Bradford) and Mar. 26, 1921 (when they were beaten 3—0 away to Manchester City). Burnley won the championship that season. Manchester City were runners-up. (Note that Burnley's run applies to League games only. It was interrupted by an F.A. Cup defeat by Hull City.)

In the Scottish League Celtic were undefeated in 63 games from Nov. 13, 1915 to April 21, 1917. Kilmarnock broke this remarkable run, winning 2—0 at Parkhead.

In International matches the longest undefeated run was made by Hungary. After losing 3—5 against Austria, May 14, 1950, they were undefeated in 29 matches before losing 2—3 to Germany in the World Cup Final, July 4, 1954.

In season 1881-2, Blackburn Rovers played 35 matches without defeat before losing 0—1 in the F.A. Cup Final to Old Etonians in Mar., 1882.

Between Mar. 17, 1928 and Mar. 27, 1929, Rangers players 38 consecutive Scottish League, Division I, games without defeat. Hamilton Academicals broke the run, 3—1, at Douglas Park.

Celtic (Glasgow) were undefeated in 33 games after losing in the Scottish Cup Final, April 1966, until beaten by Dundee United Dec. 12, 1966. In League games only this run extended over 27 from Feb. 1966.

In season 1952-3 Bristol Rovers played 27 consecutive Division III(S)

games without defeat. They were beaten 0—3 at Millwall on Sept. 13, 1952, and did not lose again until Reading beat them, 2—0, at Elm Park, Mar. 21, 1953.

Liverpool started the 1949-50 season by playing 19 consecutive Division I games without defeat. Of these they won 10. Their first defeat of the season was 2—3 at Huddersfield, Dec. 10, 1949. This is a record start for Division I since World War I.

In Division IV Millwall also played 19 games from the start of a season before suffering their first defeat. This was in 1959-60.

In the Scottish League, Division II, 1963-64, Morton actually *won* their first 23 games before losing 1—3 at East Fife.

Millwall hold the Football League record for the longest home run without defeat. After losing their last home game of 1963-4 they were unbeaten in 59 consecutive League games at The Den before losing 1—2 to Plymouth Argyle, Jan. 14, 1967.

After losing at home 1—3 to Brentford, April 8, 1933, Reading were unbeaten in the Football League on their own ground until Jan. 15, 1936, when they lost 1—2 to Queen's Park Rangers. They had then played 55 consecutive home League games without defeat.

Both Millwall's and Reading's runs were interrupted by Cup defeats at home, and the record home run which included Cup games (both F.A. and Football League Cup) was set up by Gillingham with a total of 52. After losing 2—3 at home to Barrow, April 6, 1963, they were undefeated at Priestfield Stadium until losing 0—1 to Exeter City, April 10, 1965. Gillingham's run included 48 Football League games.

Stockport County had an unbeaten home run of 48 Football League games, plus three F.A. Cup ties, April 2, 1927 to Oct. 5, 1929.

Plymouth Argyle were not beaten at home between Mar. 25, 1921 and Aug. 25, 1923, a total of 47 Football League plus three F.A. Cup games.

In the Spanish League Real Madrid were undefeated at home from Feb. 3, 1957, when they lost 2—3 to Atletico Madrid, until beaten o—1 by the same club, Mar. 7, 1965. Between these games they won 114 and drew 8 League games on their own ground.

Sunderland were not beaten at home in a Football League game from Sept. 15, 1890 (lost 3—4 to Wolverhampton Wanderers) to Dec. 9, 1893 (lost 2—3 to Blackburn Rovers); 44 home games without defeat, including six draws. There followed another run of 37 undefeated home games, including seven draws, before losing 0—1 to Bury, Sept. 1, 1896. That is a run of 82 home games with only one defeat.

Since World War II the following clubs have completed a season of League matches without a home defeat:

Cardiff City, Rotherham United, 1946-7; Portsmouth, Swansea Town, 1948-9; Mansfield Town, 1950-51; Port Vale, 1953-4; Manchester United, 1955-6; Torquay United, Colchester United, 1956-7; Walsall, 1960-61; Liverpool, 1961-2; Everton, Bournemouth, 1962-3; Tottenham Hotspurs, Northampton Town, Brighton, Millwall, 1964-5; Manchester City, Millwall, 1965-6; Manchester United, Wrexham, 1966-7; Barnsley, Crewe Alexandra 1967-8; Leeds United, Luton Town, 1968-9; Wrexham, 1969-70.

For undefeated F.A. Cup run see under FOOTBALL ASSOCIATION CHALLENGE CUP (Results).

Fewest Defeats

The fewest defeats in a season since each division of the Football League contained at least 22 clubs, are listed below:

DIVISION I

		Defeats	Games
Leeds United	1968-69	2	42
Arsenal	1930-31	4	42

DIVISION II

Leeds United	1963-64	3	42
Tottenham Hotspur	1919-20	4	42

DIVISION III(S)

Southampton	1921-22	4	42
Plymouth Argyle	1929-30	4	42

DIVISION III(N)

Wolverhampton Wanderers	1923-24	3	42
Doncaster Rovers	1946-47	3	42
Port Vale	1953-54	3	46

DIVISION III

Plymouth Argyle	1958-59	7	46

DIVISION IV

Millwall	1964-65	7	46
Luton Town	1967-68	7	46
Swansea City	1969-70	7	46
Port Vale	1969-70	7	46

Scottish League

DIVISION I
(with 20 or more clubs)

Rangers	1920-21	1	42
	1928-29	1	38
	1967-68	1	34
Celtic	1956-57	1	36
	1967-68	1	34
Hearts	1957-58	1	34

DIVISION II
(with 19 clubs)

Clyde	1956-57	1	36
Morton	1963-64	1	36
St. Mirren	1967-68	1	36

(with 18 clubs)

Raith Rovers	1937-38	2	34
Cowdenbeath	1938-39	2	34

DENMARK

Denmark is still one of the strongholds of the amateur game. There is no professionalism in this country and that is probably one of the reasons why they have not made much of an impression in the international field except, of course, in the amateur Olympic Games where they have been finalists in 1908, 1912 and 1960.

Money talks, and in recent years the Danish national side has been prevented from developing into a major force because of the regular exodus of their star players to other countries, principally Italy, France, and more recently, Scotland, where they are tempted by the professional game.

Football was begun in Denmark by British residents in about 1876 and the Danish Football Union which now controls something like 1,500 clubs, was formed in 1899.

England suffered their first-ever defeat by a side outside of the United Kingdom when they were beaten 2—1 in Copenhagen in May 1910 in an amateur international, and there was another shock in store for England's full professional side when they met Denmark for the first time in 1948. On that occasion the Danish amateurs held the English profes-

sionals to a goalless draw.
Address of the governing body:
Dansk Boldspil Union, P.H. Lings-

Allé 4, Kobenhavn V. Colours: Red
shirts, white shorts.

Sept. 26, 1948	Denmark 0, England 0; Copenhagen
May 12, 1951	Scotland 3, Denmark 1; Glasgow
May 25, 1952	Denmark 1, Scotland 2; Copenhagen
Oct. 2, 1955	Denmark 1, England 5; Copenhagen
Oct. 3, 1956*	Eire 2, Denmark 1; Dublin
Dec. 5, 1956*	England 5, Denmark 2; Wolverhampton
May 15, 1957*	Denmark 1, England 4; Copenhagen
Oct. 2, 1957*	Denmark 0, Eire 2; Copenhagen
Oct. 21, 1964*	Denmark 1, Wales 0; Copenhagen
Dec. 1, 1965*	Wales 4, Denmark 2; Wrexham
July 3, 1966	Denmark 0, England 2; Copenhagen
Oct. 16, 1968	Denmark 0, Scotland 1; Copenhagen
Dec. 1, 1968*	Eire 1, Denmark 1; Dublin†
May 27, 1969*	Denmark 2, Eire 0; Copenhagen
Oct. 15, 1969*	Eire 1, Denmark 1; Dublin

* World Cup   † Abandoned

DERBY COUNTY F.C.

Founded 1884 as the football section of Derby County Cricket Club.
One of the original members of the
Football League, 1888. Honours:
Runners-up, Division I, 1895-6, 1929-
30, 1935-6. Champions, Division II,
1911-12, 1914-15, 1968-9. Runners-up
1925-6. Champions, Division III(N),
1956-7. Runners-up, Division III(N),
1955-6. F.A. Cup: Winners, 1946.
Finalists, 1898, 1899, 1903. Record
attendance: 41,826 v. Tottenham
Hotspur, Division I, Sept. 20,
1969. Address, Baseball Ground,
Derby (Tel. 40105). Nickname: Rams.
Colours: White shirts, black shorts.
Record League goal-scorer: J. Bowers,
Division I, 1930-31, and R. Straw,
Division III(N), 1956-7, 37 goals.
Record victory: 9—0, v. Wolver-
hampton Wanderers, Division I,
Jan. 10, 1891; v. Sheffield Wednesday,
Division I, Jan. 21, 1899. Record
defeat: 11—2 v. Everton, F.A. Cup,
1st Round, 1889-90.

DIRECTORS

A director of a football club company affiliated to the Football Association is prohibited by the rules from
receiving any payment for his services
as a director and as an employee
of the club in any other capacity. In
other words, anyone who is already
on the payroll of a club, as say a

groundsman, secretary or manager,
cannot become a director and still
receive payment in respect of his other
office.

DISASTERS

The biggest disaster in the history
of sport occurred at the National
Stadium, Lima, Peru, on Sunday,
May 24, 1964. Six minutes before the
end of a match between Peru and
Argentina, the referee disallowed a
goal by the home side and a riot
quickly broke out. The police used
tear gas, and during the ensuing
panic to get out of the stadium 301
people were killed and over 500 injured.

On Mar. 9, 1946, 33 people were
killed and well over 400 injured at
Burden Park, Bolton, before an F.A.
Cup-tie between Bolton Wanderers
and Stoke City. A section of the crowd
was so tightly packed that they got
out of hand and were pushed help-
lessly upon one another as crush-
barriers broke. Several thousand
pounds were collected for the depend-
ants of those killed and for the injured.

During an International Championship match at Ibrox Park, Glasgow,
between Scotland and England on
April 5, 1902, part of the West stand
collapsed and many people were killed
and injured. Officially the casualty list
was 25 killed, 24 dangerously injured,

168 seriously injured, 153 injured, and 172 slightly injured. The game, which had been in progress for about 10 minutes, was resumed after a hold-up of half an hour. The result was a draw 1—1 but the match was subsequently declared unofficial and deleted from International records.

Manchester United lost eight of their players when the aircraft bringing the team home from Belgrade crashed at Munich Airport, Feb. 6, 1958. The players who died were R. Byrne, T. Taylor, D. Edwards, G. Bent, E. Coleman, M. Jones, D. Pegg, and W. Whelan. The club secretary, coach, trainer and eight sporting journalists were also killed.

On May 14, 1949, the whole of the Torino team, Italian League Champions, including eight internationals, were killed, when the plane returning them from a game in Lisbon crashed at Superga, outside Turin. In addition to the players including all the reserves, the club's manager, trainer and coach were also killed. The total death roll was 28.

Two people were killed and several injured when crush barriers collapsed at Ibrox Park, Glasgow, Sept. 16, 1961, during a game between Rangers and Celtic.

At Hillsborough, Sheffield, on Feb. 14, 1914, during a replayed F.A. Cup-tie between Sheffield Wednesday and Wolverhampton Wanderers, a retaining wall collapsed and 75 people were injured. The game was resumed but there was no addition to the score of 1—0 in favour of the Wednesday.

DONCASTER ROVERS F.C.

Founded 1879. Elected to Football League, Division II, 1901. Failed to gain re-election, 1903. Re-elected 1904. Failed to gain re-election 1905. Unable to gain re-admission to the League until elected to Division III(N) 1923. Honours: Champions, Division III(N), 1934-5, 1946-7, 1949-50. Runners-up, Division III(N), 1937-8, 1938-9. Champions, Division IV, 1965-6, 1968-9. Best in Division II, 7th 1901-2. Record attendance: 37,149 v. Hull City Division III(N), Oct. 2, 1948. Address: Belle Vue, Doncaster (Tel. 55281). Colours: White shirts, red shorts. Record League goalscorer: C. Jordan, 42 goals, Division

III(N), 1946-7. Record victory: 10—0 v. Darlington, Division IV, January 25, 1964. Record defeat: 12—0 v. Small Heath, Division II, April 11, 1903.

DOUBLE, THE

Only three clubs have won the Football League Championship and the F.A. Cup in the same season, Preston North End in 1888-9, Aston Villa in 1896-7, and Tottenham Hotspur in 1960-61.

The details of their records are as follows:

Preston North End

Football League:
Played 22, won 18, drawn 4, lost 0. For 74, against 15. Points 40.

F.A. Cup:
Round 1 v. Bootle (a)   3—0
Round 2 v. Grimsby Town (a) 2—0
Round 3 v. Birmingham St. George (h)   2—0
Semi-final v. West Bromwich Albion (at Bramall Lane, Sheffield)
                                         1—0
Final v. Wolverhampton Wanderers (at The Oval)   3—0

Aston Villa

Football League:
Played 30, won 21, drawn 5, lost 4. For 73, against 38. Points 47.

F.A. Cup:
Round 1 v. Newcastle United (h)
                                         5—1
Round 2 v. Notts County (h)   2—1
Round 3 v. Preston North End (after draws 1—1, 0—0, 2nd replay at Sheffield)   3—2
Semi-final v. Liverpool (at Bramall Lane, Sheffield)   3—0
Final v. Everton (at Crystal Palace)
                                         3—2

Tottenham Hotspur

Football League:
Played 42, won 31, drawn 4, lost 7. For 115, against 55. Points 66.

F.A. Cup:
Round 3 v. Charlton Athletic (h)
                                         3—2
Round 4 v. Crewe Alexandra (h)
                                         5—1
Round 5 v. Aston Villa (a)   2—0
Round 6 v. Sunderland (h) (after draw 1—1)   5—0
Semi-final v. Burnley (at Villa Park)   3—0

Final v. Leicester City (at Wembley)   2—0

In Scotland two clubs, Celtic and Rangers, have won the Scottish League and Cup in the same season on several occasions:

Celtic: 1907, 1908, 1914, 1954, 1967.

Rangers: 1928, 1930, 1934, 1935, 1949, 1950, 1953, 1963, 1964.

In seasons 1948-9 and 1963-4 Rangers also won the Scottish League Cup. Celtic achieved this in 1966-67, and 1968-69.

DRAWS

The record number of draws by a club in a single season is 21, by Plymouth Argyle in Division III(S), in 1920-21.

In the Scottish League, Division I, the record is 17, by Falkirk in 1921-2 and 1922-3.

On Saturday, Sept. 18, 1948, there were nine drawn games in Division I of the Football League, a record for any division of the League in a single day.

There were 22 drawn games in the Football League on Oct. 13, 1962.

The record for drawn games in a single round of the F.A. Cup is 15 in the 3rd Round, Jan. 9, 1954.

DUMBARTON F.C.

Founded 1872. One of the original members of Scottish League, 1890. Honours: Scottish League Champions, 1890-1 (shared), 1891-2. Champions, Division II, 1910-11. Scottish Cup, Winners, 1882-3. Finalists, 1880-1, 1881-2, 1886-7, 1890-1, 1896-7. Record attendance: 18,000 v. Raith Rovers, Scottish Cup, 7th Round, Mar. 2, 1957. Address: Boghead Park, Dumbarton (Tel. 2569). Colours: Black and gold striped shirts, black shorts. Record goal-scorer in Division I: J. Wood, 25 goals, 1921-2 Record victory: 8—0 v. Cowdenbeath, Division II, Mar. 28, 1964. Record defeat: 8—0 v. Dundee United, Division II, 1935-6, v. Morton, Division II, 1953-4, v. Third Lanark, Scottish Cup, 3rd Round, Feb. 22, 1936.

DUNDEE F.C.

Founded 1893 by the amalgamation of East End and Our Boys clubs.

Joined Scottish League, Division I, 1893. Honours: Champions, Division 1, 1961-2. Runners-up, 1902-3, 1906-7, 1908-9, 1948-9. Champions, Division B, 1946-7. Scottish Cup: Winners, 1910. Finalists, 1925, 1952, 1964. Record attendance: 43,024 v. Glasgow Rangers, Scottish Cup, 2nd Round, Feb. 7, 1953. Address: Dens Park, Dundee (Tel. 86104). Nickname: Blues. Colours: Dark blue with white collars and shorts. Record League goal-scorer in Division I, D. Halliday, 38 goals, 1923-4. Record victory: 10—1 v. Fraserburg, Scottish Cup, 1st Round, Jan. 17, 1931. Record defeat: 11—0 v. Celtic, Division I, Oct. 26, 1895.

DUNDEE UNITED F.C.

Founded 1910 as Dundee Hibernian. Changed name to Dundee United in 1923. Joined Scottish League, Division II, 1923. Honours: Champions, Division II, 1924-5, 1928-9. Runners-up, 1930-31, 1959-60. Record attendance: 26,500 v. Barcelona, Nov. 16, 1966, and v. Juventus, Mar. 8, 1967. Both Inter-Cities Fairs Cup ties. Address: Tannadice Park, Dundee (Tel. 86289). Colours: Tangerine shirts with black facings, black shorts with tangerine stripe. Record goal-scorer in Division I: K. Cameron, 27 goals, 1968-9. Record victory: 14—0 v. Nithsdale Wanderers, Scottish Cup, 1st Round, Jan. 17, 1931. Record defeat: 12—1 v. Motherwell, Division B, 1953-4.

DUNFERMLINE ATHLETIC F.C.

Founded 1907. Joined Scottish League, Division II, 1921. Honours: Champions, Division II, 1925-6. Runners-up, 1933-4, 1954-5, 1957-8. Best in Division I, 4th, 1961-2. Scottish Cup: Winners, 1961, 1968. Runners-up, 1965. Record attendance: 24,377 v. Rangers, Scottish Cup, 3rd Round, Mar. 1, 1958. Address: East End Park, Dunfermline (Tel. 24295). Colours: Black and white stripe shirts, black shorts. Record goal-scorer in Division I, R. Skinner, 25 goals, 1926-7. Record victory: 11—2 v. Stenhousemuir, Division II, 1930-31. Record defeat: 9—3 v. Motherwell, Division I, 1934-5.

E

EAST FIFE F.C.

Founded 1903. First promoted to Division I, 1930. Honours: Champions, Division B, 1947-8. Runners-up, Division II, 1929-30. Best in Division I, 3rd, 1951-2, 1952-3. Scottish Cup: Winners, 1938. Finalists, 1927, 1950. Record attendance: 22,515 v. Raith Rovers, Jan. 2, 1950. Address: Bayview Park, Methil (Tel. Leven 175). Colours: Black and gold striped shirts, white shorts. Record League goalscorer in Division I: C. Fleming, 32 goals, 1952-3. Record victory: 13—2 v. Edinburgh City, Division II, Dec. 11, 1937. Record defeat: 9—1 v. Celtic, Division I, Jan. 10, 1931.

ECUADOR

With star players emigrating to Uruguay and Brazil this small country has made little impression at International level.

The controlling body was formed in 1925. Address: Federación Deportiva Nacional del Ecudor, Apartado de correo 3409, Guayaquil.

Result of international match:

May 25, 1970   Ecuador 0, England 2; Quito

EIRE

To avoid confusion between the two Associations which control football in Ireland, i.e., the Football Association of Ireland and the Irish Football Association, the former is generally referred to throughout this encyclopaedia under the Gaelic name, Eire. " Ireland " refers to teams selected by the Irish F.A. (Belfast).

In June 1954, F.I.F.A. decided that the title for international teams representing Eire should be " Republic of Ireland ".

In 1970 Northern Ireland is entitled by F.I.F.A. to select players born in Eire for international matches with England, Scotland or Wales, but must restrict itself to its own players for matches with any other countries. The Football Association of Ireland (Dublin) has taken exception to this arrangement, and have gone so far as to compel its players, before transferring to clubs outside the country, to sign an agreement that they would not play for any country other than Eire. The F.A. of Ireland, were however, forced to abandon this rule.

On the other hand it was not so long ago that the Irish F.A. (Belfast) lifted its ban prohibiting the playing of any matches between clubs of its Association with clubs in membership with the Eire Association.

The Football Association of Ireland was formed in June 1921, shortly after many clubs in Southern Ireland broke away from the Irish F.A. (Belfast). The Football League of Ireland came into being two months later.

At first the new Association was not granted recognition by the Associations of England, Scotland and Wales, and the clubs were entirely suspended by the Irish F.A. (Belfast).

The first step towards international recognition was made in August 1923, when the F.A. of Ireland was accepted into membership with F.I.F.A. Next came recognition by the Associations of Great Britain, although this recognition did not extend to the International Championship. The Irish F.A. (Belfast) was still the only authority recognised to represent Ireland, and only its members were allowed to sit on the International Board.

Several clubs from Belfast and Derry were in membership with the F.A. of Ireland (Dublin), but one of the conditions of recognition by the other Associations of Great Britain, was that the membership of these clubs should be cancelled. Another condition was that the title of the new Association should be changed to the F.A. of the Irish Free State.

The Dublin Association tried to reach an agreement with the Irish F.A. (Belfast) whereby the selection and control of international matches concerning Ireland would be dealt with by a committee from the two Associations working on a 50-50 basis. These proposals were not accepted.

Subsequently the Dublin authorities complained to F.I.F.A. and the International Board that the Irish F.A. (Belfast) was still fielding its International XI under the title " Ireland," although it had control in only six of the 32 counties of Ireland. They demanded that the Belfast Association should adopt the title " Northern Ireland ". Although this proposal was accepted by F.I.F.A. it was not adopted by the Irish F.A. (Belfast).

In 1949 Eire became the first country outside the United Kingdom to defeat England on English soil. At Goodison Park, Everton, on Sept. 21, 1949, Eire beat England 2—0. For the teams in this game see INTERNATIONALS (England).

Address of governing body: F.A. of Ireland, 80 Merrion Square, Dublin, 2. Colours: Green shirts, white shorts.

The results of matches with foreign countries are given under each country.

Results of international matches :

Sept. 30, 1946	Eire 0, England 1; Dublin
Sept. 21, 1949	England 0, Eire 2; Everton
May 8, 1957*	England 5, Eire 1; Wembley
May 19, 1957*	Eire 1, England 1; Dublin
Sept. 28, 1960	Eire 2, Wales 3; Dublin
May 3, 1961*	Scotland 4, Eire 1; Glasgow
May 7, 1961*	Eire 0, Scotland 3; Dublin
June 9, 1963	Eire 1, Scotland 0; Dublin
May 24, 1964	Eire 1, England 3; Dublin
Sept. 21, 1969	Eire 1, Scotland 1; Dublin

* World Cup

ENGLAND
See INTERNATIONALS (England).

ENTRANCE CHARGES
See ADMISSION CHARGES.

EUROPEAN CHAMPION CLUBS CUP

This is one of the most popular football competitions and although only inaugurated in 1955 it was soon firmly established and considered by many to be the forerunner of a European Super League.

Known simply as the European Cup it was prompted by a suggestion of the French football magazine *L'Equipe* and is run under the auspices of the European Union of Football Associations.

Each season the champion club of each of the Associations in the Union are eligible to compete together with the winner of the previous season's competition. Games are played on a home and away basis with the aggregate score of the two games deciding the winner. In the final only one game is played.

Here are the results of the finals of this competition together with the attendance at each game and, in brackets, the number of clubs which competed :

1955-56	(16)	Real Madrid 4, Reims 3; Paris, 38,000
1956-57	(22)	Real Madrid 2, Fiorentina 0; Madrid, 125,000
1957-58	(24)	Real Madrid 3, A.C. Milan 2*; Brussels, 67,000
1958-59	(28)	Real Madrid 2, Reims 0; Stuttgart, 80,000
1959-60	(27)	Real Madrid 7, Eintracht-Frankfurt 3; Glasgow, 127,621
1960-61	(28)	Benfica 3, Barcelona 2; Berne, 30,000
1961-62	(29)	Benfica 5, Real Madrid 3; Amsterdam, 65,000
1962-63	(30)	A.C. Milan 2, Benfica 1; Wembley; 45,000

1963-64	(31)	Internazionale 3, Real Madrid 1; Vienna; 74,000
1964-65	(31)	Internazionale 1, Benfica 0; Milan, 80,000
1965-66	(32)	Real Madrid 2, Partizan 1; Brussels; 38,713
1966-67	(33)	Glasgow Celtic 2, Internazionale 1; Lisbon; 65,000
1967-68	(31)	Manchester United 4, Benfica 1* Wembley, 100,000
1968-69	(27)	A.C. Milan 4, Ajax Amsterdam 1; Madrid, 50,000
1969-70	(33)	Feyenoord 2, Celtic 1*; Milan, 85,000

* After extra time

EUROPEAN CUP WINNERS CUP

Run on the same system as the European Cup, the clubs eligible for this competition are the winners (or if unable to compete—the runners-up) of each of the national cups.

In the event of a drawn tie away goals count double.

Results of finals:

1960-61	(10)	Fiorentina beat Rangers (Glasgow) 2—0, 2—1.
1961-62	(23)	Atletico Madrid beat Fiorentina 3—0†
1962-63	(25)	Tottenham Hotspur beat Atletico Madrid 5—1
1963-64	(28)	Sporting Lisbon beat M.T.K. Budapest 1—0*‡
1964-65	(30)	West Ham United beat Munich 2—0
1965-66	(31)	Borussia Dortmund beat Liverpool 2—1*
1966-67	(32)	Bayern Munich beat Glasgow Rangers 1—0*
1967-68	(32)	Milan beat S.V. Hamburg 3—0
1968-69	(27)	Slovan Bratislava beat Barcelona 3—2
1969-70	(33)	Manchester City beat Gornik Zabrze 2—1

† First game drawn 1—1 after extra time
* After extra time   ‡ First game drawn 3—3

EUROPEAN FAIRS CUP

This competition was established in 1955 as the International Industries Fairs Inter-Cities Cup and was originally intended for representative sides from cities who annually hold Industries Fairs. The title was changed in 1969 to European Fairs Cup.

The first of these competitions was played over a period of three years with teams from 12 cities taking part. London and Barcelona emerged as finalists in 1958 and the Spaniards won the two-leg final 6—0 and 2—2.

The idea of entering representative sides from each city soon gave way to the entry of club teams. In the second competition which began in 1958, Chelsea represented London and Birmingham was represented by the club of that name, 16 clubs entered from 11 countries.

Birmingham City won through to the Final before losing 0—0, 4—1 to Barcelona.

Results of subsequent Finals with number of entries given in brackets:

1960-61 (16) AS Roma beat Birmingham City, 2—0, 2—2.
1961-62 (28) Valencia beat Barcelona, 6—2, 1—1.
1962-63 (32) Valencia beat Dynamo Zagreb, 2—0, 2—1.
1963-64 (32) Real Zaragoza beat Valencia, 2—1.
1964-65 (46) Ferencvaros beat Juventus, 1—0.
1965-66 (45) CF Barcelona beat Zaragoza, 0—1, 4—2.*
1966-67 (48) Dynamo Zagreb beat Leeds Utd., 2—0, 0—0.
1967-68 (44) Leeds United beat Ferencvaros 1—0, 0—0.
1968-69 (62) Newcastle United beat Ujpest Dosza 3—0, 3—2.
1969-70 (64) Arsenal beat Anderlecht 1—3, 3—0.

* After extra time

EUROPEAN FOOTBALL CHAMPIONSHIP (NATIONS CUP)

This is another competition run under the auspices of the European Union of Football Associations and in this the system of elimination is similar to that of the World Cup.

This competition was reorganised in 1966 so that it is now played partly on a League basis instead of being an entirely knock-out competition. The qualifying competition for the quarter-finals is split into eight groups with the members of each group playing each other at home and away. The British International Championship (including two seasons) is one of these groups.

The trophy is the Henri Delaunay Cup, named after the late Secretary of the French Football Federation who originally conceived this idea of an international competition among European nations. Unfortunately, Monsieur Delaunay did not live long enough to see his dream come true.

It has been agreed to run this competition every four years, in the years between the World Cup, and the first of these tournaments was completed in 1960, when Russia emerged winners.

Results of finals:

1960 (17) Russia 2, Yugoslavia, 1; Paris, 17,966.
1964 (29) Spain 2, Russia 1; Madrid, 120,000.
1968 (31) Italy 2, Yugoslavia 0; Rome, 100,000. After draw 1—1.

EUROPEAN UNION OF FOOTBALL ASSOCIATIONS

In 1952 the suggestion was made that the Football Associations of the various European countries should form themselves into a group.

A referendum was conducted among the European Associations and, upon general agreement, the European Football Union came into being in June 1954.

Mr. Ebbe Schwartz of Denmark was elected the first Chairman. The committee included one representative from the United Kingdom Associations, Sir George Graham, O.B.E., Secretary of the Scottish Football Association.

It should be noted that this Union is formed as a special group under the auspices of F.I.F.A. and is not a separate body. All members of the Union or Federation are affiliated to F.I.F.A., and the object of forming the group was to ensure a closer liaison between the European Associations.

There are now 33 members and the address of the headquarters is: U.E.F.A., Case Postale 16, Laubeggstrasse 70, 3,000 Berne 32 Switzerland.

EVERTON F.C.

Founded 1878 as St. Domingo Church Sunday School Club. Became Everton, 1879. One of the original members of the Football League, 1888. Moved to Goodison Park, 1892. Honours: Champions, Division I, 1890-91, 1914-15, 1927-8, 1931-2, 1938-9, 1962-3, 1969-70. Runners-up, 1889-90, 1894-5, 1901-2, 1904-5, 1908-9, 1911-12. Champions, Division II, 1930-31. Runners-up, 1953-4. F.A. Cup: Winners, 1906, 1933, 1966. Finalists, 1893, 1897, 1907, 1968. Record attendance: 78,299 v. Liverpool, Division I, Sept. 18, 1948. Address: Goodison Park, Liverpool 4 (Tel. 051-525 5263). Nickname: Toffees. Colours: Royal blue shirts with white collars, white shorts. Record League goal-scorer: W. Dean, 60 goals, Division I, 1927-28 (Football League record). Record victory 11—2 v. Derby County, F.A. Cup, 1st Round, 1889-90. Record defeat: 10—4 v. Tottenham Hotspur, Division I, Oct. 11, 1958.

EXETER CITY F.C.

Founded 1904 on amalgamation of St. Sidwell's United and Exeter United. Adopted professionalism and joined the Southern League as Exeter City 1908. One of the original members of the Football League, Division III, 1920. Honours: Runners-up, Division III(S), 1932-3. Record attendance: 20,984 v. Sunderland, F.A. Cup, 6th Round (replay), Mar. 4, 1931. Address: St. James's Park, Exeter (Tel. 54073). Nickname: Grecians. Colours: Red and white striped shirts, red shorts. Record League goal-scorer: F. Whitlow, 34 goals, Division III(S), 1932-3. Record victory: 8—1 v. Coventry City, Division III(S), Dec. 4, 1926; v. Aldershot, Division III(S), May 4, 1935. Record defeat: 9—0 v. Notts County, Division III(S), Oct. 16, 1948, and v. Northampton Town, Division III(S), Apl. 12, 1958.

F

FALKIRK F.C.

Founded 1876. Joined Scottish League, Division II, 1902. Division I, 1905. Honours: Runners-up, Division I, 1907-8, 1909-10. Champions, Division II, 1935-6. Runners-up, 1960-61. 1969-70. Scottish Cup: Winners, 1913, 1957. Record attendance: 23,100 v. Celtic, Scottish Cup, 3rd Round, Feb. 21, 1953. Address: Brockville Park, Falkirk (Tel. 24121). Nickname: Bairns. Colours: Navy blue shirts, white shorts. Record League goalscorer: E. Morris, 43 goals, Division I, 1928-9. Record victory: 10—0 v. Breadalbane, Scottish Cup, 1st Round, Jan. 13, 1923, and also Jan. 23, 1926. Record defeat: 11—1 v. Airdrieonians, Division A, 1950-51.

FAMILIES

Brothers

There have been many instances of brothers playing with the same League club, far too many to mention here. Included below are cases where brothers appeared together in international matches or in particularly interesting circumstances.

Two pairs of brothers in the same international side is a record set up on April 20, 1955, when L. and I. Allchurch and J. and M. Charles appeared for Wales against Ireland at Windsor Park, Belfast. They also appeared against Israel at Tel Aviv, Jan. 15, 1958, and against Brazil at Rio de Janeiro, May 12, 1962.

Abegglen. The three brothers, Jean, Max and André (" Trello ") Abegglen, all played for Switzerland during the 1930s but never more than two in the same side.

Allchurch. Ivor and Len Allchurch, appeared together in eight internationals for Wales 1955-63.

Bambridge. A. L. and E. C. appeared together for England v. Wales in 1883 and v. Ireland in 1884. Another brother, E. H., had also played for England.

Blanchflower. R. D. (" Danny ") Blanchflower, Tottenham Hotspur wing-half, and John Blanchflower, Manchester United inside-forward, appeared together for Ireland in 10 internationals 1954-58.

Browell. In season 1910-11 Andrew, Gordon and Tom Browell appeared together in Hull City's Division II side.

Carr. In season 1919-20 the brothers William (centre-half), John (outside-right) and George Carr (inside-right) appeared together in the Middlesbrough side in Division I.

Charles. John and Melvyn Charles appeared together for Wales in 15 internationals during the period 1955-62.

Charlton. John and Robert have appeared in the same England team on 28 occasions to June 1970.

Corbett. In 1937-8 West Ham United had three brothers on their books who were all recognised as right-half-backs. They were David, James and Robert Corbett.

Cursham. Arthur and Harry of Notts County appeared together for England v. Scotland and Wales in 1882-3.

Doughty. The record number of goals scored in an International Championship match by two brothers is seven by Jack and Roger Doughty of the Druids. That was the number they scored between them in Wales' 11—0 victory over Ireland at Wrexham, 1888.

Evaristo. Mario (outside-left) and Juan (right-half) are two brothers who appeared together for the Argentine in the 1930s.

Forman. The only two brothers to play together for England as professionals before the Charlton brothers were Frank and Frederick Forman of Nottingham Forest. They were in the same England team on three occasions in season 1898-99.

Goodall. John Goodall, Preston North End and Derby County, was capped for England 14 times. His younger brother, Archie, Derby County and Glossop, was capped 10 times, but for Ireland not England. They never opposed each other in these games.

Heron. The only two brothers to appear together both in an international side and an F.A. Cup winning side were Frederick and Hubert Heron of The Wanderers. They played for England v. Scotland, Mar. 4, 1876, and, two weeks later, appeared in their club side which defeated Old Etonians in the Cup Final.

Hollins. Dave Hollins, born Bangor and capped for Wales during the 1960s. Younger brother, John, born Guildford, and received first of his England caps in 1967.

Koerner. Brothers Albert (outside-left) and Robert (outside-right) appeared together for Austria in several internationals in the 1950s.

Jack. Three brothers playing together with each of two Football League clubs is a record. David, Donald and Robert Jack were all with Plymouth Argyle in 1920 and all with Bolton Wanderers in 1923.

Jones. The brothers John (Linfield) and Samuel Jones (Distillery and Blackpool), played alongside each other, as centre-half and left-half respectively, for Ireland v. England, Oct. 14, 1933, and v. Wales, Nov. 4, 1933. Against Wales, their brother-in-law, William Mitchell (Chelsea), completed the half-back line.

Keetley. Four brothers of the Keetley family all played for Doncaster Rovers. Three were with the club at the same time. On Feb. 20, 1926, Joseph, Thomas and Harold Keetley appeared together in the Rovers' forward line v. Wigan Borough in Division III(N). At the end of the season Joseph Keetley left Doncaster Rovers, but another brother, Frank, came to the club from Derby County.

Milburn. John, James and George Milburn, all brothers and full-backs, were together with Leeds United from Nov. 1935 until the summer of 1937.

Morgan. Twin brothers Ian and Roger each scored for Queen's Park Rangers in the same Football League games a number of times in the 1960s.

O'Donnell. The brothers Frank and Hugh O'Donnell played together with the following clubs: St. Agatha School, Leven, Fifeshire, Denbeath Violet, Wellesley Juniors, Celtic, Preston North End, Blackpool, and Heart of Midlothian.

O'Flanagan. Dr. Kevin and his brother, Michael O'Flanagan played outside-right and centre-forward, respectively, for Eire v. England, Dublin, Sep. 30, 1946.

Shaw. David Shaw (Hibernian) and brother Jack Shaw (Rangers), right and left-back respectively, played together for Scotland v. England and v. Switzerland in 1946.

Stephens. On Sept. 21, 1946, Swindon Town defeated Exeter City 2—0 in the Third Division (S). The Stephens twins, Alfred and William, each scored a goal, the first time that twins scored in the same Football League game (see also Morgan).

Sulon. Gerald and Albert Sulon are twin brothers who have appeared together in the Belgium National team.

Wallbanks. Five Wallbanks brothers were professionals with Football League clubs: John Wallbanks with Barnsley, Chester and Bradford, 1929-35, Frederick with Bradford City, West Ham United and Nottingham Forest, 1932-36, Harold with Fulham, 1946-8, James with Barnsley, Northampton Town, Portsmouth, Millwall and Reading, 1929-47, and Horace with Grimsby Town and Luton Town, 1946-8.

Walter. Fritz and Ottmar Walter are two brothers who have played alongside each other in several international games for Germany, they were inside-left and centre-forward respectively in the German side that won the World Cup in 1954.

Walters. The brothers A. M. and P. M. Walters (Old Carthusians) right and left-back respectively, played together for England in nine international matches in the 1880s.

Two pairs of brothers in the same Football League side is a record: Frank and Fred Forman, Arthur and Adrian Capes for Nottingham Forest, Division I, 1896-97. Samuel and John Tonner, Thomas and

Owen Williams, for Clapton Orient, Division II, 1921-2 and 1922-3. Peter and John Butler, Antony and Peter Bircumshaw for Notts County, Division III, 1961-2. Cyril and Gilbert Beech or Cliff and Bryn Jones with Ivor and Len Allchurch, Swansea Town, 1953-4. Ray and Pat Brady, Roger and Ian Morgan, Queen's Park Rangers, Division III, 1964-5.

Swansea Town had four pairs of brothers on their books as professionals during 1953-4, for in addition to those mentioned above they also had the brothers Colin and Alan Hole.

Father and Son

Two pairs of father and son have won F.A. Cup medals with the same club: Thomas Boyle and Harold Johnson won medals with Sheffield United in 1925; their fathers, Peter Boyle and Harold Johnson sen., won medals with the same club in 1899 and 1902. Another son, Thomas Johnson, was Sheffield United's centre-half in the side beaten by Arsenal in the Final of 1936.

On the same day in April 1936, Harold Wait was Walsall's first-team goalkeeper, while his son, H. C. Wait, was Walsall's reserve team goalkeeper.

It is believed that there have been only three instances in first-class football of father and son playing together in the same club side. The first pair are J. and W. Butler who appeared together for Grimsby Town during season 1916-17. The second pair are Alec and David Herd who played inside-right and inside-left respectively for Stockport County v. Hartlepools United at Edgley Park in the last Third Division (N) game of the 1950-51 season (May 5, 1951). And in the Irish League during 1954-5 George Eastham and his son, also George, appeared regularly as the inside-forwards of Ards.

FAST SCORING

See under GOAL-SCORING (Individuals) Fast Scoring, GOAL-SCORING (Teams). All scored.

FATALITIES

See CASUALTIES and DISASTERS.

FEDERATION INTER-NATIONALE DE FOOT-BALL ASSOCIATION

In 1970 there are over 130 National Associations in membership of F.I.F.A. This body was formed in 1904 for the better control of the game on an international basis; to see that it is played in all countries under the same code of rules, and to organise an international Cup competition.

Belgium, France, Switzerland and the Netherlands originated the idea of the federation. Together with Sweden and Spain they held an inaugural meeting in Paris on May 21, 1904.

The F.A. (of England) had previously suggested that some such meeting should be held—in London—to discuss the better control of international relations. This invitation was apparently ignored and the F.A. was not represented at a meeting of the new federation until June 1906, when Mr. D. B. Woolfall of Lancashire, Honorary Treasurer of the F.A., was elected President of F.I.F.A.

In 1913, F.I.F.A. was given representation on the International Football Association Board.

An article of the Federation states that only one representative association from each country can hold membership with F.I.F.A. Therefore, in 1908, membership was refused to the Amateur Football Association and even the Associations of Ireland and Scotland. It was considered that these two national associations were subsidiaries of the English F.A.

Scotland, Ireland and Wales were, however, admitted in 1910. The F.A. of Ireland (Eire) followed in 1923.

The United Kingdom associations have twice since ceased membership of the Federation.

After World War I, the United Kingdom associations, Belgium, France and Luxemburg, refused to be associated with Austria, Germany or Hungary. It was suggested that they should form a separate federation. Neutral countries such as Denmark and Norway were opposed to this and eventually the trouble was satisfactorily ironed out. The U.K. associations returned to F.I.F.A. in 1924.

The second withdrawal took place in 1928, following disagreement over the Federation's definition of amateurism and, more particularly, the question of broken time payments. This time the U.K. associations remained outside the Federation until 1946.

One of the most important aspects of F.I.F.A. is its control over the movement of players from one member country to another. No player may transfer from a club in one country to a club in another country in the Federation without the permission of the Federation. This rule prevents the poaching of valuable players without agreement or the paying of transfer fees. However, when a number of British players departed for Bogota, Colombia, in 1950, their Football League clubs were powerless to claim any compensation for the loss of these players because Colombia was not a member of F.I.F.A. That situation could not occur again for Colombia has since joined F.I.F.A.

However, a similar situation has since arisen in 1960 when several players left Austria and signed for clubs in Australia. The Austrian F.A. complained that no transfer agreements had been made and so the F.I.F.A. banned the Australian Soccer Football Association from membership for a period of three years.

The executive committee of F.I.F.A. consists of a President elected by Congress (since Sept. 1961 Sir Stanley Rous has held this post), eight vice-presidents and ten members, each nominated by different associations or groups of associations.

The headquarters of F.I.F.A. is at 11, Hitziweg, Zurich 8032, Switzerland.

FINES

Fines for players committing certain offences on the field of play were first introduced by the Football League in 1935.

In May 1970 Leeds United was fined £5,000 by the Football League for allegedly failing to field full strength teams in certain games. Everton was fined £2,000 for a similar offence in 1966.

Derby County was fined £10,000 in April 1970 and banned from Europe following allegations of irregularities in their books. Manchester United was fined £7,000 in July 1969 after similar allegations, while Leyton Orient was fined £2,000 in 1957-58.

In Nov. 1967 Peterborough United was fined £500 and demoted from the Third Division for alleged irregularities, and in 1968 Port Vale was fined £4,000 and expelled from the League for alleged breaches of regulations but the club was re-elected the following season.

Another club accused of playing a weak team in the Football League is Burnley. In Mar. 1961 this club was fined £1,000 following a game with Chelsea in which they included 10 of their reserves. Despite this they drew the game 4—4.

Tottenham Hotspur was fined £350 after their home F.A. Cup tie with Aston Villa (1903-4) had to be abandoned because the crowd had invaded the pitch. The Villa was leading 1—0 at the time, but Spurs won the replay which the F.A. ordered to be played at Villa Park.

Liverpool was fined £250 in Aug. 1911 for poaching R. R. Pursell, full-back, from Queen's Park. A director of Liverpool was also suspended for two years.

Stockport County was fined £125 and two points were deducted from its record for playing J. (Joe) Smith, whose transfer had been secured from Bolton Wanderers on Mar. 16, 1927, without permission.

Sunderland was fined £50 and two points deducted from its record for playing J. Doig, Scottish international goalkeeper, in a Football League match against West Bromwich Albion on Sept. 20, 1890, before the player had completed the qualifying period of 14 days registration—the rule at that time.

In April 1957, a joint commission of the F.A. and the Football League fined Sunderland £5,000 and ordered the club to pay the expenses of an inquiry. The commission found the club guilty of making illegal payments contrary to the regulations of the Football League.

See also SUSPENSION.

FINLAND

Football in Finland is amateur, and due largely to the climate and the lack of suitable pitches the game has been slow to develop since its was first introduced by Englishmen in 1890.

As will be seen below, Finland was

resoundingly beaten in her first game with England's full international team, all five England forwards scoring in an eight goal victory.

Their F.A. was formed in 1907 and its membership today is just over 600 clubs. The address: Suomen Pallo Liitto-Finlands Bollförbund r.y. Bulevardi 28, Helsinki 12. Colours: Blue shirts, white collars and cuffs, white shorts.

Results of international matches:

May 20, 1937	Finland 0, England 8; Helsingfors
Sept. 8, 1949*	Eire 3, Finland 0; Dublin
Oct. 9, 1949*	Finland 1, Eire 1; Helsinki
May 25, 1954	Finland 1, Scotland 2; Helsinki
May 20, 1956	Finland 1, England 5; Helsinki
Oct. 21, 1964*	Scotland 3, Finland 1; Glasgow
May 27, 1965*	Finland 1, Scotland 2; Helsinki.
June 26, 1966	Finland 0, England 3; Helsinki

* World Cup

FIXTURES

For many years after the formation of the Football League the arrangement of fixtures was left in the hands of the clubs, but as the numbers increased it became evident that some master plan for the compilation of a fixture list would have to be adopted and this work was subsequently brought to a fine art by Mr. Harold Sutcliffe who produced the League's list for many years.

For five seasons after World War I it was the practice for clubs to play each other both at home and away in successive matches. But this system was abandoned because it presented many difficulties, such as clashes of the home fixtures of neighbouring clubs and the travelling of long distances during the Christmas and Easter holidays.

Clubs are given the opportunity of appealing against the arrangement of their fixtures at the League's annual fixture meeting. Any disputes are then referred to the Management Committee. Any club in the Football League which fails to carry out a fixture on the allotted day without good reason is liable to a fine of up to £5,000.

See also under BETTING and MATCHES.

FLOODLIT FOOTBALL

The first-ever game by floodlight took place at Bramall Lane, Sheffield, Oct. 14, 1878. The teams taking part were chosen by the Sheffield Association from local clubs. The game attracted a great deal of attention for electric light was still something of a novelty in the provinces. The official attendance was given as 12,000, but it was estimated that at least another 7,000 gained admission without paying. Bearing in mind the fact that the F.A. Cup Final in 1878 attracted only 5,000 people, it will be appreciated that a crowd of nearly 20,000 was quite extraordinary. The lighting itself was considered to be a great success. The electric power was generated on the ground by two portable engines—one behind each goal—driving Siemens dynamos. The lamps—one in each corner of the ground—were erected on wooden towers, 30 ft. high. The power of each lamp was 8,000 standard candles.

The result of the match was a 2—0 victory for the team captained by W. E. Clegg, an England international, later Sir William Clegg and Lord Mayor of Sheffield. The losing side was captained by his brother, J. C. Clegg, also an England international, and who later became Sir Charles Clegg, President of the F.A.

Birmingham was beaten by only two weeks for the distinction of staging the first floodlit football match. At the Lower Aston Grounds, Aston, on Oct. 28, 1878, a Birmingham representative side beat Nottingham Forest 2—1, and the illumination was provided by 12 electric lights spaced out around the pitch.

Unfortunately, this was only a partial success, as wind and rain interfered with the lights and there were a number of stoppages while the breakdowns were put right.

A week later football by floodlight was played in London. At Kennington Oval on Nov. 4, 1878, the Wanderers met Clapham Rovers under lights. But, according to Press reports, this match was not as successful as the Sheffield match.

I am indebted to the Editor of *Sport and Country* for the following quotations which appeared in its forerunner, *Illustrated Sporting and Dramatic News* during Nov. 1878.

" The result of the light, as applied to the purpose of steadily illuminating so large a field was not, as arranged on this occasion, satisfactory . . . Although in itself wonderfully powerful, pure and brilliant, the light was in this case to be tested in its management rather than in itself, and remembering that the attempt was of necessity an experiment, its comparative failure is no very important matter. Besides who wants to play football by artificial light? As a novelty, now and then, or to attract wandering shillings after dark, it may be all very well, but for the real purpose of the game daylight is quite good enough and long enough."

In 1887 the F.A. gave permission for two floodlit games to be played in Sheffield and another early floodlit game took place at Belle Vue Gardens, Manchester, Feb. 26, 1889. On this occasion the illumination was not supplied by electricity but by Wells lights (naphtha flares with air pressure forcing the oil to the burners). The game, which was staged in aid of the Hyde Colliery Explosion Fund, was between Ardwick (later Manchester City) and Newton Heath (later Manchester United). A profit of £140 was made.

Floodlit football under more modern conditions became popular about 1929, but the F.A. refused to give its sanction. In Aug. 1930 the F.A. passed a resolution prohibiting clubs in membership from taking part in such games.

Thereafter, certain charity matches were played under lights but the resolution was not rescinded until Dec. 1950, but this was followed by the adoption of a motion, in Jan. 1951, which stated that NO competitive matches were to be played under artificial light without the permission of the F.A. or the County Association and the Competition concerned.

The first competitive fixture to be played under floodlights in Great Britain was Southampton v. Tottenham Hotspur in a Football Combination " B " match at The Dell, Oct. 1, 1951.

Although progress was slow or almost nil between 1878 and 1955, tremendous strides forward in the acceptance of floodlit football in Britain were taken in 1955 and 1956. Both the F.A. and the Football League were forced to accord more official recognition to this branch of the game. The first step towards general recognition of competition football under floodlights was made in Feb. 1955 when the F.A. decided that, as from season 1955-6, replays of F.A. Cup-ties, up to and including the Second Round, might be played under lights.

The first F.A. Cup replay to be so played was between Kidderminster Harriers and Brierley Hill Alliance, Preliminary Round, Sept. 14, 1955. The first F.A. Cup replay between Football League clubs was between Carlisle United and Darlington, 1st Round, Nov. 23, 1955.

The next official move was made by the Football League at its annual meeting in June 1955, when it adopted a Sunderland proposal that postponed League games might be played by floodlight if both clubs agreed. The first Football League game to be played under lights was between Portsmouth and Newcastle United, at Fratton Park, Feb. 22, 1956.

A further relaxation of the ban on floodlight competition games was made by the F.A. in Dec. 1955 when it decided that 3rd Round F.A. Cup-ties, due to be played on Jan. 7, might be played under lights, or might be started in daylight and lights turned on during the game if necessary. On Jan. 7, 1956, lights were turned on during the following 3rd Round ties: Arsenal v. Bedford Town, Portsmouth v. Grimsby Town, Sheffield Wednesday v. Newcastle United, Tottenham Hotspur v. Boston United, and West Ham United v. Preston North End.

The England international side had already played under floodlights abroad in a match against the United States in New York on June 8, 1953. The first international match in England of which any part was played under lights was England v. Spain, at Wembley, Nov. 30, 1955. The lights were turned on as fog reduced visibility towards the end of this game.

The introduction of floodlights to so many grounds brought an increase in matches and following disputes over payment for these the Players' Union decided to ban all floodlight games, the ban to come into force on Mar. 13, 1956. But two days before the date, the ban was lifted when the League promised to consider the Union's demands.

In June 1956 Floodlit football really came into its own when it got the blessing of the Football League at their annual meeting. It was decided that floodlit League games would be permitted providing that both clubs agree. At the same time it was also agreed that a payment of from £2 to £3 could be made to each player taking part in games extra to normal League and Cup fixtures.

It was at their annual meeting in June 1958, that the Football League made the final move which freed floodlit games from any conditions apart from the obvious one that the lights should be up to a certain standard. At this meeting they decided that it would not be necessary for both clubs to agree before a game could be played under lights.

FOOTBALL, The Game

See TACTICS and TEAM EVOLUTION. See also OFFSIDE.

FOOTBALL ASSOCIATION, THE

The Football Association is the ruling body of the game in England. As the father of all Football Associations, its influence is felt all over the world where soccer is played.

The F.A. is made up of 87 affiliated units which include 43 English County Associations, the three Services, and the various Commonwealth countries and Protectorates overseas. The major competition in England, the Football League, is an important member of the F.A. Since 1929, it has been allowed a say in the Association's affairs by having eight of its representatives sitting on the F.A. Council which controls the work of the Association.

At one time, in the early part of the century, certain foreign countries were also in membership with the F.A. The Californian Association, and the Associations of America, Argentina and Chile were among them. Subsequently they withdrew to become members of F.I.F.A. In addition to the Associations which are members of the F.A. there are also 255 clubs in full membership, plus another 112 associate members. These associate members may qualify for full membership after a period of five years and provided certain other stipulations are complied with.

All professional and amateur footballers in this country who play for recognised clubs must be registered with the F.A. in addition to any registration they may have to make with local leagues or competitions.

The F.A. has been a Limited Company since 1903. This is a formality to provide certain protection for its members and does not mean that it is a profit-making business concern. None of the shareholders is entitled to receive any bonus or dividends or any profit from membership. The whole of the profits is ploughed back into the game.

The F.A. is a democratic body governed by a Council which is freely elected by its members. In addition to the officers of the Association the Council includes 10 Divisional Representatives from all parts of the country; about 50 County, Service, University, English and Public School representatives, as well as those of the Football League and the Associations of Australia, New Zealand, Canada, the British West Indies and Guyana.

The Beginning

The original meeting convened to discuss the formation of a football association took place at the Freeman's Tavern, Great Queen Street, London, on Oct. 26, 1863. Apart from a number of independent persons interested in the scheme, the following clubs were represented at this meeting: Barnes, Blackheath, Charterhouse, Perceval House (Blackheath), Kensington School, War Office, Crystal Palace, Blackheath Proprietary School, The Crusaders, Forest (Epping Forest), No Names' (Kilburn).

It had been hoped that a larger number of the public schools, which were the most important centres of football at that time, would join the Association so that a uniform code of Charterhouse a n d Westminster, rules could be drawn up, but Harrow, decided, for the time being, to retain their independence and their own rules.

There was a considerable difference of opinion among the original members as to the laws of the game. These were not passed until the fifth meeting. (See LAWS OF THE GAME). Shortly after the laws were published, Blackheath withdrew from membership mainly because they resented the rule banning hacking. Their withdrawal marks the separation of Rugby from Soccer. (See RUGBY).

The original rules adopted by the F.A. were brief and to the point:

1. That the Association be called "The Football Association."

2. That all clubs of one year's standing be eligible for membership.

3. That the subscription for each club be 5s. per annum payable in advance.

4. That the officers be a president, a treasurer, a secretary, with a committee comprising the beforementioned officers and four other members.

5. That the officers be elected at the annual meeting by the majority of the representatives of clubs present, the retiring officers to be eligible for re-election.

6. That the general meetings be held in the month of February.

7. That each club be entitled to send two representatives to all meetings of the Association.

8. That in the event of any alteration being deemed necessary in the rules or the laws established by the Association, notice shall be sent in writing to the secretary of the proposed alteration on or before the 1st of February in each year; and the terms of the proposed alteration shall be advertised in such sporting newspapers as the committee may direct, at least 14 days prior to the annual meeting.

9. That each club shall forward to the secretary a statement of its distinguishing colours and costumes.

The biggest controversy over the Laws, apart from the abolition of hacking, concerned the "strict offside" rule, and it was not until this was altered in 1867 that the rules were more generally accepted.

In 1870 members of the Association numbered 39:

Amateur Athletic Club, Barnes, Brixton, Bramham College (York), Clapham Rovers, Cowley School (Oxford), Crystal Palace, Donington Grammar School (Lincoln), 21st Essex R.V., F o r e s t School, Garrick (Sheffield), Hampstead Heathens, Harrow Pilgrims, Hitchin, Holt (Wilts.), Hull College, Kensington School, Leamington College, Lincoln, London Scottish R.V., C.C.C. (Clapham), Charterhouse School, Chesterfield, Civil Service, London Athletic Club, Milford College, No Names' (Kilburn), Newark, Nottingham, Oxford University, Royal Engineers (Chatham), Reigate, Sheffield, Totteridge Park (Herts), Upton Park, Wanderers, Westminster School, West Brompton College, Worlabye House (Roehampton).

The move which probably did most to broaden the outlook of the F.A. and spread its influence over a greater field was made on July 20, 1871 when it was proposed that a Challenge Cup be established for competition among its members. (See FOOTBALL ASSOCIATION CHALLENGE CUP.)

After this membership increased by leaps and bounds, until in 1881 clubs and associations under the wing of the F.A. numbered 128.

Professionalism entered the game around 1881. At first the F.A. was definitely opposed to the payment of players, maintaining a strictly amateur outlook. Its attitude caused many upsets in its relations with other bodies, especially with the Football League, and the authority of the F.A. remained in the balance for a number of years until it decided to legalise professionalism in July 1885. (See PROFESSIONALISM.)

In April 1887, the rules of the Association were revised and the Association was re-constituted so as to be governed by a Council consisting originally of six officers.

As already mentioned, the F.A. became a Limited Company in 1903. The share capital consists of £100 in 2,000 shares of one shilling each.

In 1907, certain amateur clubs and associations affiliated to the F.A. objected to a new ruling insisting that all associations must permit all clubs, professional or amateur to become members. The amateurs felt that the F.A. was now becoming too professional in its outlook. They decided to break away and form their own governing body, the Amateur Football Association. See AMATEUR FOOTBALL ALLIANCE). It was not until 1914 that this new body agreed to recognise the authority of the Football Association.

The one important quarrel that the F.A. had with bodies outside the F.A. concerned the question of "broken time" payments to amateurs. The F.A.'s definition of amateurism has always been a much stricter one than that of the *foreign* members of F.I.F.A. And, in 1928, the British Associations withdrew from membership of F.I.F.A. on this account and did not return until 1946.

The F.A. functions to see that wherever football is played in this country and in the Commonwealth, it is played according to the Laws of the Game, and is controlled in an orderly and organised fashion. It protects the rights of the player, the club, the authority of the Football Association.

To deal with all the many aspects of the game the F.A. has a number of committees. Some deal with disciplinary matters, others deal with the competitions which are the immediate concern of the F.A. (i.e. the Challenge Cup, the Amateur Cup, and the Youth Cup). There is a committee which concerns itself with the rules and regulations governing the game. Another takes care of the organisation and expansion of youth football. One of the most important committees is the international committee which deals with the arrangements for international matches.

F.A. Headquarters

The headquarters of the Football Association were originally in Holborn Viaduct. Later the Association moved to 61, Chancery Lane. 1902 found it at 104, High Holborn, and in 1910 its address was 42, Russell Square. The F.A. moved to its present address, 22, Lancaster Gate, W.2, in Dec. 1929.

I am indebted for much of this information to *The History of the Football Association.*

FOOTBALL ASSOCIATION AMATEUR CHALLENGE CUP

See also CUP MEDALS.

The Amateur Cup was inaugurated in 1893. In its earliest years it did not meet with the wholehearted support and approval of many of the leading amateur clubs who resented the fact that such a competition should come under the control of the F.A., an organisation which many amateurs at that time believed to have a bias towards professional football.

The rules have been tightened since those days and the competition is now governed by an all-amateur committee. Whereas, in its early days, the competition included former professional players who had been re-instated as amateurs, this is no longer permitted.

The only club to win both the F.A. Cup and the F.A. Amateur Cup was Old Carthusians. They defeated Old Etonians, 3—0, to win the F.A. Cup in 1881, and won the F.A. Amateur Cup on two occasions, v. Casuals, 2—1, in 1894, and v. Stockton, 4—1 (after draw 1—1), in 1897.

The only former professional player to secure an F.A. Amateur Cup winner's medal after gaining a winner's medal in the F.A. Cup competition was R. Chatt. In 1895 he was inside-right in the Aston Villa team which defeated West Bromwich Albion, 1—0. Later, when he was re-instated as an amateur, he appeared in the Stockton team which won the Amateur Cup Final of 1899, beating Harwich and Parkeston, 1—0.

In 1970 over 390 clubs entered for the F.A. Amateur Cup. The competition is open to all wholly amateur clubs who are members or affiliated members of the F.A. or are playing in a senior competition as members of an Association affiliated to the F.A. The closing date for entries each year is July 1.

The clubs which have won this competition the most times in the 66 seasons to 1969 are: Bishop Auckland 10, Clapton 5, Crook Town 5, Dulwich Hamlet 4, Stockton 3, Leytonstone 3 and Bromley 3.

Bishop Auckland won the trophy three times in succession 1955-6-7, the only club to perform this feat.

FOOTBALL ASSOCIATION CHALLENGE CUP

Appearances

See PLAYERS in this section, and TRANSFERS (F.A. Cup).

The Cup

The present trophy is the third to be played for in the history of the competition. It was made for the F.A. early in 1911 by Messrs. Fattorini and Sons of Bradford. In its first year it returned to Bradford after Bradford City beat Newcastle United in the Cup Final. The cost of this trophy was 50 gns. It weighs 175 oz., and stands 19 in. high, exclusive of the ebony plinth which has a silver band around it upon which are inscribed the names of the winners.

The original trophy, which was much smaller and cost about £20, was made early in 1872 by Messrs. Martin, Hall & Co. In 1895, after Aston Villa had won the competition, the cup was stolen from the window of a firm of football outfitters in Newton Row, Birmingham, where it had been placed on display. It was never recovered, and Aston Villa were fined £25 by the F.A.

A second trophy was ordered by the F.A. to be an exact replica of the original. This was possible because of the existence of silver replicas of the trophy which had been presented to Wolverhampton Wanderers, t h e winners of 1893, by the club's chairman. This second trophy was the work of Messrs. Vaughtons Ltd. It was retained for competition until 1910, when, prompted by the fact that the design had been duplicated for another competition, the F.A. withdrew it and presented it to Lord Kinnaird, as a token of respect, on his completing 21 years as President of the F.A.

Extra Time

According to the rules of the competition an extra half-hour may be played in all ties before the semi-final round, if, after 90 minutes, the result is a draw.

However, except during the first four seasons after World War II, an extra half-hour has rarely been played in the first meeting between competing clubs. If a replay ends in a draw then the two sides are compelled by the rules to play the extra half-hour. This rule was introduced by the F.A. Council in 1896.

In the semi-finals, an extra half-hour must be played in a replayed match ending in a draw. In the final tie extra time of half an hour must be played at the end of the first meeting if necessary. This rule was introduced in 1912. Since then extra time has been played in the following finals:

1919-20—
    Aston Villa 1, Huddersfield Town 0
1937-8—
    Preston North End 1, Huddersfield Town 0
1945-6—
    Derby County 4, Charlton Athletic 1
1946-7—
    Charlton Athletic 1, Burnley 0
1964-5—
    Liverpool 2, Leeds United 1
1967-8—
    West Bromwich Albion 1, Everton 0
1969-70—
    Chelsea 2, Leeds United 2, and replay—Chelsea 2, Leeds United 1.

The Finals

			Score	Attendance Receipts
1872	Wanderers	beat Royal Engineers	1—0	2,000
1873	Wanderers	beat Oxford University	2—0	3,000
1874	Oxford University	beat Royal Engineers	2—0	2,000
1875	Royal Engineers	beat Old Etonians (replay, after draw 1—1)	2—0	3,000
1876	Wanderers	beat Old Etonians (replay, after draw 0—0)	3—0	3,500
1877	Wanderers	beat Oxford University	*2—0	3,000
1878	Wanderers	beat Royal Engineers	3—1	4,500
1879	Old Etonians	beat Clapham Rovers	1—0	5,000
1880	Clapham Rovers	beat Oxford University	1—0	6,000
1881	Old Carthusians	beat Old Etonians	3—0	4,500
1882	Old Etonians	beat Blackburn Rovers	1—0	6,500

Year	Winner	Result		Attendance	Receipts
1883	Blackburn Olympic	beat Old Etonians	*2—1	8,000	
1884	Blackburn Rovers	beat Queen's Park (Glasgow)	2—1	4,000	
1885	Blackburn Rovers	beat Queen's Park (Glasgow)	2—0	12,500	£442
1886	Blackburn Rovers	beat West Bromwich Albion (replay, after draw 0—0)	2—0	15,000	
1887	Aston Villa	beat West Bromwich Albion	2—0	15,500	
1888	West Bromwich Albion	beat Preston North End	2—1	19,000	
1889	Preston North End	beat Wolverhampton Wanderers	3—0	22,000	
1890	Blackburn Rovers	beat Sheffield Wednesday	6—1	20,000	
1891	Blackburn Rovers	beat Notts County	3—1	23,000	£1,454
1892	West Bromwich Albion	beat Aston Villa	3—0	25,000	£1,800
1893	Wolverhampton Wanderers	beat Everton	1—0	45,000	£2,559
1894	Notts County	beat Bolton Wanderers	4—1	37,000	
1895	Aston Villa	beat West Bromwich Albion	1—0	42,560	
1896	Sheffield Wednesday	beat Wolverhampton Wanderers	2—1	48,836	
1897	Aston Villa	beat Everton	3—2	65,891	
1898	Nottingham Forest	beat Derby County	3—1	62,017	
1899	Sheffield United	beat Derby County	4—1	78,833	£2,747
1900	Bury	beat Southampton	4—0	68,945	
1901	Tottenham Hotspur	beat Sheffield United (replay, after draw 2—2)	3—1	110,820‡	£3,998
1902	Sheffield United	beat Southampton (replay, after draw 1—1)	2—1	76,914	
1903	Bury	beat Derby County	6—0	63,102	
1904	Manchester City	beat Bolton Wanderers	1—0	61,374	
1905	Aston Villa	beat Newcastle United	2—0	101,117	£7,785
1906	Everton	beat Newcastle United	1—0	75,609	£6,625
1907	Sheffield Wednesday	beat Everton	2—1	84,584	£7,053
1908	Wolverhampton Wanderers	beat Newcastle United	3—1	74,967	£5,988
1909	Manchester United	beat Bristol City	1—0	71,401	£6,434
1910	Newcastle United	beat Barnsley (replay, after draw 1—1)	2—0	77,747‡	£6,898
1911	Bradford City	beat Newcastle United (replay, after draw 0—0)	1—0	69,098‡	£6,512
1912	Barnsley	beat West Bromwich Albion (replay, after draw 0—0)	†1—0	54,556‡	£6,057
1913	Aston Villa	beat Sunderland	1—0	120,081	£9,406
1914	Burnley	beat Liverpool	1—0	72,778	£6,687
1915	Sheffield United	beat Chelsea	3—0	49,557	£4,052
1920	Aston Villa	beat Huddersfield Town	*1—0	50,018	£9,722
1921	Tottenham Hotspur	beat Wolverhampton Wanderers	1—0	72,805	£13,414
1922	Huddersfield Town	beat Preston North End	1—0	53,000	£10,551
1923	Bolton Wanderers	beat West Ham United	2—0	126,047	£27,776

1924	Newcastle United	beat Aston Villa	2—0	91,695	£14,280
1925	Sheffield United	beat Cardiff City	1—0	91,763	£15,941
1926	Bolton Wanderers	beat Manchester City	1—0	91,447	£23,157
1927	Cardiff City	beat Arsenal	1—0	91,206	£23,113
1928	Blackburn Rovers	beat Huddersfield Town	3—1	92,041	£23,238
1929	Bolton Wanderers	beat Portsmouth	2—0	92,576	£23,400
1930	Arsenal	beat Huddersfield Town	2—0	92,448	£26,265
1931	West Bromwich Albion	beat Birmingham	2—1	92,406	£23,366
1932	Newcastle United	beat Arsenal	2—1	92,298	£24,688
1933	Everton	beat Manchester City	3—0	92,950	£24,831
1934	Manchester City	beat Portsmouth	2—1	93,258	£24,950
1935	Sheffield Wednesday	beat West Bromwich Albion	4—2	93,204	£24,856
1936	Arsenal	beat Sheffield United	1—0	93,384	£24,857
1937	Sunderland	beat Preston North End	3—1	93,495	£24,831
1938	Preston North End	beat Huddersfield Town	*1—0	93,497	£25,723
1939	Portsmouth	beat Wolverhampton Wanderers	4—1	99,370	£29,116
1946	Derby County	beat Charlton Athletic	*4—1	98,000	£45,000
1947	Charlton Athletic	beat Burnley	*1—0	99,000	£39,500
1948	Manchester United	beat Blackpool	4—2	99,000	£39,500
1949	Wolverhampton Wanderers	beat Leicester City	3—1	99,500	£39,300
1950	Arsenal	beat Liverpool	2—0	100,000	£39,296
1951	Newcastle United	beat Blackpool	2—0	100,000	£39,336
1952	Newcastle United	beat Arsenal	1—0	100,000	£39,351
1953	Blackpool	beat Bolton Wanderers	4—3	100,000	£49,900
1954	West Bromwich Albion	beat Preston North End	3—2	100,000	£49,883
1955	Newcastle United	beat Manchester City	3—1	100,000	£49,881
1956	Manchester City	beat Birmingham City	3—1	100,000	£49,856
1957	Aston Villa	beat Manchester United	2—1	100,000	£48,816
1958	Bolton Wanderers	beat Manchester United	2—0	100,000	£49,706
1959	Nottingham Forest	beat Luton Town	2—1	100,000	£49,708
1960	Wolverhampton Wanderers	beat Blackburn Rovers	3—0	100,000	£49,816
1961	Tottenham Hotspur	beat Leicester City	2—0	100,000	£49,813
1962	Tottenham Hotspur	beat Burnley	3—1	100,000	£53,837
1963	Manchester United	beat Leicester City	3—1	100,000	£88,882
1964	West Ham United	beat Preston North End	3—2	100,000	£89,289
1965	Liverpool	beat Leeds United	*2—1	100,000	£89,103
1966	Everton	beat Sheffield Wednesday	3—2	100,000	£109,691
1967	Tottenham Hotspur	beat Chelsea	2—1	100,000	£109,649
1968	West Bromwich Albion	beat Everton	*1—0	100,000	£110,064
1969	Manchester City	beat Leicester City	1—0	100,000	£128,238
1970	Chelsea	beat Leeds United (replay, after draw †2—2)	*2—1	100,000	£128,272

* Extra half-hour played. † Extra half-hour played in replay.

‡ The attendance shown is that of the first game. The attendance at the replays were: 1901—20,470; 1902—33,068; 1910—69,000; 1911—58,000; 1912—38,555, 1970—62,078.

The Finals (Venues)

1872, The Oval. 1873, Lillie Bridge, West Brompton. 1874-1892, The Oval. 1893, Fallowfield, Manchester. 1894, Everton. 1895-1914, Crystal Palace. 1915, Old Trafford, Manchester. 1920-22, Stamford Bridge. 1923 onward, Wembley Stadium.

The Finals (Replay Venues)

1875 and 1876, The Oval. 1886, Derby. 1901, Bolton. 1902, Crystal Palace. 1910, Everton. 1911, Old Trafford, Manchester. 1912, Bramall Lane, Sheffield. 1970, Old Trafford, Manchester.

The First

The first entrants for the F.A. Cup in season 1871-2 were Barnes, Civil Service, Crystal Palace, Clapham Rovers, Donington School (Spalding), Hampstead Heathens, H a r r o w Chequers, Hitchen, Maidenhead, Marlow, Queen's Park (Glasgow), Reigate Priory, Royal Engineers, Upton Park, and Wanderers.

Harrow Chequers, Reigate Priory and Donington School all scratched.

Wanderers, a team formed by ex-public school and university men, won the first season's competition by defeating Royal Engineers 1—0 in the final played at The Oval. The first Cup Final goal was scored by M. P. Betts who played under the assumed name of A. H. Chequer. He was an Old Harrovian who had once played for Harrow Chequers.

Fourth Division

Only one club from the Fourth Division has reached the 6th Round—Oxford United, beaten 2—1 by Preston North End, 1963-4.

General

In 1890-91 Birmingham were disqualified from the F.A. Cup for playing an ineligible player. In 1921-22 they missed the competition because they omitted to submit their entry form.

Sheffield Wednesday missed the competition in 1886-7 when they were too late with their entry.

There has never been a case of a club not turning up for the Cup Final, although this has happened in the Scottish Cup (q.v.).

The record number of times that the same clubs have met each other in consecutive seasons' cup-ties is four. Brighton and Hove Albion and Watford met in the F.A. Cup Competition in four consecutive seasons as follows:

1924-5. 1st Round—
    Watford 1, Brighton 1
    (Replay) Brighton 3, Watford 4
1925-6. 1st Round—
    Brighton 1, Watford 1
    (Replay) Watford 2, Brighton 0
1926-7. 2nd Round—
    Watford 0, Brighton 1
1927-8. 1st Round—
    Watford 1, Brighton 2

In 1947-8 Manchester United were drawn in turn against six First Division clubs in the season's F.A. Cup competition, the first and only time this has happened to any club. The teams met were Aston Villa, Liverpool, Charlton Athletic, Preston North End, Derby County, and Blackpool. Manchester United beat Blackpool in the final, 4—2.

Since the formation of the Football League in 1888, all but five F.A. Cup winners have been First Division clubs. The five—Notts County (1894), Wolverhampton Wanderers (1908), Barnsley (1912), West Bromwich (1931)—all of them Second Division sides—and Tottenham Hotspur, who were a Southern League club when they won the Cup in 1901.

Goal Records

See GOAL-SCORING (Individuals) Cup Scoring; GOAL-SCORING (Teams and General) Cup.

Ireland

Three Irish clubs have appeared in the F.A. Cup Competition Proper: Cliftonville reached the 3rd Round in 1886-7 before being beaten 11—1 by Partick Thistle; Linfield Athletic scratched after drawing, 2—2, with Nottingham Forest in 1888-9; Belfast Distillery lost 10—2 to Bolton Wanderers in the 1st Round of 1889-90.

Medals

F.A. Cup medals are 9-carat gold, the winners' medals being slightly heavier.

See also CUP MEDALS in separate section.

Non-League Clubs

Since the formation of the Football League in 1888 the following non-League clubs have reached the last eight in the F.A. Cup:

	Last Eight	Semi-final	Final
Birmingham St. George's	1889		
Bootle	1890		
Chatham	1889		
Coventry City	1910		
Crystal Palace	1907		
Fulham	1905		
Middlesbrough Ironopolis	1893		
Millwall		1900, 1903	
Nottingham Forest	1891	1892	
Portsmouth	1902		
Queen's Park Rangers	1910, 1914		
Reading	1901		
Sheffield Wednesday	1889, 1891, 1892		1890
Southampton	1899, 1905, 1906, 1908	1898	1900, 1902
Stoke	1891		
Swindon	1911	1910, 1912	
Tottenham Hotspur	1899, 1903, 1904		*1901
West Ham United	1911		

*Tottenham Hotspur are the only non-League club to win the Cup since 1888.

Since the Football League was expanded to 86 clubs in 1921 the following non-League clubs have reached the 4th Round (last 32) or the old 2nd Round equivalent in the Cup Competition Proper:

1923-4—Corinthians: 1st Round, beat Blackburn Rovers (H) 1—0; 2nd Round, lost, West Bromwich Albion (A) 5—0.

1926-7—*Corinthians: 3rd Round, beat Walsall (A) 4—0; 4th Round, lost, Newcastle United (H) 3—1.

1928-9—*Corinthians: 3rd Round, beat Norwich City (A) 5—0; 4th Round, lost West Ham United (A) 3—0. Mansfield Town: 1st Round, beat Shirebrook (A) 4—2; 2nd Round, beat Barrow (A) 2—1; 3rd Round, beat Wolves (A) 1—0; 4th Round, lost Arsenal (H) 2—0.

1933-4—Workington: 1st Round, beat Southport (H) 1—0; 2nd Round, beat Newport County (H) 3—1; 3rd Round, beat Gateshead (H) 4—1; 4th Round, lost, Preston North End (H) 2—1.

1938-9—Chelmsford City: 1st Round, beat Kidderminster (H) 4—0; 2nd Round, beat Darlington (H) 3—1; 3rd Round, beat Southampton (H) 4—1; 4th Round, lost, Birmingham (A) 6—0.

1947-8—Colchester United: 1st Round, beat Banbury Spencer (H) 2—1; 2nd Round, beat Wrexham (H) 1—0; 3rd Round, beat Huddersfield Town (H) 1—0; 4th Round, beat Bradford (H) 3—2; 5th Round, lost, Blackpool (A) 5—0.

1948-9—Yeovil Town: 1st Round, beat Runcorn (H) 2—1; 2nd Round, beat Weymouth (A) 4—0; 3rd Round, beat Bury (H) 3—1; 4th Round, beat Sunderland (H) 2—1 after extra time; 5th Round, lost, Manchester United (A) 8—0.

1952-3—Walthamstow Avenue: 1st Round, beat Wimbledon (A) 3—0 after draw 2—2; 2nd Round, beat Watford (A) 2—1 after draw 1—1; 3rd Round, beat Stockport County (H) 2—1; 4th Round, lost, Manchester United (H) 5—2 after draw 1—1.

1953-4—Headington United: 1st Round, beat Harwich and Parkeston (A) 3—2; 2nd Round, beat Millwall (A) 1—0 after draw 3—3; 3rd Round, beat Stockport County (H) 1—0 after draw 0—0; 4th Round, lost, Bolton Wanderers (H) 4—2.

1954-5—Bishop Auckland: 1st Round, beat Kettering (H) 5—1; 2nd Round, beat Crystal Palace (A) 4—2; 3rd Round, beat Ipswich Town (H) 3—0 after draw 2—2; 4th Round, lost, York City (H) 3—1.

1956-7—Rhyl: 1st Round, beat Scarborough (H) 3—2; 2nd Round, beat Bishop Auckland (H) 3—1; 3rd Round, beat Notts County (A) 3—1; 4th Round, lost, Bristol City (A) 3—0.

New Brighton: 1st Round, beat Stockport County (A) 3—2 after draw 3—3; 2nd Round, beat Derby County (A) 3—1; 3rd Round, beat Torquay United (H) 2—1; 4th Round, lost, Burnley (A) 9—0. Peterborough United: 1st Round, beat Yeovil Town (A) 3—1; 2nd Round, beat Bradford (H) 3—0; 3rd Round, beat Lincoln City (A) 5—4 after draw 2—2; 4th Round, lost, Huddersfield Town (A) 3—1.

1958-9 — Worcester City: 1st Round, beat Chelmsford City (H) 3—1 after draw 0—0; 2nd Round, beat Millwall (H) 5—2; 3rd Round, beat Liverpool (H) 2—1; 4th Round, lost, Sheffield United (H) 2—0.

1959-60—Peterborough United: 1st Round, beat Shrewsbury Town (H) 4—3; 2nd Round, beat Walsall (A) 3—2; 3rd Round, beat Ipswich Town (A) 3—2; 4th Round, lost, Sheffield Wednesday (A) 2—0.

1961-2—Weymouth: 1st Round, beat Barnet (H) 1—0; 2nd Round, beat Newport County (H) 1—0; 3rd Round, beat Morecambe (A) 1—0; 4th Round, lost, Preston North End (A) 2—0.

1962-3—Gravesend: 1st Round, beat Exeter City (H) 3—2; 2nd Round, beat Wycombe (H) 3—1; 3rd Round, beat Carlisle United (A) 1—0; 4th Round, lost, Sunderland (A) 5—2 after 1—1 draw.

1963-4—Bedford Town: 1st Round, beat Weymouth (H) 1—0 after draw 1—1; 2nd Round, beat Chelmsford (A) 1—0; 3rd Round, beat Newcastle United (A) 2—1; 4th Round, lost Carlisle United (H) 3—0.

1965-6—Bedford Town: 1st Round, beat Exeter City (A) 2—1; 2nd Round, beat Brighton (H) 2—1 after draw 1—1; 3rd Round, beat Hereford (H) 2—1; 4th Round, lost Everton (H) 0—3.

1969-70: Sutton United: 1st Round, beat Dagenham (A) 1—0; 2nd Round, beat Barnet (A) 2—0; 3rd Round, beat Willingdon (A) 4—1 after 0—0 draw; 4th Round, lost, Leeds United (H) 0—6

* Corinthians were exempt until the 3rd Round.

Players

Seven men have played in and also managed F.A. Cup winning teams:

M. Busby: Right-half in Manchester City's Cup-winning team of 1934, and manager of Manchester United, Cup-winners of 1948 and 1963.

P. McWilliam: Left-half in Newcastle United's winning team of 1910, and manager of Tottenham Hotspur, winners in 1921.

J. Mercer: Left-half in Arsenal's Cup-winning team of 1950, and manager of Manchester City, winners in 1969.

J. Seed: Inside-right in the Tottenham Hotspur Cup-winning side of 1921, and manager of Charlton Athletic, winners in 1947.

W. Shankly: Right-half for Preston North End, Cup-winners 1938, and manager of Liverpool winners 1965. He also appeared for Preston in the 1937 final.

J. (Joe) Smith: Inside-left for Bolton Wanderers when they won the Cup in 1923 and again in 1926, and manager of Blackpool, winners in 1953 when they beat Smith's old club, Bolton Wanderers.

W. Walker: Captain of Aston Villa, Cup-winners in 1920, manager of Sheffield Wednesday, winners in 1935, and of Nottingham Forest, 1959.

Most appearances in F.A. Cup winning teams: J. H. Forrest (Blackburn Rovers) 1884, 1885, 1886, 1890, 1891. Hon. A. F. Kinnaird (Wanderers) 1873, 1877, 1878, (Old Etonians) 1879, 1882. C. H. R. Wollaston (Wanderers) 1872, 1873, 1876, 1877, 1878.

Since 1900 the most appearances in F.A. Cup-winning teams is three: C. Stephenson (Aston Villa) 1913, 1920, (Huddersfield Town) 1922. W. Butler, R. Haworth, H. Nuttall, R. Pym, and J. Seddon (all Bolton Wanderers) 1923, 1926, 1929. D. Jack (Bolton Wanderers) 1923, 1926, (Arsenal) 1930. G. Cowell, J. Milburn and R. Mitchell (all Newcastle United) 1951, 1952, 1955. D. Mackay (Tottenham Hotspur) 1961, 1962, 1967.

The record for most appearances in Wembley Cup Finals is held by J. Hulme who was outside-right for Arsenal when they were winners in 1930 and 1936, and losers in 1927 and 1932. He made his fifth appearance at outside-right for Huddersfield Town, losers in 1938.

The record for the most players in a Cup Final team who had already had Cup Final experience is held by Bolton Wanderers. Their Cup-winning team of 1926 showed only one change from that which had won the Cup in 1923. West Bromwich Albion's Cup Final team of 1935 included nine men who had played in a previous Cup Final. The Blackpool side of 1953 and the Tottenham Hotspur side of 1962 included the same number.

The first club to win the F.A. Cup with an all-English side was West Bromwich Albion in 1888.

There was only one Englishman in Cardiff City's F.A. Cup winning team in 1927. W. Hardy, the left-half. The rest of the team comprised four Irishmen, three Scotsmen, and three Welshmen.

The most Scots in an F.A. Cup winning team was eight in Bradford City's team in 1911.

Only two men have won both F.A. Cup and F.A. Amateur Cup winners' medals. R. Chatt was in Aston Villa's winning team of 1895, and was later re-instated as an amateur and appeared in the Stockton side which won the Amateur Final of 1899. T. Morren was Middlesbrough's centre-half when they won the Amateur Cup in 1895, and Sheffield United's centre-half when they won the F.A. Cup in 1899.

For men who have won both F.A. and Scottish F.A. Cup medals see SCOTLAND in this section.

Replays

Four replays (five games)—the most games played in a single tie of the F.A. Cup competition—have occurred in the following ties:

New Brompton (now known as Gillingham) d e f e a t e d Woolwich Arsenal 1—0 at Gravesend, season 1899-1900, after drawing 1—1 at Plumstead, 0—0 at New Brompton, 2—2 at Millwall, and 1—1 at Tottenham. The total playing time was 9 hr. 30 min.

In 1924-25 Gillingham and Barrow met 5 times in the 6th Qualifying Round. Barrow won 2—1 at New Cross after drawing 0—0 at Gillingham, 1—1 at Barrow, 1—1 at Wolverhampton, and 1—1 at Highbury. Total 9 hr. 30 min.

Also in season 1924-25, Leyton

defeated Ilford after 5 games, lasting a record time of 9 hr. 40 min. A double period of extra time was played in two of the games.

The record time of 9 hr. 22 min. in the Competition Proper was played in a 3rd Round tie between Stoke City and Bury in 1954-5. They met at Bury, Stoke (abandoned eight minutes from the end of extra time with the home side leading 1—0), Goodison Park, Anfield and Old Trafford before Stoke City won 3—2.

Doncaster Rovers defeated Aston Villa 3—1 at The Hawthorns, West Bromwich, in the 4th replay of a 4th Round tie, 1954-5. Total playing time: 9 hr.

Chelsea defeated Burnley 2—0 at White Hart Lane, Tottenham, after four drawn games, 4th Round, 1955-6. Total playing time 9 hr.

Hull City defeated Darlington 3—0 at Middlesbrough, after four drawn games in 2nd Round, 1960-1.

Three replays (four games) have been played in the following ties:

1898-9. Sheffield United defeated Liverpool, 1—0 in the Semi-final after 2 drawn games and a game abandoned as a goalless draw after the crowd invaded the field.

1911-12. Barnsley beat Bradford City, 3—2 in the 4th Round, after three drawn games.

1922-3. Sheffield United beat Nottingham Forest, 1—0 in the 1st Round after three drawn games. In the four games only three goals were scored in a total of seven hours' play.

1923-4. Newcastle United beat Derby County, 5—3 in the 2nd Round after three drawn games.

1923-4. Crystal Palace beat Notts County, 2—1 in the 2nd Round after three drawn games. Only three goals were scored in the seven hours' play.

1925-6. Blyth Spartans beat Hartlepool United 2—1 at Sunderland in the 1st Round after three drawn games.

1938-39. Halifax Town beat Mansfield Town 2—1 in 2nd Round after three drawn games. Total playing time 7 hrs. 30 min.

1951-2. Tranmere Rovers beat Blyth Spartans, 5—1 in the 2nd Round at Everton after three drawn games. The first replay was abandoned after only 15 min. extra time owing to bad light.

1952-3. Chelsea beat West Bromwich Albion, 4—0 in the 4th Round at Highbury after three drawn games.

1953-4. Blackpool beat Luton Town, 2—0 in the 3rd Round at Wolverhampton after three drawn games.

1969-70. Barrow beat Alfreton 2—0 at Preston after three drawn games in 1st Round.

Results

Only 2 clubs have won the Cup three times in succession. Blackburn Rovers, 1884, 1885, 1886, and Wanderers, 1876, 1877, 1878.

The highest number of consecutive F.A. Cup ties played by a single club without defeat is 24 by Blackburn Rovers, set up from Dec. 1883 to Dec. 1886.

The highest number of consecutive ties without a victory (by a Football League club) is 16 by Leeds United, from 1952 to 1963.

For results of Final ties see under FINALS in this section.

Scotland

The last season in which Scottish Clubs entered the F.A. Cup competition was 1886-7. In that season Rangers reached the semi-finals in which they were beaten 1—3 by Aston Villa. Thereafter the Scottish F.A. made a rule preventing clubs from entering any national competition other than its own. Scottish clubs who have competed in the competition are Heart of Midlothian, Cowlairs, Renton, Queen's Park, Rangers, Partick Thistle.

Queen's Park reached the Final twice but were beaten by Blackburn Rovers on both occasions.

A semi-final tie in the F.A. Cup was played in Scotland in 1885 when Queen's Park defeated Nottingham Forest, 3—0 at Merchiston Castle, Edinburgh, after drawing 1—1 at Derby.

The following players have won both F.A. and Scottish F.A. Cup winners' medals:

Brady, A. Celtic 1892, Sheffield Wednesday 1896.

Campbell, H. Renton 1888, Blackburn Rovers 1890.

Campbell, J. Celtic 1892, 1899, 1900; Aston Villa 1897.

Cook, W. Celtic 1931, Everton 1933.

*Delaney, J. Celtic 1937, Manchester United 1948.

Groves, W. Hibernian 1887, West Bromwich Albion 1892.

Hall, C. Blackburn Rovers 1891, St. Bernard's 1895.

McPherson, J. Hearts 1891, Nottingham Forest 1898.

Mackay, D. Hearts, 1956, Tottenham Hotspur 1961, 1962, 1967.

Nibloe, J. Kilmarnock 1929, Sheffield Wednesday 1935.

O'Donnell, H. Celtic 1933, Preston North End 1938.

Scott, A. Rangers 1960, Everton 1966.

Simpson, R. Newcastle United 1952, 1955; Celtic 1967.

Smith, J. R. Kilmarnock 1920, Bolton Wanderers 1923, 1926.

Stevenson, W. Rangers 1960, Liverpool 1965.

Welford, J. Aston Villa, 1895, Celtic 1899.

Wilson, G. Hearts 1906, Newcastle United 1910.

Welford was the only Englishman to collect both F.A. and Scottish F.A. Cup medals.

Young, A. Hearts 1956, Everton 1966.

For the most Scots in an F.A. Cup winning team see PLAYERS in this section.

*Delaney also won Irish and F.A of Ireland Cup medals with Derry City, 1954, and Cork Athletic, 1956.

Second Division

For Division II Cup winners see GENERAL in this section.

Third Division

Clubs which have reached the 6th Round (or its earlier equivalent) whilst in Division III are:

Bournemouth and Boscombe Athletic	1956-57
Bristol Rovers	1950-51
Charlton Athletic	1922-23
Coventry City	1962-63
Exeter City	1930-31
Gateshead	1952-53
Hull City	1948-49, 1965-66
Leyton Orient	1953-54
Luton Town	1932-33
Mansfield Town	1968-69
Millwall	1921-22, 1926-27, 1936-37

Norwich City 1958-59
Peterborough United 1964-65
Port Vale 1953-54
Queen's Park Rangers
1922-23, 1947-48
Southport 1930-31
Swindon Town 1923-24
Watford 1931-32
York City 1937-38, 1954-55

Only four clubs have reached the Semi-final of the F.A. Cup while members of Division III: Millwall in 1936-7, Port Vale in 1953-4, York City in 1954-5, and Norwich City in 1958-9. York City and Norwich City each drew their first game but were beaten in the replay.

Wales

The entry of Welsh clubs into the F.A. Cup competition is restricted to 14. Their entries must be submitted by Mar. 1, not May 1, the deadline for all other accepted entries.

The only occasion when the F.A. Cup was won by a club from outside of England was in 1927 when Cardiff City beat Arsenal 1—0.

FOOTBALL ASSOCIATION CHARITY SHIELD

The annual F.A. Charity Shield match was inaugurated in 1908.

The first game was played at Stamford Bridge, April 27, 1908, between the Champions of the Football League, Manchester United, and the Champions of the Southern League, Queen's Park Rangers.

The champions of these two Leagues met in this match for the next four years. Subsequently, the game was played between teams chosen by the F.A., usually the Amateurs v. Professionals, or the F.A. Cup holders v. the League Champions. In recent years the matches have been played between the Cup holders and the League Champions.

Season	Team	Score	Opponent	Score
1908-09	Manchester United	4	Queen's Park Rangers (after drawn game 1—1)	0
1909-10	Newcastle United	2	Northampton Town	0
1910-11	Brighton and Hove Albion	1	Aston Villa	0
1911-12	Manchester United	8	Swindon Town	4
1912-13	Blackburn Rovers	2	Queen's Park Rangers	1
1913-14	Professionals	7	Amateurs	2
1919-20	West Bromwich Albion	2	Tottenham Hotspur	0
1920-21	Tottenham Hotspur	2	Burnley	0
1921-22	Huddersfield Town	1	Liverpool	0
1922-23	No match			
1923-24	Professionals	2	Amateurs	0
1924-25	Professionals	3	Amateurs	1
1925-26	Amateurs	6	Professionals	1
1926-27	Amateurs	6	Professionals	3
1927-28	Cardiff City	2	Corinthians	1
1928-29	Everton	2	Blackburn Rovers	1
1929-30	Professionals	3	Amateurs	0
1930-31	Arsenal	2	Sheffield Wednesday	1
1931-32	Arsenal	1	West Bromwich Albion	0
1932-33	Everton	5	Newcastle United	3
1933-34	Arsenal	3	Everton	0
1934-35	Arsenal	4	Manchester City	0
1935-36	Sheffield Wednesday	1	Arsenal	0
1936-37	Sunderland	2	Arsenal	1
1937-38	Manchester City	2	Sunderland	0
1938-39	Arsenal	2	Preston North End	1
1948-49	Arsenal	4	Manchester United	3
1949-50	Portsmouth	1	Wolverhampton Wanderers	1
1950-51	World Cup XI	4	Canadian Tourists	2
1951-52	Tottenham Hotspur	2	Newcastle United	1
1952-53	Manchester United	4	Newcastle United	2
1953-54	Arsenal	3	Blackpool	1
1954-55	Wolverhampton Wanderers	4	West Bromwich Albion	4
1955-56	Chelsea	3	Newcastle United	0
1956-57	Manchester United	1	Manchester City	0

1957-58	Manchester United	4	Aston Villa	0
1958-59	Bolton Wanderers	4	Wolverhampton Wanderers	1
1959-60	Wolverhampton Wanderers	3	Nottingham Forest	1
1960-61	Burnley	2	Wolverhampton Wanderers	2
1961-62	Tottenham Hotspur	3	F.A. Selection XI	2
1962-63	Tottenham Hotspur	5	Ipswich Town	1
1963-64	Everton	4	Manchester United	0
1964-65	Liverpool	2	West Ham United	2
1965-66	Liverpool	2	Manchester United	2
1966-67	Liverpool	1	Everton	0
1967-68	Manchester United	3	Tottenham Hotspur	3
1968-69	Manchester City	6	West Bromwich Albion	1
1969-70	Leeds United	2	Manchester City	1
1970-71	Everton	2	Chelsea	1

FOOTBALL ASSOCIATIONS (VARIOUS)

The title and address of the governing football body of each foreign country is given under the name of each country.

The first football association to be formed was the F.A. in London in 1863 (see under FOOTBALL ASSOCIATION, The).

The next oldest in chronological order are: Sheffield 1867, Scotland 1873, Birmingham 1875, Wales 1876, Sheffield New, Staffordshire, Surrey (reformed 1882) 1877, Berks and Bucks, Cheshire, Lancashire 1878, Northumberland and Durham 1879, Ireland 1880, Cleveland (North Riding), Lincolnshire, Norfolk 1881.

The Sheffield New was re-named Hallamshire in 1881 and subsequently amalgamated with the orginal Sheffield Association. Northumberland and Durham split in 1883.

The first of the above named associations to become affiliated to the F.A. (England) were the Sheffield, Lancashire, and Birmingham associations.

The earliest football associations to be formed outside the United Kingdom were those of Holland 1889, New Zealand 1891, Argentine 1893, Belgium, Chile and Switzerland, 1895.

FOOTBALL LEAGUE, The

This is the father of all league football competitions. Formed in 1888 it has proved a worthy model for all successive competitions of its kind.

The Football League is governed by a Management Committee of 9 elected members who have full power to deal with all matters requiring attention

outside of the Annual General Meeting which is held usually at the beginning of June.

At the A.G.M. there are 49 members entitled to vote on all proposals: 44 members of the First and Second Divisions, four representatives of the Third and Fourth Divisions, and the President. The membership of the League is limited to the 44 clubs in the first two divisions. The Third and Fourth Division clubs are merely Associate Members, limited in number to 48, and entitled to send only one representative for every eleven of their number to the A.G.M. to vote. Even then their vote is limited to certain matters.

The limited representation of the two lower Divisions has caused much discontent among the Associate Members but it must be remembered that when the members of the old Southern League approached the Football League and applied for membership and the formation of a Third Division, they accepted the status of Associate Members without any voting power whatsoever in the beginning.

The Football League owes its inception to a Scotsman, Mr. W. McGregor, an official of the Aston Villa Club. As professionalism spread throughout the North of England and the Midlands it became important for those clubs, who had to find money to pay players, to run games on business-like lines.

Football before 1888 was a carefree affair. Even when fixtures were arranged no one was certain that their opponents would turn up. When they did, it was nothing for games to be delayed an hour or so because of their late arrival. In addition, the game lacked the regular competitive element that only a league system could bring.

Mr. McGregor first wrote to five of the leading clubs, suggesting that a stricter control could be kept on the game, and more attractive fixtures arranged, if ten or twelve of the more powerful clubs formed themselves into a league. His suggested title for this organisation was The Association Football Union.

Following his circular, an informal meeting was held at Anderton's Hotel, in Fleet Street, London, on Mar. 22, 1888. There the proposal to form a League was accepted. The first formal meeting of " The Football League " took place a month later, April 17, at The Royal Hotel, Manchester.

Twelve clubs formed the new League and agreed to an annual subscription of £2 2s. They were Accrington, Aston Villa, Blackburn Rovers, Bolton Wanderers, Burnley, Derby County, Everton, Notts County, Preston North End, Stoke, West Bromwich Albion and Wolverhampton Wanderers. Three other clubs—Sheffield Wednesday, Nottingham Forest and Halliwell—applied for membership at the time but were not accepted because of the difficulty of arranging fixtures.

A Second Division consisting of 12 clubs was formed in 1892, by which time the First Division had increased to 16 clubs. There were several subsequent additions to both divisions, but they were not brought up to their present strength of 22 each until the 1919-20 season.

A Third Division was formed in 1920 with 22 clubs. This became the Third Division (Southern Section) when a Northern Section was formed in 1921. At first there were only 20 clubs in Division III (North), but the number was increased to 22 in 1923. Both these sections continued with 22 clubs each until 1950 when two more clubs were added to each.

A proposal to reorganise the League with four national divisions was turned down at the A.G.M. of 1956 but accepted the following year. And so, for season 1958-9, the Northern and Southern sections were abolished and the clubs formed into new Third and Fourth Divisions. At the same time a system of four up and down promotion and relegation between these two divisions was accepted.

FOOTBALL LEAGUE CHAMPIONS

Football League

1888-9 Preston North End; 1889-90 Preston North End; 1890-91 Everton; 1891-2 Sunderland.

First Division

1892-3 Sunderland; 1893-4 Aston Villa; 1894-5 Sunderland; 1895-6 Aston Villa; 1896-7 Aston Villa; 1897-8 Sheffield United; 1898-9 Aston Villa; 1899-1900 Aston Villa; 1900-1901 Liverpool; 1901-2 Sunderland; 1902-3 Sheffield Wednesday; 1903-4 Sheffield Wednesday; 1904-5 Newcastle United; 1905-6 Liverpool; 1906-7 Newcastle United; 1907-8 Manchester United; 1908-9 Newcastle United; 1909-10 Aston Villa; 1910-11 Manchester United; 1911-12 Blackburn Rovers; 1912-13 Sunderland; 1913-14 Blackburn Rovers; 1914-15 Everton; 1919-20 West Bromwich Albion; 1920-21 Burnley; 1921-2 Liverpool; 1922-3 Liverpool; 1923-4 *Huddersfield Town; 1924-5 Huddersfield Town; 1925-6 Huddersfield Town; 1926-7 Newcastle United; 1927-8 Everton; 1928-9 Sheffield Wednesday; 1929-30 Sheffield Wednesday; 1930-31 Arsenal; 1931-2 Everton; 1932-3 Arsenal; 1933-4 Arsenal; 1934-5 Arsenal; 1935-6 Sunderland; 1936-7 Manchester City; 1937-8 Arsenal; 1938-9 Everton; 1946-7 Liverpool; 1947-8 Arsenal; 1948-9 Portsmouth; 1949-50 *Portsmouth; 1950-51 Tottenham Hotspur; 1951-2 Manchester United; 1952-3 *Arsenal; 1953-4 Wolverhampton Wanderers; 1954-5 Chelsea; 1955-6 Manchester United; 1956-7 Manchester United; 1957-8 Wolverhampton Wanderers; 1958-9 Wolverhampton Wanderers; 1959-60 Burnley; 1960-61 Tottenham Hotspur; 1961-2 Ipswich Town; 1962-3 Everton; 1963-4 Liverpool; 1964-5 *Manchester United; 1965-6 Liverpool; 1966-7 Manchester United; 1967-8 Manchester City; 1968-9 Leeds United; 1969-70 Everton.

Second Division

1892-3 Small Heath; 1893-4 Liverpool; 1894-5 Bury; 1895-6 *Liverpool; 1896-7 Notts County; 1897-8 Burnley; 1898-9 Manchester City; 1899-1900 Sheffield Wednesday; 1900-1901 Grimsby Town, 1901-2 West Bromwich Albion; 1902-3 Manchester City; 1903-4 Preston North End; 1904-5 Liverpool; 1905-6 Bristol City; 1906-7 Nottingham Forest; 1907-8 Bradford City; 1908-9 Bolton Wanderers; 1909-10 Manchester City; 1910-11 West Bromwich Albion; 1911-12 Derby County; 1912-13 Preston North End; 1913-14 Notts County; 1914-15 Derby County; 1919-20 Tottenham Hotspur; 1920-21 *Birmingham; 1921-2 Nottingham Forest; 1922-3 Notts County; 1923-4 Leeds United; 1924-5 Leicester City; 1925-6 Sheffield Wednesday; 1926-7 Middlesbrough; 1927-8 Manchester City; 1928-9 Middlesbrough; 1929-30 Blackpool; 1930-31 Everton; 1931-2 Wolverhampton Wanderers; 1932-3 Stoke City; 1933-4 Grimsby Town; 1934-5 Brentford; 1935-6 Manchester United; 1936-7 Leicester City; 1937-8 Aston Villa; 1938-9 Blackburn Rovers; 1946-7 Manchester City; 1947-8 Birmingham City; 1948-9 Fulham; 1949-50 Tottenham Hotspur; 1950-51 Preston North End; 1951-2 Sheffield Wednesday; 1952-3 Sheffield United; 1953-4 *Leicester City; 1954-5 *Birmingham City; 1955-6 Sheffield Wednesday; 1956-7 Leicester City; 1957-8 West Ham United; 1958-9 Sheffield Wednesday; 1959-60 Aston Villa; 1960-61 Ipswich Town; 1961-2 Liverpool; 1962-3 Stoke City; 1963-4 Leeds United; 1964-5 Newcastle United; 1965-6 Manchester City; 1966-7 Coventry City; 1967-8 Ipswich Town; 1968-9 Derby County; 1969-70 Huddersfield Town.

Third Division (Southern Section)

1920-21 Crystal Palace; 1921-2 *Southampton; 1922-3 Bristol City; 1923-4 Portsmouth; 1924-5 Swansea Town; 1925-6 Reading; 1926-7 Bristol City; 1927-8 Millwall; 1928-9 *Charlton Athletic; 1929-30 Plymouth Argyle; 1930-31 Notts County; 1931-2 Fulham; 1932-3 Brentford; 1933-4 Norwich City; 1934-5 Charlton Athletic; 1935-6 Coventry City; 1936-7 Luton Town; 1937-8 Millwall; 1938-9 Newport County; 1946-7 Cardiff City; 1947-8 Queen's Park Rangers; 1948-9 Swansea Town; 1949-50 Notts County; 1950-51 Nottingham Forest; 1951-2 Plymouth Argyle; 1952-3 Bristol Rovers; 1953-4 Ipswich Town; 1954-5 Bristol City; 1955-6 Leyton Orient; 1956-7 Ipswich Town; 1957-8 Brighton and Hove Albion.

Third Division (Northern Section)

1921-2 Stockport County; 1922-3 Nelson; 1923-4 Wolverhampton Wanderers; 1924-5 Darlington; 1925-6 Grimsby Town; 1926-7 Stoke City; 1927-8 Bradford; 1928-9 Bradford City; 1929-30 Port Vale; 1930-31 Chesterfield; 1931-2 *Lincoln City; 1932-3 Hull City; 1933-4 Barnsley; 1934-5 Doncaster Rovers; 1935-6 Chesterfield; 1936-7 Stockport County; 1937-8 Tranmere Rovers; 1938-9 Barnsley; 1946-7 Doncaster Rovers; 1947-8 Lincoln City; 1948-9 Hull City; 1949-50 Doncaster Rovers; 1950-51 Rotherham United; 1951-2 Lincoln City; 1952-3 Oldham Athletic; 1953-4 Port Vale; 1954-5 Barnsley; 1955-6 Grimsby Town; 1956-7 Derby County; 1957-8 Scunthorpe and Lindsey United.

Third Division

1958-9 Plymouth Argyle; 1959-60 Southampton; 1960-61 Bury; 1961-2 Portsmouth; 1962-3 Northampton Town; 1963-4 *Coventry City; 1964-5 Carlisle United; 1965-6 Hull City; 1966-7 Queen's Park Rangers; 1967-8 Oxford United; 1968-9 *Watford; 1969-70 Orient.

Fourth Division

1958-9 Port Vale; 1959-60 Walsall; 1960-61 Peterborough United; 1961-2 Millwall; 1962-3 Brentford; 1963-4 *Gillingham; 1964-5 Brighton; 1965-6 *Doncaster Rovers; 1966-7 Stockport County; 1967-8 Luton Town; 1968-9 Doncaster Rovers; 1969-70 Chesterfield.

* Won on goal average.

FOOTBALL LEAGUE CUP

At the A.G.M. of the Football League in May 1960 a proposal that they should introduce their own Cup competition was accepted and approved by 31 votes to 16.

The competition is optional and it was not until season 1969-70 that all 92 League clubs took part.

Providing that it is a First Division club, then the winner of this competition is nominated by the League for entry into the Inter-Cities Fairs Cup.

Results of finals:

1960-61 Aston Villa beat Rotherham United on aggregate in a two-leg final, 0—2, 3—0 after extra time.

1961-62 Norwich City beat Rochdale 3—0, 1—0.

1962-63 Birmingham City beat Aston Villa, 3—0, 0—0.

1963-64 Leicester City beat Stoke City, 1—1, 3—2.

1964-65 Chelsea beat Leicester City, 3—2, 0—0.

1965-66 West Bromwich Albion beat West Ham United, 1—2, 4—1.

1966-67 Queen's Park Rangers beat West Bromwich Albion, 3—2.

1967-68 Leeds United beat Arsenal, 1—0.

1968-69 Swindon Town beat Arsenal, 3—1.

1969-70 Manchester City beat West Bromwich Albion 2—1 after extra time.

FOOTBALLER OF THE YEAR

The Football Writers' Association annual award.

1947-48	S. Matthews, Blackpool
1948-49	J. Carey, Manchester United
1949-50	J. Mercer, Arsenal
1950-51	H. Johnston, Blackpool
1951-52	W. Wright, Wolverhampton Wanderers
1952-53	N. Lofthouse, Bolton Wanderers
1953-54	T. Finney, Preston North End
1954-55	D. Revie, Manchester City
1955-56	B. Trautmann, Manchester City
1956-57	T. Finney, Preston North End
1957-58	D. Blanchflower, Tottenham Hotspur
1958-59	S. Owen, Luton Town
1959-60	W. Slater, Wolverhampton Wanderers
1960-61	D. Blanchflower, Tottenham Hotspur
1961-62	J. Adamson, Burnley
1962-63	S. Matthews, Stoke City
1963-64	R. Moore, West Ham United
1964-65	R. Collins, Leeds United
1965-66	R. Charlton, Manchester United
1966-67	J. Charlton, Leeds United
1967-68	G. Best, Manchester United
1968-69	D. Mackay, Derby County and A. Book, Manchester City
1969-70	W. Bremner, Leeds United

FOREIGN PLAYERS IN FOOTBALL LEAGUE

Several foreign born players have appeared for Football League clubs. These include:

Chinese: Cheung Chi Doy, forward, for Blackpool, 1960-62.

Danish: N. Middleboe, left-half, for Chelsea, 1913-14. H. V. Jensen, full-back, for Hull City, 1948-56.

Dutch: G. P. Keizer, goalkeeper, Arsenal and Charlton Athletic 1930-32.

Egyptian: T. Abdullah, inside-forward, Derby County, 1920-22, Hartlepools United, 1923-24. H. Hegazi, centre-forward for Fulham, 1911-12. M. Mansour, goalkeeper, for Queen's Park Rangers, 1938-9.

German: M. Seeburg, inside-forward, for Chelsea, Tottenham Hotspur, Burnley, Grimsby Town and Reading, 1907-14. A. Eisentrager, inside-forward for Bristol City, 1949-56. B. Trautmann, goalkeeper, for Manchester City, 1949-63. D. Bruck, wing-half, for Coventry City, 1960-70.

Hungarian: B. Olah, inside-forward, for Northampton Town, 1960-62. M. Nagy, for Swindon Town, 1951-2. J. Haasz, inside-forward, for Swansea Town, Workington, 1960-63.

Italian: A. Freezia, half-back, for Reading, 1913-14.

Polish: F. Staroscik, outside-left, for Northampton Town, 1953-5. S. Gerula, goalkeeper, for Leyton Orient. 1949-50.

Spanish: E. Aldecoa, forward, for Coventry City, 1946-7. J. Gallego, Brentford forward, 1946-8.

Swedish: H. Jeppson, centre-forward, for Charlton Athletic, 1950-51.

FRANCE

A football club was formed at Le Havre as long ago as 1872 following the introduction of the game to the town by English sailors in the summer of that year, but it was many years after this before the dribbling code really made any progress in France.

Rugby took a much stronger hold on the country than soccer and it was not until 1917 that widespread interest in the latter game was created by the introduction of a national cup competition run on similar lines to the F.A. Cup. This was the Charles Simon Cup, in memory of the founder of the

Comité Français Interfédéral who had been killed in the war in 1915. After that war this competition became known simply as the Coupe de France.

The controlling body of football in France is the Fédération Française du Football, formed in 1919 out of the old Comité Français Interfédéral which consisted of four separate organisations.

Professionalism in France was not approved until 1932 and even today most of the players among the first-class clubs are only part-time professionals.

The address of the governing body of football in France : Fédération Française de Football, 60 bis Avenue d'iena 75, Paris 16. Colours: Blue jerseys, white shorts, red stockings.

May 10, 1923	France 1, England 4; Paris
May 17, 1924	France 1, England 3; Paris
May 21, 1925	France 2, England 3; Paris
May 26, 1927	France 0, England 6; Paris
May 17, 1928	France 1, England 5; Paris
May 9, 1929	France 1, England 4; Paris
May 18, 1930	France 0, Scotland 2; Paris
May 14, 1931	France 5, England 2; Paris
May 8, 1932	France 1, Scotland 3; Paris
May 25, 1933	France 1, Wales 1; Paris
Dec. 6, 1933	England 4, France 1; Tottenham
May 23, 1937	Eire 2, France 0; Paris
May 26, 1938	France 2, England 4; Paris
May 20, 1939	France 2, Wales 1; Paris
May 3, 1947	England 3, France 0; Highbury
May 23, 1948	France 3, Scotland 0; Paris
April 27, 1949	Scotland 2, France 0; Hampden
May 22, 1949	France 1, England 3; Paris
May 27, 1950	France 0, Scotland 1; Paris
May 12, 1951	Ireland 2, France 2; Belfast
May 16, 1951	Scotland 1, France 0; Hampden
Oct. 3, 1951	England 2, France 2; Highbury
Nov. 11, 1952	France 3, Ireland 1; Paris
Nov. 16, 1952	Eire 1, France 1; Dublin
May 14, 1953	France 6, Wales 1; Paris
Oct. 4, 1953*	Eire 3, France 5; Dublin
Nov. 25, 1953*	France 1, Eire 0; Paris
May 15, 1955	France 1, England 0; Paris
Nov. 27, 1957	England 4, France 0; Wembley
June 15, 1958*	Scotland 1, France 2; Sweden
June 19, 1958*	Ireland 0, France 4; Sweden
Oct. 3, 1962	England 1, France 1; Sheffield
Feb. 27, 1963†	France 5, England 2; Paris
July 20, 1966*	England 2, France 0; Wembley
Mar. 12, 1969	England 5, France 0; Wembley

* World Cup   † Nations Cup

FULHAM F.C.

Founded 1880 as St. Andrew's Sunday School, West Kensington. The nearest available ground was at Fulham so went under the name of Fulham St. Andrews. Elected to Football League, Division II, 1907. Honours: Champions, Division II, 1948-9. Runners-up, 1958-9. Champions, Division III(S), 1931-2. Best in Division I, 10th, 1959-60. F.A. Cup: Semi-finalists, 1908, 1936, 1958, 1962.

Record attendance : 49,335 v. Millwall, Division II, Oct. 8, 1938. Address : Craven Cottage, Stevenage Road, S.W.6 (Tel. 01-736 5621). Nickname : Cottagers. Colours : White shirts, black shorts. Record League goal-scorer : F. Newton, 41 goals, Division III(S), 1931-32. Record victory : 10—1 v. Ipswich Town, Division I, Dec. 26, 1963. Record defeat 8—4 v. Barnsley, Division II, Jan. 28, 1928.

G

GATE RECEIPTS

European Cup

The record receipts for a European Cup match were those taken in the final between Manchester United and Benfica, Wembley, May 29, 1968. The figure was approximately £118,000.

F.A. Amateur Cup

Record receipts £29,305, Wembley Stadium, April 16, 1955. Final tie between Bishop Auckland and Hendon.

F.A. Cup

For list of receipts at F.A. Cup Finals see FOOTBALL ASSOCIATION CHALLENGE CUP (Finals). The record Cup Final receipts, £128,272 were taken in 1970 for the match, Chelsea v. Leeds United.

Rules for the division of gate receipts are laid down by the F.A., and, briefly, are as follows:

The home club is entitled to deduct match expenses such as fees to the referee and linesmen, cost of advertising, printing, police, etc., and the travelling expenses of the visiting team are also deducted. Thereafter the division is:

Round 1, 2: divided equally between the two clubs.

Rounds 3, 4, 5 and 6: divided equally between the two clubs and the Cup Pool.

Replays in these rounds are subject to a 5% levy by the F.A. before the final division is made.

Semi-finals: 25% to the F.A., 25% to the Cup Pool, and the remainder equally between the four clubs.

If both semi-finals are replayed then the division is the same as before. If one match only is replayed then the share for each of the two clubs is increased to 25% of the net proceeds.

The Final: 25% to the F.A., 25% to the Cup Pool, and 50% divided between the two clubs.

As regards the Cup Pool, this is subsequently divided equally among all the Football League clubs who entered the competition.

Non-League clubs in rounds 3, 4, 5 and 6, qualify for a half share of the gate, and, if opposed by a League club, the Cup Pool deduction comes out of the League club's share. The non-League clubs do not contribute to the pool as they do not qualify for the final share-out.

Football League

After necessary expenses have been deducted by the home club in League games the net proceeds from gate receipts is divided as follows:

4% to the Football League pool (the net amount in this case includes an appropriate proportion of the receipts from the sale of season tickets); to the visiting club an amount consisting of 1s for each adult and 6d. for each schoolchild, including all season ticket holders; the balance to the home club.

In all cases the visiting club's share must be at least £200.

Internationals

The record receipts for an international match played in the British Isles, £204,805, World Cup Final, Wembley, July 30, 1966.

Scottish Association Cup

The record receipts for a single game in this competition amounted to

£54,776 for the Final between Celtic and Rangers, Apr. 26, 1969.

In all ties of the Scottish Association Cup competition proper, excluding the semi-finals and final, the home club must guarantee their visitors a sum equivalent to the cost of 15 rail fares plus £20 if the clubs are more than 100 miles apart.

Referee's and linesmen's fees and expenses and also a levy of 5% for the Cup Pool are deducted, and then, providing that the visitors receive their guarantee as first mentioned, the receipts are divided equally between the two clubs.

In the semi-finals the total receipts are pooled and, after payment of match expenses and clubs' guarantees, the Scottish F.A. takes 5% of the balance. The remainder, less allowances for use of grounds, is then divided equally between the four clubs. There are other more complex arrangements for re-played semi-finals. The Association also takes 5% of the receipts at the Final tie. The balance is then divided equally after deduction of guarantees and expenses and allowance for use of the ground.

Scottish League

Receipts divided equally between competing clubs, providing that the visiting club receives a guarantee of £500 in the First Division and £150 in Second Division and League Cup games.

The Scottish League only takes 2% of net receipts at games played on neutral grounds and the Semi-finals and Final of the League Cup. In these games the competing clubs share the proceeds equally.

If a game is abandoned there is no guarantee for the visiting club in the replay but the proceeds are shared equally.

World Cup

The record receipts at a football match anywhere in the world is £204,805, the amount paid to see the World Cup Final at Wembley, July 30, 1966.

GERMANY

Germany was one of the first countries outside of the British Isles where football was played under Association rules. That would be in about 1870. A team from Oxford University visited Germany in 1875 and this was the first-ever overseas tour of a soccer team. Soon after this a number of German universities were encouraged to take up the game.

The oldest club still in existence in Germany, Hamburg S.V., was formed in 1887. Two years later the English F.A. sent over a representative side, and in 1900 the German F.A. was founded.

Aston Villa F.C. visited Berlin in 1901 and in the same year the Germans sent a side to meet England in games at White Hart Lane and Manchester. These two games are not ranked as official internationals. In the first, England, represented by amateurs, won 12—0. Professionals took over for England in the second game and won 10—0.

Germany played their first official representative international match in 1908 when they lost 5—3 to Switzerland at Basle.

The first full international between Germany and one of the home countries took place in 1929 against Scotland. England met Germany a year later.

Needless to say there are, today, two German F.A.s, the East and the West. Both are members of F.I.F.A. and it should be noted that there are more football clubs in West Germany than in any country in the world apart from England and, possibly, Russia. Indeed, Germany actually has more registered players than there are in England.

It is not surprising, therefore, that Germany is one of only two Continental countries (the other is Italy), to have won the World Cup. Their victory in 1954 was achieved with a side of super-fit men who played real down-to-earth football without any frills. It is generally acknowledged that they were not as good a side as the Hungarians whom they beat in the final, catching them on an off-day in conditions (it was pouring with rain) which suited the Germans better than the more artistic Hungarians, but there is no denying that the Germans' effort was a remarkable one.

That, of course, was the West German team. The East German team with only about a third as many clubs from which to select their players has so far not made anything like the same impression in world soccer. They are, however, just as enthusiastic about the game in the East and the re-organisation of their League football in 1950 has increased interest. A further re-organisation was made in the early 1960s and there is now a top division of 14 clubs, the remainder being divided into regions.

The East German Association was formed in 1947. Its address is: Deutscher Fussball-Verband, Storkower Strasse 118, Berlin 1055. Colours: Blue shirts, white shorts.

The West German Association, re-founded in 1950, is the Deutscher Fussball Bund, Zeppelinalle 77, Frankfurt a/M. Colours: White shirts with black collars and cuffs, black shorts, black stockings with white tops.

June 1, 1929	Germany 1, Scotland 1; Berlin
May 10, 1930	Germany 3, England 3; Berlin
May 8, 1935	Germany 3, Eire 1; Dortmund
Dec. 4, 1935	England 3, Germany 0; Tottenham
May 6, 1936	Germany 4, Eire 1; Cologne
Oct. 14, 1936	Scotland 2, Germany 2; Ibrox
Oct. 17, 1936	Eire 5, Germany 2; Dublin
May 14, 1938	Germany 3, England 6; Berlin
May 23, 1939	Germany 1, Eire 1; Bremen
Oct. 17, 1951	Eire 3, West Germany 2; Dublin
May 4, 1952	West Germany 3, Eire 0; Cologne
Dec. 1, 1954	England 3, West Germany 1; Wembley
May 28, 1955	West Germany 2, Eire 1; Hamburg
May 26, 1956	West Germany 1, England 3; Berlin
Nov. 25, 1956	Eire 3, West Germany 0; Dublin
May 19, 1957*	East Germany 2, Wales 1; Leipzig
May 22, 1957	West Germany 1, Scotland 3; Stuttgart
Sept. 25, 1957*	Wales 4, East Germany 1; Cardiff
June 15, 1958*	Ireland 2, West Germany 2; Sweden
May 6, 1959	Scotland 3, West Germany 2; Hampden
Oct. 26, 1960*	Ireland 3, Germany 4; Belfast
May 10, 1961*	West Germany 2, Ireland 1; Hamburg
June 2, 1963	East Germany 1, England 2; Leipzig
May 12, 1964	West Germany 2, Scotland 2; Hanover
May 12, 1965	West Germany 0, England 1; Nuremberg
Feb. 23, 1966	England 1, West Germany 0; Wembley
May 4, 1966	Eire 0, West Germany 4; Dublin
May 7, 1966	Ireland 0, West Germany 2; Belfast
July 30, 1966*	England 4, West Germany 2; Wembley†
May 8, 1968	Wales 1, West Germany 1; Cardiff
June 1, 1968	West Germany 1, England 0; Hanover
Mar. 26, 1969	West Germany 1, Wales 1; Frankfurt
Apr. 16, 1969*	East Germany 2, Wales 1; Dresden
Apr. 16, 1969*	Scotland 1, West Germany 1; Glasgow
Oct. 22, 1969*	Wales 1, East Germany 3; Cardiff
Oct. 22, 1969*	West Germany 3, Scotland 2; Hamburg
May 9, 1970	West Germany 2, Eire 1; Berlin
June 14, 1970*	England 2 West Germany 3; Leon †

* World Cup   † After extra time

GILLINGHAM F.C.

New Brompton Excelsior met with such success in local junior football that a company was formed in 1893 and the club set on a proper footing as New Brompton. It changed its name to Gillingham in 1913. One of the original members of the Football League, Division III, 1920. Dropped out, 1938. Re-elected 1950. Honours: Champions, Division IV, 1963-4. Record attendance: 23,002 v. Queens Park Rangers, F.A. Cup, 3rd Round, Jan. 10, 1948. Address: Priestfield Road, Gillingham (Tel. Medway 51854). Colours: Blue shirts, white shorts with blue stripes. Record League goal-scorer: E. Morgan, 31 goals, Division III(S), 1954-55. Record victory: 10—1 v. Gorleston, F.A. Cup, 1st Round, Nov. 16, 1957. Record defeat: 9—2 v. Nottingham Forest, Division III(S), Nov. 18, 1950.

GOAL AVERAGE

To calculate goal average the num-ber of goals for are divided by the number of goals against. The higher the result, the better is the goal aver-age.

Goal average does not count in the International Championship and it should be noted that goal average is never considered in many competitions abroad. In Belgium, for instance, the team with the greater number of vic-tories is placed highest, while many countries, including Northern Ireland, still insist on a play-off for the top places.

In the Football League and the Scottish League the championship of each division has been decided on goal average in the following instances:

Season	Champions	Goal Average	Runners-up	Goal Average
		Division I		
1923-24	Huddersfield Town	1.818	Cardiff City	1.794
1949-50	Portsmouth	1.947	Wolverhampton W.	1.551
1952-53	Arsenal	1.515	Preston North End	1.416
1964-65	Manchester United	2.282	Leeds United	1.596
		Division II		
1895-96	Liverpool	3.312	Manchester City	1.657
1911-12	Derby County	2.645	Chelsea	1.882
1920-21	Birmingham	2.078	Cardiff City	1.843
1953-54	Leicester City	1.616	Everton	1.586
1954-55	Birmingham City	1.972	Luton Town	1.660
			(3rd) Rotherham United	1.468
		Division III		
1963-64	Coventry City	1.606	Crystal Palace	1.431
1968-69	Watford	2.176	Swindon Town	2.028
		Division IV		
1963-64	Gillingham	1.966	Carlisle United	1.948
1965-66	Doncaster Rovers	1.575	Darlington	1.358
		Division III(S)		
1921-22	Southampton	3.238	Plymouth Argyle	2.625
1928-29	Charlton Athletic	1.433	Crystal Palace	1.208
		Division III(N)		
1931-32	Lincoln City	2.257	Gateshead	1.958
	Scottish League. Division I or A			
1952-53	Rangers	2.051	Hibernian	1.823
1964-65	Kilmarnock	1.878	Hearts	1.836

In 1890-91 Dumbarton and Rangers finished level on points at head of the table. A deciding match between the clubs resulted in a draw 2—2. They were held to be joint champions for the season.

Celtic and Rangers finished level on points in 1904-5. A decider was won by Celtic, 2—1.

1929-30	Leith Athletic	2.190	East Fife	1.965
1931-32	East Stirling	2.018	St. Johnstone	1.961
1948-49	Raith Rovers	1.818	Stirling Albion	1.510
1950-51	Queen of South	1.971	Stirling Albion	1.772
1969-70	Falkirk	2.764	Cowdenbeath	2.314

GOALKEEPERS

The goalkeeper, as we know him to-day, came into being about 1870. The word "goalkeeper" appeared in the Sheffield Rules before then, but not in reference to a particular individual.

The relevant passage occurs in the rule concerning "offside." It reads:

"The goalkeeper is that player on the defending side who, for the time being, is nearest his own goal."

The first mention of a goalkeeper as a player who is permitted to use his hands was made in the Football Association Rules of 1870.

Throughout the years many outstanding personalities have filled this position. The greatest have included such as these:

England:

S. Hardy: Spent most of his career with Liverpool and Aston Villa and made 23 appearances for England between 1906 and 1920.

H. Hibbs: Birmingham's goalkeeper from 1925 until World War II. Noted for his uncanny sense of anticipation. He was considered short for a goalkeeper, but played for England in 26 games.

F. Swift: Retired from League football in 1950 and was killed in the Munich plane crash disaster of 1958. One of the most popular personalities ever to gain an England cap. Played in 19 full internationals as well as 14 war-time and victory games during the 18 years he was with Manchester City.

Ireland:

E. Scott: The Liverpool and Belfast Celtic goalkeeper made 31 International Championship appearances for his country. Joined Liverpool in season 1911-12 and remained with them for more than 22 years.

Scotland:

J. Brownlie: Goalkeeper for Third Lanark in the early 1900s. Made 16 appearances for Scotland.

E. Doig: One of the outstanding personalities among the earliest professional players. Kept goal for Sunderland for 14 seasons from 1890. Previously played for Arbroath and made a brief appearance with Blackburn Rovers. Scotland capped him six times.

J. Dawson: Not to be confused with Burnley's long-service goalkeeper. This Scot helped Glasgow Rangers win the Scottish League championship five times and the Cup twice. Scotland capped him 14 times.

Wales:

J. Trainor: In the 80s and 90s he was known as the "Prince of Goalkeepers." Wrexham and Preston North End were his principal clubs. Played in 21 International Championship games.

L. R. Roose: One of the greatest amateur goalkeepers to play in the International Championship. Played for Aberystwyth, London Welsh, Stoke (two separate periods), Everton, Sunderland, Huddersfield Town, Aston Villa and Woolwich Arsenal, between 1899 and 1912. Made 25 international appearances including one amateur game.

Four Goalkeepers

Four goalkeepers were called upon to take part in the England v. Wales game at Wrexham, Mar. 16, 1908. England's goalkeeper was H. Bailey (Leicester Fosse). The Welsh goalkeeper, L. R. Roose (Sunderland) was injured in the first half and his place was taken by full-back C. Morris (Derby County). In the second half England agreed to D. Davies (Bolton Wanderers) substituting in goal, and Morris returned to his original position.

Goalkeepers' Jerseys

At the annual meeting of the Football League, June 8, 1909, it was decided that goalkeepers must play in distinctive colours of either scarlet, royal blue or white, to assist the referee. Royal green was added on June 3, 1912.

On June 3, 1921, it was ruled that

goalkeepers in international matches should wear jerseys of deep yellow. This colour is also compulsory in Scottish Association Cup-ties.

Goalkeeper Goal-scorers

The only occasion on record in which opposing goalkeepers each scored for their own side in a first-class game was in 1910 when J. Brownlie netted for Third Lanark and C. Hampton for Motherwell.

The Football League goalscoring record for a goalkeeper was set up in season 1923-24 by A. Birch of Chesterfield. He played in every one of Chesterfield's Division III(N) matches that season and scored five goals, all from penalties.

C. Williams, playing in goal for Manchester City, scored with a goal kick against Sunderland in a Division I game, April 14, 1900. The Sunderland goalkeeper, E. Doig, touched the ball as it entered the net. Sunderland won 3—1. In those days the full-back (in this instance, D. Jones) tapped the ball into the goalkeeper's hands to enable him to take a drop kick.

Two other goalkeepers who have scored with long kicks are P. Jennings (Tottenham Hotspur) v. Manchester United, Charity Shield, Aug. 12, 1967, and P. Shilton (Leicester City) v. Southampton, Division I, Oct. 14, 1967.

A goalkeeper's " own goal " was scored at Home Park, Plymouth, 16 minutes after the start of a Division II game between Plymouth Argyle and Fulham, on Oct. 2, 1954, when F. Elliott, the Fulham goalkeeper, in trying to cut out a cross shot while the Plymouth Argyle centre-forward Langman, challenged him, fell as he smothered the ball and rolled over on his back, injured. As he lay on the ground he threw the ball back over his head and it rolled gently into his own goal.

Other goalkeepers who have suffered the misfortune of scoring in their own goal include: H. Brown (Queen's Park Rangers) v. Northampton Town, Dec. 27, 1954; R. Drinkwater (Queen's Park Rangers) v. Brentford, Nov. 22, 1958; G. Wright (Colchester United) v. Torquay United, Feb. 16, 1952; H. Gregg

(Manchester United) v. Tottenham Hotspur, Nov. 9, 1963; G. Sprake (Leeds United) v. Liverpool, Dec. 9, 1967; M. Gibson (Bristol City) v. Manchester City, Aug. 28, 1965.

There have been several instances of goalkeepers giving up their position during a game because of injury, continuing in another position and scoring. Examples include T. Adlington (Torquay United) v. Barnet, F.A. Cup, 1st Round, Nov. 16, 1963, I. Black (Fulham) v. Leicester City, Division II, Aug. 25, 1952; G. Bradley (Notts County) v. Leicester City, Division II, Sept. 22, 1956; H. Dowd (Manchester City) v. Bury, Division II, Feb. 8, 1964; G. Farm (Blackpool) v. Preston North End, Division I, Oct. 20, 1955; M. Granger (Halifax Town) v. Workington, F.A. Cup, 1st Round, Nov. 16, 1963; D. Herod (Stoke City) v. Aston Villa, Division I, Feb. 16, 1952; F. Moss (Arsenal) v. Everton, Division I, Mar. 16, 1935; B. Singleton (Exeter City) v. Aldershot, Division III(S), Dec. 25, 1950; J. Savage (Halifax Town) v. Bradford, Division III(N), Dec. 27, 1952; C. Tinsley (Exeter City) v. Workington, Division IV, Sept. 20, 1962; A. Wilkie (Reading) v. Halifax Town (2 goals), Division III, Aug. 31, 1962.

GOAL NETS

Goal nets were invented and patented by J. A. Brodie of Liverpool in 1890. The first important game in which nets were used was North v. South, at Nottingham, Jan. 1891. Nets were first used in the F.A. Cup Final in 1891 at the Oval.

GOAL SCORING (INDIVIDUALS)

Aggregate Record for Single Season

Football League:

Division I:

		Goals	Games
W. R. Dean (Everton)	1927-28	60	39
T. Waring (Aston Villa)	1930-31	49	39

Division II:

		Goals	Games
G. Camsell (Middlesbrough)	1926-27	59	37
D. Dooley (Sheffield Wednesday)	1951-52	46	30

Division III(S):
J. Payne (Luton Town)
1936-37 55 39
C. Bourton (Coventry City)
1931-32 49 40
Division III(N):
E. Harston (Mansfield Town)
1936-37 55 41
A. Lythgoe (Stockport
County) 1933-34 46 39
Division III:
D. Reeves (Southampton)
1959-60 39 46
Division IV:
T. Bly (Peterborough United)
1960-61 52 46
Scottish League:
Division I:
W. McFadyen (Motherwell)
1931-32 52 34

Division II:
J. Smith (Ayr United)
1927-28 66 38

Highest aggregate of goals in a
single season of first-class football in
any of the home countries is 96 by F.
Roberts, Glentoran centre-forward, in
season 1930-31.

Irish League	55
Irish Cup	4
Belfast City Cup	28
County Antrim Shield	7
Belfast Charity Cup	2
	—
	96

J. Bambrick, Linfield centre-forward, scored 94 goals in season 1929-
30:

Irish League	50
Irish Cup	7
Belfast City Cup	10
County Antrim Shield	5
Belfast Charity Cup	9
Inter-League games	5
Irish Gold Cup	1
Conder Cup	1
International games	6
	—
	94

J. Smith, Ayr United centre-forward
scored 84 goals in season 1927-8.

Scottish League, Division II	66
Scottish F.A. Cup	2
Ayr Charity Cup	1
Other Games	15
	—
	84
	—

W. Dean, Everton centre-forward
scored 82 goals in season 1927-8.

Football League, Division I	60
F.A. Cup	3
Inter-League games	6
International trial games	8
Internationals	5
	—
	82
	—

G. Camsell, Middlesbrough centre-
forward, scored 79 goals in season
1926-7.

Football League, Division II	59
F.A. Cup	5
North-Eastern League	12
International trial games	3
	—
	79
	—

Top goal-scorers in each division for
every season since World War I:

Division I

1919-20	F. Morris, West Bromwich Albion	37
1920-21	J. Smith, Bolton Wanderers	38
1921-22	A. Wilson, Middlesbrough	31
1922-23	C. Buchan, Sunderland	30
1923-24	W. Chadwick, Everton	28
1924-25	F. Roberts, Manchester City	31
1925-26	E. Harper, Blackburn Rovers	43
1926-27	J. Trotter, Sheffield Wednesday	37
1927-28	W. Dean, Everton	60
1928-29	D. Halliday, Sunderland	43
1929-30	V. Watson, West Ham United	41
1930-31	T. Waring, Aston Villa	49
1931-32	W. Dean, Everton	44
1932-33	J. Bowers, Derby County	35
1933-34	J. Bowers, Derby County	35
1934-35	E. Drake, Arsenal	42
1935-36	E. Glover, Grimsby Town	31
	H. Carter, Sunderland	31
	R. Gurney, Sunderland	31
1936-37	F. Steel, Stoke City	33
1937-38	T. Lawton, Everton	28
1938-39	T. Lawton, Everton	35
1946-47	D. Westcott, Wolverhampton Wanderers	37
1947-48	R. Rooke, Arsenal	33
1948-49	W. Moir, Bolton Wanderers	25
1949-50	D. Davis, Sunderland	25
1950-51	S. Mortensen, Blackpool	30

1951-52 G. Robledo, Newcastle United 33
1952-53 C. Wayman, Preston North End 24
1953-54 J. Glazzard, Huddersfield Town 29
1954-55 R. Allen, West Bromwich Albion 27
1955-56 N. Lofthouse, Bolton Wanderers 33
1956-57 J. Charles, Leeds United 38
1957-58 R. Smith, Tottenham Hotspur 36
1958-59 J. Greaves, Chelsea 33
1959-60 D. Viollet, Manchester United 32
1960-61 J. Greaves, Chelsea 41
1961-62 R. Crawford, Ipswich Town 33
1962-63 J. Greaves, Tottenham Hotspur 37
1963-64 J. Greaves, Tottenham Hotspur 35
1964-65 A. McEvoy, Blackburn Rovers 29
        J. Greaves, Tottenham Hotspur 29
1965-66 W. Irvine, Burnley 29
1966-67 R. Davies, Southampton 37
1967-68 G. Best, Manchester United 28
        R. Davies, Southampton 28
1968-69 J. Greaves, Tottenham Hotspur 27
1969-70 J. Astle, West Bromwich Albion 25

Division II

1919-20 S. Taylor, Huddersfield Town 35
1920-21 S. Puddefoot, West Ham United 29
1921-22 J. Broad, Stoke City 25
1922-23 H. Bedford, Blackpool 32
1923-24 H. Bedford, Blackpool 34
1924-25 A. Chandler, Leicester City 33
1925-26 J. Trotter, Sheffield Wednesday 37
1926-27 G. Camsell, Middlesbrough 59
1927-28 J. Cookson, West Bromwich Albion 38
1928-29 J. Hampson, Blackpool 40
1929-30 J. Hampson, Blackpool 45
1930-31 W. Dean, Everton 39
1931-32 C. Pearce, Swansea Town 35
1932-33 E. Harper, Preston North End 37
1933-34 E. Glover, Grimsby Town 42

1934-35 J. Milsom, Bolton Wanderers 31
1935-36 R. Finan, Blackpool 34
        E. Dodds, Sheffield United 34
1936-37 J. Bowers, Leicester City 33
1937-38 G. Henson, Bradford 27
1938-39 H. Billington, Luton Town 28
1946-47 C. Wayman, Newcastle United 30
1947-48 E. Quigley, Sheffield Wednesday 23
1948-49 C. Wayman, Southampton 32
1949-50 T. Briggs, Grimsby Town 35
1950-51 J. McCormack, Barnsley 33
1951-52 D. Dooley, Sheffield Wednesday 46
1952-53 A. Rowley, Leicester City 39
1953-54 J. Charles, Leeds United 42
1954-55 T. Briggs, Blackburn Rovers 33
1955-56 W. Gardiner, Leicester City 34
1956-57 A. Rowley, Leicester City 44
1957-58 B. Clough, Middlesbrough 40
1958-59 B. Clough, Middlesbrough 42
1959-60 B. Clough, Middlesbrough 39
1960-61 R. Crawford, Ipswich Town 39
1961-62 R. Hunt, Liverpool 41
1962-63 R. Tambling, Chelsea 35
1963-64 R. Saunders, Portsmouth 33
1964-65 G. O'Brien, Southampton 34
1965-66 M. Chivers, Southampton 30
1966-67 R. Gould, Coventry City 24
1967-68 J. Hickton, Middlesbrough 24
1968-69 J. Toshack, Cardiff City 22
1969-70 J. Hickton, Middlesbrough 24

Division III(S)

1920-21 J. Connor, Crystal Palace 28
        E. Simms, Luton Town 28
        G. Whitworth, Northampton Town 28
1921-22 F. Richardson, Plymouth Argyle 31
1922-23 F. Pagnam, Watford 30
1923-24 W. P. Haines, Portsmouth 28
1924-25 J. Fowler, Swansea Town 28
1925-26 J. Cock, Plymouth Argyle 32
1926-27 D. Morris, Swindon Town 47
1927-28 D. Morris, Swindon Town 38
1928-29 A. Rennie, Luton Town 43
1929-30 G. Goddard, Queen's Park Rangers 37
1930-31 P. Simpson, Crystal Palace 46

1931-32 C. Bourton, Coventry
City 49
1932-33 C. Bourton, Coventry
City 40
1933-34 A. Dawes, Northampton
Town and Crystal Palace 27
1934-35 R. Allen, Charlton
Athletic 32
1935-36 A. Dawes, Crystal Palace 38
1936-37 J. Payne, Luton Town 55
1937-38 H. Crawshaw, Mansfield
Town 25
1938-39 G. Morton, Swindon
Town 28
1946-47 D. Clarke, Bristol City 36
1947-48 L. Townsend, Bristol City 29
1948-49 D. McGibbon, Bournemouth and Boscombe
United 30
1949-50 T. Lawton, Notts County 31
1950-51 W. Ardron, Nottingham
Forest 36
1951-52 R. Blackman, Reading 39
1952-53 G. Bradford, Bristol Rov. 33
1953-54 J. English, Northampton
Town 28
1954-55 E. Morgan, Gillingham 31
1955-56 R. Collins, Torquay
United 40
1956-57 E. Phillips, Ipswich Town 41
1957-58 S. McGrory, Southend
United 31
D. Reeves, Southampton 31

Division III(N)
1921-22 J. Carmichael, Grimsby
Town 37
1922-23 G. Beel, Chesterfield 23
J. Carmichael, Grimsby
Town 23
1923-24 D. Brown, Darlington 27
1924-25 D. Brown, Darlington 39
1925-26 J. Cookson, Chesterfield 44
1926-27 A. Whitehurst, Rochdale 44
1927-28 J. Smith, Stockport
County 38
1928-29 J. McConnell, Carlisle
United 43
1929-30 F. Newton, Stockport
County 36
1930-31 J. McConnell, Carlisle
United 37
1931-32 B. Hall, Lincoln City 42
1932-33 W. McNaughton, Hull
City 39
1933-34 A. Lythgoe, Stockport
County 46
1934-35 G. Alsop, Walsall 39
1935-36 R. Bell, Tranmere Rovers 33
1936-37 E. Harston, Mansfield
Town 55
1937-38 J. Roberts, Port Vale 28

1938-39 S. Hunt, Carlisle United 32
1946-47 C. Jordan, Doncaster
Rovers 41
1947-48 J. Hutchinson, Lincoln
City 32
1948-49 W. Ardron, Rotherham
United 29
1949-50 R. Phillips, Crewe
Alexandra 26
P. Doherty, Doncaster
Rovers 26
1950-51 J. Shaw, Rotherham
United 37
1951-52 A. Graver, Lincoln City 36
1952-53 J. Whitehouse, Carlisle
United 29
1953-54 G. Ashman, Carlisle
United 30
1954-55 A. Bottom, York City 30
D. Travis, Oldham
Athletic 30
J. Connor, Stockport
County 30
1955-56 R. Crosbie, Grimsby
Town 36
1956-57 R. Straw, Derby County 37
1957-58 A. Ackerman, Carlisle
United 35

Division III
1958-59 E. Towers, Brentford 32
1959-60 D. Reeves, Southampton 39
1960-61 A. Richards, Walsall 36
1961-62 C. Holton, Watford and
Northampton 37
1962-63 G. Hudson, Coventry
City 30
1963-64 A. Biggs, Bristol Rovers 30
1964-65 K. Wagstaff, Mansfield
Town and Hull City 34
1965-66 L. Allen, Queen's Park
Rangers 30
1966-67 R. Marsh, Queen's Park
Rangers 30
1967-68 D. Rogers, Swindon
Town 25
1968-69 D. Rogers, Swindon
Town 22
1969-70 G. Jones, Bury 26

Division IV
1958-59 A. Rowley, Shrewsbury
Town 37
1959-60 C. Holton, Watford 42
1960-61 T. Bly, Peterborough
United 52
1961-62 R. R. Hunt, Colchester
United 37
1962-63 K. Wagstaff, Mansfield
Town 34
1963-64 H. McIlmoyle, Carlisle
United 39

1964-65	A. Jeffrey, Doncaster Rovers	36
1965-66	K. Hector, Bradford	44
1966-67	E. Phythian, Hartlepools United	23
1967-68	L. Massie, Halifax Town	25
	R. Chapman, Port Vale	25
1968-69	G. Talbot, Chester	22
1969-70	A. Kinsey, Wrexham	27

Scottish League
Division I (A)

1919-20	H. Ferguson, Motherwell	33
1920-21	H. Ferguson, Motherwell	43
1921-22	D. Walker, St. Mirren	45
1922-23	J. White, Hearts	30
1923-24	D. Halliday, Dundee	38
1924-25	W. Devlin, Cowdenbeath	33
1925-26	W. Devlin, Cowdenbeath	37
1926-27	J. McGrory, Celtic	49
1927-28	J. McGrory, Celtic	47
1928-29	E. Morrison, Falkirk	43
1929-30	B. Yorston, Aberdeen	38
1930-31	B. Battles, Hearts	44
1931-32	W. McFadyen, Motherwell	52
1932-33	W. McFadyen, Motherwell	45
1933-34	J. Smith, Rangers	41
1934-35	D. McCulloch, Hearts	38
1935-36	J. McGrory, Celtic	50

1936-37	D. Wilson, Hamilton Academicals	34
1937-38	A. Black, Hearts	40
1938-39	A. Venters, Rangers	34
1946-47	R. Mitchell, Third Lanark	22
1947-48	A. Aikman, Falkirk	20
1948-49	A. Stott, Dundee	30
1949-50	W. Bauld, Hearts	30
1950-51	L. Reilly, Hibernian	22
1951-52	L. Reilly, Hibernian	27
1952-53	C. Fleming, East Fife	30
	L. Reilly, Hibernian	30
1953-54	J. Wardhaugh, Hearts	27
1954-55	W. Bauld, Hearts	21
1955-56	J. Wardhaugh, Hearts	30
1956-57	H. Baird, Airdrieonians	33
1957-58	J. Wardhaugh, Hearts	28
1958-59	J. Baker, Hibernian	25
1959-60	J. Baker, Hibernian	42
1960-61	J. Harley, Third Lanark	42
1961-62	A. Gilzean, Dundee	24
1962-63	J. Millar, Rangers	25
1963-64	A. Gilzean, Dundee	32
1964-65	J. Forrest, Rangers	30
1965-66	J. McBride, Celtic	31
1966-67	S. Chalmers, Celtic	23
1967-68	R. Lennox, Celtic	32
1968-69	K. Cameron, Dundee United	27
1969-70	C. Stein, Rangers	24

Aggregate Record in League Career

Here are listed the men who have scored 250 or more goals in Football League and Scottish League games:

A. G. Rowley	c.f.	West Bromwich Albion, Fulham, Leicester City, Shrewsbury Town	1946-65	434
J. McGrory	c.f.	Celtic, Clydebank	1922-38	410
H. Gallacher	c.f.	Airdrieonians, Newcastle United, Chelsea, Derby County, Notts County, Grimsby Town, Gateshead	1921-39	387
W. R. Dean	c.f.	Tranmere Rovers, Everton, Notts County	1923-37	379
H. Ferguson	c.f.	Motherwell, Cardiff City, Dundee	1916-30	363
S. Bloomer	i.r.	Derby County (twice), Middlesbrough	1892-1914	352
J. Greaves	i.f.	Chelsea, Tottenham Hotspur, West Ham United	1957-70	348*
G. Camsell	c.f.	Durham City, Middlesbrough	1923-39	345
D. Halliday	c.f.	St. Mirren, Dundee, Sunderland, Arsenal, Manchester City, Clapton Orient	1920-35	338
V. Watson	c.f.	West Ham United, Southampton	1920-36	317
J. Atyeo	c.f.	Bristol City	1951-66	315
Joe Smith	i.l.	Bolton Wanderers, Stockport County	1908-29	314
H. Johnson	c.f.	Sheffield United, Mansfield Town	1919-36	309

H. Bedford	c.f. or .i.f.	Nottingham Forest, Blackpool, Derby County, Newcastle United, Sunderland, Bradford, Chester-field	1919-34	309
R. McPhail	i.l.	Airdrieonians, Rangers	1923-39	305
C. Holton	c.f.	Arsenal, Watford, Northampton Town, Crystal Palace, Charlton Athletic, Leyton Orient	1950-68	295
G. Hodgson	c.f. or i.f.	Liverpool, Aston Villa, Leeds United	1925-39	296
D. H. Morris	c.f.	Fulham, Brentford, Millwall, Swansea Town, Swindon Town, Clapton Orient	1920-34	294
J. Hampson	i.f.	Nelson, Blackpool	1925-38	289
E. Hine	i.r.	Barnsley (twice), Leicester City, Huddersfield Town, Manchester United	1921-38	287
A. Chandler	c.f.	Queen's Park Rangers, Leicester City	1920-35	278
T. Keetley	c.f.	Bradford, Doncaster Rovers, Notts County	1919-33	277
R. Allen	**c.f.**	Port Vale, West Bromwich Albion, Crystal Palace	1946-65	274
W. McFadyen	c.f.	Motherwell, Huddersfield Town	1923-39	269
G. Brown	c.f.	Huddersfield Town, Aston Villa, Burnley, Leeds United, Dar-lington	1921-38	268
R. Crawford	c.f.	Portsmouth, Ipswich Town (twice) Wolverhampton Wanderers, W.B.A., Charlton Athletic	1957-70	265*
E. C. Harper	c.f.	Blackburn Rovers (twice), Sheffield Wednesday, Tottenham Hot-spur, Preston North End	1923-35	260
D. B. N. Jack	i.f.	Plymouth Argyle, Bolton Wan-derers, Arsenal	1920-34	261
C. M. Buchan	i.r.	Sunderland, Arsenal	1910-28	258
R. Ferrier	o.l.	Motherwell	1918-37	256
J. Cookson	c.f.	Chesterfield, West Bromwich Albion, Plymouth Argyle, Swindon Town	1925-39	256
T. Briggs	c.f.	Grimsby Town (twice), Coventry City, Birmingham City, Black-burn Rovers	1947-59	255
N. Lofthouse	c.f.	Bolton Wanderers	1946-61	255
C. Wayman	c.f.	Newcastle United, Southampton, Preston North End, Middles-brough, Darlington	1946-58	254
B. Clough	**c.f.**	Middlesbrough, Sunderland	1955-64	252
J. A. Bradford	c.f.	Birmingham, Bristol City	1920-36	251
I. Allchurch	i.f.	Swansea Town (twice), Newcastle United, Cardiff City	1949-68	250
R. Hunt	i.f.	Liverpool, Bolton Wanderers	1960-70	250*

* May still add to this total in 1970-71.

Aggregate Record in League
Career for a single club

Here are listed the men who have scored 200 or more goals *for a single club* in either the Football League or the Scottish League. Only League games are included.

J. McGrory	c.f.	Celtic	1922-38	397
W. R. Dean	c.f.	Everton	1925-37	349

G. Camsell	c.f.	Middlesbrough		1925-39	325
J. Atyeo	c.f.	Bristol City		1951-66	315
V. Watson	c.f.	West Ham United		1920-35	306
S. Bloomer	i.r.	Derby County	1892-1906,	1910-14	291
H. Ferguson	c.f.	Motherwell		1916-25	283
A. Chandler	c.f.	Leicester City		1923-35	262
R. Ferrier	o.l.	Motherwell		1918-37	256
N. Lofthouse	c.f.	Bolton Wanderers		1946-61	255
Joe Smith	i.l.	Bolton Wanderers		1908-26	254
A. G. Rowley	c.f.	Leicester City		1950-58	251
J. A. Bradford	c.f.	Birmingham		1920-35	250
W. McFadyen	c.f.	Motherwell		1923-37	250
J. Hampson	i.f.	Blackpool		1927-38	247
D. Wilson	c.f.	Hamilton Academicals		1928-39	246
G. Bradford	c.f.	Bristol Rovers		1949-64	245
R. Hunt	i.f.	Liverpool		1960-69	245
G. Turner	i.f.	Luton Town		1949-64	243
R. McPhail	i.l.	Rangers		1927-39	233
G. Hodgson c.f. or i.f.		Liverpool		1925-26	233
J. Smith	c.f.	Rangers		1929-39	224
D. McCrae	c.f.	St. Mirren		1923-34	223
J. Greaves	i.f.	Tottenham Hotspur		1961-70	220
D. H. Morris	c.f.	Swindon Town		1926-33	216
W. Liddell o.l. or c.f.		Liverpool		1946-60	216
H. Hampton	c.f.	Aston Villa		1904-20	213
W. Walker	i.f.	Aston Villa		1919-34	213
C. M. Buchan	i.r.	Sunderland		1911-25	209
J Wardhaugh	i.l.	Hearts		1946-59	206
R. Allen	c.f.	West Bromwich Albion		1950-61	206
H. Johnson	c.f.	Sheffield United		1919-30	205
R. Gurney	c.f.	Sunderland		1925-39	205
R. Collins o.l. or c.f.		Torquay United		1948-58	204
G. W. Elliott	c.f.	Middlesbrough		1909-25	202
C. R. Eyre	c.f.	Bournemouth and Boscombe		1924-33	202
J. Patterson i.f. or c.f.		Queen of the South		1949-63	201
A. Wilson	c.f.	Sheffield Wednesday		1900-19	200

* May still add to this total in 1970-71.

Averages

Averages are not normally associated with soccer but readers may be interested to see how the players who have scored over 300 League goals in the Football League or Scottish League figure in such a list. The figures quoted are the average of goals per game.

J. McGrory (Celtic, Clydebank) 1·004, W. R. Dean (Everton, etc) ·867, H. Ferguson (Motherwell, Cardiff City, Dundee) ·858, G. Camsell (Durham City, Middlesbrough) ·780, D. Halliday (Dundee, Sunderland, etc.) ·751, J. Greaves (Chelsea, Spurs) .746, H. Gallacher (Airdrie, Newcastle United, etc.) .712, A. G. Rowley (West Bromwich Albion, Fulham, etc.) .701, H. Johnson (Sheffield United, Mansfield Town), .653, R. McPhail (Airdrie, Rangers), .650, V. Watson (West Ham United, Southampton) .636, H. Bedford (Nottingham Forest, Blackpool, etc.) .634, S. Bloomer (Derby County, Middlesbrough) .586, Joe Smith (Bolton Wanderers, Stockport Cty) .582. J. Atyeo (Portsmouth, Bristol City) .525.

Both Sides

The only player to score two goals for each side in a single Football League game—S. Wynne, Oldham Athletic v. Manchester United, Division II, Oct. 6, 1923. He scored with a free kick and a penalty kick for his own side but also put two through his own goal.

Consecutive Games

A. Chandler created a record in 1924-25 by scoring in 16 consecutive Football League games for Leicester City in Division II.

Cup Scoring

The record individual score in a

national cup-tie is 13 goals by J. Petrie, Arbroath outside-right, v. Bon Accord (Aberdeen) in Scottish Cup, Sept. 5, 1885.

The most goals for a defeated side was scored by W. H. Minter of St. Albans City who scored seven goals v. Dulwich Hamlet in a replayed 4th Qualifying Round tie of the F.A. Cup, Nov. 22, 1922. Result 8—7. Minter's side lost.

The following players have scored in every round of the F.A. Cup competition in a single season:

A. Brown, Tottenham Hotspur, 1900-01; E. Rimmer, Sheffield Wednesday 1934-35; F. O'Donnell, Preston North End 1936-37; S. Mortensen, Blackpool 1947-48; J. Milburn, Newcastle United 1950-51; N. Lofthouse, Bolton Wanderers 1952-53; C. Wayman, Preston North End 1953-54; J. Astle, West Bromwich Albion 1967-68; P. Osgood, Chelsea, 1969-70.

A. Brown scored the record number of 15 goals in the F.A. Cup, 1900-1901.

The individual F.A. Cup Final goal-scoring record is held jointly by three players. Each scored three Cup Final goals:

W. Townley, Blackburn Rovers 1890
J. Logan, Notts County 1894
S. Mortensen, Blackpool* 1953

*One of his goals went in off a Bolton defender and is given as "Hassell, own goal" in some records.

The first full-back to score in an F.A. Cup Final at Wembley was E. Shimwell who scored with a penalty kick for Blackpool against Manchester United in 1948.

The highest number of goals scored by any player during this century, in one F.A. Cup-tie, in or after the third round (or the old first round equivalent) is six: G. Hilsdon for Chelsea v. Worksop Town, 1st Round, Jan. 11, 1908; R. Rooke, Fulham v. Bury, 3rd Round, Jan. 7, 1939; G. Best, Manchester United v. Northampton Town (A), 5th Round, Feb. 7, 1970.

D. Law also scored six goals in a cup-tie, Manchester City v. Luton Town, 4th Round, Jan. 28, 1961, but this game had to be abandoned.

The quickest goal scored in an F.A. Cup Final occurred 40 sec. after the start of the Aston Villa v. West Bromwich Albion Final in 1895. It was scored by J. Devey although it is

sometimes credited to R. Chatt.

J. Milburn scored for Newcastle United 45 sec. after the start of the 1955 Final v. Manchester City.

Blackburn Rovers' centre-forward, J. Roscamp, scored inside a minute against Huddersfield Town in the 1928 Cup Final.

Debuts, Goal-scoring

The record number of goals scored by a player making his debut in first-class football is eight by J. Dyet, making his first appearance for King's Park v. Forfar Athletic in the Scottish League, Division II, Jan. 2, 1930. Result 12—2.

In the Football League the goal-scoring record for a player making his first appearance is five. G. Hilsdon scored that number for Chelsea v. Glossop, Division II, Sept. 1, 1906.

Five players have each scored four goals in League *debut*:

A. Gardiner, centre-forward for Leicester City v. Portsmouth, Feb. 21, 1934.

T. Hall, for Rotherham v. Wigan Borough, Nov. 5, 1927.

F. Howard, centre-forward for Manchester City v. Liverpool, Jan. 18, 1913.

J. Shepherd, centre-forward for Millwall v. Leyton Orient (A.), Oct. 25, 1952.

R. Turnbull, centre-forward for Sunderland v. Portsmouth, Nov. 29, 1947.

One other player scored four goals when making his debut for a Football League club, but this was in the F.A. Cup, 3rd Round, Jan. 5, 1957. Seventeen-year-old Ian Lawson scored four goals for Burnley v. Chesterfield.

Many players have scored three goals when making their Football League debut. They include:

J. Downing, Darlington v. Carlisle United, April 29, 1933.

W. Hales, Gillingham v. Port Vale (A), Mar. 31, 1951.

R. Hollis, Norwich City v. Queen's Park Rangers, April 21, 1948.

T. Francis, Hartlepools United v. Bradford, Nov. 30, 1963.

R. Graham, Liverpool v. Aston Villa, Sept. 26, 1964.

P. Laraman, Torquay United v. Barnsley, Sept. 7, 1961.

T. Lowder, Rotherham United v.

Carlisle United, Dec. 4, 1948.

H. Nash, Aston Villa v. Liverpool, April 3, 1915.

N. O'Halloran, Cardiff City v. Charlton Athletic, Dec. 10, 1955.

M. Owen, Swindon Town v. Watford, Jan. 11, 1947.

J. Pye, Notts County, 1945. Wartime League.

G. Robledo, Barnsley v. Nottingham Forest, Aug. 31, 1946.

A. Rowles, Bristol City v. Exeter City, Jan. 15, 1938.

K. Tucker, West Ham United v. Chesterfield, Oct. 4, 1947.

C. Viljoen, Ipswich Town v. Portsmouth, Mar. 25, 1967.

R. Wainscoat, Barnsley v. Fulham, Mar. 6, 1920.

J. Welsh (3 in 6 min.) Queen of the South v. Cowdenbeath, Nov. 16, 1968.

A Whittaker, Blackburn Rovers v. Preston North End, Oct. 14, 1899.

C. Wilson, Tottenham Hotspur v. South Shields, Sept. 20, 1919.

A. Withers, Blackpool v. Huddersfield Town, Nov. 18, 1950.

Fast Scoring

See also CUP SCORING in this section. Four goals in five minutes were scored by:

J. McIntyre for Blackburn Rovers v. Everton, at Ewood Park, Division I, Sept. 16, 1922.

W. Richardson, West Bromwich Albion, centre-forward, at West Ham, Division I, Nov. 7, 1931.

W. Best, Rangers v. Arbroath, Scottish League, Division I, Nov. 2, 1968. Three goals in three minutes were scored by:

W. Best, Southend United v. Brentwood, F.A. Cup, 2nd Round, Dec. 7, 1968.

J. Hartburn, Leyton Orient v. Shrewsbury Town, Division III(S), Jan. 22, 1955.

W. Lane, Watford v. Clapton Orient, Division III(S), Dec. 12, 1933.

G. Leggatt, Fulham v. Ipswich Town, Division I, Dec. 26, 1963.

J. Lindsay, Southport v. Scunthorpe United, Division III(N), Feb. 9, 1952.

J. McGrory, Celtic v. Motherwell, Scottish League, Division I, Mar. 14, 1936.

I. St. John, Motherwell v. Hibernian, Scottish League Cup, Aug. 15, 1959.

J. Scarth, Gillingham v. Leyton Orient, Division III(S), Nov. 1, 1952.

J. Swindells, Altrincham v. Scarborough, F.A. Cup, 1st Round, Nov. 13, 1965.

G. Talbot, Chester v. Crewe Alexandra, F.A. Cup, 1st Round, Nov. 14, 1964.

Six goals were scored in 21 min. by F. Keetley, Lincoln City v. Halifax Town, Division III(N), Jan. 16, 1932.

The record of having scored the quickest goal in first-class football is credited to J. Fryatt who is considered to have scored only four seconds after the kick-off for Bradford v. Tranmere Rovers, April 25, 1964. This time is fantastic but it was confirmed by referee R. J. Simon.

Three men have each scored only six seconds after the kick-off: A. Mundy for Aldershot at Hartlepools, Division IV, Oct. 25, 1958: B. Jones for Notts County v. Torquay United, Division III, Mar. 31, 1962. Jones was making his League debut; K. Smith for Crystal Palace v. Derby County, at Derby, Division II, Dec. 12, 1964.

Other quick goals:

7 sec. W. Sharp for Partick Thistle v. Queen of the South, Scottish League, Division A, Dec. 20, 1947; R. Langton for Preston North End v. Manchester City, Division I, Aug. 25, 1948; R. Drake for Stockport County v. Accrington Stanley, Division III(N), Dec. 25, 1956.

8 sec. K. East for Bournemouth v. Shrewsbury Town, Division III, at Bournemouth Aug. 31, 1968. G. Hudson, Tranmere Rovers v. Bury, Division III Dec. 2, 1967. V. Lambden, Bristol Rovers v. Aldershot, F.A. Cup, 3rd Round, Jan 6, 1951.

Fewest Goals

W. Milne, Swansea Town full-back, 1919-37, played in 500 Football League games before scoring his first League goal.

Full-Backs

The probable record number of goals netted by a full-back in a Football League game is four, scored by T. Wynne, left-back of Oldham Athletic v. Manchester United, Division II, Oct. 10, 1923. Wynne scored once with a penalty, once with a free kick, and also put the ball twice into his own goal.

In season 1921-2, J. Evans, Southend United full-back, scored a total of

10 goals in the Football League, Division III(S). All the goals were scored from penalties. In season 1964-5, S. Lynn, Birmingham City's full-back also scored 10 goals (8 penalties). Each of these players ended the season as his club's top League goal-scorer (Lynn actually shared top) and are the only full-backs who have achieved this distinction with Football League clubs.

Goalkeepers, Goal-scoring

See GOALKEEPERS in separate section.

Half-Backs

The record number of Football League goals scored by any player other than a forward in a single season is 15, by Reading's right-half, J. Lewis, in Division III(S), 1951-2.

His runner-up is A. Grimsdell who scored 14 goals from left-half for Tottenham Hotspur in Division II, 1919-20.

The record number of goals scored by a half-back in a single game in the Football League is three, by T. McDonald for Newcastle United v. Cardiff City, Division I, Dec. 25, 1926; by W. Imrie for Newcastle United v. Wolverhampton Wanderers, Division I, April 21, 1934; J. Muir for Bristol Rovers v. Crystal Palace, Division III (S), Sept. 5, 1931; D. Mackay, Tottenham Hotspur v. West Ham United, Division I, Dec. 22, 1962; R. Rooks, Middlesbrough v. Cardiff City, Division II, May 3, 1966; D. Webb, Chelsea v. Ipswich Town (A.), Division I, Dec. 26, 1968; E. Winstanley, Barnsley v. Watford, Division III, Apl. 22, 1969.

In the Football Combination, May 1, 1961. Swindon Town's left half-back, P. Chamberlain, scored five goals against Crystal Palace.

"Hat-Tricks"

The record number of "hat-tricks" scored in the Football League is 37 by W. Dean in 18 seasons.

The record number of "hat-tricks" in a season of League Football is nine by G. Camsell for Middlesbrough in Division II, 1926-7.

T. Keetley scored three goals in each of three consecutive Football League, Division II matches, away from home with Notts County, 1931:
v. Plymouth Argyle, Oct. 10, 1931;

v. Manchester United, Oct. 24, 1931;
v. Chesterfield, Nov. 7, 1931.
T. Holford scored "hat-tricks" for Manchester City in three out of four consecutive matches at Hyde Road in Jan. 1909:
v. Bradford City, League, Division I. Jan. 9, 1909; v. Tottenham Hotspur, Cup, 1st Round, Jan. 16, 1909; v. Everton, League, Division I, Jan. 30, 1909.

Heading Goals

The following are reckoned to be the record long-distance goal-scoring headers in the Football League:
In Division I, Sept. 1, 1952, P. Aldis, Aston Villa full-back, headed a goal against Sunderland from 35yd. This was his first goal in League football.

On Boxing Day, 1921, the winning goal for Aston Villa against Sheffield United in a Division I match, was headed from 30yd. by centre-half F. Barson.

Internationals and Inter-League

The individual goal-scoring record in international matches is held by G. Fuchs, who scored 10 goals for Germany v. Russia in the Consolation Tournament of the Olympic Games of 1912. Germany won 16—0.

When Denmark beat France 'A' 17—1 in 1908 S. Nielsen scored seven goals.

International and Inter-League records of British players are as follows:

Eight Goals:
V. J. Woodward, England v. France (Amateur), Paris, Nov. 1, 1906.

Six Goals:
J. Bambrick, Ireland v. Wales, Belfast, Feb. 1, 1930.
R. E. Foster, England v. Germany, Tottenham, Sept. 1901.
(N.B. This game is not recognised as an official international match).
W. O. Jordan, England v. France (Amateur) at Park Royal, London, Mar. 23, 1908.
N. Lofthouse, Football League v. League of Ireland, Wolverhampton, Sept. 24, 1952.
H. A. Walden, England v. Hungary (Amateur), Olympic Games, Stockholm, July 1, 1912.
V. J. Woodward, England v. Holland

FOOTBALL ASSOCIATION CHALLENGE CUP. General view of the Cup Final
between Liverpool and Burnley at the Crystal Palace, April 1914.

GOAL SCORERS (INDIVIDUALS). Two record-breakers, W. R. "Dixie" Dean
(*left*) and Hughie Gallacher.

GOAL SCORERS (INDIVIDUALS). Record international goal scorers: Bobby Charlton (*above left*), Denis Law (*above right*), Billy Gillespie (*below left*) and Trevor Ford.

(Amateur), Stamford Bridge, Chelsea, Dec. 11, 1909.

Five Goals:

B. Battles, Scottish League v. Irish League, Firhill Park, Glasgow, Oct. 31, 1928.

J. Bradford, Football League v. Irish League, Goodison Park, Liverpool, Sept. 25, 1929.

S. Bloomer, England v. Wales, Cardiff, Mar. 16, 1896.

B. Clough, Football League v. Irish League, Windsor Park, Belfast, Sept. 23, 1959.

R. Flavell, Scottish League v. Irish League, Windsor Park, Belfast, April 30, 1947.

H. Gallacher, Scottish League v. Irish League, Belfast, Nov. 11, 1925.

G. W. Hall, England v. Ireland, Old Trafford, Manchester, Nov. 16, 1938 (including three goals in 3½ min.).

G. O. Smith, England v. Ireland at Sunderland, Feb. 18, 1899.

A. Stubbins, Football League v. Irish League, Bloomfield Road, Blackpool, Oct. 18, 1950.

Four goals is the individual record for England v. Scotland, scored by D. Wilshaw in the 7—2 England victory at Wembley, April 2, 1955.

England's greatest goal-scorer in the International Championship is S. Bloomer. He scored 28 goals in 23 games : 12 v. Wales, 8 v. Scotland, 8 v. Ireland.

The only player to score more than one goal for England in a Home International while playing in a position other than in the forward line was A. Grimsdell (Tottenham Hotspur), left-half, who scored two goals against Scotland in a Victory International, Hampden Park, May 3, 1919.

Leading International goal-scorers :

England:

	*I.C.	V.I.	O.	T.
R. Charlton (Manchester United)	16	—	33	49
J. Greaves (Chelsea, Tottenham Hotspur)	19	—	25	44
N. Lofthouse (Bolton Wanderers)	10	—	20	30
T. Finney (Preston North End)	10	—	20	30
V. J. Woodward (Tottenham Hotspur, Chelsea)	14	—	15	29
S. Bloomer (Derby County, Middlesbrough)	28	—	—	28
S. Mortensen (Blackpool)	8	1	15	24
T. Lawton (Everton, Chelsea, Notts County)	7	1	15	23[1]

Scotland:

D. Law (Huddersfield Town, Manchester City, Torino, Manchester United)	12	—	16	28
H. Gallacher (Airdrieonians, Newcastle United, Chelsea, Derby County)	22	—	2	24
L. Reilly (Hibernian)	11	—	11	22
A. N. Wilson (Dunfermline, Middlesbrough)	13	4	—	17
W. Steel (Morton, Derby County, Dundee)	7	—	6	13[2]
A. Gilzean (Dundee, Tottenham Hotspur)	7	—	5	12

Ireland:

W. Gillespie (Sheffield United)	7	—	6	13
J. Bambrick (Linfield, Chelsea)	11	—	—	11

Wales:

T. Ford (Swansea Town, Aston Villa, Sunderland, Cardiff City)	11	—	12	23
I. Allchurch (Swansea Town, Newcastle United, Cardiff City)	8	—	14	22
C. Jones (Swansea Town, Tottenham Hotspur)	10	—	6	16
W. J. Charles (Leeds United, Juventus)	13	—	2	15[3]

[1] Also scored 2 for Great Britain v. Rest of Europe, 1947.
[2] Also scored 1 for Great Britain v. Rest of Europe, 1947.
[3] Also scored 1 (own goal) for England, 1956.
*I.C.—International Championship. V.I.—Victory Internationals (not ranked as full internationals). O—Overseas countries.

Long-distance Goals

Full-backs who have scored goals with big kicks from their own half of the field, include:

S. Barkas, Bradford City v. West Ham United, Division II, Sept. 7, 1932.

A. Black, Leicester City v. Sunderland, Division I, April 22, 1933.

D. Burnett, West Ham United v. Oldham Athletic, F.A. Cup, 3rd Round, Jan. 22, 1966.

A. Chalkley, West Ham United v. Manchester City, Division I, Mar. 2, 1932.

T. Garrett, Blackpool v. Huddersfield Town, F.A. Cup, 4th Round, Jan. 31, 1953.

A. Ingham, Queen's Park Rangers v. Gillingham, Division III(S), Jan. 31, 1953.

R. Kirk, Coventry City v. Northampton Town, F.A. Cup, 1st Round, Nov. 20, 1954.

W. Lowton, Wolverhampton Wanderers v. Nottingham Forest, Division II, Nov. 16, 1929.

P. Roscoe, Halifax Town v. Gateshead, F.A. Cup, 1st Round, Nov. 14, 1959.

Match Records

The individual goal-scoring record for a single game in first-class football was set up by J. Petrie who scored 13 for Arbroath v. Bon Accord in the Scottish Cup, Sept. 5, 1885.

Next to Petrie the top goal-scoring feats by British players are as follows:

Ten Goals:

G. Baker, St. Mirren v. Glasgow University, Scottish Cup, 1st Round, Jan. 30, 1960.

J. Payne, Luton Town v. Bristol Rovers, Division III(S), April 13, 1936.

Nine Goals:

J. Baker, Hibernian v. Peebles Rovers, Scottish Cup, 2nd Round, Feb. 11, 1961.

R. Bell, Tranmere Rovers v. Oldham Athletic, Division III(N), Dec. 26, 1935.

J. Simpson, Partick Thistle v. Royal Albert, Scottish Cup, 1st Round, Jan. 17, 1931.

J. Smith, Rangers v. Blairgowrie, Scottish Cup, 1st Round, Jan. 20, 1934.

Eight Goals:

J. Calder, Morton v. Raith Rovers, Scottish League, Division II, April 18, 1936.

J. Dyet, King's Park v. Forfar Athletic, Scottish League, Division II, Jan. 2, 1930.

J. McGrory, Celtic v. Dunfermline, Scottish League, Division I, Jan. 14, 1928.

O. McNally, Arthurlie v. Armadale, Scottish League, Division II, Oct. 1, 1927.

D. Weir, Halliwell v. Notts County (8 consecutive goals) 1887-88.

W. Walsh, Hearts v. King's Park, Scottish Cup, 2nd Round, Feb. 13, 1937.

Seven Goals:

T. Briggs, Blackburn Rovers v. Bristol Rovers, Division II, Feb. 5, 1955.

A. Brown, Southampton v. Northampton Town, Southern League, Dec. 28, 1901.

N. J. Coleman, Stoke City v. Lincoln City, Division II, Feb. 23, 1957.

E. Drake, Arsenal v. Aston Villa, at Villa Park, Division I, Dec. 14, 1935.

E. Gemmell, Oldham Athletic v. Chester, Division III(N), Jan. 19, 1952.

A. Gilzean, Dundee v. Queen of the South, Scottish League, Division I, Dec. 1, 1962.

E. Harston, Mansfield Town v. Hartlepools United, Division III(N), Jan. 12, 1937.

A. Juliussen, Dundee v. Dunfermline, Scottish League, Division B, Mar. 22, 1947.

H. Maxwell, Falkirk v. Clyde, Scottish League, Division I, Dec. 8, 1962.

W. H. Minter, St. Albans City v. Dulwich Hamlet, replayed F.A. Cuptie, 4th Qualifying Round, Nov. 22, 1922.

J. Ross (jnr.), Preston North End v. Stoke, Division I, Oct. 6, 1888.

R. Thompson, Chelsea v. Luton Town, London Combination, Mar. 3, 1916.

A. J. Whitehurst, Bradford City v. Tranmere Rovers, Division III(N), Mar. 6, 1929.

Six Goals:

E. Addison, Berwick Rangers v. Dundee United, Scottish League, Division II, Feb. 21, 1959.

M. Armstrong, Aberdeen v. Ayr United, Scottish League, Division I, Feb. 16, 1935.

H. Atkinson, Tranmere Rovers v. Ashington, F.A. Cup, 1st Round, Nov. 22, 1952.

A. Bacon, Reading v. Stoke City, Division II, April 3, 1931.

J. Bambrick, Ireland v. Wales, Feb. 1, 1930.

G. Best, Manchester United v. Northampton Town (A.), F.A. Cup, 5th Round, Feb. 7, 1970.

S. Bloomer, Derby County v. Sheffield Wednesday, Division I, Jan. 21, 1899.

A. Bown, Swindon Town v. Watford, Southern League, April 6, 1915.

D. F. Brown, Dundee v. Raith Rovers, Scottish League, Dec. 9, 1916.

F. Cheesemuir, Gillingham v. Merthyr Town, Division III(S), April 26, 1930.

S. Curran, Belfast Celtic v. Newry Town, Dec. 18, 1926.

A. Chandler, Leicester City v. Portsmouth, Division I, Oct. 20, 1928.

J. Cookson, West Bromwich Albion v. Blackpool (including two penalties), Division II, Sept. 17, 1927.

C. Dickson, Dunfermline v. St. Mirren, Scottish League, Division I, Dec. 30, 1961.

J. Duncan, Leicester City v. Port Vale, Division II, Dec. 25, 1924.

J. Fleming, Rangers v. Clyde, Glasgow Cup, Sept. 26, 1927.

R. E. Foster, England v. Germany, White Hart Lane, Sept. 1901 (not a full international).

J. W. Glover, Southport v. Grimsby Town, Division III(N), Oct. 22, 1921.

A. Graver, Lincoln City v. Crewe Alexandra, Division III(N), Sept. 29, 1951.

G. Henson, Bradford v. Blackburn Rovers, Division II, Jan. 29, 1938.

D. Hunt, Sheffield Wednesday v. Norwich City, Division II, Nov. 19, 1938.

H. Halse, Manchester United v. Swindon Town, F.A. Charity Shield, Sept. 25, 1911.

G. Hilsdon, Chelsea v. Worksop, F.A. Cup, 1st Round, Jan. 11, 1908.

W. Humphries, Motherwell v. Dundee United, Scottish League, Division B, Jan. 23, 1954.

G. Hurst, West Ham United v.

Sunderland, Division I, Oct. 19, 1968.

W. C. Jordan, England v. France (Amateur), Park Royal, Mar. 23, 1908.

A. Juliussen, Dundee v. Alloa Athletic, Scottish League, Division B, Mar. 8, 1947. Juliussen scored 13 goals in two successive League games at this time.

F. Keetley, Lincoln City v. Halifax Town (six in 21 min.) Division III(N), Jan. 19, 1932.

T. Keetley, Doncaster Rovers v. Ashington, Division III(N), Feb. 16, 1929.

D. Law, Manchester City v. Luton Town (at Luton), F.A. Cup, 4th Round, Jan. 28, 1961. Match abandoned.

D. Lindsay, Cowdenbeath v. St. Johnstone, Scottish Cup, 1st Round, Jan. 21, 1928.

H. Lister, Oldham Athletic v. Southport, Division IV, Dec. 26, 1962.

S. Littlewood, Port Vale v. Chesterfield, Division II, Sept. 24, 1932.

N. Lofthouse, Football League v. League of Ireland, Sept. 24, 1952.

R. S. McColl, Queen's Park v. Port Glasgow Athletic, Scottish League, April 26, 1910.

L. McBain, Queen's Park v. Partick Thistle, Scottish League, Feb. 8, 1927.

H. Melrose, Dunfermline Athletic v. Partick Thistle, Scottish League, Division I, April 18, 1959.

J. Miller, Sunderland v. Fairfield, F.A. Cup, 1st Round, 1894-95.

J. Milsom, Bolton Wanderers v. Burnley, Division II, Jan. 2, 1935.

L. Page, Burnley v. Birmingham, at St. Andrews, Division I, April 10, 1926.

J. Patterson, Queen of the South v. Cowdenbeath, Scottish League, Division II, Dec. 16, 1961.

R. Rooke, Fulham v. Bury, F.A. Cup, 3rd Round, Jan. 7, 1939.

L. Shackleton, Newcastle United v. Newport County, Division II, Oct. 5, 1946.

P. Simpson, Crystal Palace v. Exeter City, Division III(S), Oct. 4, 1930.

J. Southworth, Everton v. West Bromwich Albion, Division I, Dec. 30, 1893.

T. Tippett, Rochdale v. Hartlepools United, Division III(N), April 21, 1930.

H. A. Walden, England v. Hungary,

H. A. Walden, England v. Hungary (Olympic Games, Stockholm), July 1, 1912.

T. Walsh, Bristol City v. Gillingham, Division III(S), Jan. 15, 1927.

T. Waring, Tranmere Rovers v. Durham City, Division III(N), Jan. 7, 1928.

G. Watson, Motherwell v. Falkirk, Scottish League, Oct. 27, 1928.

V. Watson, West Ham United v. Leeds United, Division I, Feb. 9, 1929.

D. Wilson, Rangers v. Falkirk, Scottish League, Mar. 17, 1962.

V. J. Woodward, England v. Holland (Amateur), Chelsea, Dec. 11, 1909.

J. Greaves has created a record by scoring five goals in a Football League game on four separate occasions.

Own Goal

See also GOALKEEPERS (Goalscorers).

Goals which are shared between two players are rare, but an "own goal" shared in a First Division game at Stamford Bridge, Dec. 18, 1954, is unique. Leicester City defenders, Milburn and Froggatt, were involved in a misunderstanding in front of their own goal. Going for the ball together, they connected with it simultaneously and sent it into their own net. The players themselves confirmed that each had got his boot to the ball at the same time. The result was a 3—1 win for Chelsea and one of their goals is entered in the records as "Milburn and Froggatt, shared one own goal."

A most remarkable "own goal" was scored by D. Evans, the Arsenal leftback, in a Division I game at Highbury, Dec. 17, 1955. The game appeared to be running over time and an agitated spectator blew a whistle. Thinking it was the referee's signal to end the game, Evans kicked the ball into his own net and several players began to leave the field. But the referee, F. B. Coultas, pointed to the centre spot, signalling for a goal.

The record for the quickest "own goal" probably belongs to A. Mullery (Fulham) who scored for Sheffield Wednesday within 30 seconds of the start and before any Sheffield player had touched the ball. Jan. 31, 1961.

Penalty Goals

See PENALTIES in separate section.

Wingmen Scoring

The record aggregates of goals scored by wing forwards is as follows:

Football League: 33 goals, C. Bastin, outside-left, Arsenal, Division I, 1932-3. C. Taylor, outside-left, Walsall, Division III, 1960-61.

Scottish League: 39 goals, K. Dawson, outside-left, Falkirk, Division II, 1935-6.

32 goals, T. McCall, Queen of the South, Division II, 1932-3; also 32 goals, R. Ferrier, outside-left, Motherwell, Division I, 1929-30.

The record number of goals by a wing-forward in a single match is 13, scored by J. Petrie, Arbroath v. Bon Accord, Scottish Cup, Sept. 5, 1885.

The Football League record: N. J. Coleman, seven goals for Stoke City v. Lincoln City, Division II, Feb. 23, 1957.

The Scottish League record: H. Melrose, six goals for Dunfermline Athletic v. Partick Thistle, Scottish League, Division I, April 18, 1959.

The following wing-forwards have scored five goals in a match:

R. Auld, Celtic v. Airdrie (A), Scottish League, Division I, Mar. 10, 1965. Included two penalties.

T. Eglington, Everton v. Doncaster Rovers, Football League, Division II, Sept. 27, 1952.

P. Harris, Portsmouth v. Aston Villa, Division I, Sept. 3, 1958 (including a penalty).

A. McGuigan, Liverpool v. Stoke, Division I, Jan. 4, 1902.

H. Melrose, Dunfermline Athletic v. Falkirk, Scottish League, Division I, Sept. 5, 1964.

W. Robbins, Cardiff City v. Thames Association, Division III(S), Feb. 6, 1932.

G. Smith, Hibernian v. Third Lanark, Scottish League, Division A, Nov. 8, 1947.

J. Summers, Charlton Athletic v. Huddersfield Town, Division II, Dec. 21, 1957, and v. Portsmouth, Division II, Oct. 1, 1960.

R. Tambling, Chelsea v. Aston Villa, at Villa Park, Division I, Sept. 17, 1966.

A. Turner, Doncaster Rovers v. New Brighton, Division III(N), Feb. 16, 1935.

GOAL-SCORING (TEAMS and GENERAL)

All Scored

In season 1912-13 every one of the Greenock Morton players who appeared in the Scottish League, Division I, scored a goal. The goalkeeper scored from a penalty.

Several times each member of a team's forward-line has scored in a single game, but the outstanding example was when all the Everton forwards scored against Charlton Athletic at The Valley in an 18 min. spell. The Everton forwards were Stein, Dean, Dunn, Critchley and Johnson. Everton won 7—0 in Division II, Feb. 7, 1931.

Double Figures

Here are listed all the clubs who have scored double figures in peacetime Football League games:

Five times

Birmingham City (originally known as Small Heath): v. Walsall Town Swifts 12—0, Division II, Dec. 17, 1892; v. Ardwick 10—2, Division II, Mar. 17, 1894; v. Blackpool 10—1, Division II, Mar. 2, 1901; v. Doncaster Rovers 12—0, Division II, April 11, 1903; v. Glossop 11—1, Division II, Jan. 6, 1915.

Four times

Hull City: v. Wolverhampton Wanderers 10—3, Division II, Dec. 12, 1919; v Halifax Town 10—0, Division III(N), Dec. 26, 1930; v. Southport 10—1, Division III(N), Jan. 13, 1938; v. Carlisle United 11—1, Division III(N), Jan. 14, 1939.

Aston Villa: v. Accrington 12—2, Division I, March 12, 1892; v. Sheffield Wednesday 10—0, Division I, Oct. 5, 1912; v. Burnley 10—0, Division I, Aug. 29, 1925; v. Charlton Athletic 11—1, Division II, Nov. 14, 1959.

Three times

Sheffield United: v. Burslem Port Vale 10—0*, Division II, Dec. 10, 1892; v. Cardiff City 11—2, Division I, Jan. 1, 1926; v. Burnley 10—0, Division I, Jan. 19, 1929.

Twice

Darwen: v. Rotherham Town 10—2, Division II, Jan. 13, 1896; v. Walsall 12—0, Division II, Dec. 26, 1896.

Fulham v. Torquay United 10—2,

Division III(S), Sept. 7, 1931; v. Ipswich Town, Division I, Dec. 26, 1963.

Luton Town: v. Torquay United 10—2, Division III(S), Sept. 2, 1933; v. Bristol Rovers 12—0, Division III(S), April 13, 1936.

Manchester City: v. Lincoln City 11—3, Division II, Mar. 23, 1895; v. Darwen 10—0, Division II, Feb. 4, 1899.

Notts County: v. Burslem Port Vale 10—0, Division II, Feb. 26, 1895; v. Newport County 11—1, Division III(S), Jan. 15, 1949.

Oldham Athletic: v. Chester 11—2, Division III(N), Jan. 19, 1952; v. Southport 11—0, Division IV, Dec. 26, 1962.

Tranmere Rovers: v. Durham City 11—1, Division III(N), Jan. 7, 1928; v. Oldham Athletic 13—4, Division III(N), Dec. 26, 1935.

Once

Barrow: v. Gateshead 12—1, Division III(N), May 5, 1934.

Bournemouth and Boscombe Athletic: v. Northampton Town 10—0, Division III(S), Sept. 2, 1939.

Bradford City: v. Rotherham United 11—1, Division III(N), Aug. 25, 1928.

Chester v. York City 12—0, Division III(N), Feb. 1, 1936.

Chesterfield: v. Glossop 10—0, Division II, Jan. 17, 1903.

Doncaster Rovers: v. Darlington 10—0, Division IV, Jan. 25, 1964.

South Shields†: v. Rotherham United 10—1, Division III(N), Mar. 16, 1929.

Hartlepools: v. Barrow 10—1, Division IV, April 14, 1959.

Huddersfield Town: v. Blackpool 10—1, Division I, Dec. 13, 1930.

Leicester City: v. Portsmouth 10—0, Division I, Oct. 20, 1928.

Lincoln City: v. Crewe Alexandra 11—1, Division III(N), Sept. 29, 1951.

Liverpool: v. Rotherham United 10—1, Division II, Feb. 18, 1896.

Loughborough Town: v. Darwen 10—0, Division II, April 1, 1899.

Newton Heath‡: v. Wolverhampton Wanderers 10—1, Division I, Oct. 15, 1892.

Middlesbrough: v. Sheffield United 10—3, Division I, Nov. 18, 1933.

Newcastle United: v. Newport County 13—0, Division II, Oct. 5, 1946.

Newport County: v. Merthyr Town 10—0, Division III(S), April 10, 1930.

Northampton Town: v. Walsall 10—0, Division III(S), Nov. 5, 1927.

Norwich City: v. Coventry City 10—2, Division III(S), Mar. 15, 1930.

Nottingham Forest: v. Leicester Fosse 12—0, Division I, April 21, 1909.

Preston North End: v. Stoke 10—0, Division I, Sept. 14, 1889.

Reading: v. Crystal Palace 10—2, Division III(S), Sept. 4, 1946.

Stockport County: v. Halifax Town 13—0, Division III(N), Jan. 6, 1934.

Stoke City: v. West Bromwich Albion 10—3, Division I, Feb. 4, 1937.

Tottenham Hotspur: v. Everton 10—4, Division I, Oct. 11, 1958.

Walsall: v. Darwen 10—0, Division II, Mar. 4, 1899.

West Bromwich Albion: v. Darwen 12—0, Division I, Mar. 4, 1892.

Wolverhampton Wanderers: v. Leicester City 10—1, Division I, April 15, 1938.

Woolwich Arsenal: v. Loughborough Town 12—0, Division II, Mar. 12, 1900.

Wrexham v. Hartlepools United 10—1, Division IV, Mar. 3, 1962.

*All the above matches resulted in home wins with the exception of this game which stands as the record away win in the Football League.

†Now known as Gateshead.

‡Now known as Manchester United.

Failed to Score

After losing at home 1—2 to Leicester City, Oct. 4, 1919, Coventry City did not score another goal in Division II until Dec. 25, 1919 when they defeated Stoke 3—2 at home. In the interim period they played 11 games without scoring.

Fast Scoring

Preston North End scored six goals in seven minutes when they defeated Hyde 26—0, F.A. Cup, Oct. 15, 1887.

Highest Score in Cup Games

The record score in an F.A. Cuptie: Preston North End 26, Hyde 0, 1st Series, 1st Round, Oct. 15, 1887. Every player except the goalkeeper scored.

This game is believed to have run more than half an hour over time because of an error by the referee.

Other big scores in the F.A. Cup Competition proper are:

Preston North End	18	Reading	0	1st Round	1893-94
Wanderers	16	Farningham	0	1st Round	1874-75
Royal Engineers	15	High Wycombe	0	1st Round	1875-76
Darwen	15	Romford	0	5th Round	1880-81
Wolverhampton Wanderers	14	Crosswells Brewery	0	2nd Round	1886-87
Clapton	0	Nottingham Forest	14	1st Round	1890-91
Bolton Wanderers	13	Sheffield United	0	2nd Round	1889-90
Aston Villa	13	Casuals	1	1st Round	1890-91
Aston Villa	13	Wednesbury Old Athletic	0	1st Round	1886-87
Darwen	13	Kidderminster	0	1st Round	1890-91*
Tottenham Hotspur	13	Crewe Alexandra	2	4th Round	1959-60*
Clapham Rovers	12	Leyton	0	2nd Round	1875-76
Bury	12	Stockton	1	1st Round	1896-97*
Sheffield Wednesday	12	Halliwell	0	1st Round	1890-91

*Replay

The record F.A. Cup Final victory: Bury 6, Derby County 0, April 18, 1903. Semi-finals: Newcastle United 6, Fulham 0, 1908; West Bromwich Albion 6, Nottingham Forest 2, 2nd replay, 1892.

Scottish Association Cup

The record score in a Scottish Association Cup-tie: Arbroath 36, Bon Accord 0; Dundee Harp 35, Aberdeen Rovers 0. Both were 1st Round ties played on the same day, Sept. 5, 1885.

Other high scores:

Queen's Park	16	St. Peter's	0	1st Round	1885-86
Partick Thistle	16	Royal Albert	0	1st Round	1930-31
St. Mirren	15	Glasgow United	0	1st Round	1959-60
Hearts	15	King's Park	0	2nd Round	1936-37
Vale of Leven	15	Jamestown	0	3rd Round	1878-79
Hibernian	15	Peebles Rovers	1	2nd Round	1960-61
Queen's Park	15	Hurlford	1	5th Round	1879-80
Queen's Park	15	Shotts	0	6th Round	1881-82

The record victory in a Scottish Association Cup Final: Renton 6, Cambuslang 1, Hampden Park, 1888.

Scottish League Cup:
The record victory in a Scottish League Cup Final: Celtic 7, Rangers 1, Hampden Park, Oct. 19, 1957.

Foreign:
In European Cup Winners' Cup, 1st Round, 1963-4, Sporting Lisbon beat Apoel (Cyprus) 16—1.

Highest Score in Internationals

See also INTERNATIONALS (ENGLAND, IRELAND, SCOTLAND, WALES).

Record victory in the International Championship: England 13, Ireland 0, Belfast, Feb. 18, 1882.

Record victory for any international match which included at least one of the home countries: Australia 0, England 17, Sydney, June 30, 1951.

Record victory in an amateur international match between any two of the home countries: England 9, Wales 0, Merthyr Tydfil, Jan. 24, 1920. England 9, Wales 1, Plymouth, Feb. 2, 1914.

Record victory in any amateur international match which included at least one of the home countries: England 15, France 0, Paris, Nov. 1, 1906.

In 1910 at Ipswich England beat France 20—0, but this was under the auspices at the breakaway A.F.A.

Other big scores in internationals:
Denmark 17, France 'A' 1, 1908. Germany 16, Russia 0 (Olympic Games), 1912. Germany 13, Finland 0, 1940. Spain 13, Bulgaria 0, 1933. England 13, Ireland 2, Sunderland, 1899. Hungary 13, France 1, 1927.

Highest Score in League Games

Division I					
West Bromwich Albion	12	Darwen	0	Mar. 4, 1892	
Nottingham Forest	12	Leicester Fosse	0	April 21, 1909	
Aston Villa	12	Accrington	2	Mar. 12, 1892	
Division II					
Newcastle United	13	Newport County	0	Oct. 5, 1946	
Small Heath	12	Walsall Town Swifts	0	Dec. 17, 1892	
Small Heath	12	Doncaster Rovers	0	April 11, 1903	
Darwen	12	Walsall	0	Dec. 26, 1896	
Woolwich Arsenal	12	Loughborough Town	0	Mar. 12, 1900	
Division III(S)					
Luton Town	12	Bristol Rovers	0	April 13, 1936	
Division III(N)					
Stockport County	13	Halifax Town	0	Jan. 6, 1934	
Tranmere Rovers	13	Oldham Athletic	4	Dec. 26, 1935	
Barrow	12	Gateshead	1	May 5, 1934	
Chester	12	York City	0	Feb. 1, 1936	
Division III					
Tranmere Rovers	9	Accrington Stanley	0	April 18, 1959	
Brentford	9	Wrexham	0	Oct. 15, 1963	
Brighton	9	Southend United	1	Nov. 27, 1965	
Queen's Park Rangers	9	Tranmere Rovers	2	Dec. 3, 1960	
Division IV					
Oldham Athletic	11	Southport	0	Dec. 26. 1962	

Division I (A)

Celtic	11	Dundee	0	Oct. 26, 1895
Airdrieonians	11	Falkirk	1	April 28, 1951
Airdrieonians	1	Hibernian	11	Oct. 24, 1959
Hibernian	11	Hamilton Academicals	1	Nov. 6, 1965

Division II (B)

| East Fife | 13 | Edinburgh City | 2 | Dec. 11, 1937 |

Highest Score in a League Season

The record aggregate of goals in a single season:

Football League

Division I: 128 goals, 42 games, Aston Villa, 1930-31.

Division II: 122 goals, 42 games, Middlesbrough, 1926-7.

Division III(S): 127 goals, 42 games, Millwall, 1927-8.

Division III(N): 128 goals, 42 games, Bradford City, 1928-9.

Division III: 111 goals, 46 games, Queen's Park Rangers, 1961-2.

Division IV: 134 goals, 46 games, Peterborough United, 1960-61.

Scottish League

Division I: 132 goals, 34 games, Heart of Midlothian, 1957-8.

Division II: 142 goals, 34 games, Raith Rovers, 1937-8.

Own Goals

Three "own goals" for the same side in a single Football League game were registered when Carlisle defeated Rochdale, 7—2, on Dec. 25, 1954. Three of Carlisle United's goals were scored by Rochdale players—Underwood, Boyle and Murphy.

West Bromwich Albion's score included three "own goals" by Sheffield Wed. players (Kenny, Curtis, and Gannon) at Hillsborough, Division I, Dec. 26, 1952. Albion won 5-4.

GREECE

Soccer was played in Greece in the 1890s but little progress was made before World War I and it was not until several years after the formation of their F.A. in 1926 that they were able to make much of an impression on the European international game.

Professionalism has been introduced into Greek football in recent years, and in 1960 the League was reorganised with a First Division of 16 clubs (since increased to 18) formed on a national basis in place of the old regional system. There are at present about 1,000 clubs affiliated to the National Association.

Address of the governing body: Elliniki Podosferiki Omospondia, 93 Rue de l'Académie, Athens. Colours: White shirts, blue shorts.

Results of internationals:

May 3, 1961*	Greece 2, Ireland 1; Athens
Oct. 17, 1961*	Ireland 2, Greece 0; Belfast
Dec. 9, 1964*	Greece 2, Wales 0; Athens
Mar. 17, 1965*	Wales 4, Greece 1; Cardiff

* World Cup

GRIMSBY TOWN F.C.

Founded as Grimsby Pelham 1878. Dropped the name "Pelham" 1879. One of the original members of the Football League, Division II, 1892. Honours: Champions, Division II, 1900-1901, 1933-4. Runners-up, 1928-9. Champions, Division III(N), 1925-6, 1955-6. Runners-up, 1951-2. Runners-up, Division III, 1961-2. Best in Division I, 5th, 1934-5. Record attendance: 31,651 v. Wolverhampton Wanderers, F.A. Cup, 5th Round, Feb. 20, 1937. Address: Blundell Park, Cleethorpes (Tel. Cleethorpes 61420). Nickname: M a r i n e r s. Colours: Black and white striped shirts, black shorts. Record League goal-scorer: E. Glover, 42 goals, Division II, 1933-4. Record victory: 9—2 v. Darwen, Division II, April 15, 1899. Record defeat: 9—1 v. Arsenal, Division I, Jan. 28, 1931.

GROUNDS

The club grounds in the U.K. with the greatest capacities are:

England: The Valley (Charlton Athletic), 73,500.

Ireland: Windsor Park, Belfast (Linfield), 60,000.

Scotland: Hampden Park, Glasgow (Queen's Park), 150,000 (now restricted to 135,000).

Wales: Ninian Park (Cardiff City), 60,000.

H

HALF-BACKS

See Goal-Scoring, Tactics and Team Evolution, Offside.

HALIFAX TOWN F.C.

Founded 1911 and played in the Yorkshire Combination. Eventually joined the Midland League. Joined Football League, Division III(N), on its formation, 1921. Honours: Runners-up, Division III(N), 1934-5. Runners-up, Division IV, 1968-9. Address: The Shay Ground, Halifax. (Tel. 53423). Record attendance: 36,995 v. Tottenham Hotspur, F.A. Cup, 5th Round, Feb. 14, 1953. Colours: Tangerine shirts with white trim, blue shorts. Record League goal-scorer: A. Valentine, 34 goals, Division III(N), 1934-5. Record victory: 7—3 v. Rochdale, F.A. Cup, 1st Round, Nov. 26, 1938. Record defeat: 13—0 v. Stockport County, Division III(N), Jan. 6, 1934.

HAMILTON ACADEMICALS F.C.

Founded 1870. Joined Scottish League, Division I, 1906. Honours: Champions, Division II, 1903-4. Runners-up (B), 1952-3. Runners-up, Division II, 1964-5. Scottish Cup: Finalists, 1911, 1935. Address: Douglas Park, Hamilton (Tel. 23108). Record attendance: 28,281 v. Hearts, Scottish Cup, 3rd Round, Mar. 3, 1937. Nickname: Accies. Colours: Red and white hooped shirts, white shorts. Record League goal-scorer in Division I: D. Wilson, 34 goals, 1936-7. Record victory: 10—2 v. Cowdenbeath, Division I, 1932-3. Record defeat: 11—1 v. Hibernian, Division I, Nov. 6, 1965.

HARTLEPOOL F.C.

Founded 1908. One of the original members of Division III(N) on its formation, 1921. Honours: Runners-up, Division III(N), 1956-7. Record attendance: 17,300 v. Nottingham Forest, F.A. Cup, 4th Round, Jan. 29, 1955. Address: Victoria Ground, West Hartlepool (Tel. 3492). Nickname: Pools. Colours: Blue shirts, white shorts. Record League goal-scorer: W. Robinson, 28 goals, Division III(N), 1927-8. Record victory: 10—1 v. Barrow, Division IV, April 4, 1959. Record defeat: 10—1 v. Wrexham, Division IV, Mar. 3, 1962.

HAT-TRICKS

See also Goal-Scoring (Individuals), Hat-tricks.

The term "hat-trick," used in football to denote three consecutive goals for a team scored by the same player, originates from cricket. It dates back to the days when a bowler was presented with a new hat by his club whenever he succeeded in taking three wickets with three balls.

Strictly speaking, it is not correct to credit a player with a "hat-trick" in football if his sequence of three goals is broken by a goal from another player for the same side.

HEADING

See Goal-Scoring (Individuals), Heading.

HEART OF MIDLOTHIAN F.C.

Founded 1873. Moved to present headquarters, 1886. One of the original members of the Scottish League in 1890. Honours: Champions, Division 1, 1894-5, 1896-7, 1957-8, 1959-60. Runners-up, 1893-4, 1898-9, 1903-4, 1905-6, 1914-15, 1937-8, 1953-4, 1955-6, 1956-7, 1958-9, 1964-5. Scottish Cup: Winners, 1891, 1896, 1901,

1906, 1956. Finalists, 1903, 1907, 1968. Record attendance: 53,490 v. Rangers, Scottish Cup, 3rd Round, Feb. 13, 1932. Address: Tyne-castle Park, Edinburgh (Tel. 031-337 6132). Colours: Maroon shirts, white shorts. Record goal-scorer in Division I: B. Battles, 44 goals, 1930-31. Record victory: 15—0 v. King's Park, Scottish Cup, 2nd Round, Feb. 13, 1937. Record defeat: 7—1 v. Dundee (H), Division I, Feb. 27, 1965.

HEIGHT
Shortest

The shortest player to appear in Football League matches is outside-right F. le May. He was 5ft. high. He played for Thames 1930-31, Watford 1931-2, and Clapton Orient 1932-3.

C. Nastri, an outside-right, made two Football League appearances for Crystal Palace in 1958-9 when he was 5ft. 1in.

The shortest goalkeeper to play for England is E. Davison (Sheffield Wednesday) v. Wales, Mar. 13, 1922. Height: 5ft. 7in.

The shortest full-back to play for England is H. Burgess (Manchester City) who made four appearances between 1904 and 1906. Height: 5ft. 5in.

The shortest centre-half for England, J. Holt (Everton) who appeared in the 1890s, and W. Wedlock (Bristol City) who appeared in the early 1900s up to World War I. Both were 5ft. 4½in.

The shortest wing-half to appear in an England side is T. Magee of West Bromwich Albion. He was 5ft. 3in. A right-half, he was capped five times in the 1920s.

The shortest England international forward is probably F. Walden, Tottenham Hotspur's 5ft. 3in. outside-right who was capped once before, and once after World War I.

S. Tufnell, who played for Blackpool from 1927 to 1934, was the shortest half-back ever to appear in Football League matches. Height 5ft. 2¾in.

Tallest

The tallest players to appear in Football League matches include:

S. Taylor, centre-half, Bristol Rovers, 1966-70; 6ft. 5in.

A Iremonger, goalkeeper, Notts County and Lincoln City, 1904-27; 6ft. 5in.

G. Ephgrave, goalkeeper, Aston Villa, Swindon Town, Southampton, Norwich City and Watford, 1938-53; 6ft. 4½in.

H. Liley, goalkeeper, Bristol Rovers, 1946-51; 6ft. 4½in.

J. Nicholls, goalkeeper, Tottenham Hotspur, Bristol Rovers, 1926-39; M. Deacy, half-back, Newport County, 1968-70; 6ft. 4 in.

Ivan Horrath, Dynamo (Zagreb) and Yugoslavian international centre-half of the post-war era stands 6ft. 5in. tall.

HIBERNIAN F.C.

Founded 1875 by Irishmen in Edin-burgh. One of the original members of the Scottish League, Division II, 1893. Honours: Champions, Division I, 1902-3, 1947-8, 1950-1, 1951-2. Runners-up, 1896-7, 1946-7, 1949-50, 1952-3. Champions, Division II, 1893-4, 1894-5, 1932-3. Scottish Cup: Winners, 1887, 1902. Finalists, 1896, 1914, 1923, 1924, 1947. Record attendance: 65,850 v. Hearts, Division A, Jan. 2, 1950. Address: Easter Road Park, Edinburgh (Tel. 031-661 2159). Nickname: Hibs. Colours: Green shirts, white sleeves, white shorts. Record League goal-scorer: J. Baker, 42 goals, Division I, 1959-60. Record victory: 15—1 v. Peebles Rovers, Scottish Cup, 2nd Round, Feb. 11, 1961. Record defeat: 9—2 v. Greenock Morton, Division I, 1918-19.

HOLLAND

The Netherlands F.A. was founded in 1889 and is the oldest outside of Great Britain. There was a soccer club in Haarlem as long ago as 1879, but due to the reluctance of the governing body to accept professionalism the game in that country made only limited progress in the 50-odd years before World War II.

With the football boom in other European countries after World War II and Holland's continued refusal to adopt professionalism several of their best players departed for France, Italy and Germany. The matter was then brought to a head by the formation of rival Football Association backed by several of the more progressive clubs who preferred to pay their players.

So, in Nov. 1954, professionalism was officially recognised, a new professional League inaugurated, and Dutch football embarked on a new era of expansion and improvement. A number of their leading players were encouraged to return home, other professionals joined Dutch clubs, and a number of experienced coaches were brought in to help develop the game.

Address of governing body: Koninklijke Nederlandsche Voetbalbond, Verlengde Tolweg 6, 's—Gravenhage. Colours: Orange shirts, white shorts.

Results of internationals:

June 4, 1929	Holland 0, Scotland 2; Amsterdam
May 8, 1932	Holland 0, Eire 2; Amsterdam
April 8, 1934	Holland 5, Eire 2; Amsterdam
May 18, 1935	Holland 0, England 1; Amsterdam
Dec. 8, 1935	Eire 3, Holland 5; Dublin
May 21, 1938	Holland 1, Scotland 3; Amsterdam
Nov. 27, 1946	England 8, Holland 2; Huddersfield
May 1, 1955	Eire 1, Holland 0; Dublin
May 10, 1956	Holland 1, Eire 4; Rotterdam
May 27, 1959	Holland 1, Scotland 2; Amsterdam
May 9, 1962	Holland 4, Ireland 0; Rotterdam
Dec. 9, 1964	Holland 1, England 1; Amsterdam
Mar. 17, 1965*	Ireland 2, Holland 1; Belfast
April 7, 1965*	Holland 0, Ireland 0; Rotterdam
May 11, 1966	Scotland 0, Holland 3; Hampden Park
May 30, 1968	Holland 0, Scotland 0; Amsterdam
Nov. 5, 1969	Holland 0, England 1; Amsterdam
Jan. 15, 1970	England 0; Holland 0; Wembley

* World Cup

HOME DEFEATS

The record number of consecutive home defeats in one season in the Football League is 13 by Rochdale. After defeating New Brighton, 3—2 on Nov. 7, 1931, they were beaten in all 13 remaining home matches that season.

Rochdale also suffered defeat in their first home game of the following season and it was not until their second home game that they broke the spell by drawing 0—0 with Barrow.

Barrow lost a total of 15 home matches in Division III(N), 1925-6.

HOME WINS

The record for home wins in a single season of Football League matches is held by Brentford. In Division III(S) in 1929-30, Brentford won all 21 of their home matches.

Brentford Reserves won all their 23 home matches in the London Combination in 1932-3. In fact, they won 44 successive home games in that competition from Nov. 1931 to Nov. 1933.

Five other clubs in addition to Brentford have won all of their home matches in the Football League during a single season:

Sunderland	Division I	1891-2	13	games
Liverpool	Division II	1893-4	15	„
Bury	Division II	1894-5	16	„
Sheffield Wednesday	Division II	1899-1900	18	„
Small Heath (Birmingham)	Division II	1902-3	18	„

Since World War I all 11 matches in a single division of the Football League have resulted in home wins on four occasions:

Division I: Feb. 13, 1926; Dec. 10, 1955.

Division III(N), April 3, 1926; Mar. 14, 1931.

In Division I on Christmas Day, 1936, 10 of the 11 games resulted in home wins. The remaining game was a draw. This also occurred Sept. 1, 1956.

HUDDERSFIELD TOWN F.C.

Founded 1908. Played one season in North-Eastern League, then joined Midland League. Elected to Football League, Division II, 1910. The club nearly went out of existence in 1919 but local supporters collected a substantial amount of money and the club was kept going. Honours: Champions, Division I, 1923-4, 1924-5, 1925-6. Runners-up, 1926-7, 1927-8, 1933-4. Champions, Division II, 1969-70. Runners-up, 1919-20, 1952-3. F.A. Cup: winners, 1922. Finalists, 1920, 1928, 1930, 1938. Record attendance: 67,037 v. Arsenal, F.A. Cup, 6th Round, Feb. 27, 1932. Address: Leeds Road, Huddersfield (Tel. 20335). Colours: Blue and white striped shirts, white shorts. Record League goal-scorer: S. J. Taylor, 35 goals, Division II, 1919-20, and G. Brown, 35 goals, Division I, 1925-26. Record victory: 10—1 v. Blackpool, Division I, Dec. 13, 1930. Record defeat: 7—1 v. Bolton Wanderers, Division I, Jan. 1, 1930, and v. Wolverhampton Wanderers, Division I, Oct. 2, 1948.

HULL CITY F.C.

Founded 1904. Formed into a limited company, 1905. Elected to Football League, Division II, 1905. Honours: Champions, Division III, 1965-6. Champions, Division III(N), 1932-3, 1948-9. Runners-up, Division III, 1958-9. Best in Division II, 3rd, 1909-10. Record attendance: 55,019 v. Manchester United, F.A. Cup, 6th Round, Feb. 26, 1949. Address: Boothferry Park, Hull (Tel. 04-82 52195). Nickname: Tigers. Colours: Old gold with black edgings, black shorts. Record League goal-scorer: W. F. McNaughton, 39 goals, Division III (N), 1932-3. Record victory: 11—1 v. Carlisle United, Division III(N), Jan. 14, 1939. Record defeat: 8—0 v. Wolverhampton Wanderers, Division II, Nov. 4, 1911.

HUNGARY

The Hungarian national team of the 1950s will never be forgotten. They were, undoubtedly, the finest national soccer combination of all time. Unfortunately, however, all the more recent performances of Hungarian XIs are judged by the standard set by those Mighty Magyars of the previous decade and one is apt to miss the fact that although they have slipped from that once high pinnacle they are still not far behind the most powerful nations in world soccer.

Hungary went 13 years undefeated at home in international games—from their 7—2 defeat by Sweden in 1943 to their 4—2 defeat by Czechoslovakia in 1956. At home and away their crack teams of the 1950s played 29 matches without defeat over a period of more than four years. The defeat which ended that run was the one suffered in the final of the World Cup of 1954 when they lost 3—2 to West Germany.

The defeat of England, 6—3 at Wembley in Nov. 1953, is a game that shook British football to the core. Not only because it was England's first-ever home defeat by a continental side, but because of the immaculate display of the Hungarians which proved how far the old masters had slipped behind.

Here are details of that historical match:

Nov. 25, 1953, at Wembley Stadium.

Referee: Mr. L. Horn of Holland.

Hungary 6 (scorers—Hidegkuti 3, Puskas 2, Bozsik).

England 3 (scorers—Sewell, Mortensen, Ramsey—penalty).

England: Merrick; Ramsey, Eckersley; Wright, Johnston, Dickinson; Matthews, Taylor, Mortensen, Sewell, Robb.

Hungary: Grosics; Buzansky, Lantos; Bozsik, Lorant, Zakarias; Budai, Kocsis, Hidegkuti, Puskas, Czibor.

Apart from the precision of the Hungarian team and the power of its shooting, one of the features of their play was the terrific speed and anticipation of its wing-men. As soon as a wing-half or inside-forward gained possession, the winger immediately raced away up the touch-line and gained several yards before the ball was lobbed ahead of him. This running into position to receive the ball was carried out with great success by every man in the side.

As if to prove that this was no flash in the pan Hungary gave England an even bigger beating six months later, winning 7—1 in Budapest, May 23, 1954.

In case one is led to believe that Hungarian football begins and ends with this brilliant national team of the 1950s perhaps it should be pointed out that Hungary first beat England in 1934 in Budapest, and were World Cup finalists in 1938 when they lost 4—2 to Italy. Indeed, Hungarian footballers have long been respected for their ability and Hungarian soccer coaches have been accepted in many parts of the world and acknowledged as among the finest the game has ever produced.

The Hungarian F.A. was formed in 1901, the same year as a National League was inaugurated, and now there are more than 104,000 players registered, all of them amateurs.

Hungarian football went through a bad spell during the early part of 1956, and then, in October of that year, just when they were showing signs of recovery, the Revolution sent many of their best players fleeing abroad. Many returned and Hungary have since recaptured some of their former glory, reaching the Quarter-finals of the 1966 World Cup, and winning the 1964 and 1968 Olympic Tournaments.

In the Qualifying Competition for the 1970 World Cup Hungary were eliminated by Czechoslovakia in a play-off at the head of their group.

The address of the governing body of football in Hungary is the Magyar Labdarugok Szövetsége, Nepköztarsasag Utja 47, Budapest VI. Colours: Red shirts, white shorts, green stockings.

Results of internationals:

May 10, 1934	Hungary 2, England 1; Budapest
Dec. 15, 1934	Eire 2, Hungary 4; Dublin
May 3, 1936	Hungary 3, Eire 3; Budapest
Dec. 2, 1936	England 6, Hungary 2; Highbury
Dec. 6, 1936	Eire 2, Hungary 3; Dublin
Dec. 7, 1938	Scotland 3, Hungary 1; Ibrox Park
Mar. 19, 1939	Eire 2, Hungary 2; Cork
May 18, 1939	Hungary 2, Eire 2; Budapest
Nov. 25, 1953	England 3, Hungary 6; Wembley
May 23, 1954	Hungary 7, England 1; Budapest
May 29, 1955	Hungary 3, Scotland 1; Budapest
May 7, 1958	Scotland 1, Hungary 1; Hampden Park
June 8, 1958*	Wales 1, Hungary 1; Sweden
June 17, 1958*	Wales 2, Hungary 1; Sweden
May 22, 1960	Hungary 2, England 0; Budapest
June 5, 1960	Hungary 3, Scotland 3; Budapest
May 28, 1961	Hungary 3, Wales 2; Budapest
May 31, 1962*	Hungary 2, England 1; Chile
May 5, 1965	England 1, Hungary 0; Wembley
June 8, 1969*	Eire 1, Hungary 2; Dublin
Nov. 5, 1969*	Hungary 4, Eire 0; Budapest

*World Cup

I

ICELAND

An island with a population only roughly equivalent to that of a town the size of Southend or Wolverhampton could not be expected to make much of an impression in international soccer, but the Republic of Iceland have not been without their successes.

In 1948 they beat Finland 2—0, and in 1951 they gained a 4—3 victory over Sweden. They have also beaten Norway twice (in 1954 and 1955) and gained a 3—2 win over U.S.A. in 1955.

The first club was formed in 1899 and a national league was inaugurated in 1912. But it was not until after World War II that Icelandic football really began to develop. In 1946 they played their first International—with Denmark, and that same year they sent a touring side to play amateur clubs in England. That team's star inside-foward, Albert Gudmundsson, subsequently made two First Division appearances for Arsenal.

Iceland's first application for entry into the World Cup Competition in 1953-4 arrived too late for acceptance, and when they were grouped with France and Belgium in the 1958 Qualifying Competition they were outclassed. They have not entered since.

The address of the governing body: Knattspyrnusamband Islands—K.S.I., P.O. Box 1011, Reykjavik. Colours: Red shirts, white shorts.

Results of international matches:

Aug. 12, 1962   Eire 4, Iceland 2; Dublin
Sept. 2, 1962   Iceland 1, Eire 1; Reykjavik

Both Nations Cup games

INJURIES

The only four Football League players who have fractured a leg as many as four times during their playing careers are L. Ritson, Leyton Orient f.b., 1946-9; A. Evans, Aston Villa and West Bromwich Albion, f.b., 1896-1908; D. Smith, Burnley, Brighton and Bristol City f.b., 1950-63 (five times); A. Davidson, Hull City f.b., 1950-68; L. Leslie, Airdrie, West Ham United, Stoke City, Millwall, Southend United, gl., 1959-69.

In a Division IV game at Chester, Jan. 1, 1966, the home side lost both of their full-backs, R. Jones and B. Jones, with broken legs. Even so, Chester beat Aldershot 3—2.

In September 1964 D. Mackay of Tottenham Hotspur was unlucky enough to break a leg for the second time in nine months.

See also under CASUALTIES.

INTER-LEAGUE

The first Inter-League game took place on April 20, 1891, at Sheffield, between the Football League and the Football Alliance.

Next came the Football League's first game with the Scottish League, played at Bolton, April 11, 1892, ending in a draw 2—2. The Football League side included four Scots, T. McInnes (Lincoln City), D. Gow (Sunderland), W. Groves (West Bromwich

Albion), and H. Gardiner (Bolton Wanderers). It was the last time that the Football League knowingly included Scottish players until D. Mackay (Tottenham Hotspur) played against the Scottish League in Mar. 1960. On one other occasion a Scottish-born player, A. Maitland (South Shields) unwittingly was chosen to play against the Irish League, at Bolton, in Oct. 1922. The selectors discovered their error before the match, but decided to let Maitland play.

The first game between the Football League and the Irish League was played at Belfast, Feb. 10, 1894.

The first game between the Football League and the League of Ireland (Eire), took place at Dalymount Park, Dublin, April 30, 1947.

Before World War I, the old Southern League also entered into competition with the three other big leagues. They met the Football League six times between 1909 and 1915, and the Scottish and Irish Leagues five times each during the same period.

The Football League enjoyed a record run of 24 games without defeat 1914-29. After losing 3—2 to the Scottish League at Burnley, Mar. 21, 1914 the Football League was not beaten again in an official peace-time match until they lost 2—1 to the Scottish League, Glasgow, Nov. 2, 1929. Between those dates the Football League met the Scottish League 11 times, Irish League 11 times, The Army once, and the Southern League once.

Here is a summary of the results of Inter-League games correct to c.s. 1970.

Football League v Scottish League: Played 67, Football League won 36, Scottish League won 18, drawn 13.

Football League v. Irish League: Played 60, Football League won 53, Irish League won 3, drawn 4.

Football League v. League of Ireland (Eire): Played 20, Football League won 17, League of Ireland won 1, drawn 2.

Football League v. Southern League: Played 6, Football League won 4, Southern League won 1, drawn 1.

Scottish League v. Irish League: Played 60, Scottish League won 55, Irish League won 5, drawn 0.

Scottish League v. Southern League: Played 5, Scottish League won 2, Southern League won 2, drawn 1.

Scottish League v. League of Ireland (Eire): Played 19, Scottish League won 16, League of Ireland won 1, drawn 2.

Irish League v. Southern League: Played 5, Irish League won 0, Southern League won 3, drawn 2.

Football League v. International Football Combination of Denmark: Played 1, Football League won 1.

Football League v. Italian League: Played 4, Football League won 1, Italian League won 3, drawn 0.

Football League v. Belgian League: Played 1, drawn 1.

Scottish League v. Italian League: Played 2, Scottish League won 0, Italian League won 1, drawn 1.

Irish League v. Italian League: Played 1, Irish League won 1, Italian League won 0, drawn 0.

INTERNATIONAL FOOTBALL ASSOCIATION BOARD

In 1882 the Football Association proposed that there should be a meeting between the four national associations of the United Kingdom to agree on the Laws of the Game.

At first the Scottish F.A. was reluctant to participate at such a meeting. They preferred to retain their own version of the rules and would not tolerate any interference with their independence. The English F.A. threatened to discontinue international matches with Scotland and a serious breakdown of negotiations seemed imminent before the Scottish F.A. relented and agreed to the meeting.

This was held at Manchester, Dec. 6, 1882, and was attended by two members of each of the four Associations of England, Scotland, Ireland and Wales. It was an immediate success. A uniform code of rules was drawn up, being subsequently agreed upon by all four countries, and the International Association Board came into being.

At the present time the Board meets at least once a year and in addition to four representatives from the four United Kingdom Associations, four members of the Fédération Internationale de Football Association are entitled to attend.

The prime object of the Board is the same today as it was originally, that is, to discuss proposed alterations to the Laws of the Game. They reserve the right alone to make any such alterations as they may agree upon from time to time. Furthermore, in accordance with present agreements, no single Association can themselves make any alterations to the Laws of the Game unless these are passed by the Board.

INTERNATIONAL FOOT-BALL LEAGUE BOARD

This was formed in 1897 when the Football League and the Scottish League agreed to meet to draw up some uniform code of rules regarding the rights of clubs to retain players, and in particular, the recognition of these rights by each League, so that " poaching " of players by one League from another could be prevented.

The board is made up of twelve representatives, four each from the Football League and the Scottish League, and two each from the Irish Football League and the Football League of Ireland.

It is because of the agreements drawn up by this board that no player retained or transfer-listed by any club in any one of those four Leagues can play for any other club in the Leagues without a proper transfer.

INTERNATIONALS

See also AMATEURS (INTER-NATIONALS), APPEARANCES (INTER-NATIONALS), ATTENDANCES, AGE (of players), GOAL-SCORING, and also various International Cup Competitions.

International Championship data concerning England, Ireland, Scotland and Wales appear in this section. Details of other countries are to be found under the respective names of those countries.

Club Records

Rangers have supplied more international players to any one of the home countries than any other club. 100 of their players have been honoured by Scotland.

This number has not been exceeded by any other club, even when internationals to all four home countries are included, and the Rangers' record figure in this respect is increased to 108 with the addition of eight Irish internationals.

Juventus (Turin) had 10 players in the Italian side v. Hungary, May 11, 1947. This is a world record. The fact that Queen's Park provided all the players for Scotland v. England in the first official international of 1872 could not be considered a genuine record as no attempt was made to choose a representative team.

The greatest number of players from one club appearing in the International Championship on the same day is seven. Tottenham Hotspur had this number playing on Oct. 12, 1963: Norman, Greaves, and Smith, for England v. Wales; C. Jones, for Wales; and Brown, Mackay, and White for Scotland v. Ireland.

Cardiff City also had seven players in the International Championship on Feb. 28, 1925. Keenor, Thomas, Davies, Nicholls and Beadles for Wales v. England, Nelson for Scotland and Farquharson for Ireland.

Arsenal had seven players in the England team v. Italy, Nov. 14, 1934: Moss, Male, Hapgood, Copping, Bowden, Drake and Bastin. This is a record for the home countries.

Blackburn Rovers supplied five men for the England team v. Ireland, Mar. 15, 1890: Forrest, Lofthouse, Townley, Barton and Walton. Arsenal also provided five men for this match, Feb. 6, 1935: Male, Hapgood, Copping,

INTERNATIONALS. England *v.* Scotland in 1879 at Kennington Oval.

INTERNATIONALS. An aerial view of Britain's largest soccer stadium—
Hampden Park, Glasgow.

ORIGINS OF THE GAME. (*Above*) Village boys playing football, painted in 1839 by Thomas Webster. (*Below*) A finely-coloured cartoon published by Robert Cruikshank in 1827.

Drake and Bastin.

W. Rowley, T. Clare, A. Underwood, all of Stoke, formed the England defence v. Ireland, Mar. 5, 1892.

Other instances of a one-club-defence in an England team was v. Wales, in a war-time international, May 9, 1942. Marks, Scott and Hapgood of Arsenal were the players, and v. Ireland, Oct. 2, 1954, when Manchester United provided R. Wood, W. Foulkes and R. Byrne.

The only instance of a club half-back line playing on one side in an International Championship match was when Muirhead, Meiklejohn and Craig of Rangers played for Scotland v. Ireland, Feb. 25, 1928.

Wolverhampton Wanderers provided England's half-back line v. Russia (twice), Brazil and Austria, in May and June, 1958. The players were E. Clamp, W. Wright and W. Slater.

Tottenham Hotspur had four men in the England team v. Scotland, Apr. 9, 1921 : B. Smith, A. Grimsdell, B. Bliss, and J. H. Dimmock.

The England team v. Scotland has included as many as three forwards from the same club on five occasions: 1875—C. H. Wollaston, C. W. Alcock and H. E. Heron (Wanderers). 1878—H. Wace, J. G. Wylie and H. E. Heron (Wanderers). 1891—F. Geary, E. Chadwick and A. Milward (Everton). 1908—V. J. Woodward, G. Hilsdon and J. Windridge (Chelsea). 1937—S. Matthews, F. C. Steele and J. A. Johnson (Stoke).

The three Chelsea forwards mentioned above were also together in England's side in the other two home internationals of season 1907-8, as well as v. Austria, Hungary and Bohemia in the summer of 1908.

The England team which met Hungary at Wembley, Nov. 25, 1953, included three forwards from Blackpool : S. Matthews, E. Taylor and S. Mortensen. In addition, H. Johnston of Blackpool was at centre-half in the same side.

The England team which defeated Wales 5—1 at Wrexham, Mar. 5, 1894, and also that which drew with the Principality, 1—1, at Queen's Club, London, Mar. 18, 1895, consisted entirely of Corinthian players. This cannot be considered a club record in the ordinary way, because the Corinthian team was for the most part a combined eleven made up of players from various schools, colleges and universities.

Scotland's side which beat England, 2—1, at Sheffield, April 4, 1903, included a one-club defence, Doig, McCombie and Watson, from an English club —Sunderland.

Arsenal's best season for internationals on their books was 1936-7. By the end of the season, 13 Arsenal players had been capped by their respective countries. The selection of A. Kirchen for England v. Norway, May 14, 1937, brought the total to 14. C. Bastin, R. Bowden, W. Copping, J. Crayston, E. Drake, E. Hapgood, J. Hulme, B. Joy, A. Kirchen, G. Male, F. Moss and H. Roberts were the England internationals. A. James (Scotland) and R. John (Wales) brought up the total.

Cardiff City had 14 players towards the end of the 1925-6 season, who had all been capped. They were : Keenor, Davies (W.), Davies (L.), Beadles, Evans (J.), Evans (H.), for Wales. Cassidy, Nelson, Blair and Lawson for Scotland. Farquharson, McIlvenny, Watson and Sloan for Ireland.

In 1933-4, Aston Villa possessed 14 men who had played for their respective countries : Beresford, Brown, Cunliffe, Gardener, Houghton, Mort, Tate, Smart, Walker and Waring for England. Blair, Gibson and Nibloe for Scotland.

At the start of season 1965-6 Manchester United had 15 internationals on their books including Amateur cap, D. Sadler. The other full internationals were P. Dunne, H. Gregg, S. Brennan, N. Cantwell, A. Dunne, P. Crerand, W. Foulkes, N. Stiles, G. Best, R. Charlton, J. Connelly, D. Herd, D. Law and G. Moore. United had as many as 13 internationals for a long spell in the 1960s.

Towards the end of the season 1932-33, Rangers possessed 13 international players : Archibald, Brown, Craig, Fleming, Gray, Hamilton (T.), McPhail, Marshall, Meiklejohn and Morton for Scotland; English, Hamilton (R.), and McDonald for Ireland.

Rangers also had 13 international players near the end of the previous season. But R. McAuley, a Scottish international was transferred during the summer of 1932 to Chelsea. However the total of 13 was maintained, by the capping of English for Ireland v. Scotland in Sept. 1932.

When Wales and Scotland met in the International Championship at Ninian Park, Feb. 16, 1924, Wales were captained by F. Keenor of Cardiff City, and Scotland were captained by J. Blair, also of Cardiff City. This is a club record.

Consecutive Appearances

See APPEARANCES (INTERNATIONALS).

England

England's first home defeat by an international team took place on Sept. 21, 1949 at Goodison Park. Result, England 0, Eire 2. Teams: *England:* Williams (Wolverhampton Wanderers); Mozley (Derby County), Aston (Manchester United); Wright (Wolverhampton Wanderers), (capt.), Franklin (Stoke City), Dickinson (Portsmouth); Harris (Portsmouth), Morris (Derby County), Pye (Wolverhampton Wanderers), Mannion (Middlesbrough), Finney (Preston North End).

Eire: Godwin (Shamrock Rovers); Carey (Manchester United) (capt.), Aherne (Luton Town), Walsh (W.) (Manchester City), Martin (Aston Villa), Moroney (West Ham United); Corr (Everton), Farrell (Everton), Walsh (D.) (West Bromwich Albion), Desmond (Middlesbrough), O'Conner (Shamrock Rovers). Scorers: Martin and Farrell.

However, as some may not consider Eire to be foreign it must be noted that the first Continental team to beat England on English soil was Hungary. Details are given under the heading, HUNGARY.

England's first defeat abroad was against Spain at Madrid, May 15, 1929. Result 3—4. In fact, this was the first defeat abroad of an England team including professionals, for an England all-amateur side was beaten abroad at Copenhagen, May 5, 1910, Denmark winning 2—1. The teams in England's first professional defeat were:

England: Hufton (West Ham United); Cooper (Derby County), Blenkinsop (Sheffield Wednesday); Kean (Bolton Wanderers), Hill (Newcastle United) Peacock (Middlesbrough); Adcock (Leicester City), E. Kail (Dulwich Hamlet), Carter (West Bromwich Albion), Bradford (Birmingham), Barry (Leicester City).

Spain: Zamora (Club Deportive Espanol of Barcelona); Queseda (Real Madrid), Quincoces (Club Deportive Alaves of Vittoria); Prats (Real Madrid), Marculeta (Real Sociedad of San Sebastian), J. M. Pena (Real Madrid); Lazcano (Real Madrid), Goiburu (Osasuna Club of Pampona), Rubio (Real Madrid), Padron (Club Deportive of Barcelona), Yurrita (Real Sociedad of San Sebastian).

Scorers: Spain—Rubio, Lazcano 2, Goiburu. England—Carter 2, Hill.

England have won the International Championship outright 26 times—more times than any other country.

v. Scotland. Played 87, won 30, lost 35, drawn 22.
Biggest win: 9—3 at Wembley, April 15, 1961.
Biggest defeat: 2—7 at Old Hampden, Mar. 2, 1878.
v. Ireland. Played 77, won 60, lost 5, drawn 12.
Biggest win: 13—0 at Belfast, Feb. 18, 1882.
Biggest defeat: 0—3 at Middlesbrough, Feb. 14, 1914.
v. Wales. Played 80, won 53, lost 11, drawn 16.
Biggest win 9—1 at Cardiff, Mar. 16, 1896.
Biggest defeat: 3—5 at Wrexham, Mar. 13, 1882.

First

The first international matches were those played between England and Scotland in 1870, 1871 and 1872 and the series owes its beginning to the enterprise of Mr. C. W. Alcock shortly after his appointment as Honorary Secretary of the Football Association in 1870.

Mr. Alcock first wrote a letter to a Glasgow newspaper inviting applications from or nomination of Scottish players who would be prepared to take part in an England v. Scotland game he proposed to stage in London.

The Queen's Park Club immediately took an interest in this idea and subsequently played a leading part in the establishment of these games as a regular feature of the football scene.

They proposed the name of one of their players, R. Smith, then resident in London, and he appeared in the first and second games played in Nov. 1870 and Feb. 1871.

These games, however, are no longer considered as official internationals, and neither are the third and fourth games. In none of these early games were the Scottish teams representative of Scottish football but merely made up of Scots resident in England. As a matter of record the results of these games were as follows:

Nov. 19, 1870 England 1, Scotland 0.
Feb. 28, 1871 England 1, Scotland 1.
Nov. 18, 1871 England 2, Scotland 1.
Feb. 24, 1872 England 1, Scotland 0.

The first official international was played at the ground of the West of Scotland Cricket Club at Partick, near Glasgow, on Saturday, Nov. 30, 1872.

As already indicated the idea of such a meeting had been contemplated for some time past, but the definite plans were set in motion following discussions between leading members of the Queen's Park Club, the F.A., and the Wanderers F.C., when the Scottish enthusiasts had travelled down to London to meet the Wanderers in the first semi-final of the new F.A. Cup Competition in Feb. 1872.

As may be seen in this section under RESULTS the game ended in a goalless draw. Bell's Life described it as " one of the jolliest, one of the most spirited and most pleasant matches that have ever been played according to Association Rules . . . and each member of the two sides was greeted with a volley of applause as he entered the pavilion." The spectators numbered about 4,000.

The Scottish side in that game consisted entirely of members of the Queen's Park Club, but that was fair enough considering that they were then the most powerful combination north of the Border.

When the return game took place four months later, at the Oval, to economise in train fares the Scottish selectors included three Scots resident in London.

The dates of the earliest internationals between the other home countries are as follow:

Mar. 25, 1876, Scotland v. Wales at Glasgow.

Jan. 18, 1879, England v. Wales at The Oval.

Feb. 18, 1882, England v. Ireland at Belfast.

Feb. 25, 1882, Wales v. Ireland at Wrexham.

Jan. 28, 1884, Ireland v. Scotland at Belfast.

The first official international between any of the home countries and a foreign country was that between England and Austria, in Vienna, June 6, 1908. Two earlier games between England and a visiting German side which were played in Sept. 1901 are not ranked as official.

The first international played in Europe—Austria 5, Hungary 0, Oct. 12, 1902.

The first international played in South America—Argentine 1, Uruguay 1, 1905.

Fourth Division

The first player to win a full international cap while on the books of a Fourth Division club—V. Rouse of Crystal Palace, who kept goal for Wales v. Ireland, April 22, 1959.

General

In 1955-6 all four countries in the International tournament finished level with three points each, the first time that this has happened.

The only instance of an International Championship game being played outside the two countries concerned was at Shrewsbury, Feb. 8, 1890, when Wales played Ireland.

The only non-British-born player to appear in the International Championship was W. Andrews the Glentoran and Grimsby Town half-back. Born Kansas City, U.S.A., he made three appearances for Ireland: 1907-8, v. Scotland, 1912-13 v. England and Scotland.

The only gipsy ever to play for England was R. Howell, Sheffield United and Liverpool half-back, who made two appearances in the 1890s. He was born in a caravan near Sheffield.

Goal-scoring

See GOAL-SCORING (INTERNATIONALS).

Individual Appearances

See APPEARANCES (INTERNATIONALS).

Ireland

This section refers to Northern Ireland. International matches concerning the Football Association of Ireland (Dublin) appear under the heading, EIRE.

The Irish Football Association (Belfast) are entitled by F.I.F.A. ruling to include players from Eire in International Championship matches with either England, Scotland or Wales, but must restrict their choice to players born in Northern Ireland for all other international matches. In June 1954, F.I.F.A. ruled that the official designation for international teams under the jurisdiction of the Irish F.A. should be "Northern Ireland".

Ireland gained her only outright International Championship title in 1913-14, although in 1902-3, 1955-6, 1957-8, 1958-9 and 1963-4 she shared the Championship.

In that Championship winning season Ireland defeated Wales 2—1 at Wrexham, and England 3—0 at Middlesbrough, and drew with Scotland 1—1 at Belfast.

The men who took part in Ireland's most successful season were:

Goal: McKee (Belfast Celtic) v. W. E. S.

Full-backs: McConnell (Bohemians) v. W. E. S., Craig (Morton) v. W. E. S.

Half-backs: Harris (Everton) v. W. S., Hampton (Bradford City) v. E., O'Connell (Hull City) v. W. E. S., Rollo (Linfield) v. W., Hamill (Manchester United) v. E. S.

Forwards: Seymour (Bohemians) v. W., Rollo (Linfield) v. E., Houston (Everton) v. S., Young (Linfield) v. W. E. S., Nixon (Linfield) v. S., Gillespie (Sheffield United) v. W. E., Lacey (Liverpool) v. W. E. S., Brookman (Bradford City) v. W., Thompson (Clyde) v. E. S.

Goal-scorers: v. Wales, Gillespie (2). v. England, Gillespie and Lacey (2). v. Scotland, Young.

v. *Scotland.* Played 75, won 10, lost 54, drawn 11.

Biggest win: 2—0 at Glasgow, Mar. 21, 1903. Also at Belfast, Oct. 4, 1947. Biggest defeat: 0—11 at Glasgow, Feb. 23, 1901.

v. *Wales.* Played 77, won 23, lost 37, drawn 17.

Biggest win: 7—0 at Belfast, Feb. 1, 1930. Biggest defeat: 0—11 at Wrexham, Mar. 3, 1888.

v. *England.* Played 77, won 5, lost 60, drawn 12.

Biggest win: 3—0 at Middlesbrough, Feb. 14, 1914. Biggest defeat: 0—13 at Belfast, Feb. 18, 1882.

The highest individual scorer for Ireland in a single game is J. Bambrick who scored six goals v. Wales at Belfast, Feb. 1, 1930.

Qualifications

In international matches the qualification of players appearing for any of the home countries is birth within the area of the National Association. In the case of British subjects born abroad, their nationality is decided by the nationality of their fathers.

For cases of players appearing for countries other than that for which they were rightly qualified, see APPEARANCES (INTERNATIONALS); General.

Results

Here follow the results of internationals between the home countries. Results of internationals with all foreign countries are given under those countries.

England v. Scotland

*Year	Venue	E.	S.
1873	Glasgow	0	0
1873	Kennington Oval	4	2
1874	Glasgow	1	2
1875	Kennington Oval	2	2
1876	Glasgow	0	3
1877	Kennington Oval	1	3
1878	Glasgow	2	7
1879	Kennington Oval	5	4
1880	Glasgow	4	5
1881	Kennington Oval	1	6
1882	Glasgow	1	5
1883	Sheffield	2	3
1884	Glasgow	0	1
1885	Kennington Oval	1	1
1886	Glasgow	1	1
1887	Blackburn	2	3
1888	Glasgow	5	0
1889	Kennington Oval	2	3
1890	Glasgow	1	1
1891	Blackburn	2	1
1892	Glasgow	4	0
1893	Richmond	5	2

*Year	Venue	E.	S.
1894	Glasgow	2	2
1895	Everton	3	0
1896	Glasgow	1	2
1897	Crystal Palace	1	2
1898	Glasgow	3	1
1899	Birmingham	2	1
1900	Glasgow	1	4
1901	Crystal Palace	2	2
1902	Birmingham	2	2
1903	Sheffield	1	2
1904	Glasgow	1	0
1905	Crystal Palace	1	0
1906	Glasgow	1	2
1907	Newcastle	1	1
1908	Glasgow	1	1
1909	Crystal Palace	2	0
1910	Glasgow	0	2
1911	Everton	1	1
1912	Glasgow	1	1
1913	Chelsea	1	0
1914	Glasgow	1	3
1919	‡Everton	2	2
1919	‡Glasgow	4	3
1920	Sheffield	5	4
1921	Glasgow	0	3
1922	Villa Park	0	1
1923	Glasgow	2	2
1924	Wembley	1	1
1925	Glasgow	0	2
1926	Manchester	0	1
1927	Glasgow	2	1
1928	Wembley	1	5
1929	Glasgow	0	1
1930	Wembley	5	2
1931	Glasgow	0	2
1932	Wembley	3	0
1933	Glasgow	1	2
1934	Wembley	3	0
1935	Glasgow	0	2
1936	Wembley	1	1
1937	Glasgow	1	3
1938	Wembley	0	1
1939	Glasgow	2	1
1946	‡Glasgow	0	1
1947	Wembley	1	1
1948	Glasgow	2	0
1949	Wembley	1	3
1950	Glasgow	1	0
1951	Wembley	2	3
1952	Glasgow	2	1
1953	Wembley	2	2
1954	Glasgow	4	2
1955	Wembley	7	2
1956	Glasgow	1	1
1957	Wembley	2	1
1958	Glasgow	4	0
1959	Wembley	1	0
1960	Glasgow	1	1
1961	Wembley	9	3
1962	Glasgow	0	2

*Year	Venue	E.	I.
1963	Wembley	1	2
1964	Glasgow	0	1
1965	Wembley	2	2
1966	Glasgow	4	3
1967	Wembley	2	3
1968	Glasgow	1	1
1969	Wembley	4	1
1970	Glasgow	0	0

England v. Ireland

*Year	Venue	E.	I.
1882	Belfast	13	0
1883	Liverpool	7	0
1884	Belfast	8	1
1885	Manchester	4	0
1886	Belfast	6	1
1887	Sheffield	7	0
1888	Belfast	5	1
1889	Everton	6	1
1890	Belfast	9	1
1891	Wolverhampton	6	1
1892	Belfast	2	0
1893	Birmingham	6	1
1894	Belfast	2	2
1895	Derby	9	0
1896	Belfast	2	0
1897	Nottingham	6	0
1898	Belfast	3	2
1899	Sunderland	13	2
1900	Dublin	2	0
1901	Southampton	3	0
1902	Belfast	1	0
1903	Wolverhampton	4	0
1904	Belfast	3	1
1905	Middlesbrough	1	1
1906	Belfast	5	0
1907	Everton	1	0
1908	Belfast	3	1
1909	Bradford	4	0
1910	Belfast	1	1
1911	Derby	2	1
1912	Dublin	6	1
1913	Belfast	1	2
1914	Middlesbrough	0	3
1920	Belfast	1	1
1921	Sunderland	2	0
1922	Belfast	1	1
1923	West Bromwich	2	0
1924	Belfast	1	2
1925	Everton	3	1
1926	Belfast	0	0
1927	Liverpool	3	3
1928	Belfast	0	2
1929	Everton	2	1
1930	Belfast	6	2
1931	Sheffield	5	1
1932	Belfast	6	2
1933	Blackpool	1	0
1934	Belfast	3	0
1935	Everton	2	1
1936	Belfast	3	1

*Year	Venue	E.	I.
1937	Stoke	3	1
1938	Belfast	5	1
1939	Manchester	7	0
1946	‡Belfast	1	0
1947	Belfast	7	2
1948	Everton	2	2
1949	Belfast	6	2
1950	Manchester	9	2
1951	Belfast	4	1
1952	Villa Park	2	0
1953	Belfast	2	2
1954	Liverpool	3	1
1955	Belfast	2	0
1956	Wembley	3	0
1957	Belfast	1	1
1958	Wembley	2	3
1959	Belfast	3	3
1960	Wembley	2	1
1961	Belfast	5	2
1962	Wembley	1	1
1963	Belfast	3	1
1964	Wembley	8	3
1965	Belfast	4	3
1966	Wembley	2	1
1967	Belfast	2	0
1968	Wembley	2	0
1969	Belfast	3	1
1970	Wembley	3	1

England v. Wales

*Year	Venue	E.	W.
1879	Kennington Oval	2	1
1880	Wrexham	3	2
1881	Blackburn	0	1
1882	Wrexham	3	5
1883	Kennington Oval	5	0
1884	Wrexham	4	0
1885	Blackburn	1	1
1886	Wrexham	3	1
1887	Kennington Oval	4	0
1888	Crewe	5	1
1889	Stoke-on-Trent	4	1
1890	Wrexham	3	1
1891	Sunderland	4	1
1892	Wrexham	2	0
1893	Stoke-on-Trent	6	0
1894	Wrexham	5	1
1895	London	1	1
1896	Cardiff	9	1
1897	Sheffield	4	0
1898	Wrexham	3	0
1899	Bristol	4	1
1900	Cardiff	1	1
1901	Newcastle	6	0
1902	Wrexham	0	0
1903	Portsmouth	2	1
1904	Wrexham	2	2
1905	Liverpool	3	1
1906	Cardiff	1	0
1907	Fulham	1	1
1908	Wrexham	7	1

*Year	Venue	E.	W.
1909	Nottingham	2	0
1910	Cardiff	1	0
1911	Millwall	3	0
1912	Wrexham	2	0
1913	Bristol	4	3
1914	Cardiff	2	0
1920	‡Cardiff	1	2
1920	‡Stoke	2	0
1920	Highbury	1	2
1921	Cardiff	0	0
1922	Liverpool	1	0
1923	Cardiff	2	2
1924	Blackburn	1	2
1925	Swansea	2	1
1926	London (Selhurst)	1	3
1927	Wrexham	3	3
1928	Burnley	1	2
1929	Swansea	3	2
1930	Stamford Bridge	6	0
1931	Wrexham	4	0
1932	Liverpool	3	1
1933	Wrexham	0	0
1934	Newcastle	1	2
1935	Cardiff	4	0
1936	Wolverhampton	1	2
1937	Cardiff	1	2
1938	Middlesbrough	2	1
1939	Cardiff	2	4
1946	‡West Bromwich	0	1
1947	Manchester	3	0
1948	Cardiff	3	0
1949	Villa Park	1	0
1950	Cardiff	4	1
1951	Sunderland	4	2
1952	Cardiff	1	1
1953	Wembley	5	2
1954	Cardiff	4	1
1955	Wembley	3	2
1956	Cardiff	1	2
1957	Wembley	3	1
1958	Cardiff	4	0
1959	Villa Park	2	2
1960	Cardiff	1	1
1961	Wembley	5	1
1962	Cardiff	1	1
1963	Wembley	4	0
1964	Cardiff	4	0
1965	Wembley	2	1
1966	Cardiff	0	1
1967	Wembley	5	1
1968	Cardiff	3	0
1969	Wembley	3	1
1970	Cardiff	1	1

Scotland v. Wales

*Year	Venue	S.	W.
1876	Glasgow	4	0
1877	Wrexham	2	0
1878	Glasgow	9	0
1879	Wrexham	3	0
1880	Glasgow	5	1

*Year	Venue	S.	W.	*Year	Venue	S.	W.
1881	Wrexham	5	1	1953	Cardiff	2	1
1882	Glasgow	5	0	1954	Glasgow	3	3
1883	Wrexham	3	0	1955	Cardiff	1	0
1884	Glasgow	4	1	1956	Glasgow	3	0
1885	Wrexham	8	1	1957	Cardiff	2	2
1886	Glasgow	4	1	1958	Glasgow	1	1
1887	Wrexham	2	0	1959	Cardiff	3	0
1888	Edinburgh	5	1	1960	Glasgow	1	1
1889	Wrexham	0	0	1961	Cardiff	0	2
1890	Paisley	5	0	1962	Glasgow	2	0
1891	Wrexham	4	3	1963	Cardiff	3	2
1892	Edinburgh	6	1	1964	Glasgow	2	1
1893	Wrexham	8	0	1965	Cardiff	2	3
1894	Kilmarnock	5	2	1966	Glasgow	4	1
1895	Wrexham	2	2	1967	Cardiff	1	1
1896	Dundee	4	0	1968	Glasgow	3	2
1897	Wrexham	2	2	1969	Wrexham	5	3
1898	Motherwell	5	2	1970	Glasgow	0	0
1899	Wrexham	6	0				
1900	Aberdeen	5	2				

Scotland v. Ireland

*Year	Venue	S.	I.
1884	Belfast	5	0
1885	Glasgow	8	2
1886	Belfast	7	2
1887	Glasgow	4	1
1888	Belfast	10	2
1889	Glasgow	7	0
1890	Belfast	4	1
1891	Glasgow	2	1
1892	Belfast	3	2
1893	Glasgow	6	1
1894	Belfast	2	1
1895	Glasgow	3	1
1896	Belfast	3	3
1897	Glasgow	5	1
1898	Belfast	3	0
1899	Glasgow	9	1
1900	Belfast	3	0
1901	Glasgow	11	0
1902	Belfast	5	1
1903	Glasgow	0	2
1904	Dublin	1	1
1905	Glasgow	4	0
1906	Dublin	1	0
1907	Glasgow	3	0
1908	Dublin	5	0
1909	Glasgow	5	0
1910	Belfast	0	1
1911	Glasgow	2	0
1912	Belfast	4	1
1913	Dublin	2	1
1914	Belfast	1	1
1919	‡Glasgow	2	1
1919	‡Belfast	0	0
1920	Glasgow	3	0
1921	Belfast	2	0
1922	Glasgow	2	1
1923	Belfast	1	0
1924	Glasgow	2	0
1925	Belfast	3	0
1926	Glasgow	4	0

The following continues the left column (Scotland v. Wales):

*Year	Venue	S.	W.
1901	Wrexham	1	1
1902	Greenock	5	1
1903	Cardiff	1	0
1904	Dundee	1	1
1905	Wrexham	1	3
1906	Edinburgh	0	2
1907	Wrexham	0	1
1908	Dundee	2	1
1909	Wrexham	2	3
1910	Kilmarnock	1	0
1911	Cardiff	2	2
1912	Tynecastle	1	0
1913	Wrexham	0	0
1914	Glasgow	0	0
1920	Cardiff	1	1
1921	Aberdeen	2	1
1922	Wrexham	1	2
1923	Paisley	2	0
1924	Cardiff	0	2
1925	Tynecastle	3	1
1926	Cardiff	3	0
1927	Glasgow	3	0
1928	Wrexham	2	2
1929	Glasgow	4	2
1930	Cardiff	4	2
1931	Glasgow	1	1
1932	Wrexham	3	2
1933	Edinburgh	2	5
1934	Cardiff	2	3
1935	Aberdeen	3	2
1936	Cardiff	1	1
1937	Dundee	1	2
1938	Cardiff	1	2
1939	Edinburgh	3	2
1946	‡Glasgow	2	0
1947	Wrexham	1	3
1948	Glasgow	1	2
1949	Cardiff	3	1
1950	Glasgow	2	0
1951	Cardiff	3	1
1952	Glasgow	0	1

*Year	Venue	S.	I.
1927	Belfast	2	0
1928	Glasgow	0	1
1929	Belfast	7	3
1930	Glasgow	3	1
1931	Belfast	0	0
1932	Glasgow	3	1
1933	Belfast	4	0
1934	Glasgow	1	2
1935	Belfast	1	2
1936	Edinburgh	2	1
1937	Belfast	3	1
1938	Aberdeen	1	1
1939	Belfast	2	0
1946	‡Belfast	3	2
1947	Glasgow	0	2
1948	Belfast	0	2
1949	Glasgow	3	2
1950	Belfast	8	2
1951	Glasgow	6	1
1952	Belfast	3	0
1953	Glasgow	1	1
1954	Belfast	3	1
1955	Glasgow	2	2
1956	Belfast	1	2
1957	Glasgow	1	0
1958	Belfast	1	1
1959	Glasgow	2	2
1960	Belfast	4	0
1961	Glasgow	5	2
1962	Belfast	6	1
1963	Glasgow	5	1
1964	Belfast	1	2
1965	Glasgow	3	2
1966	Belfast	2	3
1967	Glasgow	2	1
1968	Belfast	0	1
1969	Glasgow	1	1
1970	Belfast	1	0

Wales v. Ireland

*Year	Venue	W.	I.
1882	Wrexham	7	1
1883	Belfast	1	1
1884	Wrexham	6	0
1885	Belfast	8	2
1886	Wrexham	5	0
1887	Belfast	1	4
1888	Wrexham	11	0
1889	Belfast	3	1
1890	Shrewsbury	5	2
1891	Belfast	2	7
1892	Bangor	1	1
1893	Belfast	3	4
1894	Swansea	4	1
1895	Belfast	2	2
1896	Wrexham	6	1
1897	Belfast	3	4
1898	Llandudno	0	1
1899	Belfast	0	1
1900	Llandudno	2	0
1901	Belfast	1	0

*Year	Venue	W.	I.
1902	Cardiff	0	3
1903	Belfast	0	2
1904	Bangor	0	1
1905	Belfast	2	2
1906	Wrexham	4	4
1907	Belfast	3	2
1908	Aberdare	0	1
1909	Belfast	3	2
1910	Wrexham	4	1
1911	Belfast	2	1
1912	Cardiff	2	3
1913	Belfast	1	0
1914	Wrexham	1	2
1920	Belfast	2	2
1921	Swansea	2	1
1922	Belfast	1	1
1923	Wrexham	0	3
1925	Wrexham	0	0
1926	Belfast	0	3
1927	Cardiff	2	2
1928	Belfast	2	1
1929	Wrexham	2	2
1930	Belfast	0	7
1931	Wrexham	3	2
1932	Belfast	0	4
1933	Wrexham	4	1
1934	Belfast	1	1
1935	Wrexham	3	1
1936	Belfast	2	3
1937	Wrexham	4	1
1938	Belfast	0	1
1939	Wrexham	3	1
1946	‡Cardiff	0	1
1947	Belfast	1	2
1948	Wrexham	2	0
1949	Belfast	2	0
1950	Wrexham	0	0
1951	Belfast	2	1
1952	Swansea	3	0
1953	Belfast	3	2
1954	Wrexham	1	2
1955	Belfast	3	2
1956	Cardiff	1	1
1957	Belfast	0	0
1958	Cardiff	1	1
1959	Belfast	1	4
1960	Wrexham	3	2
1961	Belfast	5	1
1962	Cardiff	4	0
1963	Belfast	4	1
1964	Cardiff	2	3
1965	Belfast	5	0
1966	Cardiff	1	4
1967	Belfast	0	0
1968	Wrexham	2	0
1969	Belfast	0	0
1970	Swansea	1	0

* The year is the last year of the season, i.e. 1959 means season 1958-9.

‡ Victory international.

Rules

By a law drawn up in 1921, every goalkeeper appearing in an International Championship game has to wear a jersey of deep yellow.

It has been agreed that any National Association wishing to utilise the services of a Football League player for an international match must insure the players' club against permanent total disablement in an amount of not less than £25,000.

Football League clubs still retain the right to refuse to release players for international matches to any National Association except the F.A.

Scotland

Scotland has won the International Championship outright 22 times including a run of five Championships in six seasons from 1920 to 1926.

The 1920s were halcyon years for Scottish international football when such great players as goalkeeper W. Harper; full-backs W. McStay and D. Meiklejohn; wing-half J. McMullan and outside-left A. Morton were at the peak of their careers.

v. *England*. Played 87, won 35, lost 30, drawn 22. Biggest win: 7—2 at Old Hampden, Mar. 2, 1878. Biggest defeat: 3—9 at Wembley, April 15, 1961.

v. *Ireland*. Played 75, won 54, lost 10, drawn 11. Biggest win: 11—0 at Hampden Park, Feb. 23, 1901. Biggest defeat: 0—2 at Hampden Park, Mar. 21, 1903, and also at Belfast, Oct. 4, 1947.

v. *Wales*. Played 83, won 50, lost 15, drawn 18. Biggest win: 9—0 at Old Hampden, Mar. 23, 1878. Biggest defeat: 2—5 at Edinburgh, Oct. 26, 1932.

Scotland's first defeat by a foreign country took place on May 16, 1932, at Vienna when Austria won 5—0.

The record number of Anglo-Scots in a Scottish international team is nine, when Scotland played England on April 6, 1907. The Scotland team on that occasion was: McBride (Preston North End); Thomson (Hearts), Sharp (Woolwich Arsenal); Aitken (Middlesbrough), Raisbeck (Liverpool), McWilliam (Newcastle United); Stewart (Manchester City), Walker (Hearts), A. Wilson (Sheffield Wednesday), White (Bolton Wanderers) and G. Wilson (Everton).

Substitutes

These were not allowed until 1966 when it was decided to permit substitute goalkeepers only in International Championship matches, but at Wrexham in 1908, L. R. Roose was injured playing for Wales against England and the F.A. consented to D. Davies of Bolton Wanderers appearing in goal for Wales in the second half.

See also under separate section—SUBSTITUTES.

Third Division

Only three players from the Third Division have played for England in the International Championship since World War II: T. Lawton, who was with Notts County when he played centre-forward against Scotland at Hampden Park, April 10, 1948; R. Matthews of Coventry City, played in goal v. Scotland, at Hampden Park, April 14, 1956, and v. Ireland at Windsor Park, Oct. 6, 1956; and J. Byrne of Crystal Palace, inside-right v. Ireland, at Wembley, Nov. 22, 1961.

While still in the Third Division Lawton also played against Sweden, Italy and Denmark; and Matthews played against Brazil, Sweden and Germany.

Wales

The outstanding period in the history of Welsh international football was in the 1930s. From 1932 to 1934 a great Welsh side won the Championship two seasons running being undefeated throughout the two seasons.

The following players represented Wales during that time:

Goal: R. John (Stoke City), L. Evans (Birmingham).

Full backs: B. Williams (Everton), B. Ellis (Motherwell), R. John (Arsenal), S. Lawrence (Swansea Town), D. Jones (Leicester City).

Half-backs: J. Murphy (West Bromwich Albion), F. Keenor (Crewe Alexandra), A. Day (Tottenham Hotspur), T. Griffiths (Bolton Wanderers and Middlesbrough), H. Hanford (Swansea Town), D. Richards (Wolverhampton Wanderers).

Forwards: F. Warren (Middlesbrough), C. Phillips (Wolverhampton Wanderers), W. Richards (Fulham), E. O'Callaghan (Tottenham Hotspur), D.

Astley (Aston Villa), E. Glover (Grimsby Town), W. Robbins (West Bromwich Albion), T. Mills (Clapton Orient), D. Lewis (Swansea Town), W. Evans (Tottenham Hotspur), E. Curtis (Birmingham).

The highest individual scorer in a single Championship match for Wales since World War I is M. Charles (Cardiff City), 4 goals v. Ireland at Cardiff, April 11, 1962.

v. *England*. Played 80, won 11, lost 53, drawn 16. Biggest win: 5—3 at Wrexham, Mar. 13, 1882. Biggest defeat: 1—9 at Cardiff, Mar. 16, 1896.

v. *Ireland*. Played 77, won 37, lost 23, drawn 17. Biggest win: 11—0 at Wrexham, Mar. 3, 1888. Biggest defeat: 0—7 at Belfast, Feb. 1, 1930.

v. *Scotland*. Played 83, won 15, lost 50, drawn 18. Biggest win: 5—2 at Edinburgh, Oct. 26, 1932. Biggest defeat: 0—9 at Glasgow, Mar. 23, 1878.

Wales won the International Championship outright in 1906-7, 1919-20, 1923-4, 1927-8, 1932-3, 1933-4, 1936-7

IPSWICH TOWN F.C.

Founded 1880. Adopted professionalism, 1936. Elected to Football League, Division III(S), 1938. Honours: Champions, Division I, 1961-2. Champions, Division II, 1960-1, 1967-8. Champions, Division III(S), 1953-4, 1956-7. Record attendance: 30,837 v. Manchester United, Division 1, Feb. 1, 1969. Address: Portman Road, Ipswich (Tel. 51306). Colours: Royal blue shirts, white shorts. Record League goal-scorer: E. Phillips, 41 goals. Division III(S), 1956-7. Record victory: 7—0 v. Portsmouth, Division II, Nov. 7, 1964. Record defeat: 10—1 v. Fulham, Division I, Dec. 26th, 1963.

IRELAND

See under IRISH FOOTBALL ASSOCIATION, IRISH FOOTBALL ASSOCIATION CUP, IRISH LEAGUE, INTERNATIONALS (IRELAND) and (RESULTS).

The oldest club in Ireland is Cliftonville formed in 1879 by Mr. J. M. McAlery who introduced the game into Ireland and also formed the Irish F.A. (q.v.).

Cliftonville played their first match on the ground of the local cricket club on Oct. 11, 1879, but, sad to relate, these enterprising sportsmen were defeated 2—1 by a team consisting largely of rugby players.

Other clubs formed almost immediately after Cliftonville included Banbridge Academy, Ulster, Ardee, Knock, Portland and Moyola Park, but none of these has maintained a continuous existence as a senior club.

IRELAND, FOOTBALL ASSOCIATION OF

See EIRE.

IRISH FOOTBALL ASSOCIATON

The "father" of Association Football in Ireland was Mr. J. M. McAlery, a keen Belfast sportsman. He was so impressed by what he saw of the game on a visit to Scotland in 1877 that he determined to introduce it to his home town.

After calling a meeting of other sporting personalities, Mr. McAlery wrote to Mr. J. Allen, the honorary secretary of Glasgow Caledonian F.C., with an invitation to him to stage an exhibition match in Belfast.

Mr. Allen liked the idea and contacted the neighbouring Queen's Park Club asking them to provide the opposition for such a game.

Association Football came to Ireland on Oct. 24, 1878, when, on the ground of the Ulster Cricket Club, Belfast, Queen's Park defeated Caledonian F.C. by three goals to two.

Soon after this, another Scottish club, Lenzie F.C., visited Ireland and met the newly formed Ulster F.C.

These games were sufficient to arouse enthusiasm for the dribbling code, and despite the strength of the established Rugby game, Soccer clubs began to form in Ireland.

In 1880 Mr. McAlery called meetings to organise the formation of an Irish F.A. and this was estabished Nov. 18 of that year. Mr. McAlery was made the first Honorary Secretary of the Association, and the first President was Major (afterwards Lord) Spencer Chichester.

The Association became a limited company in 1909. Three years later such serious disputes arose between this governing body and a large number of the senior clubs that the Association's authority and existence was threatened. Agreement, however, was reached and differences settled before the final break was made a few years later.

This break came in 1921 when clubs in the South of Ireland formed what was then known as the Irish Free State F.A. (For more details of this and other matters which concern both the Belfast and Dublin Associations, see EIRE).

When the country was split politically in 1923, a meeting of the four home Associations was held at Liverpool. The I.F.S.A. received official recognition, and it was agreed that the Irish F.A.'s jurisdiction should be restricted to Northern Ireland. The Irish F.A. (Northern Ireland), however, is the only one of the two Irish Associations to be a member of the International Board and take part in the International Championship.

The address of the Irish F.A. is Windsor Avenue, Belfast. Colours: Green shirts, white shorts.

IRISH FOOTBALL ASSOCIATION CUP

This trophy was purchased for £55 18s. 6d. and put up for competition for the first time in 1880 when seven clubs took part after paying an entrance fee of 10s. each. Those seven clubs were Alexander (Limavady), Avoniel, Cliftonville, Distillery, Knock, Oldpark, and Moyola Park, and the latter became the first winners defeating Cliftonville 1—0.

Linfield are by the far the most successful club, winning the trophy on 30 occasions. Next comes Distillery with 11 wins. Linfield also hold the record for the highest score in the Cup Final, 10—1 v. Bohemians, 1895.

No Final tie was played in season 1911-12 because of the football split in the country at that time, but the Cup was awarded to Linfield. Similarly there was no Final in season 1919-20 when it was decided not to play the game because of the riots at

the replayed semi-final tie between Belfast Celtic and Glentoran on the Cliftonville ground. Shelbourne, who had qualified for the Final, were awarded the trophy.

IRISH INTERNATIONALS
See INTERNATIONALS (IRELAND), APPEARANCES (INTERNATIONAL).

IRISH LEAGUE
Eight clubs formed the Irish League in 1890. They were Clarence, Cliftonville, Distillery, Glentoran, Linfield, Milford, Old Park and Ulster. The first President was Mr. McNiece of Cliftonville.

In 1911-12 season the Belfast clubs withdrew their reserve teams from the Irish Junior League after a dispute with the F.A. and formed a Second Division of the Irish League as well as instituting the Irish Gold Cup competition.

At the end of the 1920-21 season the Southern clubs, Shelbourne and the Bohemians, broke away from the Irish League and together with other clubs in the South formed their own Association and League.

The Irish League has enjoyed a continuous existence since its inaugural season of 1890-91 with the exception of three seasons during World War I when it was suspended and substituted by the Belfast League competition, and during the second World War from season 1940-41 to 1946-7 inclusive when the competition was known as the Northern Ireland Regional League.

ISRAEL
The Israel F.A.—Hitachdut Lekadrugel Beisrael—was founded in 1928 and now has a membership of more than 80 clubs, all amateur.

The address of the Israel F.A. is P.O. Box 88, Tel-Aviv. Colours: White shirts with blue collars, blue shorts.

Israel first appeared in the World Cup Final Tourament in 1970 but finished bottom of their group.

Results of international matches:

Jan. 15, 1958*	Israel 0, Wales 2;	Tel-Aviv.
Feb. 5, 1958*	Wales 2, Israel 0;	Cardiff.
May 16, 1967	Israel 1, Scotland 2;	Tel-Aviv.
Sept. 10, 1968	Israel 2, Ireland 3;	Tel-Aviv.

* World Cup.

ITALY

Italian footballers are among the highest-paid players in the world. Such are the wages that the Italian clubs attract many stars from foreign countries, and, in all, over 300 overseas players have signed for Italian clubs since World War II.

Many of the leading clubs are sponsored by wealthy industrialists who appear to have unlimited supplies of money for the purchase of star players and the payment of top bonuses.

On the other hand, however, as these wealthy club presidents are prepared to pay so well to get the best they are less tolerant of sub-standard performances, and the constant striving to satisfy their masters means that Italian professionals must be exceptionally dedicated to the game and prepared to work and play under a strict disciplinary code.

The Italians won the World Cup in 1934 when the competition was held in their country, and, two years later, they won the soccer tournament of the Olympic Games in Berlin. They confirmed their supremacy in 1938 by retaining the World Cup, defeating Hungary 4—2 in the Final.

At international level Italy went through a bad spell after World War II. Their failure to qualify for the World Cup in 1958 caused quite a commotion, and their defensive complex showed up in the 1962 and 1966 tournaments. The side returned home in disgrace after a 1—0 defeat by North Korea in 1966.

Lost prestige was restored in 1970 when they reached the Final before losing 4—1 to Brazil, but their defensive complex still showed through and they have yet to recapture the all-round brilliance of pre-war days when they produced such grand attackers as Meazza, Piola, Ferrari and Schiavio.

The Italian F.A. was formed in 1898, and today it has a membership of over 5,000 clubs. The oldest of these is Genoa, formed in 1893.

The address of the governing body is: Federazione Italiana Giuoco Calcio, Via Gregorio Allegri 14, Roma
Colours: Blue shirts, white shorts.

Results of international matches:

Mar. 21, 1926	Italy 3, Eire 0; Turin.
May 20, 1931	Italy 3, Scotland 0; Rome.
May 13, 1933	Italy 1, England 1; Rome.
Nov. 14, 1934	England 3, Italy 2; Highbury.
May 13, 1939	Italy 2, England 2; Milan.
May 16, 1948	Italy 0, England 4; Turin.
Nov. 30, 1949	England 2, Italy 0; Tottenham.
May 18, 1952	Italy 1, England 1; Florence.
April 25, 1957*	Italy 1, Ireland 0; Rome.
Dec. 4, 1957	Ireland 2, Italy 2; Belfast
Jan. 15, 1958*	Ireland 2, Italy 1; Belfast.
May 6, 1959	England 2, Italy 2; Wembley.
April 25, 1961	Italy 3, Ireland 2; Bologna.
May 24, 1961	Italy 2, England 3; Rome.
May 1, 1965	Italy 4, Wales 1; Florence
Nov. 9, 1965*	Scotland 1, Italy 0; Hampden Park
Dec. 7, 1965*	Italy 3, Scotland 0; Naples
Oct. 23, 1968*	Wales 0, Italy 1; Cardiff
Nov. 4, 1969*	Italy 4, Wales 1; Rome

* World Cup.

K

KICKING

See GOAL-SCORING (INDIVIDUALS), Long-distance goals; GOALKEEPERS (GOAL-SCORING).

R. Whiting, a 6ft. goalkeeper who played with Chelsea and Brighton immediately before World War I, could kick a ball from his goal-line over the bar of the goal at the other end.

KILMARNOCK F.C.

Founded 1869. The club originally played rugby (hence the name of their ground) but when rugby fixtures became difficult to arrange the club changed to soccer. Became a limited company in 1906. Honours: Champions, Division I, 1964-5. Runners-up, Division I, 1959-60, 1960-1, 1962-3, 1963-4, Champions Division II, 1898, 1899. Runners-up (B), 1953-4. Scottish Cup: Finalists, 1898, 1932, 1957, 1960. Record attendance: 33,545 v. Rangers, Scottish Cup, 2nd Round (replay), Feb. 17, 1954. Address: Rugby Park, Kilmarnock (Tel. 25184). Nickname: Killies. Colours: Blue and white striped shirts, white shorts. Record League goal-scorer: H. Cunningham, 35 goals, Division I, 1927-8. Record victory: 11—1 v. Paisley Academicals, Scottish Cup, 1st Round, Jan. 18, 1930. Record defeat: 8—0 v. Hibernian, Division I, 1925-6, and v. Rangers, Division I, 1936-7.

L

LAW, THE, and FOOTBALL

The validity of the Football League's retain and transfer system was put to the test in law in 1912 when L. J. Kingaby and the Players' Union brought an action against Aston Villa.

Details of this case appear under the heading TRANSFERS, but the outcome of it was that the League's regulations were upheld.

In 1963, however, when G. Eastham brought a case against his old club, Newcastle United, the F.A., and the Football League, he was successful in so far as a declaration was made to the effect that the system of retaining a player after the expiration of his contract was not binding in law.

Since then, of course, certain alterations and additions have been made to the wording of players' contracts, but the system remains very much the same.

LAWS OF THE GAME

Football of sorts was played at the public schools as long ago as the middle of the 18th century. Each school, however, had its own rules and these often varied considerably from school to school. None bore much resemblance to the modern game.

It is generally considered that it was at Cambridge University that the first code of rules was compiled which closely resembles that we know today.

The date of these first rules is believed to be 1848. But although the existence of these rules has been definitely established, no copy of them has ever been traced.

Enough of them is known, however, to judge that the major differences between them and the original Football Association rules, published in 1863, were that at Cambridge handling was permitted to a greater degree, and the offside rule was more severely applied.

The earliest set of Cambridge University rules still in existence is dated 1856 and the reference to handling the ball and to "offside" make interesting reading:

"When a player catches the ball directly from the foot, he may kick it as he can without running with it. In no other case may the ball be touched with the hands, except to stop it.

"If the ball has passed a player and has come from the direction of his goal, he may not touch it till the other side have kicked it, unless there are more than three of the other side before him. No player is allowed to loiter between the ball and the adversaries' goal."

Another of the earliest set of rules, details of which have been traced, were those drawn up by a master at Uppingham School, Mr. J. C. Thring. They are dated June 1862, and are worth a close examination:

1. A goal is scored whenever the ball is forced through the goal and under the bar, except it be thrown by the hand.

2. Hands may be used only to stop the ball and place it on the ground before the feet.

3. Kicks must be aimed only at the ball.

4. A player may not kick the ball whilst in the air.

5. No tripping up or heel kicking is allowed.

6. Whenever a ball is kicked beyond the side-flags, it must be returned by the player who kicked it, from the spot it passed the flag-line in a straight line towards the middle of the ground.

7. When a ball is kicked behind the line of goal, it shall be kicked off from that line by one of the side whose goal it is.

8. No player may stand within six paces of the kicker when he is kicking off.

9. A player is "out of play" immediately he is in front of the ball, and must return behind the ball as soon as possible. If the ball is kicked by his own side past a player, he may not touch it, kick it, or advance, until one of the other side has first kicked it, or one of his own side, having followed up, has been able, when in front of him, to kick it.

10. No charging allowed when a player is out of play, i.e. immediately the ball is behind him.

Clubs other than those drawn from the public schools became more numerous about this time, and each had their own code of rules. A further effort was made at Cambridge to draw up a uniform code of rules more acceptable to all clubs. The result of this effort was published in Oct. 1863:

1. The length of the ground should not be more than 150yd. and the breadth not more than 100yd. The ground shall be marked out by posts, and two posts shall be placed on each side line, at distance 25yd. from each goal-line.

2. The goals shall consist of two upright poles at a distance of 15ft. from each other.

3. The choice of goals and kick-off shall be determined by tossing, and the ball shall be kicked off from the middle of the ground.

4 In a match, when half the time agreed upon has elapsed, the sides shall change goals when the ball is next out of play. After a change or a goal obtained, the kick-off shall be from the middle of the ground in the same direction as before. The time during which the match shall last, and the number on each side, are settled by the heads of the sides.

5. When a player has kicked the ball, any one of the same side who is nearer to the opponents' goal-line is out of play, and may not touch the ball himself, nor in any way whatsoever prevent any other player from doing so.

6. When the ball goes out of the ground by crossing the side lines, it is out of play, and shall be kicked straight into the ground again from the point where it first stopped.

7. When a player has kicked the ball beyond the opponents' goal-line, whoever first touches the ball when it is on the ground with his hand may have a free-kick, bringing the ball 25yd. straight out from the goal-line.

8. No player may touch the ball behind his opponent's goal-line, who is behind it when the ball is kicked there.

9. If the ball is touched down behind the goal-line and beyond the line of the side posts, the free-kick shall be from the 25yd. post.

10. When a player has a free-kick no one of his own side may be between him and his opponents' goal-line, and no one of the opposite side may stand within 10yd. of him.

11. A free-kick may be taken in any manner the player may choose.

12. A goal is obtained when the ball goes out of the ground by passing between the poles, or in such a manner that it would have passed between them had they been of sufficient height.

13. The ball when in play may be stopped by any part of the body, but may not be held or hit by the hands, arms or shoulders.

14. All charging is fair; but holding, pushing with the hands, tripping up and shinning are forbidden.

These rules were published about the time the Football Association was holding its inaugural meeting and drafting its own rules for the game.

There is no doubt it was greatly influenced by the Cambridge rules, but the fact that these rules did not permit "hacking", nor handling the ball while in play, caused much argument in the newly-formed Association. Although there was a majority vote in favour of the ban on "hacking" the F.A. did not feel inclined to dispense entirely with the use of the hands.

It was not without more than one resignation that the F.A. rules were eventually agreed upon and published in Dec. 1863. Here they are:

1. The maximum length of the ground shall be 200yd.; the maximum breadth shall be 100yd.; the length and breadth shall be marked off with flags; and the goals shall be defined

by two upright posts, 8yd. apart, without any tape or bar across them.

2. The winners of the toss shall have the choice of goals. The game shall be commenced by a place-kick from the centre of the ground by the side losing toss. The other side shall not approach within 10yd. of the ball until it is kicked off.

3. After a goal is won, the losing side shall kick off, and goals shall be changed.

4. A goal shall be won when the ball passes between the posts or over the space between the posts (at whatever height), not being thrown, knocked on, or carried.

5. When the ball is in touch, the first player who touches it shall throw it from the point on the boundary-line where it left the ground in a direction at right angles with the boundary-line, and it shall not be in play until it has touched the ground.

6. When a player has kicked the ball, any one of the same side who is nearer the opponents' goal-line is out of play, and may not touch the ball himself nor in any way whatever prevent any other player from doing so until the ball has been played; but no player is out of play when the ball is kicked from behind the goal-line.

7. In case the ball goes behind the goal-line, if a player on the same side to whom the goal belongs first touches the ball, one of his side shall be entitled to a free-kick from the goal-line at the point opposite the place where the ball shall be touched. If a player of the opposite side first touches the ball, one of his side shall be entitled to a free-kick (but at the goal only) from a point 15yd. from the goal-line opposite the place where the ball is touched; the opposing side shall stand behind the goal-line until he has had his kick.

8. If a player makes a fair catch,* he shall be entitled to a free-kick, provided he claims it by making a mark with his heel at once; and in order to take such a kick he may go as far back as he pleases, and no player on the opposite side shall advance beyond his mark until he has kicked.

9. No player shall carry the ball.

10. Neither tripping nor hacking shall be allowed, and no player shall use his hands to hold or push an adversary.

11. A player shall not throw the ball or pass it to another.

12. No player shall take the ball from the ground with his hands while it is in play under any pretence whatever.

13. A player shall be allowed to throw the ball or pass it to another if he made a fair catch or catches the ball on the first bounce.

14. No player shall be allowed to wear projecting nails, iron plates or gutta percha on the soles or heels of his boots.

For the sake of brevity and easy reference the principal alterations in the Laws of the Game from the original F.A. laws, are set out below in chronological order:

1865: Tape to be stretched across the goals 6ft. from the ground.

1866: Offside rule altered to allow a player to be onside when three of the opposing team are nearer their own goal-line.

1866: Fair catch rule omitted.

Kick-out rule altered and goal-kicks introduced.

1871: Goalkeepers mentioned in the laws for the first time.

1872: Corner kick adopted.

1874: Umpires first mentioned.

1875: Tapes may be replaced by crossbar.

1877: The London Association and the Sheffield Association agreed to use the same rules.

A player may be charged if he is facing his own goal.

1881: Referees mentioned. The referee was empowered to give a goal against a player who handled in attempting to prevent the ball crossing the goal-line.

1882: Handling rule of 1881 rescinded.

Two-handed throw-in introduced.

1883: The four home countries' F.A.s agreed on uniform set of rules.

1890: Penalty-kick introduced after suggestion of the Irish F.A.

* A Fair Catch is when the ball is caught after it has touched the person of an adversary, or has been kicked or knocked on by an adversary, and before it has touched the ground or one of the side catching it; but if the ball is kicked from behind the goal-line, a fair catch cannot be made.

1891: Linesmen replaced umpires.

1892: Penalty kicker must not play ball twice.

Extra time allowed for taking of penalty.

1894: Referee given complete control of the game. No longer necessary for players to appeal to him for a decision.

Goalkeeper could only be charged when "playing the ball or obstructing opponent".

1895: Goalposts and crossbars must not exceed 5in. in width.

Player taking throw-in must stand on touch-line. (No run-up.)

1897: The word "intentional" introduced into the law on handling.

1912: Goalkeeper not permitted to handle the ball outside his own penalty area.

1913: Opposing players not to approach within 10yd. (instead of 6yd.) of ball when free-kick is being taken.

1914: Above alteration applied to corner kicks.

1920: Players cannot be offside at a throw-in.

1924: Goal may be scored direct from a corner kick.

1925: Following proposal of the Scottish F.A., the offside rule was changed so that a player could not be offside when two opponents instead of three were between himself and the opposing goal-line.

Player taking throw-in must have both feet on the touch-line.

1929: Goalkeeper compelled to stand still on his goal-line when penalty-kick is being taken.

1931: Goalkeeper permitted to carry ball four steps instead of two.

Instead of a free-kick for foul throw-in, reverts to opposing side.

1936: Defending players no longer permitted to tap ball into goalkeeper's hands when goal-kick is being taken.

1937: Defending player no longer permitted to tap ball into goalkeeper's hands when a free-kick is being taken inside the penalty area.

Weight of ball increased from 13-15oz. to 14-16oz.

Arc of circle 10yd. radius from penalty spot to be drawn outside the penalty area.

1951: Obstruction included as one of the offences punishable by an indirect free-kick.

Studs may project three-quarters of an inch instead of half an inch.

1954: Ball shall not be changed during the game unless authorised by the Referee.

The Laws of the Game as they stand in 1970 are as follows:

Law 1. The Field of Play

(1) *Dimensions.* The field of play shall be rectangular, its length being not more than 130yd. nor less than 100yd., and its breadth not more than 100yd nor less than 50yd. (In international matches the length shall not be more than 120yd. nor less than 110yd., and the breadth not more than 80yd. nor less than 70yd.) The length shall in all cases exceed the breadth.

(2) *Marking.* The field of play shall be marked with distinctive lines, not more than 5in. in width, not by a V-shaped rut, in accordance with the plan, the longer boundary line being called the touch-lines and the shorter the goal-lines.

A flag on a post not less than 5ft. high and having a non-pointed top, shall be placed at each corner, a similar flag-post may be placed opposite the half-way line on each side of the field of play, not less than one yard outside the touch-line. A half-way line shall be marked out across the field of play. The centre of the field of play shall be indicated by a suitable mark and a circle of 10yd radius shall be marked round it.

(3) *The Goal Area.* At each end of the field of play two lines shall be drawn at right angles to the goal-line, 6yd. from each goal-post. These shall extend into the field of play for a distance of 6yd. and shall be joined by a line drawn parallel with the goal-line. Each of the spaces enclosed by these lines and the goal-line shall be called a goal area.

(4) *The Penalty Area.* At each end of the field of play two lines shall be drawn at right angles to the goal-line, 18yd. from each goal-post. These shall extend into the field of play for a distance of 18yd. and shall be joined by a line drawn parallel with the goal-line. Each of the spaces enclosed by these lines and the goal-line shall be called a penalty area A suitable mark shall be made within each penalty

area, 12yd. from the mid-point of the goal-line, measured along an undrawn line at right angles thereto. These shall be the penalty kick marks. From each penalty kick mark an arc of a circle, having a radius of 10yd. shall be drawn outside the penalty area.

(5) *Corner Area.* From each corner flag-post a quarter circle having a radius of 1yd., shall be drawn inside the field of play.

(6) *The Goals.* The goals shall be placed on the centre of each goal-line and shall consist of two upright posts, equidistant from the corner flags and 8yd. apart (inside measurement), joined by a horizontal crossbar, the lower edge of which shall be 8ft. from the ground. The width and depth of the goal-posts and the width and depth of the crossbars shall not exceed 5in. The goal-posts and the crossbars shall have the same width.

Nets may be attached to the posts, crossbars and ground behind the goals. They should be appropriately supported and be so placed as to allow the goalkeeper ample room.

Law 2. The Ball

The ball shall be spherical; the outer casing shall be leather or other approved materials. No material shall be used in its construction which might prove dangerous to the players. The circumference of the ball shall not be more than 28in. nor less than 27in. The weight of the ball at the start of the game shall not be more than 16oz. no less than 14oz. The pressure shall be equal to atmospheric pressure (15lb. per sq. in. i.e. 1 kg. per sq. cm.) at sea level. The ball shall not be changed during the game unless authorised by the Referee.

Law 3. Number of Players

(1) A game shall be played by two teams, each consisting of not more than eleven players, one of whom shall be the goalkeeper.

(2) Substitutes, up to a maximum of two per team, are permitted in a friendly match and also, provided that the authority of the International Association(s) or National Association(s) concerned, has been obtained, in a match played under the rules of of a competition. The Referee shall be informed of the names of the sub-stitutes (if any) before the start of the match.

(3) One of the other players, or a named substitute (if allowed) may change places with the goalkeeper, provided that notice is given to the Referee before the change is made.

Punishment. If, without the Referee being notified, a player, or a named substitute, changes places with the goalkeeper during the game, at the half-time interval, or at any other interval in a game in which extra time is played and then handles the ball within the penalty area, a penalty kick shall be awarded.

Law 4. Player's Equipment

A player shall not wear anything which is dangerous to another player. Boots must conform to the following standard : (a) Bars shall be made of leather or rubber and shall be transverse and flat, not less than half an inch in width and they shall extend the total width of the boot and be rounded at the corners. (b) Studs shall be made of leather, rubber, aluminium, plastic or similar material and shall be solid and not less than half an inch in diameter. With the exception of that part of the stud forming the base, which shall not protrude from the sole more than one quarter of an inch, studs shall be round in plan. Where studs are tapered the minimum diameter of any section of a stud must not be less than half an inch. Where metal seating for a screw type is used, this seating must be embedded in the sole of the boot and any attachment screw shall be part of the stud. Other than the metal seating for the screw type of stud, no metal plates, even though covered with leather or rubber shall be worn; neither studs which are threaded to allow them to be screwed on to a base screw that is fixed by nails or otherwise to the soles of boots, nor studs with any form of protruding edge, rim, or relief marking or ornament shall be allowed. (c) Combined bars and studs may be worn, provided the whole conforms to the general requirements of this law; neither bars nor studs on the soles or heels shall project more than three-quarters of an inch. If nails are used they shall be driven in flush with the surface.

(N.B.—The usual equipment of a

player consists of a jersey or shirt, shorts, stockings and boots. A goalkeeper shall wear colours which distinguish him from the other players.)

Punishment. For any infringement of this Law, the player at fault shall be sent off the field of play to adjust his equipment and he shall not return without first reporting to the Referee. who shall satisfy himself that the player's equipment is in order; the player shall only re-enter the game at a moment when the ball has ceased to be in play.

Law 5. Referees

A referee shall be appointed to officiate in each game. He shall:

(a) Enforce the Laws and decide any disputed point. His decision on points of fact connected with the play shall be final so far as the result of the game is concerned. His jurisdiction begins from the time he signals for the kick-off, and his power of penalising shall extend to offences committed when play has been temporarily suspended or when the ball is out of play. He shall, however, refrain from penalising in cases, where he is satisfied that by doing so he would be giving an advantage to the offending team.

(b) Keep a record of the game, act as timekeeper and allow the full or agreed time, adding there to all time lost through accident or other cause.

(c) Have discretionary power to stop the game for any infringement of the Laws and to suspend or terminate the game whenever, by reason of the elements, interference by spectators or other cause, he deems such stoppage necessary. In such a case he shall report the matter to the National or Affiliated Association under whose jurisdiction the game was played, within two days (Sundays not included). Reports will be deemed to be made when received in the ordinary course of post.

(d) Have discretionary power from the time he enters the field of play, to caution the player guilty of misconduct or ungentlemanly behaviour and, if he persists, to suspend him from further participation in the game. In such cases the Referee shall send the name of the offender to the National or Affiliated Association concerned, within two days after the occurrence (Sundays not included). Reports will be deemed to be made when received in the ordinary course of post.

(e) Allow no person other than the players and linesmen to enter the field of play without his permission.

(f) Stop the game if, in his opinion, a player has been seriously injured, have the player removed as soon as possible from the field of play, and immediately resume the game. If a player is slightly injured, the game shall not be stopped until the ball has ceased to be in play. A player who is able to go to the touch or goalline for attention of any kind, shall not be treated on the field of play.

(g) Have discretionary powers to suspend from further participation in the game, without previous caution, a player guilty of violent conduct.

(h) Signal for recommencement of the game after all stoppages.

(i) Decide that the ball provided for a match meets the requirements of Law 2.

Law 6. Linesmen

Two linesmen shall be appointed whose duty (subject to the decision of the Referee) shall be to indicate when the ball is out of play and which side is entitled to the corner kick, a goalkick or throw-in. They shall also assist the Referee to control the game in accordance with the Laws. In the event of undue interference or improper conduct by a linesman, the Referee shall dispense with his services and arrange for a substitute to be appointed. (The matter shall be reported by the Referee to the National or Affiliated Association having jurisdiction over the offending linesman.) The linesmen should be equipped with flags by the club on whose ground the match is played.

Law 7. Duration of Game

The duration of the game shall be

two equal periods of 45min., unless otherwise mutually agreed upon, subject to the following: (a) Allowance shall be made in either period for all time lost through accident or other cause, the amount of which shall be a matter for the discretion of the Referee. (b) Time shall be extended to permit of a penalty kick being taken at or after the expiration of the normal period in either half.

At half time the interval shall not exceed five minutes, except by the consent of the Referee.

Law 8. The Start of Play

(a) *At the beginning of the game,* choice of ends and the kick-off shall be decided by the toss of a coin. The team winning the toss shall have the option of choice of ends or the kick-off.

The Referee, having given the signal, the game shall be started by a player taking a place-kick (i.e. a kick at the ball while it is stationary on the ground in the centre of the field of play) into his opponents' half of the field of play. Every player shall be in his own half of the field and every player of the team opposing that of the kicker shall remain not less than 10yd. from the ball until it has been kicked off: it shall not be deemed in play until it has travelled the distance of its own circumference. The kicker shall not play the ball a second time until it has been played or touched by another player.

(b) *After a goal has been scored,* the game shall be re-started in like manner by a player of the team losing the goal.

(c) *After half time;* when re-starting after half time, ends shall be changed and the kick-off shall be taken by a player of the opposite team to that of the player who started the game.

Punishment. For any infringement of this Law, the kick-off shall be re-taken, except in the case of the kicker playing the ball again before it has been touched or played by another player; for this offence, an indirect free-kick shall be taken by a player of the opposing team from the place where the infringement occurred. A goal shall not be scored direct from a kick-off.

(d) *After any temporary suspension;* when re-starting the game after a temporary suspension of play from any cause not mentioned elsewhere in these Laws, provided that immediately prior to the suspension the ball has not passed over the touch or goal-lines, the Referee shall drop the ball at the place where it was when play was suspended and it shall be deemed in play when it has touched the ground, if, however, it goes over the touch or goal-lines after it has been dropped by the Referee, but before it is touched by a player, the Referee shall again drop it. A player shall not play the ball until it has touched the ground. If this section of the Law is not complied with, the Referee shall again drop the ball.

Law 9. Ball In and Out of Play

The ball is out of play:
(a) When it has wholly crossed the goal-line or touch-line, whether on the ground or in the air.
(b) When the game has been stopped by the Referee.

The ball is in play at all other times from the start of the match to the finish, including:
(a) If it rebounds from a goal-post, crossbar or corner flagpost into the field of play.
(b) It rebounds off either the Referee or Linesmen when they are in the field of play.
(c) In the event of a supposed infringement of the Laws, until a decision is given.

Law 10. Method of Scoring

Except as otherwise provided in these Laws, a goal is scored when the whole of the ball has passed over the goal-line, between the goal-posts and under the crossbar, provided it has not been thrown, carried or propelled by hand or arm, by a player of the attacking side except in the case of a goalkeeper, who is within his own penalty area. Should the crossbar become displaced for any reason during the game, and the ball crosses the goal-line at a point which, in the opinion of the Referee, is below where the crossbar should have been, he shall award a goal.

The team scoring the greater number of goals during the game shall be the winner, if no goals, or an equal number of goals are scored the game shall be termed a "draw".

Law 11. Offside

A player is offside if he is nearer his opponents' goal-line than the ball at the moment the ball is played unless:
(a) He is in his own half of the field of play.
(b) There are two of his opponents nearer to their own goal-line than he is.
(c) The ball last touched an opponent or was last played by him.
(d) He received the ball direct from a goal-kick, a corner kick, a throw-in, or when it is dropped by the Referee.

Punishment. For an infringement of this Law, an indirect free-kick shall be taken by a player of the opposing team, from the place where the infringement occurred.

A player in an offside position shall not be penalised unless, in the opinion of the Referee he is interfering with the play or with an opponent, or is seeking to gain an advantage by being in an offside position.

Law 12. Fouls and Misconduct

A player who intentionally commits any of the following nine offences:
(a) Kicks or attempts to kick an opponent;
(b) Trips an opponent, i.e., throwing or attempting to throw him by the use of the legs, or by stooping in front of or behind him;
(c) Jumps at an opponent;
(d) Charges an opponent in a violent or dangerous manner;
(e) Charges an opponent from behind unless the latter be obstructing;
(f) Strikes or attempts to strike an opponent;
(g) Holds an opponent with his hand or any part of his arm;
(h) Pushes an opponent with his hand or any part of his arm;
(i) Handles the ball, i.e. carries, strikes or propels the ball with his hand or arm (this does not apply to the goalkeeper within his own penalty area);
shall be penalised by the award of a DIRECT FREE-KICK to be taken by the opposing side from the place where the offence occurred.

Should a player of the defending side intentionally commit one of the above nine offences within the penalty area he shall be penalised by a PENALTY KICK.

A penalty kick can be awarded irrespective of the position of the ball, if in play, at the time an offence within the penalty area is committed.

A player committing any of the five following offences:
(1) Playing in a manner considered by the Referee to be dangerous, e.g. attempting to kick the ball while held by the goalkeeper;
(2) Charging fairly, i.e. with the shoulder when the ball is not within playing distance of the players concerned and they are definitely not trying to play it;
(3) When not playing the ball, intentionally obstructing an opponent, i.e. running between the opponent and the ball, or interposing the body so as to form an obstacle to an opponent;
(4) Charging the goalkeeper except when he—
  (a) is holding the ball;
  (b) is obstructing an opponent;
  (c) has passed outside his goal-area;
(5)
(a) When playing as goalkeeper takes more than four steps whilst holding, bouncing or throwing the ball in the air and catching it again without releasing it so that it is played by another player, or
(b) indulges in tactics which, in the opinion of the Referee, are designed merely to hold up the game and thus waste time and so give an unfair advantage to his own team
shall be penalised by the award of an INDIRECT FREE-KICK to be taken by the opposing side from the place where the infringement occurred.

A player shall be CAUTIONED if;
(j) He enters the field of play to join or rejoin his team after the game has commenced without first having received a signal from the Referee showing him that he is in order to do so.
If the game has been stopped (to administer the caution) it shall be re-started by the Referee dropping the ball at the place where the infringement occurred, but if the player has committed a more important offence he shall be

penalised according to that section of the Law infringed;

(k) He persistently infringes the Laws of the game;

(l) He shows by word or action, dissent from any decision given by the Referee;

(m) He is guilty of ungentlemanly conduct.

For any of these last three offences, in addition to the caution, an INDIRECT FREE-KICK shall also be awarded to the opposing side from the place where the offence occurred.

A player shall be SENT OFF the field of play if:

(n) In the opinion of the Referee, he is guilty of violent conduct or serious foul play;

(o) He uses foul or abusive language;

(p) He persists in misconduct after having received a caution.

If play be stopped by reason of a player being ordered from the field for an offence without a separate breach of the Law having been committed, the game shall be resumed by an INDIRECT FREE-KICK awarded to the opposing side from the place where the infringement occurred.

Law 13. Free-Kick

Free-kicks shall be classified under two heads:

" Direct " (from which a goal can be scored direct against the offending side), and " Indirect " (from which the goal cannot be scored unless the ball has been played or touched by a player other than the kicker before passing through the goal).

When a player is taking a direct or an indirect free-kick inside his own penalty area, all of the opposing players shall remain outside the area, and shall be at least ten yards from the ball whilst the kick is being taken. The ball shall be in play immediately it has travelled the distance of its own circumference and is beyond the penalty area. The goalkeeper shall not receive the ball into his hands, in order that he may thereafter kick it into play. If the ball is not kicked direct into play, beyond the penalty area the kick shall be retaken.

When a player is taking a direct or an indirect free-kick outside his own penalty area, all of the opposing players shall be at least ten yards from the ball, until it is in play, unless they are standing on their own goal line, between the goalposts. The ball shall be in play when it has travelled the distance of its own circumference.

If a player of the opposing side encroaches into the penalty area, or within ten yards of the ball, as the case may be, before a free-kick is taken, the Referee shall delay the taking of the kick, until the Law is complied with.

The ball must be stationary when a free-kick is taken, and the kicker shall not play the ball a second time, until it has been touched or played by another player.

Punishment. If the kicker, after taking the free-kick, plays the ball a second time before it has been touched or played by another player, an indirect free-kick shall be taken by a player of the opposing team from the spot where the infringement occurred.

Law 14. Penalty Kick

A penalty kick shall be taken from the penalty mark and when it is being taken all players with the exception of the player taking the kick, and the opposing goalkeeper shall be within the field of play, but outside the penalty area, and at least 10yd. from the penalty mark. The opposing goalkeeper must stand (without moving his feet) on his own goal-line, between the goal-posts, until the ball is kicked. The player taking the kick must kick the ball forward; he shall not play the ball a second time until it has been touched or played by another player. The ball shall be deemed in play directly it is kicked, i.e. travelled the distance of its own circumference, and a goal may be scored direct from such a penalty kick. If the ball touches the goalkeeper before passing between the posts, when a penalty kick is being taken at or after the expiration of half time or full time, it does not nullify a goal. If necessary, time of play shall be extended at half time or full time to allow a penalty kick to be taken.

Punishment.

For any infringement.

(a) By the defending team the kick

shall be re-taken, if a goal has not resulted.

(b) By the attacking team other than by the player taking the kick, if a goal is scored, it shall be disallowed and the kick re-taken.

(c) By the player taking the penalty kick, committed after the ball is in play, a player of the opposing team shall take an indirect free-kick from the spot where the infringement occurred.

Law 15. Throw-In

When the whole of the ball passes over the touch-line either on the ground or in the air, it shall be thrown in from the point where it crossed the line, in any direction, by a player of the team opposite to that of the player who last touched it. The thrower at the moment of delivering the ball must face the field of play and part of each foot shall be either on the touch-line or on the ground outside the touch-line. The thrower shall use both hands and shall deliver the ball from behind and over his head. The ball shall be in play immediately it enters the field of play, but the thrower shall not again play the ball until it has been touched or played by another player. A goal shall not be scored direct from a throw-in.

Punishment.

(a) If the ball is improperly thrown in, the throw-in shall be taken by a player of the opposing team.

(b) If the thrower plays the ball a second time before it has been touched or played by another player, an indirect free-kick shall be taken by a player of the opposing team from the place where the infringement occurred.

Law 16. Goal-Kick

When the whole of the ball passes over the goal-line, excluding the portion between the goal-posts, either in the air or on the ground, having last been played by one of the attacking team, it shall be kicked direct into play beyond the penalty area, from a point within that half of the goal area nearest to where it crossed the line, by a player of the defending team. A goalkeeper shall not receive the ball into his hands from a goal-kick in order that he may thereafter kick it into play. If the ball is not kicked beyond the penalty area i.e. direct into play, the kick shall be re-taken. The kicker shall not play the ball a second time until it has touched or been played by another player. A goal shall not be scored direct from such a kick. Players of the team opposing that of the player taking the goal-kick shall remain outside the penalty area whilst the kick is being taken.

Punishment. If a player taking a goal-kick plays the ball a second time after it has passed beyond the penalty area, but before it has touched or been played by another player, an indirect free-kick shall be awarded to the opposing team, to be taken from the place where the infringement occurred.

Law 17. Corner Kick

When the whole of the ball passes over the goal-line, excluding that portion between the goal-posts, either in the air or on the ground, having last been played by one of the defending team, a member of the attacking team shall take a kick from within the quarter circle at the nearest corner flagpost, which must not be moved, i.e. a corner kick. A goal may be scored direct from such a kick. Players of the team opposing that of the player taking the corner kick shall not approach within 10yd. of the ball until it is in play, i.e. it has travelled the distance of its own circumference, nor shall the kicker play the ball a second time until it has been touched or played by another player.

Punishment. For an infringement of this Law, an indirect free-kick shall be awarded to the opposing team, to be taken from the place where the infringement occurred.

The introduction of other rules which may be of some interest were made as follows:

1896: An extra half-hour to be played in all replayed cup ties, if drawing at the end of 90min.

1912: An extra half-hour must be played in the Cup Final if the sides are drawing at full time.

1924: Where colours clash, visitors must change.

1927: Professionals reinstated as amateurs not permitted to play in amateur international matches.

1931: Two years' residential qualification for non-British born subjects registering as professionals in the Football League.

1939: Watering pitches permitted except during November, December, January and February. Players in Football League matches must be numbered.

LEEDS UNITED F.C.

Founded 1920 after Leeds City club was wound up. (Leeds City had been in existence since 1904, and was a member of the Football League, Division II, from 1905.) Leeds United was elected to the Football League, Division II, in 1920. Honours: Champions Division I, 1968-9. Runners-up, 1964-5, 1965-6, 1969-70. Champions, Division II, 1923-4, 1963-4. Runners-up, 1927-8, 1931-2, 1955-6. F.A. Cup: Finalists, 1965, 1970. League Cup Winners, 1968. Fairs Cup: Winners, 1968. Finalists, 1967. Record attendance: 57,892 v. Sunderland, F.A. Cup, 5th Round (replay), Mar. 15, 1967. Cup Final receipts, £128,272 were taken in 1970 for the match, Chelsea v. Leeds United.

Address: Elland Road, Leeds (Tel. 76037). Nickname: Peacocks. Colours: White shirts and shorts. Record League goal-scorer: J. Charles, 42 goals, Division II, 1953-4. Record victory: 8—0 v. Leicester City, Division I, April 7, 1934; (as Leeds City) v. Nottingham Forest, Division II, Nov. 29, 1913. Record defeat: 8—2 v. West Ham United, Division I, Feb. 9, 1929.

LEICESTER CITY F.C.

Founded 1884 by old boys of Wyggeston School and adopted the name Leicester Fosse. Changed to Leicester City, 1919. Elected to Football League, Division II, 1894. Honours: Runners-up, Division I, 1928-9. Champions, Division II, 1924-5, 1936-7, 1953-4, 1956-7. Runners-up, 1907-8. F.A. Cup: Finalists, 1949, 1961, 1963, 1969. F.L. Cup: Winners, 1964. Finalists, 1965. Record attendance: 47,298 v. Tottenham Hotspur, F.A. Cup, 5th Round, Feb. 18, 1928. Address: Filbert Street Ground, Leicester (Tel. 57111). Nickname: Filberts. Colours: Royal blue shirts, white shorts. Record League goal-

scorer: A. Rowley, 44 goals, Division II, 1956-7. Record victory: 10—0 v. Portsmouth, Division I, Oct. 20, 1928. Record defeat: 12—0 (as Leicester Fosse) v. Nottingham Forest, Division I, April 21, 1909.

LIMITED COMPANIES

The first football club to become a Limited Liability Company was Small Heath (now Birmingham City) in 1888.

All of the present members of the Football League are limited companies with the exception of Nottingham Forest.

F.A. regulations applying to club companies restrict the dividend payable in respect of any year to a maximum of 7½%, or in the case of tax free dividends—5%.

Preference shares may be issued with cumulative preference dividend not exceeding £7 10s. per cent for a period not exceeding three years, but the company may not issue more Preference Shares than its subscribed Ordinary Shares.

LINCOLN CITY F.C.

Founded 1883. One of the original members of the Football League, Division II, 1892. Lincoln City failed to gain immediate re-election to the League on three separate occasions, 1908, 1911 and 1920. Each time, however, the club has been out of the League for only one season before regaining admission. On the last occasion (after dropping out of Division II in 1920), the club returned a year later as a member of the newly-formed Division III(N). Honours: Champions, Division III(N), 1931-2, 1947-8, 1951-2. Runners-up, 1927-8, 1930-31, 1936-7. Best in Division II, 5th, 1901-2. Record attendance: 25,000 v. Wolverhampton Wanderers, F.A. Cup, 3rd Round, Jan. 4, 1958. Address: Sincil Bank, Lincoln (Tel. 21912). Nickname: Imps. Colours: Red shirts with white trim, white shorts. Record League goal-scorer: A. Hall, 42 goals, Division III(N), 1931-2. Record victory: 11—1 v. Crewe Alexandra, Division III(N), Sept. 29, 1951. Record defeat: 11—3 v. Manchester City, Division II, Mar. 23, 1895.

LINESMEN

See REFEREES AND LINESMEN.

LIVERPOOL F.C.

Founded 1892 after the majority of the members of Everton F.C. left their ground at Anfield Road for Goodison Park following a rent dispute. Those who remained behind formed a new club, Liverpool. Elected to the Football League, Division II, 1893. Honours: Champions Division I, 1900-1901, 1905-6, 1921-2, 1922-3, 1946-7, 1963-4, 1965-6. Runners-up, 1898-9, 1909-10, 1968-9. Champions Division II, 1893-4, 1895-6, 1904-5, 1961-2. F.A. Cup: Winners, 1965. Finalists, 1914, 1950. European Cup Winners Cup: Finalists, 1966. Record attendance: 61,905 v. Wolverhampton Wanderers, F.A. Cup, 4th Round, Feb. 2, 1952. Address: Anfield Road, Liverpool 4 (Tel. Anfield 2361-2). Nickname: Reds. Colours: Red shirts with white trim, red shorts. Record League goal-scorer: R. Hunt, 41 goals, Division II, 1961-2. Record victory: 10—1 v. Rotherham United, Division II, Feb. 18, 1896. Record defeat: 9—1 v. Birmingham City, Division II, Dec. 11. 1954.

LONG SERVICE
Managers

It is difficult to establish the record for long service as manager with a single club for in the old days the men who were managers were not accorded that title and there is some confusion between men who would now be regarded simply as secretaries and those who had anything at all to do with team management.

However, if we restrict our choice to men who have managed Football League clubs since World War II then the record belongs to Sir Matt Busby, C.B.E., who has been manager of Manchester United since Oct. 1945.

Next comes J. Seed who was manager of Charlton Athletic from May 1933 to Sept. 1956.

J. (Joe) Smith was appointed manager of Blackpool in the summer of 1935 and remained with them until May 1958.

W. H. Walker was manager at Nottingham Forest from 1939 to 1960.

J. E. Davison was manager of Sheffield United for 20 years, from June 1932 until the summer of 1952.

Another post-war manager with a distinguished record including 18 years as manager of West Ham United is C. Paynter. In all, Mr. Paynter served West Ham United for 50 years. Joining them as a player in 1900, he became assistant trainer in 1902, trainer 1912, team-manager 1932, and secretary-manager during World War II. He retired in 1950.

Other Officials

Here are some details of long service among club, F.A. and League officials.

Sir Charles Clegg (b. June 1850; d. June 1937) was connected with the administration of the F.A. for 51 years. He became a member of the F.A. Council in 1886. In 1889 he was elected a Vice-President of the F.A. The following year he became Chairman. In 1923 he became President, a position he held until his death.

Mr. W. C. Cuff became a director of Everton F.C. in 1895 and—with the exception of one short break—was connected with the club's affairs until 1948. He was a leading figure in the management of the Football League. He was elected a member of the League's committee in 1925 and became Vice-President in 1937. Two years later Mr. Cuff was elected President, a position he held until his death in Feb. 1949.

Mr. Fred Everiss was appointed secretary of West Bromwich Albion in 1902 and retained the position for 46 years. He then became a director of the club and was still on the board when he died three years later in 1951. Prior to his appointment as secretary he had been office boy, so that his service to the club extended over more than 50 years.

Mr. H. J. Huband, founder of the Isthmian League, was a member of the F.A. Council for 45 years. He was for several years a member of the International Selection Committee. In addition, Mr. Huband gave more than 50 years' service to the London F.A. He died in 1952.

Lord Kinnaird, the famous Old Etonian, served the F.A. for 55 years. Elected to the Committee in 1868, he became Honorary Treasurer in 1877, and President in 1890. Lord Kinnaird was President of the F.A. until his death at the age of 75, on Jan. 30, 1923. In his younger days, Lord Kinnaird won five F.A. Cup-winners' medals with the Wanderers and Old Etonians.

Mr. John K. McDowall was Secretary of the Scottish Football League for over 46 years—from April 26, 1882, until he died on Sept. 6, 1928.

Mr. John McKenna, founder and chairman of Liverpool F.C. was connected with Football League administration for 34 years. He was elected a member of the Management Committee in 1902. He became a Vice-President in 1908 and President in 1910. He was President until his death in Mar. 1937. Mr. McKenna was also a Vice-President of the F.A.

Mr. William Pickford of Bournemouth was elected a member of the F.A. Council in 1888 and continued his association with the game until his death in Nov. 1938. He became President of the F.A. in 1937, and was also one of the men responsible for the early development of the Referees' Association.

Mr. George B. Ramsay served Aston Villa for 59 years. Joining them in 1876 he was in turn player, captain, member of the committee and secretary. Finally he was consulting adviser to the club.

Mr. Ted Robbins of Wrexham was Secretary of the F.A. of Wales from 1910 until his death in Jan. 1946.

Mr. Eph Smith was 54 years with West Bromwich Albion as office boy, assistant secretary, and secretary, from June 1906 until 1960.

Mr. Charles E. Sutcliffe of Rawtenstall who died in Jan. 1939, first became a member of the Football League Management Committee in 1898. He was a Vice-President from 1927 until he became President in 1937.

Sir Frederick Wall: Secretary of the F.A. for 39 years, 1895-1934. He was the man chiefly responsible for the formation of the Referees' Association and was also for many years one of the leading figures in the London Football Association and the Middlesex Association. He died in 1944.

Players

The long-service record for a player with a single club goes to E. Sagar who joined Everton, Mar. 26, 1929, and retired May 1953. This represents 24 years 1 month's service.

The previous long-service record for a player was held by R. Crompton who was a Blackburn Rovers' full-back for 23 years 7 months. Crompton, one of England's greatest defenders, signed for Blackburn Rovers in Oct. 1896, and remained with them as a player until May 1920.

In the Scottish League the record was set up by outside-left A. Smith. He made his debut for the Rangers in April 1894 and his playing career with them extended over 21 seasons.

Right back A. McNair equalled this record completing 21 seasons with Celtic to 1925.

LONGEST GAME

The longest game on record in first-class football was that between Stockport County and Doncaster Rovers on Mar. 30, 1946. This was a 2nd leg tie in the Third Division (N) Cup, and in an effort to reach a decisive result the game lasted for 205min. before bad light forced them to stop play.

In the 2nd Round, Football League North, War Cup, 2nd leg match, at Ninian Park, Cardiff, April 14, 1945, Cardiff City and Bristol City played for 3hr. 22min. before a deciding goal was scored. The teams were drawing 2—2 after 90min., and, in accordance with war-time rules, they played an extra 10min. each way, but still without a winning goal. They then continued to play until a goal was scored (by Cardiff City).

A Western Hemisphere club championship game between Santos (Brazil) and Penarol (Uruguay) at Santos Aug. 2-3, 1962 began at 9.30 p.m. and finished 3½ hours later with the score 3—3, but the actual playing time was less than the games mentioned above.

LOSING RUN

See under DEFEATS and WITHOUT A WIN.

LUTON TOWN F.C.

Founded 1885 by the amalgamation of Wanderers and Excelsior. Luton Town were the pioneers of professional football in the South of England, employing paid players as early as 1890. Elected to the Football League, Division II, 1897. Failed to gain re-election 1900. Re-entered Football League as members of Division III, 1920. Honours: Runners-up, Division II, 1954-5, Champions, Division III(S), 1936-7. Runners-up, 1935-6. Champions, Division III, 1967-8. Runners-up, 1969-70. F.A. Cup: Finalists, 1959. Record attendance: 30,069 v. Blackpool, F.A. Cup, 6th Round (replay), Mar. 4, 1959. Address: Kenilworth Road, Luton (Tel. 23151). Nickname: Hatters or Strawplaiters. Colours: White shirts, black shorts. Record League goal-scorer: J. Payne, 55 goals, Division III(S), 1936-7 (this is a record for the Southern Section). Record victory: 12—0 v. Bristol Rovers, Division III(S), April 13, 1936. Record defeat: 9—1 v. Swindon Town, Division III(S), Aug. 28, 1921.

LUXEMBOURG

Considering that Luxembourg has a population of only about 300,000 it is not surprising that they have not had much success in international matches.

The country is, however, a long established member of F.I.F.A., and its governing body, the Luxembourg Football Federation, was founded as long ago as 1908.

Luxembourg has never beaten any of the home countries in a full international but their finest win, undoubtedly, was that obtained in a World Cup game in 1961 when they beat Portugal 4—2.

They are as keen about football in Luxembourg as anywhere on the Continent and their leading clubs compete regularly in the principal international cup competitions. All players in Luxembourg are amateur and at the present time the Federation has a membership of 178 clubs.

Address of governing body: Fédération Luxembourgeoise de Football, 50 Rue de Strasbourg, Luxembourg. Colours: Red shirts, white shorts, blue stockings.

Results of international matches:

May 21, 1927	Luxembourg 2, England 5; Luxembourg.
May 9, 1936	Luxembourg 1, Eire 5; Luxembourg.
May 24, 1947	Luxembourg 0, Scotland 6; Luxembourg.
Oct. 28, 1953*	Eire 4, Luxembourg 0; Dublin.
Mar. 7, 1954*	Luxembourg, 0, Eire 1; Luxembourg.
Oct. 19, 1960*	Luxembourg 0, England 9; Luxembourg.
Sept. 28, 1961*	England 4, Luxembourg 1; Highbury.

* World Cup.

M

MANAGERS

For the names of individuals who have both played in and managed F.A. Cup winning teams see FOOTBALL ASSOCIATION CHALLENGE CUP (PLAYERS).

Only four men have both played for and subsequently managed Football League championship winning sides. E. Drake, Arsenal, centre-forward, 1933-4, 1934-5, 1937-8; Chelsea, manager, 1954-5. W. Nicholson, Tottenham Hotspur, right half-back, 1950-51; manager, 1960-61. A. E. Ramsey, right-back, Tottenham Hotspur, 1950-51, manager, Ipswich Town, 1961-2. J. Mercer left-half, Everton 1938-9, Arsenal 1947-8, 1952-3; manager, Manchester City, 1967-8.

The late W. McCandless set up a managers' record for promoting teams from the Third Division. He managed three—all Welsh: 1938-9 Newport County, 1946-7 Cardiff City, and 1948-9 Swansea Town. Mr. McCandless was himself an Irishman from Ballymena.

Managers of Football League clubs today hold extremely precarious positions. Since World War II over 700 have been sacked or left their clubs in the Football League.

The shortest time anyone has served as manager with a Football League club is 13 days. Mar. 31, 1939 to April 13, 1939 was the duration of J. Cochrane's managership at Reading.

T. Ward was appointed manager of Exeter City in Mar. 1953 but returned to Barnsley as their manager 25 days later.

W. Lambton was appointed manager of Scunthorpe United, April 21, 1959, but the agreement was only a verbal one and the appointment was cancelled three days later.

In Scotland R. Flavell was manager of Ayr United for only 17 days in Dec. 1961 before returning to St. Mirren as that club's manager. He had previously been coach at St. Mirren.

For manager with longest service see under separate section LONG SERVICE (Managers).

One of the most famous managers of all time was Herbert Chapman. No manager met with greater success. He was the only one who has managed four different Football League clubs when they won either the League Championship or the F.A. Cup. Here is his record:

Manager of Northampton Town, Southern League Champions, 1908-09.

Manager of Leeds City, Champions of the Midland Section of the Football League, 1916-17, 1917-18.

Manager of Huddersfield Town when they won the F.A. Cup, 1922, and the League Championship, 1923-4, 1924-5.

Manager of Arsenal, F.A. Cup winners, 1930. League Champions, 1930-31, 1932-3.

Mr. Chapman died after a short illness, Jan. 6, 1934, leaving £6,780.

When Andrew Beattie was appointed General Manager of Notts County in Mar. 1967 he created a record by managing his eighth Football League club. He had previously managed Barrow, Stockport County, Huddersfield Town, Carlisle United, Nottingham Forest, Plymouth Argyle and Wolverhampton Wanderers.

Major Frank Buckley was manager of seven different clubs—Norwich City, Blackpool, Wolverhampton Wanderers, Notts County, Hull City, Leeds United, and Walsall, before he retired in Sept. 1955.

MANCHESTER CITY F.C.

Founded 1894. The club is descended from the West Gorton club

(1880-83), Gorton Athletic (1884-7) and Ardwick (1887-94). Ardwick had been one of the original members of the Football League, Division II in 1892. A limited company was formed and the title changed to Manchester City in 1894. Honours: Champions, Division I, 1936-7, 1967-8. Runners-up Division I, 1903-4, 1920-21. Champions, Division II, 1898-9, 1902-3, 1909-10, 1927-8, 1946-7, 1965-6. Runners-up Division II, 1895-6, 1950-51. F.A. Cup: Winners, 1904, 1934, 1956, 1969. Finalists, 1926, 1933, 1955. League Cup: Winners, 1970. European Cup Winners Cup: Winners, 1970. Record attendance: 84,569 v. Stoke City, F.A. Cup, 6th Round, Mar. 3, 1934. Address: Maine Road, Manchester (Tel. 061-607 1191). Nickname: The Blues or Citizens. Colours: Sky blue shirts, white shorts. Record League goal-scorer: T. Johnson, 38 goals, Division I, 1928-9. Record victory: 11—3 v. Lincoln City, Division II, Mar. 23, 1895. Record defeat: 9—1 v. Everton, Division I, Sept. 3, 1906.

MANCHESTER UNITED F.C.

Founded by workmen employed by the Lancashire and Yorkshire Railway Company, probably in 1878. First known as Newton Heath but re-formed under its present title in 1902. Elected to Football League, Division I, 1892. Honours: Champions, Division I, 1907-8, 1910-11, 1951-2, 1955-6, 1956-7, 1964-5, 1966-7. Runners-up, 1946-7, 1947-8, 1948-9, 1950-51, 1958-9 1963-4, 1967-8. Champions, Division II, 1935-6. Runners-up, 1905-6, 1924-5, 1937-8. F.A. Cup: Winners, 1909, 1948, 1963. Finalists, 1957, 1958. European Cup: Winners, 1968. Record attendance: 76,962, Wolverhampton Wanderers v. Grimsby Town. F.A. Cup Semi-final, Mar. 25, 1939. Manchester United game, 70,504 v. Aston Villa, Division I, Dec. 27, 1920. Address: Old Trafford, Manchester 16 (Tel. Trafford Park 1661). Colours: Red shirts, with white trimmings, white shorts. Record League goal-scorer: D. Viollet, 32 goals, Division I, 1959-60. Record victory: 10—1 v. Wolverhampton Wanderers, Division I, Oct. 15, 1892. Record defeat: 7—0 v. Aston Villa, Division I, Dec. 27, 1930.

MANSFIELD TOWN F.C.

Founded 1905. Elected to Football League, Division III(S), 1931. Honours: Runners-up, Division III(N), 1950-51. Record attendance: 24,479 v. Nottingham Forest, F.A. Cup 3rd Round, Jan. 10, 1953. Address: Field Mill, Mansfield (Tel. 567). Nickname: Stags. Colours: White shirts with blue and amber collar and cuffs, royal blue shorts with amber stripe. Record league goal-scorer: E. Harston, 55 goals, Division III(N), 1936-7 (this is a record for the Northern Section). Record victory: 9—2 v. Rotherham United, Division III(N), Dec. 27, 1932, and v. Hounslow, F.A. Cup, 1st Round (replay), Nov. 5, 1962. Record defeat: 8—1 v. Walsall, Division III(N), Jan. 19, 1933.

MATCHES

A number of clubs have met the same opponents in the Football League, League Cup, and F.A. Cup, in the one season, but including replays Plymouth Argyle and Huddersfield Town met six times in these three competitions during 1963-4.

In season 1911-12 West Bromwich Albion played in two F.A. Cup Finals and five Division I games in 10 days: April 20, Cup Final, 0—0 v. Barnsley; April 22, 0—3(A) Everton; April 24, Cup Final (replay), 0—1 (after half-hour extra time) v. Barnsley; April 25, 1—4(A) Blackburn Rovers; April 26, 0—0(H) Bradford City; April 27, 1—5(H) Sheffield Wednesday; April 29, 0—0(H) Oldham Athletic.

See SCOTTISH ASSOCIATION CUP (replays) and SCOTTISH LEAGUE for details of clubs that played two matches in a day.

MEDALS

See CUP MEDALS, and also TROPHIES.

MEXICO

Considering that Mexico have appeared in seven of the World Cup final tournaments they must at least be ranked as the soccer champions of North America. Possibly their finest performance in this competition was their surprise 3—1 victory over Czechoslovakia in Chile in 1962.

The Mexican F.A. was founded in

1927 and now has a membership of about 360 clubs including a limited number of professionals.

The address of the governing body: Federación Mexicana de Futbol Asociación, Abraham Gonzalez 3, Mexico D.F. Colours: Green shirts, white shorts, black stockings.

Results of international matches:

June 11, 1958*	Wales 1, Mexico 1; Sweden.
May 24, 1959	Mexico 2, England 1; Mexico City.
May 10, 1961	England 8, Mexico 0; Wembley.
May 22, 1962	Mexico 2, Wales 1; Mexico City.
June 22, 1966	Ireland 4, Mexico 1; Belfast
July 16, 1966*	England 2, Mexico 0; Wembley
June 1, 1969	Mexico 0, England 0; Mexico City

* World Cup.

MIDDLESBROUGH F.C.

Founded 1876. Adopted professionalism 1889. Reverted to amateur status 1892 but turned professional again in 1899. Elected to Football League, Division II, 1899. Honours: Champions, Division II, 1926-7, 1928-9. Runners-up, Division II, 1901-2. Runners-up, Division III, 1966-7. Best in Division I, 3rd, 1913-14. F.A. Amateur Cup: Winners, 1895, 1898. Record attendance: 53,596 v. Newcastle United, Division I, Dec. 27, 1949. Address: Ayresome Park, Middlesbrough (Tel. 89659). Nickname: Ironsides or Borough. Colours: Red shirts, white shorts. Record League goal-scorer: G. Camsell, 59 goals, Division II, 1926-7 (a record for this Division). Record victory: 10—3 v. Sheffield United, Division I, Nov. 18, 1933. Record defeat: 9—0 v. Blackburn Rovers, Division II, Nov. 6, 1954.

MILLWALL F.C.

Founded 1885 as Millwall Rovers. One of the original members of Division III, 1920. Honours: Champions, Division III(S), 1927-8, 1937-8. Runners up, Division III, 1965-6. Champions, Division IV, 1961-2. Runners-up, 1964-5. Best in Division II, 7th, 1932-3. F.A. Cup: Semi-finalists, 1900, 1903, 1937. Record attendance: 48,672 v. Derby County, F.A. Cup, 5th Round, Feb. 20, 1937. Address: The Den, Cold Blow Lane, London S.E. 14 (Tel. 01-639 3143). Nickname: Lions. Colours: All white. Record League goal-scorer: R. Parker, 37 goals, Division III(S), 1926-7. Record victory: 9—1 v. Torquay United, Division III(S), Aug. 29, 1927,

and v. Coventry City, Division III(S), Nov. 19, 1927. Record defeat: 9—1 v. Aston Villa, F.A. Cup 4th Round, Jan. 28, 1946.

MORTON F.C.

Founded 1896. First entered Scottish League Division I in 1900. Honours: Champions, Division II, 1949-50, 1963-4, 1966-7. Runners-up, 1928-9, 1936-7. Scottish Cup: Winners, 1922, Finalists, 1948. Record attendance: 23,500 v. Celtic, 1921 and v, Rangers, Scottish Cup, 3rd Round, Feb. 21, 1953. Address. Cappielow Park, Greenock (Tel. 21933). Colours: White shirts, blue shorts. Record League goal-scorer: A. McGraw, 51 goals, Division II, 1963-4. Record victory: 11—1 v. Blairgowrie, Scottish Cup, 1st Round, Feb. 1, 1936. Record defeat: 10—2 v. Rangers, Division 1, Dec. 6, 1913.

MOTHERWELL F.C.

Founded 1885. First entered Scottish League, Division I in 1904. Honours: Champions, Division I, 1931-2. Runners-up, 1926-7, 1929-30, 1932-3, 1933-4. Champions, Division B, 1953-4. Scottish Cup: Winners, 1952. Finalists, 1931, 1933, 1939, 1951. Record attendance: 36,750 v. Rangers, Scottish Cup, 4th Round (replay), Mar. 12, 1952. Address: Fir Park, Motherwell (Tel. 3229). Colours: Amber shirts with claret hoop, amber shorts. Record goalscorer in Division I, William McFadyen, 52 goals, 1931-2 (Scottish League Division I record). Record victory: 12—1 v. Dundee United, Division B, 1953-4. Record defeat: 10—0 v. St. Mirren, Division A, 1945-6.

N

NAMES
Former Names of Clubs

Arsenal: Royal Arsenal, Woolwich Arsenal.

Barnsley: Barnsley St. Peters.

Birmingham City: Small Heath Alliance.

Blackpool: Blackpool St. John's.

Bolton Wanderers: Christ Church Sunday School.

Bournemouth and Boscombe Athletic: Boscombe St. John's.

Brighton and Hove Albion: Brighton and Hove Rangers.

Bristol City: Bristol South End.

Bristol Rovers: Black Arabs, Eastville Rovers.

Burnley: Burnley Rovers.

Cardiff City: Riverside.

Coventry City: Singers.

Everton: St. Domingo.

Exeter City: St. Sidwell's Old Boys.

Fulham: St. Andrew's.

Gillingham: New Brompton Excelsior.

Grimsby Town: Grimsby Pelham.

Leeds United: Leeds City.

Leicester City: Leicester Fosse.

Manchester City: West Gorton, Gorton Association, Ardwick.

Manchester United: Newton Heath.

Millwall: Millwall Rovers.

Motherwell: Wee Alpha.

Newcastle United: Newcastle East End.

Oldham Athletic: Pine Villa.

Orient The: Leyton Orient, Clapton Orient.

Oxford United: Headington United.

Port Vale: Burslem Port Vale.

Queen's Park Rangers: St. Jude's Institute.

Rochdale: Rochdale Town.

Rotherham United: Thornhill United, Rotherham County.

Southampton: Southampton St. Mary's.

Southend United: Southend Athletic.

Southport: Southport Central.

Stockport County: Heaton Norris Rovers, Heaton Norris on the Ash.

Stoke City: Stoke.

Sunderland: Sunderland Teachers' A.F.C.

Third Lanark: Third Lanark Athletic.

Walsall: Walsall Town Swifts.

West Bromwich Albion: West Bromwich Strollers.

West Ham Utd: Thames Ironworks.

NETHERLANDS
See HOLLAND.

NEWCASTLE UNITED F.C.

Founded 1882 as Newcastle East End. Changed to Newcastle United 1892. Elected to the Football League, Division II, 1893. Honours: Champions, Division I, 1904-5, 1906-7, 1908-9, 1926-7. Champions, Division II, 1964-5. Runners-up, Division II, 1897-8, 1947-8. F.A. Cup: Winners, 1910, 1924, 1932, 1951, 1952, 1955. Finalists: 1905, 1906, 1908, 1911. Fairs Cup: Winners, 1969. Record attendance: 68,386 v. Chelsea, Division I, Sept. 3, 1930. Address: St. James's Park, Newcastle-upon-Tyne (Tel. 28361). Nickname: Magpies. Colours: Black and white striped shirts, black shorts. Record League goal-scorer: H. Gallacher, 36 goals, Division I, 1926-7. Record victory: 13—0 v. Newport County, Division II, Oct. 5, 1946. Record defeat: 9—1 v. Sunderland (H), Division I, Dec. 5, 1908.

NEWPORT COUNTY F.C.

Founded 1911 by employees of local ironworks. One of the original members of the Football League, Division III, 1920. Honours: Champions, Division III(S), 1938-9. Record attendance: 24,268 v. Cardiff City, Division III(S), Oct. 16, 1937. Address:

Somerton Park, Newport, Mon. (Tel. 71543). Nickname: Ironsides. Colours: Amber shirts with black collars and cuffs, black shorts. Record League goal-scorer: T. Martin, 34 goals, Division III(S), 1929-30. Record victory: 10—0 v. Merthyr Town, Division III(S), April 10, 1930. Record defeat: 13—0 v. Newcastle United, Division II, Oct. 5, 1946.

NEW ZEALAND

Soccer has made tremendous progress in New Zealand since about 1954 when their F.A. did some re-organising and established a coaching scheme for schoolboys.

The New Zealand F.A. was formed as long ago as 1891 but for the greater part of its history interest in the dribbling code in these islands has taken a very poor second place to the Kiwis' favourite sport—rugby.

Now, however, with so much progress being made in the schools the future seems much brighter as the youngsters take to soccer in ever increasing numbers.

All the major associations (Auckland, Wellington, Canterbury and Otago) together with the majority of minor associations (altogether there are 21 associations in New Zealand) are going all out to coach as many schoolboys as possible. The game has also established itself in the universities.

New Zealand has not yet played any full internationals with teams from the British Isles but there have been a number of " Tests " with F.A. touring teams of 1937, 1961, and 1969, and against an F.A. XI when the New Zealanders visited England in 1964.

The supreme trophy among the associations is the " English Trophy " which was presented to the N.Z.F.A. by the English F.A.

All clubs in New Zealand may enter for the Chatham Cup, the equivalent of the English F.A. Cup. The competition is played off on a regional basis with the North Island finalists meeting the South Island finalists in Wellington, usually during the month of August.

Address of the governing body: New Zealand F.A. (Inc.), P.O. Box 1771, 23 Waring Taylor Street, Wellington, C.1. Colours: Black shirts with silver fern leaf, white shorts, black stockings.

Results of Test matches:

June 5, 1937	New Zealand 0, England (F.A.) 12, Dunedin.	
June 19, 1937	New Zealand 0, England (F.A.) 6; Auckland.	
June 26, 1937	New Zealand 1, England (F.A.) 12; Wellington.	
June 5, 1961	New Zealand 0, England (F.A.) 8; Wellington.	
June 10, 1961	New Zealand 1, England (F.A.) 6, Auckland.	
April 13, 1964	F.A. XI 4, New Zealand 0; Northampton.	
June 11, 1969	New Zealand 0, England (F.A.) 5; Newmarket	

NICKNAMES

Club nicknames appear under the respective club titles.

NORTHAMPTON TOWN F.C.

Founded 1897, largely through the enterprise of teachers connected with the local Elementary Schools' Athletic Association. One of the original members of the Football League, Division III, 1920. Honours: Runners-up, Division II, 1964-5. Champions, Division III, 1962-3. Runners-up, Division III(S), 1927-8, 1949-50. Record attendance: 24,523 v. Fulham, Division I, Apr. 23, 1966. Address: County Ground, Northampton (Tel. 35346). Nickname: Cobblers. Colours: White shirts with claret trim and band around chest, white shorts with claret stripe. Record League goal-scorer: C. Holton, 36 goals, Division III, 1961-2. Record victory: 10—0 v. Walsall, Division III(S), Nov. 5, 1927. In the old Southern League, 11—1 v. Southend United, Dec. 30, 1909. Record defeat: No score over seven in either Football League or F.A. Cup. 11—0 v. Southampton, Southern League, Dec. 28, 1901.

NORTHERN IRELAND

See IRISH FOOTBALL ASSOCIATION and INTERNATIONALS.

NORWAY

Norway has never adopted professionalism and their most brilliant players have had to go elsewhere to make the most of their talent and gain suitable financial reward.

It is largely because of this that Norway has rarely been able to make much of an impression in international soccer although they have not been entirely without success.

In the Olympic Games of 1920 Norway defeated Great Britain 3—1, and in the 1936 Olympics they gained their most glorious victory by defeating the German "amateurs" 2—0 and went on to gain third place in the Games.

Norway has qualified once for the World Cup Tournament and on that occasion, in 1938, they gave another fine display only losing 2—1 to Italy in extra time. Italy were the holders of the trophy at that time and went on to retain it.

The Norwegian F.A. was formed in 1902 and it is an organisation that must be commended for the way in which it has encouraged the game's development even in the country's northernmost parts where competitions are difficult to organise owing to the distances involved and consequent travelling expenses.

Today there are about 1,200 clubs registered with the Association. The First Division of the National League includes 10 clubs and the season extends from mid-April to mid-October.

Address of the governing body: Norges Fotballforbund, Ullevaal Stadion, Sognsveien 75, Post Box 42, Oslo 8. Colours: Red shirts with white collars, white shorts, blue stockings.

Results of international matches:

May 28, 1929	Norway 3, Scotland 7; Oslo.	
May 14, 1937	Norway 0, England 6; Oslo.	
Oct. 10, 1937*	Norway 3, Eire 2; Oslo.	
Nov. 7, 1937*	Eire 3, Norway 3; Dublin.	
Nov. 9, 1938	England 4, Norway 0; Newcastle.	
May 18, 1949	Norway 1, England 4; Oslo.	
Nov. 26, 1950	Eire 2, Norway 2; Dublin.	
May 30, 1951	Norway 2, Eire 3; Oslo.	
May 5, 1954	Scotland 1, Norway 0; Glasgow.	
May 19, 1954	Norway 1, Scotland 1; Oslo.	
Nov. 8, 1954	Eire 2, Norway 1; Dublin.	
May 25, 1955	Norway 1, Eire 3; Oslo.	
Nov. 6, 1960	Eire 3, Norway 1; Dublin.	
June 4, 1963	Norway 4, Scotland 3; Bergen.	
Nov. 7, 1963	Scotland 6, Norway 1; Glasgow.	
May 13, 1964	Norway 1, Eire 4; Oslo.	
June 29, 1966	Norway 1, England 6; Oslo	

* World Cup.

NORWICH CITY F.C.

Founded 1905 and joined the Southern League. One of the original members of the Football League, Division III, 1920. Honours: Champions, Division III(S), 1933-4. Runners-up, Division III, 1959-60. Football League Cup Winners, 1962. Best in Division II, 4th, 1960-61. Record attendance: 43,984 v. Leicester City, F.A. Cup 6th Round, Mar. 30, 1963. Address: Carrow Road, Norwich (Tel. 21514). Nickname: Canaries. Colours: Yellow shirts with green collars and cuffs, green shorts. Record League goalscorer: R. Hunt, 31 goals, Division III(S), 1955-56. Record victory: 10—2 v. Coventry City, Division III(S) Mar. 15, 1930. Record defeat: No score over seven in Football League or F.A. Cup. 10—2 v. Swindon Town, Southern League, 1908-9.

NOTTINGHAM FOREST F.C.

Founded 1865. Elected to Football League, Division I, 1892. Honours: Runners-up, Division I, 1966-7. Champions, Division II, 1906-7, 1921-2. Runners-up, 1956-7. Champions: Division III(S), 1950-51. F.A. Cup: Winners, 1898, 1959. Record attendance: 49,946 v. Manchester United, Division I, Oct. 28, 1967. Address: City Ground, Nottingham (Tel.

88236). Nickname: Reds. Colours:
Red shirts with white trim, white
shorts. Record League goal-scorer: W.
Ardron, 36 goals, Division III(S),
1950-51. Record victory: 14—0 v.
Clapton (A), F.A. Cup, 1st Round,
1890-91. Record defeat: 9—1 v.
Blackburn Rovers, Division II, April
10, 1937.

NOTTS COUNTY F.C.

The oldest Football League club,
formed 1862. Notts County were one
of the original members of the Football
League in 1888. Honours: Champions,
Division II, 1896-7, 1913-14 1922-3.
Runners-up, 1894-5. Champions, Division III(S), 1930-31, 1949-50. Runners-up, 1936-7. Best in Division I,
3rd, 1890-91, 1900-1901. Runners-up,
Division IV, 1959-60. F.A. Cup: Winners, 1894. Runners-up, 1891. Record
attendance: 47,301 v. York City,
F.A. Cup, 6th Round, Mar. 12, 1955.
Address: Meadow Lane, Nottingham

(Tel. 84152). Nickname: Magpies.
Colours: Black and white striped
shirts, black shorts. Record League
goal-scorer: T. Keetley, 39 goals,
Division III(S), 1930-31. Record
victory: 13—0 v. Basford Rovers,
F.A. Cup, 1st Round (1st series)
1886-7. Record defeat: 9—1 v.
Blackburn Rovers, Division I, Nov.
16, 1889; v. Aston Villa, Division I,
Sept. 29, 1888; v. Portsmouth, Division II, April 9, 1927.

NUMBERING PLAYERS

Players were first numbered in the
F.A. Cup Final in 1933. Then the
numbers ran from 1 to 22.

In the same year a proposal was
made by Tottenham Hotspur that
players should be numbered in Football League games, but it was defeated
at the A.G.M.

The proposal was not adopted by
the League until 1939 when it was
passed by 24 votes to 20.

O

The offside rule is the most discussed in the laws of the game. It is
also the most misunderstood. The law
referring to "offside" is Law 11 and
it can be seen in full under LAWS OF
THE GAME.

It must always be understood that
a player cannot move into an offside
position *after* the ball was last played,
nor can he be offside if the ball was
last played by an opponent, or if he
receives the ball direct from a goal-
kick, a corner kick, a throw-in, or
when dropped by the Referee.

The degree to which the offside
law affects tactics can be appreciated
from a consideration of the game both
before and after the law was changed
in 1925.

In that year, following a proposal
of the Scottish F.A., the law was
altered so that a player could not be
offside if two (instead of three) opponents were nearer their own goal-line
when the ball was last played.

Under the old rule, which had been
in force since 1867, the full-backs
could afford to play much further up
the field providing they kept in a diagonal line. As soon as a forward got
behind the advanced full-back he
could be in an offside position. And
should he run through after a long
ball between the backs, he still had
the other full-back to beat.

In the early 1920s, full-backs had
moved up almost to the halfway line,
one operating slightly behind the
other. They had the offside trap
worked to a fine art, and stoppages for
offside became monotonous.

When the law was changed stoppages for offside decreased considerably and for a while many more goals
were scored. In 1924-5 a total of 4,700
goals were scored in the Football

League. In the first season of the new
offside law the total rose by almost a
third to 6,373. Defensive re-organisation was inevitable.

If the full-backs continued to play
well up and on a slant, an attacker
could lie behind one of them *at all
times* and only have the other to beat.
Obviously after 1925 full-backs were
forced to play squarer and nearer
their own goal. But if they lay too
near their own goal they gave the
attackers the chance to shoot without
first beating them with the ball.

Playing square but up field meant
that a long ball down the middle
might beat them both. And if they
moved into the centre to cover this
possibility the wingers were given too
much freedom.

The obvious move was to close the
gap in the middle. So a new defensive
position—the third back—was created
and was filled by the centre-half. As
a result, we now have one less player
concentrating on attack. Great centre-
halves who were always among the
goal-scorers or giving the passes that
provided their colleagues with goal-
scoring chances, men like T. Boyle of
Burnley and J. Cowan of Aston Villa,
are no longer to be seen in football.
Nowadays we have the "stopper" or
"policeman" centre-half, considered
to have been introduced by Arsenal's
famous manager, the late Herbert
Chapman.

The change in the offside law not
only brought about an enforced
change in the positioning of the
defence, but it has had a tremendous
effect on play throughout the team.
No one can say definitely how much
the change in the law has changed the
style of the game, but it certainly encouraged a negative type of defensive
play. In this style team-work also has
become much looser, because the full-

backs are not always in such close touch with their wing half-backs.

OLDHAM ATHLETIC F.C.

Founded in 1899 in succession to Pine Villa, a club which had been in existence for a year. Elected to the Football League, Division II, 1907. Honours: Runners-up, Division I, 1914-15. Runners-up, Division II, 1909-10. Champions, Division III(N), 1952-3. Runners-up, Division IV, 1962-3. Record attendance: 47,671 v. Sheffield Wednesday, F.A. Cup, 4th Round, Jan. 25, 1930. Address: Boundary Park, Oldham (Tel. 061-624 4972). Nickname: Latics. Colours: Tangerine with blue and white collars and cuffs, blue shorts with white stripe. Record League goal-scorer: T. Davis, 33 goals, Division III(N), 1936-7. Record victory: 11—0 v. Southport, Division IV, Dec. 26, 1962. Record defeat: 13—4 v. Tranmere Rovers, Division III(N), Dec. 26, 1935.

OLYMPIC GAMES

Association Football was first introduced into the Olympic Games in 1900 in Paris, but this was only an exhibition match between the Upton Park Club and a French side which the Londoners won 4—0.

The 1904 Olympics in St. Louis included a soccer tournament which was won by Galt F.C., representing Canada, and soccer was also included in the intermediate Olympics of 1906 in Athens where Denmark emerged the winners. But the first Olympic soccer tournament to come under the auspices of F.I.F.A. was that in London in 1908.

Today the Olympic soccer tournament is open to all National Associations who are affiliated to F.I.F.A., and the players must, of course, be amateur.

Here are the results of the Finals:
1908 London,
  United Kingdom 2, Denmark 0.
1912 Stockholm,
  United Kingdom 4, Denmark 2.
1920 Antwerp,
  Belgium 2, Czechoslovakia 0.
1924 Paris,
  Uruguay 3, Switzerland 0.
1928 Amsterdam,
  Uruguay 2, Argentine 1 (after draw 1—1).

1932 Los Angeles,
  No Football Competition.
1936 Berlin,
  Italy 2, Austria 1.
1948 London,
  Sweden 3, Yugoslavia 1.
1952 Helsinki,
  Hungary 2, Yugoslavia 0.
1956 Melbourne,
  Russia 1, Yugoslavia 0.
1960 Rome,
  Yugoslavia 3, Denmark 1.
1964 Tokyo,
  Hungary 2, Czechoslovakia 1.
1968 Mexico City
  Hungary 4, Bulgaria 1.

In 1920 the Final was awarded to Belgium, leading 2—0 when the Czechs left the field before half-time after one of their number had been sent off by the referee for kicking an opponent.

The United Kingdom did not enter in 1924 or 1928 because of the split between the Football Association and F.I.F.A. over the question of broken time payments to amateurs.

The United Kingdom were knocked out in the first round by Norway 3—1, in the 1920 tournament.
1936: U.K. 2, China, 0, Round 1.
  U.K. 4, Poland 5, Round 2.
1948: U.K. 4, Holland 3, Round 1 (after extra time).
  U.K. 1, France 0, Round 2.
  U.K. 1, Yugoslavia 3, Semi finals.
1952: U.K. 3, Luxembourg 5, Preliminary Round (after extra time).
1956: Bulgaria 2, Great Britain 0, Great Britain 3, Bulgaria 3 Preliminary Round.

Despite this defeat the F.A. accepted an invitation to compete at Melbourne to fill a vacancy.

Results in Melbourne:
  Great Britain 9, Thailand 0.
  Great Britain 1, Bulgaria 6.

In 1960 the 16 teams in the final competition were divided into four groups with the winners of each group going into the semi-finals.
  Great Britain 3, Brazil 4.
  Great Britain 2, Italy 2.
  Great Britain 3, Taiwan 2.

Great Britain was eliminated, Italy winning the group and going forward to the semi-finals.
1964: Preliminary Rounds.
  Iceland 0, G.B. 6.

G.B. 4, Iceland 0.
G.B. 2, Greece 1.
Greece 4, G.B. 1.
1968 : Preliminary Rounds.
Spain 1, G.B. 0.
G.B. 0, Spain 0.

The United Kingdom's two successful teams were:

1908—H. P. Bailey (Leicester Fosse); W. S. Corbett (Birmingham), H. Smith (Oxford City); K. R. G. Hunt (Wolverhampton Wanderers), F. W. Chapman (South Nottingham), R. M. Hawkes (Luton); A. Berry (Oxford University), V. J. Woodward (Tottenham Hotspur), H. Stapley (Glossop), C. C. Purnell (Clapton), H. P. Hardman (Northern Nomads).

1912—R. G. Brebner (Northern Nomads); T. C. Burn (London Caledonians), A. E. Knight (Portsmouth); D. McWhirter (Bromley), H. C. Littlewort (Glossop), J. Dines (Ilford); A. Berry (Oxford City), V. J. Woodward (Chelsea), H. A. Walden (Bradford City), G. R. Hoare (Glossop), L. G. A. Sharpe (Derby County).

ORIENT, F.C., THE

Founded 1881. Reconstituted and adopted professionalism, 1901. The club was known as Clapton Orient until 1946 when they became Leyton Orient. Dropped Leyton from the title, 1967. Elected to Football League, Div. II, 1905. Honours: Runners-up, Division II, 1961-2. Champions, Division III, 1969-70. Champions, Division III(S), 1955-6. Runners-up, 1954-5. Record attendance: 34,345 v. West Ham United, F.A. Cup, 4th Round, Jan. 25, 1964. Address: Brisbane Road, E.10. (Tel. 01-539 1368). Nickname: The "Os". Colours: All red. Record League goal-scorer: T. Johnston, 35 goals, Division II, 1957-8. Record victory: 9—2 (as Clapton Orient) v. Aldershot, Division III(S), Feb. 10, 1934 and v. Chester, League Cup, 3rd Round, Oct. 17, 1962. Record defeat: 8—0 (as Clapton Orient) v. Aston Villa, F.A. Cup, 4th Round, Jan. 30, 1929.

ORDERED OFF

See also REFEREES.

In the England v. Argentine World Cup game at Wembley, July 23, 1966, play was held up for seven minutes before the Argentine captain A. Rat-tin would leave the field after being ordered off by Referee R. Kreitlin (W. Germany).

ORIGIN OF THE GAME

Considering that soccer and rugby are branches of the same tree then anyone trying to trace the origin of one of these games as distinct from the other is bound to run into a hopeless muddle if any attempt is made to go far beyond the middle of the 19th century.

Football historians are able to refer to the Shrovetide games played in many places including Derbyshire, Chester, Corfe Castle in Dorset, and Scone in the county of Perthshire, but with all due respect to the rugby game those boisterous medieval encounters bear more resemblance (be it only slight) to the handling code than to the game of soccer.

The same historians often claim some connections with various ball games played by the Greeks and Romans, but here again it must be pointed out that the Greek episkyros and the Roman harpastum was more rugby than soccer if only because carrying the ball was a feature of their play.

No indeed, soccer, the game not the name, cannot safely be traced beyond the 1830s when it had its origins in the public schools, but if one really insists on something earlier then we could go to the extreme and mention a form of football that was played with a leather ball in China at least as early as 200 B.C. and probably much earlier.

Professor H. A. Giles, classical and antiquarian writer who was Professor of Chinese at Cambridge University, proved by his research into the subject that in this game real emphasis was placed upon the ability of the players to dribble the ball, and his findings on this aspect of this ancient Chinese pastime are interesting because it would seem that it bore a much closer resemblance to soccer than any of the Greek and Roman games or the medieval games of mob football.

As has already been mentioned, the modern game of soccer has its origins in the public schools where various forms of football were revived after it had been almost entirely abandoned as a pastime of the working classes.

The rules differed so much from one school to another that although they all played football, some would be more appropriately mentioned in a history of rugby than of soccer, but as far as we are concerned here we can be more specific in mentioning Eton, Westminster, and Charterhouse, as the schools which laid the foundations of the game of Association Football.

From the public schools the obvious course of events was a spread to the universities and it was at Cambridge that one of the earliest attempts was made to adopt a uniform code of rules.

A number of Old Boys got together and formed the first football club, at Sheffield in 1856, and it was the Old Boys and university men who played a leading part in the formation of the Football Association (q.v.) in 1863, and this body originally decided to accept the Cambridge University Rules as a basis upon which to draw up their own rules.

It is well known that the withdrawal of the Blackheath Club two months after the inaugural F.A. meeting in 1863, marks the establishment of the separate games of soccer and rugby. The break, however, did not come, as may be supposed, on the question of handling, but on a disagreement over the F.A.'s ban on running with the ball and 'hacking' (the practice of using the toe either to kick an opponent's shins, or else to trip him up). Strange to relate it was the Blackheath Club which subsequently led a movement to ban 'hacking' from their own game, culminating in the formation of the Rugby Union in 1871.

OVERSEAS TOUR

See TOURS.

OWN GOALS

See GOAL-SCORING (INDIVIDUALS and (TEAMS), Own Goals.

OXFORD UNITED F.C.

Founded 1896 as Headington United. Adopted professionalism 1940 and changed name to Oxford United 1961. Elected to Football League Division IV, 1962. Honours: Champions, Division III, 1967-8. Record attendance: 22,730 v. Preston North End, F.A. Cup, 6th Round, Feb. 29 1964. Address: Manor Ground, London Road, Headington, Oxford (Tel 61503). Colours: Gold shirts, black shorts. Record League goal-scorer C. Booth, 23 goals, Division IV 1964-5. Record victory: 7—0 v. Barrow, Division IV, Dec. 19, 1964 Record defeat: 5—1 v. Brentford Division III, Feb. 26, 1966.

P

PARAGUAY

Paraguay reached their peak in the 1950s when they not only won the South American Championships (1953) but qualified for the World Cup Tournament both in 1950 and 1958.

They had also competed back in 1930 but then they were eliminated with defeats by the United States and Belgium. In 1950 they gained a 2—2 draw with Sweden and were only beaten 2—0 by Italy. In 1958 they defeated Scotland 3—2 and drew with Yugoslavia 3—3, but in that year it was their 7—3 defeat by France which lost them a place in the semi-finals.

These successes, however, attracted the attention of the wealthier footballing fraternity and Paraguay very soon lost their finest internationals, tempted away by high wages and bonuses.

With a population of only about 1,700,000 and less than 700 clubs affiliated to their F.A., Paraguay's past performances are remarkable indeed, and there seems no doubt that more outstanding performances may be seen in the international field by a country that has a penchant for soccer.

The address of the governing body formed in 1906: Liga Paraquaya de Football, Calle 25 de Mayo 884, Asunción. Colours: Red and white shirts, blue shorts.

Result of international match:

June 11, 1958*   Scotland 2, Paraguay 3; Sweden.

* World Cup.

PARTICK THISTLE F.C.

Founded 1876. First promoted to Scottish League, Division I, 1897. Honours: Champions, Division II, 1896-7, 1899-1900. Best in Division I, 3rd, 1947-8, 1953-4. Scottish Cup: Winners, 1921, Finalists, 1930. Record attendance: 54,723, Scotland v. Ireland, Feb. 25, 1928. Address: Firhill Park, Glasgow, N.W. (Tel. Maryhill 2673). Nickname: Jags. Colours: Red and yellow hooped shirts, white shorts. Record goal-scorer in Division I, A. Hair, 41 goals, 1926-7. Record victory: 16—0 v. Royal Albert, Scottish Cup, 1st Round, Jan. 17, 1931. Record defeat: 10—1 v. Dunfermline Athletic, Division I, 1958-9.

PENALTIES

The penalty kick was introduced by the Irish F.A. in season 1890-91. The F.A. (England) accepted it in September 1891.

Cup Final

All four penalty kicks taken in Wembley Cup Finals have been successful.

In the 1937-8 Final, G. Mutch of Preston North End scored the winning goal from the penalty spot in the last minute of extra time. Result: Preston North End 1, Huddersfield Town 0.

In the 1947-8 Final, E. Shimwell scored for Blackpool in the 14th minute. But Blackpool were beaten 4—2 by Manchester United.

In the 1953-4 Final, R. Allen scored a penalty for West Bromwich Albion against Preston North End 19min. after the interval. West Bromwich Albion won 3—2.

In the 1961-2 Final, D. Blanchflower scored for Tottenham Hotspur from a penalty awarded against Burnley for "hands" 9min. from the end. Tottenham Hotspur won 3—1.

Goalkeepers

A. Birch scored five penalties for Chesterfield in season 1923-4, a record for a goalkeeper in the Football League.

The record number of penalties saved in a Football League game is three. W. Scott saved three for Grimsby Town against Burnley, Feb. 13, 1909. But despite his valiant efforts, Burnley won 2—0.

Headed

Five players have headed a goal from a penalty kick. On Jan 5, 1935, in the match Arsenal v. Liverpool, the Arsenal full-back, E. Hapgood, took a penalty kick which Liverpool's goalkeeper, Riley, fisted back, Hapgood headed home the rebound. Arsenal won 2—0. W. R. Dean (Everton) also performed the same feat against West Bromwich Albion (goalkeeper H. F. Pearson), Nov. 7, 1936. Everton won 4—2.

W. Hopper (Workington) headed a similar goal against Aldershot (goalkeeper D. Jones), Division IV, Feb. 14, 1964; also by S. Harland (Bradford City) v. Tranmere Rovers (goalkeeper J. Heath) Division IV, Apr. 11, 1962; D. Simmons (Bournemouth) v. Tranmere Rovers (goalkeeper J. Cumbes) Division III, Jan. 4, 1969.

Missed

The greatest number of penalties missed by one side in a Football League, Division I, match is three. On Jan. 27, 1912, Fletcher (2) and Thornley missed penalties for Manchester City against Newcastle United. The game resulted in a draw 1—1.

Burnley missed three out of four v. Grimsby Town, Division II, Feb. 13, 1909.

In the last match of the 1923-4 season, L. Davies missed a penalty for Cardiff City v. Birmingham. The result was a goalless draw. If Cardiff City had won they would have been Football League Champions. As it was, they were runners-up on goal average and have never yet won the Championship.

Relegated

Manchester City missed a penalty against Newcastle United in the last match of the season 1925-6 and were relegated from the First Division. The result was a 3—2 defeat for Manchester City. A draw would have saved them from relegation.

Season's Aggregates

The highest number of penalties converted in one season of League football by single players are:

11—J. Ball, Sheffield Wednesday's centre-forward, 1932-3. W. Evans, Tottenham Hotspur's outside-left, 1932-3.

10—T. Callendar, Gateshead's centre half-back, 1949-50. J. Evans, Southend United's left-back, 1921-2. P. Morris, Mansfield Town's right-half, 1966-7.

Single Games

Three players have scored three penalties in a single Division I match:

W. Walker for Aston Villa v. Bradford City, Nov. 21, 1921; C. Mitten for Manchester United v. Aston Villa, Mar. 8, 1950, and K. Barnes for Manchester City v. Everton, Dec. 7, 1957.

During the Division III(N) match between Crewe Alexandra and Bradford on Mar. 8, 1924, there were four penalty kicks in five minutes—a league record.

There were five penalty kicks in the Argentine v. Mexico World Cup game at Montevideo in 1930. Argentine won 6—3.

W. Cook scored from the penalty spot in three consecutive Football League, Division I, games for Everton at Christmas, 1938 v. Blackpool (H), Dec. 24; v. Derby County (H), Dec. 26; and v. Derby County (A), Dec. 27.

PERU

Peru is another of the smaller countries that have suffered through the loss of their star players to richer clubs of other lands.

Since the war Peru reached their peak in the international field around 1958-9, years in which they not only defeated England 4—1 but twice held mighty Brazil to a draw, 1—1 in the World Cup and 2—2 in the South American Championships.

Following a period in which the exodus of their best players to other countries marred the progress of the game at home, Peru recovered to qualify for the 1970 World Cup in which they reached the quarter-finals.

The address of the governing body which was founded in 1922: Federación Peruana de Football, Estadio Nacional, Calle José Diaz, Puerta 4, Lima. Colours: White shirts with red diagonal stripe, white shorts, grey stockings.

Results of international matches:
May 17, 1959   Peru 4, England 1; Lima.
May 20, 1962   Peru 0, England 4; Lima.

PETERBOROUGH UNITED F.C.

Formed 1923. Elected to Division IV 1960. Honours: Champions, Division IV, 1960-61. Record attendance: 30,096 v. Swansea Town, F.A. Cup, 5th Round, Feb. 20, 1965. Address: London Road, Peterborough (Tel. 3623). Colours: Royal blue with white trim, white shorts. Record League goal-scorer: T. Bly, 52 goals, Division IV, 1960-61. Record victory 8—1 v. Oldham Athletic, Division IV, Nov. 26, 1969. Record defeat: 8—1 v. Northampton Town, F.A. Cup, 2nd Round (2nd replay), 1946-7.

PLAYERS

The least number of players to appear for a Football League club in one season's competition is 14. Liverpool called on this number when winning the Championship in 1965-6.

In the Scottish League, Division I, the record is 15—Dundee, 1961-2.

At the other end of the scale Coventry City in 1919-20, Sheffield Wednesday in 1919-20, and Hull City in 1946-7, each used as many as 42 players in the season. In the Scottish League, Falkirk and Raith Rovers in 1919-20, each used 38 players.

In the Scottish League, Division B, Albion Rovers called on 41 players during season 1952-3.

See also under TEAM CHANGES.

PLAYERS' UNION, THE

See under PROFESSIONAL FOOTBALLERS' ASSOCIATION, THE.

PLYMOUTH ARGYLE F.C.

Founded 1886. Reconstituted as a professional club 1903. One of the original clubs forming the Football League, Division III, in 1920. Honours: Champions, Division III(S), 1929-30, 1951-2. Runners-up, 1921-2, 1922-3, 1923-4, 1924-5, 1925-6, 1926-7. Champions, Division III, 1958-9. Best in Division II, 4th, 1931-2. Record attendance: 43,596 v. Aston Villa, Division II, Oct. 10, 1936. Address: Home Park, Plymouth (Tel. 52561). Nickname: Pilgrims. Colours: White shirts with green and black circlet around chest, white shorts. Record League goal-scorer: J. Cock, 32 goals, Division III(S), 1925-6. Record victory: 8—1 v. Millwall, Division II, Jan. 16, 1932. Record defeat: 9—0 v. Stoke City, Division II, Dec. 17, 1960.

POINTS

The record number of points gained by clubs in the Football League are:

Division I—1968-9, Leed United 67.

Division II—1919-20, Tottenham Hotspur 70.

Division III—1965-66, Hull City 69.

Division III(S)—1950-51, Nottingham Forest 70. 1954-5, Bristol City 70.

Division III(N)—1946-7, Doncaster Rovers 72.

Division IV—1960-61, Peterborough United 66. 1967-8, Luton Town 66.

Scottish League:

Division I—1920-21, Rangers 76.

Division II—1966-67, Morton 69.

Five times only in the history of the Football League have the champions of any division finished the season with more points than goals: Nottingham Forest (Division II), 1921-2, 56 points, 51 goals. Notts County (Division II), 1922-3, 53 points, 46 goals. Birmingham City (Division II), 1947-8, 59 points, 55 goals. Gillingham (Division IV), 1963-4, 60 points, 59 goals. Leeds United (Division I), 1968-9, 67 points, 66 goals.

In three successive seasons, 1928-9, 1929-30, and 1930-31, Millwall finished in the same position and with the same number of points. They were 14th with 39 points.

Points Deducted

Stockport County had two points deducted from their record for playing J. Smith without permission on Mar. 26, 1927. Sunderland also had two points deducted for playing J. E. Doig on Sept. 20, 1890, before he was eligible.

Fewest Points

The lowest number of points obtained in any one season in the Football League is eight by Doncaster Rovers in Division II, 1904-5. The club's record was won 3, lost 29, drawn 2.

In the Scottish League Division A, 1954-5 Stirling Albion gained only 6 points—2 wins and 2 draws in 30 games. A record low.

The fewest number of points to separate the top and bottom teams in any division of the Football League at the end of a season is 16. This happened three times in Division I: in 1901-2, 1927-8 and 1937-8.

The fewest points gained by a Championship winning Football League club in a 42-match season is 52. Sheffield Wednesday in Division I, 1928-9, Arsenal in Division I, 1937-8 and Chelsea in Division I, 1954-5, all won the Championship with only 52 points.

Most Points

The highest number of points secured by a club relegated from either Division I or II of the Football League is 38 in 1927-8 when Tottenham Hotspur were relegated from the First Division.

The record number of points collected in any one season in the Football League is 72 by Doncaster Rovers in Division III(N), 1946-7.

POLAND

Before the outbreak of World War II Poland was swiftly developing into one of the leading powers in the football world and although they have not been able to break into the upper crust of football's *élite* during the post-war years they have some notable victories to their credit.

In the 1936 Olympics Poland defeated the United Kingdom 5—4 and finished up in fourth place. In 1938 they defeated Ireland 6—0, and, when that year they appeared in the World Cup Finals for the first time, they surprised the critics by making one of the favourites, Brazil, fight all the way for a 6—5 victory. It was only after extra time that the Poles were beaten.

Soccer was played in Poland long before the country was declared independent in 1918. For many years before that most of the area now known as Poland was Russian territory and although the formation of football clubs was frowned upon by the Czar some British enthusiasts working in Lodz started a team and interest in the game spread rapidly.

Apparently, however, those British were not quite the first footballers in Poland for the oldest club was formed at Cracow in 1906 when that city was just over the border inside what was then part of Austrian Galicia. There, in 1911, a touring side from Aberdeen created great enthusiasm by playing two games winning them both, 11—1 and 8—1.

The Polish F.A. was formed in 1919. A National League was established in 1927.

Address of the governing body: Polska Sekcja Pilki Noznej, Ujazdowskie 22, Warsaw C.1. Colours: White shirts, red shorts, red and white stockings.

Results of international matches:

May 22, 1938	Poland 6, Eire 0; Warsaw.
Nov. 13, 1938	Eire 3, Poland 2; Dublin.
May 11, 1958	Poland 2, Eire 2; Katowice.
June 1, 1958	Poland 1, Scotland 2; Warsaw.
Oct. 5, 1958	Eire 2, Poland 2; Dublin.
May 4, 1960	Scotland 2, Poland 3; Hampden Park.
Oct. 10, 1962†	Poland 0, Ireland 2; Katowice.
Nov. 28, 1962†	Ireland 2, Poland 0; Belfast.
Oct. 25, 1964	Eire 3, Poland 2; Dublin.
May 10, 1964	Poland 3, Eire 1; Cracow.
May 23, 1965*	Poland 1, Scotland 1; Chorzow.

Oct. 13, 1965*	Scotland 1, Poland 2; Hampden Park
Jan. 5, 1966	England 1, Poland 1; Goodison Park
July 5, 1966	Poland 0, England 1; Katowice
May 15, 1968	Eire 2, Poland 2; Dublin
Oct. 30, 1968	Poland 1, Eire 0; Katowice
May 6, 1970	Poland 2, Eire 1; Poznan
* World Cup	† Nations Cup

PORTSMOUTH F.C.

Founded 1898. Joined Southern League 1899. Joined Football League, Division III, 1920. Honours: Champions, Division I, 1948-9, 1949-50. Runners-up, Division II, 1926-7. Champions, Division III(S), 1923-4. Champions, Division III, 1961-2. F.A. Cup: Winners, 1939. Finalists, 1929, 1934. Record attendance: 51,385 v. Derby County, F.A. Cup, 6th Round, Feb. 26, 1949. Address: Fratton Park, Portsmouth (Tel. 31204). Nickname: Pompey. Colours: Royal blue shirts with red, white and blue trim, royal blue shorts. Record League goalscorer: W. Haines, 40 goals, Division II, 1926-7. Record victory: 9—1 v. Notts County, Division II, April 9, 1927. Record defeat: 10—0 v. Leicester City, Division I, Oct. 20, 1928.

PORTUGAL

Football was introduced into Portugal by English residents of Lisbon in the 1870s and the Lisbon Club was formed in 1875. The game was established on a national basis in 1893 and with a vast increase about that time among the number of boys from Portugal receiving their education in England, the game's popularity developed rapidly. The Portuguese F.A. was formed in 1912.

Portugal reached their peak in 1966 when they proved to be one of the best footballing sides in the World Cup and won third place.

The address of the governing body: Federaçao Portuguesa de Futebol, Praça da Alegria 25, Lisbon. Colours: Red shirts, white shorts, green stockings.

Results of international matches:

June 16, 1946	Portugal 3, Eire 1; Lisbon.
May 4, 1947	Eire 0, Portugal 2; Dublin.
May 27, 1947	Portugal 0, England 10; Lisbon.
May 23, 1948	Portugal 2, Eire 0; Lisbon.
May 15, 1949	Portugal 3, Wales 2; Lisbon.
May 22, 1949	Eire 1, Portugal 0; Dublin.
May 14, 1950	Portugal 3, England 5; Lisbon.
May 21, 1950	Portugal 2, Scotland 2; Lisbon.
May 12, 1951	Wales 2, Portugal 1; Cardiff.
May 19, 1951	England 5, Portugal 2; Everton.
May 4, 1955	Scotland 3, Portugal 0; Hampden Park
May 22, 1955	Portugal, 3, England 1; Oporto.
Jan. 1, 1957*	Portugal 1, Ireland 1; Lisbon.
May 1, 1957*	Ireland 3, Portugal 0; Belfast.
May 7, 1958	England 2, Portugal 1; Wembley.
June 3, 1959	Portugal 1, Scotland 0; Lisbon.
May 21, 1961*	Portugal 1, England 1; Lisbon.
Oct. 25, 1961*	England 2, Portugal 0; Wembley.
May 17, 1964	Portugal 3, England 4; Lisbon.
June 4, 1964	Portugal 1, England 1; Sao Paulo, Brazil.
June 18, 1966	Scotland 0, Portugal 1; Hampden Park
July 26, 1966*	England 2, Portugal 1; Wembley
Dec. 10, 1969	England 1, Portugal 0; Wembley
* World Cup.	

PORT VALE F.C.

Founded 1876 as Burslem Port Vale. One of the original members of the Football League, Division II, 1892. Failed to gain re-election, 1896. Returned to Division II two years later but resigned in 1907. Next appeared in Division II when they took over the fixtures of Leeds City in Oct. 1919.

Honours: Champions, Division III(N), 1929-30, 1953-4. Runners-up, 1952-3. Champions, Division IV, 1958-9. F.A. Cup: Semi-finalists, 1954 (only the second Division III club to reach this stage of the competition). Record attendance: 49,000 v. Aston Villa, F.A. Cup, 5th Round, Feb. 20, 1960. Address: Vale Park, Burslem, Stoke-on-Trent (Tel. Stoke-on-Trent 87626). Nickname: Valiants. Colours: All white. Record League goal-scorer: W. Kirkham, 38 goals, Division II, 1926-7. Record victory: 9—1 v. Chesterfield, Division II, Sept. 24, 1932. Record defeat: 10—0 v. Sheffield United (H), Division II, Dec. 10, 1892; v. Notts County, Division II, Feb. 26, 1895.

POSTPONED MATCHES

Football League regulations do not permit members to play postponed or replayed F.A. Cup ties on a Saturday.

Where a Football League game is postponed because of an F.A. Cup tie then the two clubs are entitled to claim a sum based on the home club's average gross gate receipts. This money is paid out of the F.A. Cup Pool.

However, such compensation is not paid where games are re-arranged for a Saturday date.

See also WEATHER.

PRACTICE MATCHES

Practice matches may be played in public during the 14 days prior to the opening of the season, but the receipts must be distributed in accordance with certain rules.

In Scotland the net receipts must be handed over to charity. The F.A. (England) stipulates that 10% goes to a fund administered by them for the development of Youth Football; not less than 25% to the club's or clubs' County association(s), and the remainder in such manner as the clubs may decide.

Clubs are given until Sept. 15 (in Scotland 21 days after season opens) in which to settle-up practice match receipts.

In 1907 Woolwich Arsenal was fined £25 for delay in handing over practice match receipts to charities.

PRESTON NORTH END F.C.

Founded in 1880 by members of the North End Cricket Club, which had been in existence since 1867. Immediately prior to 1880 they had preferred rugby as their winter game. Became one of the original members of the Football League in 1888 and the first Champions. Honours: Champions, Division I, 1888-89, 1889-90. Runners-up, 1890-91, 1891-2, 1892-3, 1905-6, 1952-3, 1957-8. Champions, Division II, 1903-4, 1912-13, 1950-51. Runners-up, 1914-15, 1933-4. F.A. Cup: Winners, 1889, 1938. Finalists, 1888, 1922, 1937, 1954, 1964. Record attendance: 42,684 v. Arsenal, Division I, April 23, 1938. Address: Deepdale, Preston (Tel. 53818). Nickname: Lily whites. Colours: White shirts, dark blue shorts. Record League goal-scorer: E. Harper, 37 goals, Division II, 1932-3. Preston North End is one of the only three clubs ever to achieve "the double"—the League Championship and the F.A. Cup in the same season. They did so in 1888-9. Record victory: 26—0 v. Hyde, F.A. Cup, 1st Round, 1st Series, Oct. 15, 1887. Record defeat: 7—0 v. Blackpool (H), Division I, May 1, 1948.

PROFESSIONAL FOOT-BALLERS ASSOCIATION, THE

See also WAGES.

The first attempt to form a Players' Union was made in Oct. 1893, by W. C. Rose, a goalkeeper with Wolverhampton Wanderers. He sent letters to all the captains of clubs in Division I, proposing the formation of a Union "to protect professional interests".

A Union known as the National Union of Association Players was subsequently formed in 1899 but it soon became defunct.

The present, more powerful and fully recognised body was formed at a meeting held on Dec. 2, 1907, and registered as a trade union on Mar. 10, 1908. It was then known as the Football Players' and Trainers' Union.

In 1908 the F.A. gave official recognition to this Union but when the new body became affiliated with the Federation of Trade Unions trouble started with the F.A. and the Football League. These two organisations feared that football might be suspended through *any* subsequent union strike.

The F.A. withdrew recognition of

the Union in 1909, and gave the officials an ultimatum to resign or be forever banned from football. Several Union committeemen chose to obey the F.A.'s instructions, but not all did so, and the Chairman and Secretary were suspended by the F.A.

At the time of the ban, a strike of players was threatened. Several did in fact stand out without pay for 14 weeks before a conference was called at Birmingham in Aug. 1909. The outcome of the meeting was that the players got their wages, and the F.A. and the Union recognised each other.

Since then the Union has done much to improve the lot of the professional footballer. For many years their main bone of contention was the form of contract and the maximum wage rule, and on at least two occasions after World War II the Union threatened to strike to back up their demands.

Fortunately, strikes have been averted and while the Union or the Professional Footballers' Association (they adopted this title in 1958) has not yet gained all its demands concerning the form of contract, in 1961 they at last got their way with the abolition of the maximum wage rule.

Scotland

Scottish players have their own Union. It was formed in 1946, 33 years after the original Scottish Players' Union was dissolved when only two years old.

PROFESSIONALISM

Today there are about 7,000 registered professional footballers in Britain, but the identity of the first man to receive payment for playing football will never be definitely established. In its earliest days professionalism was an "under the counter" affair. It was frowned on by the Football Association and, indeed, banned by a rule made in 1882 which permitted only payment for actual wages lost in addition to normal expenses.

However the player who is generally considered to have been the first professional footballer was a Scot, J. J. Lang. North of the Border he had played for Clydesdale and for Glasgow Eastern, but in 1876 he joined Sheffield Wednesday. It is difficult now to prove that he was paid by the Yorkshire club but in later years when he was a steward at Ibrox Park he always claimed that he had been the first Scot to go South solely for the purpose of playing football.

Professionalism was the inevitable outcome of the spread of the game from the schools and universities to the industrial centres in the North and Midlands. It was among the clubs of the industrial North that the practice of paying players first began. As soon as it was seen that so many people were interested in watching football, someone decided to collect "gate money". The money collected was most acceptable for it meant that the clubs could buy better kit and improve their grounds so helping towards attracting bigger crowds.

There was growing enthusiasm for the F.A. Cup. None of the bigger clubs could afford to be out of the competition, but entry meant high travelling expenses so that there was a considerable need to increase revenue.

It is obvious that only winning teams can attract bigger crowds. So that when a club found that it could not form a winning combination from local talent, it looked further afield. Players who were induced to give up their jobs in other towns and move into the neighbourhood of their new clubs naturally needed some incentive other than their love of the game.

About the time that the competition among the Northern clubs for new and more attractive players was becoming so intense (about 1880) Scotland took the lead in the production of talented footballers. The Scots had developed a style of close passing which, as was proved by international results, was far more effective than the old English individual play.

The first clubs to import Scotsmen in any number were Blackburn Rovers and Darwen, between 1879 and 1882. They were soon followed by Preston North End and Bolton Wanderers.

The advent of so many imported players obviously meant professionalism, but the traditionally amateur Football Association seemed peculiarly reluctant to take any definite action against the offending clubs. They introduced a rule in 1882 which stated that any player who received remuneration or consideration of any sort above his actual expenses and any wages lost would be debarred from the Cup or any Association or international matches, and the employing club would be excluded from the Association; but the governing body did not take much action to back up the rule.

The first definite step to bar professionalism was taken by the Lancashire and Birmingham Associations. Their investigations shook the Football Association into action, and early in 1883 a sub-committee was appointed to investigate alleged professionalism. The outcome was disappointing to the opponents of professionalism, for the committee were unable to find proof of payment to players.

There was an ever-growing wave of resentment against professionalism among the amateur clubs. They expressed reluctance in competing for the F.A. Cup while professional players were also engaged in the competition. On the other hand, however, many individuals who had earlier expressed themselves against the growth of professionalism were now beginning to wonder whether professionalism was not, after all, doing the game good.

It seemed that professionalism was encouraging new players from a wider sphere of life; bringing men into the game who would normally have been unable to afford to take part. This meant an increase in the number of expert exponents of the game among men who were not only fighting to keep their places in the team purely for the game's sake, but also because it was their bread and butter. What greater inducement to play well?

The first real move made by the Football Association against professionalism came late in 1883 when it suspended Accrington for paying one of their players. As a result, there was a great deal of bad feeling directed towards the F.A. especially from the Northern clubs. The credit for clearing the air and bringing professionalism into the open belongs to the Preston North End club, and in particular to its President, Major W. Sudell. After Preston North End had drawn with Upton Park in the 4th Round of the F.A. Cup, Jan. 1884, the London club protested to the F.A. insisting that Preston had included professionals in their team.

A special meeting of the F.A. Committee was called, and to everyone's amazement, when Major Sudell came before them, instead of attempting to hide the facts, the Preston chief quite openly admitted professionalism. More than that, he announced that he could provide proof to show that most of the clubs in his part of the country were also paying their players.

Preston North End were disqualified from the competition. But Major Sudell's frankness precipitated the legalisation of professionalism.

However, the lifting of the ban on professionalism was not made immediately. Certain members of the F.A. were not prepared to give up the fight easily. A proposal by Mr. C. W. Alcock (Hon. Sec. of the F.A.) that professionalism should be legalised was countered by a proposal that it was an evil. The latter proposal was carried.

One of the leading opponents of the adoption of professionalism at this time was Mr. J. C. Clegg then the representative of the Sheffield Association, and later to become Sir Charles Clegg, President of the F.A. He considered that the legalisation of professionalism would " place more power in the hands of betting-men and encourage gambling ".

In June 1884, the Association passed new rules in their last effort to stem the tide. Under these, payment for wages lost was not allowed for more than one day in any week, and receipts were to be produced by the clubs. But a more drastic rule was that which prevented any but Englishmen from taking part in F.A. Cup ties.

Few, if any, of the clubs who were already paying their players, appeared to take heed of these new rules. Indeed, many preferred to retire from the competition rather than lay themselves open to investigation. A major split was threatened when there was a movement to form a British Football Association in which professionalism would be permitted.

The F.A. now began to realise the futility of their efforts to repress the payment of players. A sub-committee was formed to consider the question afresh. Innumerable meetings took place, proposals and counter-proposals were made, questionnaires circularised to the clubs, until eventually, at a Special General Meeting on July 20, 1885, professionalism was at last recognised. But it was to be strictly controlled. In all Cup matches only professionals who were qualified by birth or residence during the past two years within six miles of the headquarters of their respective clubs, were permitted to take part. This rule was not expunged until four years later.

The other home countries, Scotland in particular, continued to wage war against "this evil" of professionalism, but all in turn, had to submit to the inevitable. Scotland lifted her ban in May 1893.

At first there were no professional clubs in England south of Birmingham. But gradually southern clubs took the plunge, Luton Town (1890), Woolwich Arsenal (1891), Southampton (1892), Millwall (1893). and Tottenham Hotspur (1894), were among the first.

The London F.A. was the last of the leading authorities in this country to accept professionalism. They held out until Feb. 1906.

The spread of professionalism brought the need for more earnest consideration of club fixtures. Football was now a business: the various professional clubs were not in it just for the love of it. More attractive and keener games had to be organised. The outcome of these considerations was the formation of the Football League in 1888 (q.v.).

For more details of the actual payments made to players, see WAGES.

PROMOTION

Automatic promotion and relegation for the bottom two and the top two teams of Divisions I and II was first introduced in season 1898-9. Before this, promotion and relegation had been decided by a series of Test Matches.

The Test Match system was adopted in 1893, the end of the first season of the new Division II. At first, the bottom three teams in Division I met the top three clubs in Division II. Only three matches were played: one Division I team met one of the Division II teams. The winners either retained Division I status or gained promotion accordingly.

This system was revised in season 1895-6 when the bottom two Division I teams played each of the top two Division II teams twice. Promotion and relegation were decided on the points obtained by each club from its four games.

See also GOAL AVERAGE.

Fees

Clubs promoted to Division II have to pay £200 League membership fee. This figure represents the difference between the initial membership fee of £100 charged to clubs joining Division IV (or who joined the old Third Division) as Associate Members of the Football League, and the fee of £300 charged to Full Members, i.e. those 44 clubs in the top two Divisions.

Four up and Down

A proposal that four teams instead of two from each division should change places at the end of each season was made by Derby County as long ago as 1933, but although that same proposal has been made at nearly every A.G.M. of the Football League ever since it has not yet received the three-quarters majority needed for its adoption.

The main reason usually given by those who are against this proposal is that the increase in the scramble for league points would mean more dog fights and less football. However, considering the fact that it is the Division I clubs who have formed the majority of those against the proposal then it is obvious that their thoughts are mainly centred upon preserving their position in the senior section. Little consideration seems to have been given to the point that acceptance of this proposal would also mean that clubs relegated might find it easier to regain the higher status.

In 1956 the Football League Management Committee issued a five-point plan for reorganisation and it was one of their suggestions that there should be an increase in the number of teams promoted and relegated so as to give the clubs in the lower divisions greater incentive and create new interest.

It was subsequently decided to try four-up and four-down promotion and relegation when the two sections of the Third Division were formed into a Third and Fourth Division, but the increased number up and down was only between these two divisions.

See also FOOTBALL LEAGUE.

Q

QUEEN OF THE SOUTH F.C.

Formed 1919 by the amalgamation of Arrol-Johnston F.C., Dumfries F.C., and K.O.S.B. Elected to Scottish League, Division III, 1923. Reached Division I, 1933. Honours: Champions, Division B, 1950-51, Runners-up, Division II, 1932-3, 1961-2. Runners-up, Division III, 1924-5. Best in Division I, 4th, 1933-4. Record attendance: 25,000 v. Hearts, Scottish Cup, 3rd Round, Feb. 23, 1952. Address: Palmerston Park, Dumfries (Tel. 4853). Colours: Royal blue shirts, white shorts. Record goal-scorer: in Division I: J. Patterson, 26 goals, 1955-6. Record victory: 11—1 v. Stranraer, Scottish Cup, 1st Round, Jan. 16, 1932. Record defeat: 10—2 v. Dundee, Division I, Dec. 1, 1962.

QUEEN'S PARK A.F.C.

Founded 1867. Entered Division I of Scottish League, 1900-1901. Honours: Champions, Division II, 1922-3, 1955-6. Scottish Cup: Winners, 1874, 1875, 1876, 1880, 1881, 1882, 1884, 1886, 1890, 1893. Finalists, 1892, 1900. Record attendance: 149,547, Scotland v. England, April 17, 1937. Address: 55 West Regent Street, Glasgow, C.2 (Tel. Langside 1275). Colours: Black and white hooped shirts, white shorts. Record League goal-scorer: W. Martin, 30

goals, Division I, 1937-8. Record victory: 9—1 v. Cowdenbeath (A), Division II, 1959-60. Record defeat: 9—0 v. Motherwell, Division I, April 26, 1930.

QUEEN'S PARK RANGERS F.C.

Founded 1885 as St. Jude's Institute F.C. Changed to present title in 1888. Adopted professionalism 1898. Joined Football League, Division III, 1920. Honours: Champions, Division III, 1966-7. Champions, Division III(S), 1947-8. Runners-up, 1946-7. Runners-up, Division II, 1967-8. League Cup Winners, 1967. Record attendance: 33,572 v. Chelsea, F.A. Cup, 6th Round, Feb. 21, 1970. At White City —42,000 v. Leeds United, F.A. Cup, 3rd Round, Jan. 9, 1932. Address: Ellerslie Road, Shepherd's Bush, London, W.12 (Tel. Shepherd's Bush 2618). Nickname: The "R's". Colours: Blue and white hooped shirts, white shorts. Record League goal-scorer: G. Goddard, 37 goals, Division III(S), 1929-30. Record victory: 9—2 v. Tranmere Rovers, Division III, Dec. 3, 1960. Record defeat: 8—1 v. Mansfield Town, Division III, Mar. 15, 1965.

QUICKEST GOALS

See GOAL-SCORING (Fast scoring).

R

RAITH ROVERS F.C.

Founded 1883. Became Limited Liability Company, 1907. Elected to Scottish League, Division II, 1902. Honours: Champions, Division II, 1907-8, 1937-8. Runners-up, 1966-7. Best in Division I, 3rd, 1921-2. Scottish Cup: Runners-up, 1913. Record attendance: 32,000 v. Hearts, Scottish Cup, 2nd Round, Feb. 7, 1953. Address: Stark's Park, Kirkcaldy (Tel. 3514). Colours: White shirts with two blue hoops, white shorts. Record League goal-scorer: T. Jennings, 27 goals, Division I, 1923-4. Record victory: 10—1 v. Coldstream (A), Scottish Cup, 2nd Round, Feb. 13, 1954. Record defeat: 11—2 v. Morton, Division II, 1935-6.

RANGERS F.C.

Founded 1873. One of the original members of the Scottish League, 1890. Honours: Champions, Division I, 1890-91 (jointly with Dumbarton), 1898-9, 1899-1900, 1900-1901, 1901-2, 1910-11, 1911-12, 1912-13, 1917-18, 1919-20, 1920-21, 1922-3, 1923-4, 1924-5, 1926-7, 1927-8, 1928-9, 1929-30, 1930-31, 1932-3, 1933-4, 1934-5, 1936-7, 1938-9, 1946-7, 1948-9, 1949-50, 1952-3, 1955-6, 1956-7, 1958-9, 1960-61, 1962-3, 1963-4. Runners-up, 1892-3, 1895-6, 1897-8, 1904-5, 1913-14, 1915-16, 1918-19, 1921-2, 1931-2, 1935-6, 1947-8, 1950-1, 1951-2, 1957-8, 1961-2, 1965-6, 1966-7, 1967-8, 1968-9, 1969-70. Scottish Cup: Winners (19 times), 1894, 1897, 1898, 1903, 1928, 1930, 1932, 1934, 1935, 1936, 1948, 1949, 1950, 1953, 1960, 1962, 1963, 1964, 1966. Runners-up, 1877, 1899, 1904, 1905, 1921, 1922, 1929, 1969, Rangers were also finalists in 1908-9 when, after drawing with Celtic, the Cup was withheld because of a riot. European Cup Winners Cup:

Runners-up, 1961, 1967. Record attendance: 118,567 v. Celtic, Division I, Jan. 2, 1939. Address: Ibrox Stadium, Glasgow S.W.1 (Tel. Ibrox 0159). Nickname: The Blues. Colours: Royal blue shirts, white shorts. Record League goal-scorer: S. English, 44 goals, Division I, 1931-2, Record victory: 14—2 v. Blairgowrie, Scottish Cup, 1st Round, Jan. 20, 1934. Record defeat: 6—0 v. Dumbarton, Scottish League, 1891-2.

READING F.C.

Founded 1871 and subsequently strengthened by amalgamation with The Hornets (1877) and Earley (1889). One of the original members of the Southern League in 1894, and of the Football League, Division III, 1920. Honours: Champions, Division III(S), 1925-6. Runners-up, 1931-2, 1934-5, 1948-9, 1951-2. Best in Division II, 14th, 1926-7. Record attendance: 33,042 v. Brentford, F.A. Cup, 5th Round, Feb. 19, 1927. Address: Elm Park, Norfolk Road, Reading (Tel. 57878). Nickname: Biscuitmen. Colours: Sky blue shirts and shorts. Record League goal-scorer: R. Blackman, 39 goals, Division III(S), 1951-2. Record victory: 10—2 v. Crystal Palace, Division III(S), 1946-7. Record defeat: 18—0 v. Preston North End, F.A. Cup, 1st Round, 1893-4.

RECEIPTS

See GATE RECEIPTS.

RE-ELECTION

Originally it was decided that the bottom four clubs in the Football League should have to apply for re-election at the end of each season. To be precise the rule agreed upon was that the bottom four *in each class* should retire, but be eligible for re-election.

However, a second class, or second division, did not come into existence until 1892 and at the end of season 1892-3 the original rule was not adhered to and only the bottom four in Division II had to apply for re-election.

This system continued until 1896 when it was reduced to the bottom three clubs. In 1909 it became only the last two who had to retire and make a fresh application for membership.

When the Third Division was formed in 1920 the bottom two had to apply for re-election at the end of the first season, and thereafter, with the addition of a Northern Section, the bottom two in each section.

Since the formation of the Fourth Division in 1958 it is the bottom four clubs of this division that have to apply for re-election.

Going back only to the beginning of the Third Division these are the clubs that have had to apply:

Nine times: Barrow, Hartlepools United.

Eight times: Newport County, Southport.

Seven Times: Exeter City, Halifax Town, Walsall.

Six times: Chester, Rochdale.

Five times: Accrington Stanley, Bradford, Gillingham, New Brighton, York City.

Four times: Darlington, Lincoln City, Norwich City.

Three times: Aldershot, Bradford City, Crystal Palace, Crewe Alexandra, Merthyr, Swindon Town, Workington.

Twice: Aberdare, Ashington, Bournemouth, Brentford, Colchester United, Gateshead, Millwall, Durham City, Grimsby Town, Nelson, Oldham Athletic, Queen's Park Rangers, Rotherham United, Southend United, Tranmere Rovers, Watford.

Once: Brighton, Bristol Rovers, Cardiff City, Carlisle United, Charlton Athletic, Doncaster Rovers, Mansfield Town, Shrewsbury Town, Stockport County, Torquay United, Wrexham.

Thames finished bottom of Division III(S) in 1931-2 but did not seek re-election.

REFEREES AND LINESMEN

The first mention of a referee in any of the early rules of football (though not specifically soccer) is that found in those which governed the game as played at Cheltenham College in 1867.

For some time prior to this it had become the practice in most important games to appoint two umpires. This had generally been adopted by most of the public schools and one umpire was usually provided by each side. At Cheltenham, however, it was decided that " In every important match there shall be an umpire for each side (each captain to choose his own), and a referee, to be chosen by these umpires. Any point on which the umpires cannot agree shall be decided by the referee."

It should be pointed out, however, that the game which was played at Cheltenham at that time was certainly not soccer. It had been introduced into the college by young men from Rugby where it had been the practice to " run with the ball " since about 1823, and Cheltenham College then eventually adopted the Rugby Union rules.

The first official reference to a referee in Association Football did not appear until 1871 when Rule 15 of the new F.A. Challenge Cup Competition read as follows:

" The Committee shall appoint two umpires and a referee to act at each of the matches in the Final Ties. Neither the umpires nor the referee shall be members of either of the contending clubs and the decision of the umpires shall be final except in the case of the umpires disagreeing when an appeal shall be made to the referee, whose decision shall be final."

The wording of this rule shows just how much the increased competition was already beginning to change the attitude of the players. The days of the gentlemen players, who were proud of the manner in which rival teams generally conducted themselves, and settled any disputes, were beginning to fade. The time had come not only to specify the appointment of both umpires and referees but to insist upon these men being NEUTRAL.

Umpires were first mentioned in the actual laws of Association Football in 1874, but no mention of referees is made until 1881 when the following appeared:

" By mutual consent of the competing clubs in matches, a referee shall be appointed whose duty shall be to decide in all cases of dispute between umpires. He shall also keep a record of the game and act as timekeeper, and in the event of ungentlemanly behaviour on the part of any of the contestants, the offender or offenders shall, in the presence of the umpires, be cautioned, and in the case of violent conduct, the referee shall have power to rule the offending player or players out of play, and order him or them off the ground, transmitting name or names to the committee of the Association under whom rules the game was played, and in whom shall be solely vested the right of accepting an apology."

The umpires were abolished in favour of linesmen in 1891 when the referee was moved from the touchline on to the field of play and empowered to give decisions without waiting for appeals.

The referee was now in complete control and soon after this the demand for their services increased so quickly that in Mar. 1893, a Referees' Association was formed.

At its annual meeting on June 4, 1928, the F.A. Council decided that referees should be classified as follows:

Class I. To consist of referees whose competency is guaranteed by their County Associations. Referees of experience recommended for F.A. Cup ties to be starred.

Class II. Other senior referees.

Class III. Junior referees.

Today this classification by the Football Association remains very much the same (there is a similar form of classification in Scotland), although only referees whose ages do not exceed 50 are eligible for classification by the F.A. under I or II.

The Football League draws up a list of referees every season. It normally includes about 80 names. The age limit for the Football League is 47 except in special cases where an extension is granted by the management committee.

The fee for referees originally fixed by the Football League in 1888 was 10s. 6d. per match. Fees for linesmen were fixed at 5s. in 1896. The more recent increases have been made as follows:

May 30, 1938. A uniform scale of payment for referees was instituted:

3gn. for any League game, linesmen to receive 1½gn.

From 1921 to 1938 the fee for referees was 3gn. for Division I and II matches, and 2gn. for Division III matches, linesmen 1½gn. for Division I and II, 1gn. for Division III.

In 1946 there was an increase to 4gn. per match for referees and 2gn. for linesmen. This was further increased in 1948 to 5gn. and 2½gn., in 1958 to 7 gn. and 3½gn., and in 1965 to 10gn. and 5 gn.

In addition, these match officials are entitled to first class railway fare or 6d. per mile if travelling by private car to and from the match, and a meal allowance of from £1 to £3 according to travelling time. Hotel expenses of 4gns. per night are also paid where a night stay is necessary.

The scale of fees for referees and linesmen is also 10gn. and 5gn. in all Rounds of the F.A. Cup Competition proper, prior to the Final. But in the Final the referee receives 15gn. and the linesmen 7gn. In addition to these fees, the officials are entitled to travelling expenses, and are also presented with a gold medal each.

Fees for referees and linesmen in international matches are now £18 and £9 each respectively.

Two Referees

The proposal that all games should be controlled by two referees has been brought up from time to time during the past 30 years. The suggestion was given lengthy consideration for the first time in 1935 when the proposal was put to the Annual Meeting of the Football League. It was rejected by 31 votes to 18.

The prime mover of the proposal was the Everton club, and their chairman, Mr. W. C. Cuff, made strong pleas for its introduction.

The dual control plan was tried out in an international trial game, England v. The Rest, at West Bromwich, Mar. 27, 1935, as well as at the game between a Football League XI and West Bromwich Albion on May 8, 1935.

The proposal came forward again in 1937 when it was put to the A.G.M. of the Football Association.

It was suggested that the system be given a trial in practice matches before the opening of the new season and then in certain League games. The proposal was defeated.

Whistle

It is generally believed that the first time a whistle was used by a referee was in a game between Nottingham Forest and Sheffield Norfolk at Nottingham in 1878.

Sent Off

The famous occasion on which the referee was " sent off " by a team captain occurred in the annual Sheffield v. Glasgow Inter-City match, Sept. 22, 1930, at Hampden Park, Glasgow. Sheffield were playing in white shirts and black shorts. The referee, Mr. J. Thomson of Burnbank, wore a white shirt without a jacket. Captaining Sheffield was inside-right, J. Seed. As soon as he found that he was passing the ball to the referee in error, he asked Mr. Thomson to stop the game and put on a jacket. Mr. Thomson obliged.

F.A. Cup

The referee of the F.A. Cup Semi-final game between Huddersfield Town and Sheffield Wednesday, Mar. 22, 1930, blew for time as a shot from Sheffield Wednesday's centre-forward, J. Allen, was entering the net. The ball had not crossed the line so no goal was awarded. Huddersfield won 2—1.

The youngest referee ever to control an F.A. Cup Final was H. Bamlett of Gateshead. Born Mar. 1, 1882, he was 32 when he took charge of the Final tie between Burnley and Liverpool at the Crystal Palace, 1914.

Internationals

At the International Board meeting in June 1950, it was decided that referees for international matches must be from a neutral country unless otherwise agreed by the countries concerned.

REGISTRATION OF PLAYERS

See also TRANSFERS.

A player must be seventeen years of age before he can be registered as a professional with any club under the jurisdiction of the Football Association or the Scottish F.A.

However, under F.A. rules, youths between the ages of 15 and 17 may be registered as apprentice professionals, each Football League club being limited to 15 of these. As soon as these apprentice professionals have passed their 17th birthday they may register as full professionals. They have until their 18th birthday to decide whether to make this move or, if they wish, they can decide to revert to amateur status.

In Scotland players under 17 may be registered for a club on what is known as " Provisional Form ", but such registration does not become operative until the player is 17 years of age.

The minimum age at which Football League clubs are permitted to register schoolboys is 13 on the 1st September in any season.

However, this is for the purpose of training and coaching only, and no boy under the age of 15 on 1st September in any season is permitted to play for the club in the League.

Football League clubs are each limited to a maximum of 40 of these schoolboy registrations at any one time.

For many years the form of contract which entitled a club to retain a player indefinitely, providing they were prepared to pay him a certain minimum as laid down by the Football Association, was the main bone of contention when the players threatened to strike on Jan. 21, 1961. The strike was averted and a number of alterations in players' contracts were agreed during protracted discussions which extended over a period of six months and about 17 meetings between Football League representatives and leaders of the Professional Footballer's Association.

While retaining the same broad principles the F.A. originally accommodated the new agreement between the players and the Football League by inserting in their rules the words "subject to the provisions of the competition in which they compete ". However, they have since considerably amended their rules.

The Football League would not agree to abandon their right to retain players after the individual registrations expired but they did make certain concessions.

At the present time the rules are such that if a player refuses to resign by 30th June (the date when contracts normally expire) then a dispute is deemed to exist between player and club, and either may appeal to the Management Committee who shall adjudicate by not later than 31st July.

If the player has still not re-signed by 31st August then an Independent Tribunal shall determine the dispute not later than 30th September.

Until such time as the dispute is settled the player remains in the employment of his club on the terms of the existing contract.

Another aspect of players' contracts which was discussed in 1961 concerned the maximum period of time for which a player could sign for a club.

For many years it had been the practice to allow clubs to register professionals for one whole season, or during the season for the remainder of that season. If a player joined a club during the last three months of a particular season then he could be registered for the remainder of the current season and the whole of the next.

In 1961 this was amended so that a player in the Football League could be signed for any period up to two years. But even this rule has since been abolished so that now there is no limit to length of contract.

No player can play for his club until his registration has been received and acknowledged at both the Football League and Football Association headquarters. One often hears of last minute registrations, even of a player signing in the morning and playing for his club the same afternoon. This is no longer possible in the Football League where the forms must be received 48 hours before the player is deemed to be registered, but the F.A. provide special facilities for speedy registrations.

The forms and a copy of the agreement entered into between the player and the club (no registration is accepted without this agreement), is sent by registered post (or recorded delivery) to the F.A., and, at the same time, a telegram is despatched, stating that these forms have been duly signed and posted. Providing the registration is otherwise acceptable, the club may consider the player eligible to play for them from the time such telegram is received at Paddington District Post Office.

There is often some misunderstanding about players in the Southern League who are said to be on the books of Football League clubs. The explanation is that these players are not *retained* by their original clubs but placed on the *open to transfer list*. A Football League player on the transfer list cannot play for another Football League club without a proper transfer agreement, but he can play for another club outside the Football League without a fee changing hands if his new club is a member of a League which has no agreement to recognise Football League transfer registrations. The Southern League has no such agreement. Hence the fact that a number of former Football League players are now engaged with Southern League clubs who have never paid transfer fees for them.

Non-British born players cannot be registered as professionals by the F.A. unless they have resided here for at least two years.

Should a professional player wish to continue to play without remuneration (there is no such thing as reverting to amateur status; in the eyes of the Football Association—once a professional always a professional), he has to make application to the F.A., and this costs him 10s. He may then be granted a Permit.*

The Permit entitles him to play for only one club and he may not move to another club during the same season. If he continues with the same club no further Permit is necessary, but a new Permit must be obtained should he move to another club at the end of the season. In any case no Permit is given after Jan. 31 in any season, and never more than one Permit to a player in a single season. A professional playing as an " amateur " under such conditions is termed as " playing under licence ".

In 1960 the Football League decided to permit clubs to place amateurs on their retained list at the end of each season.

F.A. Cup

In all Rounds before the Third Round of the Qualifying competition

* Apprentice professionals up to the age of 18 are exempt from this rule.

only professionals who have been registered with their clubs for at least 48 hours before the Cup Tie are eligible to play. In the remaining Rounds the qualifying period is 14 days.

These qualifying periods are the same for amateurs.

Scottish Cup

The qualifying period for professionals in the Scottish Cup is 14 days unless he was last registered for, or a playing member of, a club in membership of an affiliated national association.

RELEGATION

The keenest relegation struggle in the history of the Football League was in Division I in 1927-8. Of the last nine clubs, seven had 39 points, one had 38, and one 37. Tottenham Hotspur and Middlesbrough were relegated.

The only clubs to be relegated twice in successive seasons are Bradford, Brighton, Doncaster Rovers, Fulham, Lincoln City, Northampton Town and Notts County.

Bradford dropped from Division I to Division III in seasons 1920-21 and 1921-2. They missed promotion the following season when they finished runners-up to Nelson.

Fulham dropped from Division I to Division III in seasons 1967-8 and 1968-9.

Brighton went down from Division II to Division IV in seasons 1961-2 and 1962-3.

Doncaster Rovers and Notts County dropped from Division II to Division IV together in seasons 1957-8 and 1958-9.

Lincoln City dropped from Division II to IV in seasons 1960-61 and 1961-2, while Northampton went down from Division I to III in seasons 1965-6 and 1966-7.

Port Vale also slipped from Division II to Division IV in two seasons but their case is a little different. They were relegated to Division III(S) in 1957 and when, in the following year, the two sections of the Third Division were re-arranged into a new Third and Fourth Division, Port Vale dropped into the lower Division because they were below the halfway mark in the Southern Section. The

lower half of each Third Division section made up the new Fourth Division.

The Football League ordered that Peterborough United be relegated from Division III at the end of 1967-8 as punishment for offering players illegal payments.

See also PROMOTION.

REPUBLIC OF IRELAND

See EIRE.

RESIGNED

In 1929 Bathgate and Arthurlie were forced to resign from the Scottish League, Division II, through lack of funds.

Wigan Borough resigned from Division III(N) of the Football League on Oct. 26, 1931. The club's record for the season was cancelled.

Leeds City were wound up for alleged irregular practices in Oct. 1919. The remainder of their season's fixtures were taken on by Port Vale.

Stoke resigned from Division II on June 17, 1908 and were replaced by Tottenham Hotspur. Stoke was re-formed almost immediately but failed to regain admission to the Football League until 1919.

Other clubs that have resigned from the Football League are Accrington Stanley 1893 and 1962; Glossop North End 1919; New Brighton 1901; and Stalybridge Celtic 1923.

Please note that the above does not include clubs who dropped out of the Football League when they failed to gain re-election.

Thames finished bottom of the Third Division (S) in 1932 and although they did not actually resign, the fact that they did not apply for re-election amounted to the same thing.

ROCHDALE F.C.

Founded 1900 as Rochdale Town. Became limited company as Rochdale A.F.C. in 1910. One of the original members of Division III(N) in 1921. Honours: Runners-up, Division III(N), 1923-4, 1926-7. League Cup: Runners-up, 1962. Record attendance: 24,231 v. Notts County, F.A. Cup, 2nd Round, Dec. 10, 1949. Address: Willbutts Ground, Spotland, Rochdale (Tel. 32698). Nickname: Vallians. Colours: Royal blue shirts with white trim, white shorts. Record League goal-scorer: A. J. Whitehurst, 44 goals, Division III(N), 1926-7. Record victory: 8—1 v. Chesterfield, Division III(N), Dec. 18, 1926. Record defeat: 8—0 v. Wrexham, Division III(N), Dec. 28, 1929.

ROTHERHAM UNITED F.C.

Founded as Thornhill United in 1884. Became Rotherham County, 1905. Amalgamated with Rotherham Town, with the present title of Rotherham United, 1925. Elected to Football League, Division II, 1893. Dropped out, 1896; re-elected to Division II, 1919. Honours: Champions, Division III(N), 1950-51. Runners-up, 1946-7, 1947-8, 1948-9. Best in Division II, 3rd, 1954-5. League Cup: Runners-up, 1961. Record attendance: 25,000 v. Sheffield Wednesday, Division II, Jan. 26, 1952, and v. Sheffield United, Division II, Dec. 13, 1952. Address: Millmoor Ground, Rotherham (Tel. 2434). Nickname: Merry Millers. Colours: All red. Record League goal-scorer: W. Ardron, 38 goals, Division III(N), 1946-7. Record victory: 8—0 v. Oldham Athletic, Division III(N), May 26, 1947. Record defeat: 11—1 v. Bradford City, Division III(N), Aug. 25, 1928.

ROYALTY AND FOOTBALL

It is impossible to trace the history of soccer as opposed to rugby much before the middle of the 19th century for there was then only one game—football. Therefore, most of the following references may be included in the history of both codes.

Edward II

April 13, 1314. Issued proclamation banning the playing of football.

Edward III

June 12, 1349. Royal proclamation issued deploring the falling off in the popularity of archery, and commanding that all able-bodied men should pass their leisure time with bows and arrows to ensure an adequate supply of archers in the event of war.

So that men would be compelled to adopt this pastime they were prevented, under penalty of imprisonment, from "attending to throwing stones, skittles, quoits, fives, football or hockey, or wrestling, or cock-fighting or other foolish games like these which are of no use."

Richard III

Passed a statute in 1389 forbidding "all playing at tennise, football, and other games called corts, dice, casting of the stones, railes, and other such importune games."

James II of Scotland

Issued a proclamation in 1457: "footballe and golfe be utterly cryed down and not be used."

James IV of Scotland

Proclaimed in 1491 that nowhere in the realm "ther be used futeball, golfe, or other sik unprofitable sports."

Elizabeth I

1572 proclamation: "No foteballe play to be used or suffered within the City of London."

Charles II

He is considered to have been the first monarch to show favour towards the game of football. He patronised a game between his servants and the servants of the Duke of Albemarle in 1681.

Edward VII

While Prince of Wales he became the Patron of the F.A. in 1892. He had first patronised the game in Mar. 1886 when he visited Kennington Oval for a Charity Festival which included a soccer match between the Gentlemen and Players.

George V

The first reigning monarch to attend a Football League match outside of London. On Mar. 27, 1920, he saw the Manchester City v. Liverpool, Division I, game at Hyde Road.

King George V was also the first reigning monarch to attend an F.A. Cup Final. On April 25, 1914, he watched the Burnley v. Liverpool Final at the Crystal Palace.

RUGBY

The split which established the separate games of Association and Rugby Football is marked by the breaking away of the Blackheath Club from any agreement with the newly formed Football Association in Dec. 1863.

Blackheath objected to the banning of running with the ball and 'hacking' in the Association rules (hacking is the practice of using the toe either to kick an opponent's shins or to trip him up). They insisted that "hacking was the true football game". Despite the fact that the break was made over this question of ' hacking' the Rugby Union immediately banned ' hacking' on its formation eight years later.

See also ORIGIN OF THE GAME.

The following have gained international caps both at soccer and rugby:

England

R. H. Birkett (Clapham Rovers). Soccer: v. Scotland 1879. Rugby: v. Scotland 1871, 1875 and 1876; v. Ireland 1877.

J. W. Sutcliffe (Heckmondwike and Bolton Wanderers). Soccer: v. Scotland 1895 and 1901; v. Wales 1893 and 1903; v. Ireland 1895. Rugby: v. Maoris 1889.

C. P. Wilson (Hendon and Cambridge University). Soccer: v. Scotland and Wales 1884. Rugby: v. Wales 1881.

Scotland

H. W. Renny-Tailyour (Royal Engineers). Soccer: v. England 1873. Rugby: v. England 1872.

Ireland and Eire

Dr. K. O'Flanagan (London Irish and Arsenal). Soccer: (Eire) v. England, Portugal and Spain 1947. Also for Ireland (Belfast) v. Scotland and Wales. Victory Internationals 1946. Rugby: (Ireland) v. Australia 1948.

M. O'Flanagan (Bohemians and Lansdowne). Soccer: (Eire) v. England 1947. Rugby: (Ireland) v. Scotland 1948.

E. Hammett (Treharris Newport and Blackheath) played as an amateur international for Wales at Association Football (v. England 1912) and a

Rugby Union international for England v. Scotland 1920 and 1921; v. Ireland 1921; v. Wales 1920, 1921 and 1922; v. France 1920 and 1921.

D. Davies of Bolton Wanderers was capped at Association Football for Wales and also got his cap in Rugby League Football.

RUMANIA

Football was introduced to Rumania by British engineers working at the oilfields and the oldest club in that country was formed at Ploesti in 1905.

A National Championship competition was begun in 1910 but progress was interrupted by the First World War and other political upheavals which followed and the game was not established on a proper footing until the return from exile of King Carol in 1930.

This monarch was a real soccer enthusiast and he backed the newly formed Football Association to the hilt. This Association had only been in existence since Feb. 1930 or about four months before Carol's return to his country.

Rumania appeared in the World Cup Finals in 1930, 1934, 1938 and 1970. Their only victories in any of these finals was in 1930 when they defeated Peru 3—1, and in 1970— 2—1 v. Czechoslovakia.

The Football season in Rumania is split into two halves. It extends from March to July and from September to December.

The address of the governing body: Federatia Romina de Fotbal, Vasile Conta 16, Bucharest. Colours: Yellow shirts, blue shorts.

Results of international matches:

May 24, 1939	Rumania 0, England 2; Bucharest.
Nov. 6, 1968	Rumania 0, England 0; Bucharest.
Jan. 15, 1969	England 1, Rumania 1; Wembley.
June 2, 1970*	England 1, Rumania 0; Guadalajara.

* World Cup

RUSSIA

The British introduced the Russians to football as long ago as 1887 but nearly 60 years had elapsed before the British at home were awakened to the fact that this huge country had quietly developed into a leading soccer nation.

That rude awakening came in Nov. 1945 with the visit of their League champions, Moscow Dynamo.

Interest in this Russian club had reached fever pitch by the time of their first game, with Chelsea at Stamford Bridge, and although it was played in mid-week well over 80,000 spectators crammed the stadium. The result was a draw, 3—3.

The Russians played three more games before returning home undefeated. They beat Cardiff City 10—1, Arsenal 4—3 (in a fog at Tottenham), and drew 2—2 with Rangers at Ibrox Park.

A Russian referee controlled the Arsenal game. He insisted on the match being played to a finish despite the fog which made it impossible to see more than a few yards across the field long before the final whistle was sounded.

The outstanding feature of the Russians' play in all these games was the precision of their forwards' passing. This allied to their strong shooting made them the most accomplished foreign team seen in England up to that time.

Almost immediately after this 1945 visit the Russians withdrew behind their Iron Curtain and little or nothing was seen of their footballers abroad until 1952, since when renewed efforts have been made to establish the Soviet Union as a major force in international football.

The Russians have by now gained victories over all of the world's leading international combinations with the exception of Brazil.

The first football club to be established in Russia was Morozowstky in 1887, a team of workers from a cotton mill run by the Charnock brothers from England.

A League was formed in Moscow as early as 1903 and representative matches between the Muscovites and the other principal soccer centre, St. Petersburg, began in 1908.

The first British team to visit Russia was the Wanderers; not the famous old 19th century side, but a combined Oxford and Cambridge team. They won their three games with an aggregate score of 31—0. This was in 1911.

The First World War and the Russian Revolution put a stop to any further development for a number of years, and indeed, little was seen of the Russian footballers in the international field between the two World Wars. Their matches with other countries were limited to less than a dozen during the period 1920-45 and there is no record of them ever defeating any foreign opposition in those games.

We have already mentioned the Russian post-war revival, but the really big effort to put the Russians in the top football bracket began in 1960 with the re-organisation of their League and Cup competitions and the placing of an even greater emphasis on the development of youth.

The address of the governing body: F.A. of the U.S.S.R., 4 Skatertny Pereulok, Moscow 69. Colours: Red shirts, white shorts.

Results of international matches:

May 18, 1958	Russia 1, England 1; Moscow.
June 8, 1958*	England 2, Russia 2; Sweden.
June 17, 1958*	England 0, Russia 1; Sweden.
Oct. 22, 1958	England 5, Russia 0; Wembley.
May 30, 1965*	Russia, 2, Wales 1; Moscow.
Oct. 27, 1965*	Wales 2, Russia 1; Cardiff
May 10, 1967	Scotland 0, Russia 2; Hampden Park
Dec. 6, 1967	England 2, Russia 2; Wembley
June 8, 1968†	England 2, Russia 0; Rome
Sept. 9, 1969*	Ireland 0, Russia 0; Belfast
Oct. 22, 1969*	Russia 2, Ireland 0; Moscow

* World Cup   † Nations Cup

S

ST. JOHNSTONE F.C.

Founded 1884. Joined Scottish League, Division II, 1921. Honours: Champions, Division II, 1923-4, 1959-60, 1962-3. Runners-up, 1931-2. Best in Division I, 5th, 1934-5. Record attendance: 29,972 v. Dundee, Scottish Cup, 2nd Round, Feb. 10, 1952. Address: Muirton Park, Perth (Tel. 26961). Colours: Royal blue shirts, white shorts. Record goal-scorer in Division I: J. Munro, 1926-7, and A. McCall, 1936-7, both with 28 goals. Record victory: 7—0 v. Partick Thistle, Division I, 1938-9, and v. Alloa Athletic, Division B, 1947-8 (A) and 1953-4. Record defeat: 9—2 v. Third Lanark, Division B, 1953-4.

ST. MIRREN F.C.

Founded 1876 by members of a rugby club. One of the original members of the Scottish League, 1890. Best in Division I, 3rd, 1892-3. Champions, Division II, 1967-8. Runners-up, 1935-6. Scottish Cup: Winners, 1926, 1959. Runners-up, 1908, 1934, 1962. Record attendance: 47,428 v. Celtic, Scottish Cup, 4th Round, Mar. 7, 1925. Address: St. Mirren Park, Love Street, Paisley (Tel. 2558). Nickname: Saints. Colours: Black with white stripes, white shorts. Record goal-scorer in Division I: D. Walker, 45 goals, 1921-2. Record victory: 15—0 v. Glasgow United, Scottish Cup, 1st Round, Jan. 30, 1960. Record defeat: 9—2 v. Dundee, Division I, Feb. 29, 1964.

SCOTLAND

While it is true that soccer was first popularised in England it was the Scots who first polished up the game and introduced a really high degree of skill.

The oldest club in Scotland is Queen's Park, formed by members of the Glasgow Y.M.C.A. in July 1867, and it is to this club that Scotland owes most for the speedy development of the game in its earliest days north of the Border.

Queen's Park were first to practise the passing game in the 1870s and 1880s and this quickly proved itself to be much superior to the individual style of dribbling then favoured by the Sassenachs.

The Queen's Park club staged the first official international played by their country, it was against England, in Nov. 1872, and they also provided every player in the team. Indeed Queen's Park players in the first half dozen Scotland-England internationals totalled 39 out of the 66 required.

Scotland's superior style of play brought them six wins to England's two, with two games drawn, in the first 10 meetings, and this not only caused the England selectors great concern but made the more enterprising English clubs turn to Scotland for players to strengthen their sides. It is quite likely that Scots and not Englishmen were the first professional soccer players in the history of the game. (See PROFESSIONALISM).

It was not until these pioneering Scots had spread the gospel of the passing game among the clubs south of the Border, and it had been taken up by such English soccer dignitaries as N. L. Jackson who formed the Corinthians, that England began to hold their own with Scotland in their international matches. Scotland won more than half of their first 20 meetings (to 1891) but the score in the next 20 (to 1911) was 8—6 to England.

There is no doubt that Scottish football as a whole has suffered through the continuous loss of many of their best players to clubs south of the Border, but they have also been hampered by a shortage of really big clubs in their own country. The great traditions of the Scottish game are wrapped up in such fine clubs as Rangers, Celtic, and Hearts (Queen's Park's reluctance to turn professional put them out of the running nearly 50 years ago), but aside from these and a handful of others the League competition has been forced to include a large number of tail-enders.

Scotland has appeared in the final rounds of only two of the World Cup competitions, but their record has been a dismal one. The two years were 1954 and 1958 but they failed to win any of their five games, their only point being secured from a 1—1 draw with Yugoslavia in 1958. A sad state of affairs for a country that may justly claim to have laid the foundations of the skilful passing game we know to-day.

Address of the governing body: The Scottish F.A., 6 Park Gardens, Glasgow, C.3 Colours: Navy blue shirts, white shorts.

References to Scottish football are made in various sections throughout this book. Special sections devoted to football in Scotland are: SCOTTISH ASSOCIATION CUP, SCOTTISH FOOTBALL ASSOCIATION CUP, SCOTTISH FOOTBALL ASSOCIATION, SCOTTISH FOOTBALL (GENERAL), SCOTTISH LEAGUE, INTERNATIONALS (SCOTLAND).

SCOTTISH ASSOCIATION CUP

The Scottish Cup competition came into being at the same time as the Scottish Football Association in 1873. The original meeting called by the Queen's Park club was, in fact, called primarily to organise a Cup competition on similar lines to that which had already begun in England. The meeting was held on Mar. 13, 1873, and the eight clubs represented decided not only to have a Cup competition but also to form " The Scottish Football Association ". The new Association bought a trophy and 12 medals for the winners at a cost of £56.

Sixteen clubs took part in the first season's competition which was won by Queen's Park. They also won the tournament in its second and third seasons. No club has yet succeeded in winning the trophy more than three times in succession although the treble has been achieved five times. Queen's Park won the cup in 1874, 1875 and 1876, and in 1880, 1881 and 1882. Vale of Leven won it in 1877, 1878, 1879. On the last occasion they were awarded the trophy when Rangers failed to turn up for a Final replay. Rangers are the other club that has completed the treble. They were winners in 1934, 1935 and 1936; 1948, 1949, 1950; and in 1962, 1963, 1964.

Appearances

For men who have won both Scottish Cup and F.A. Cup medals see FOOTBALL ASSOCIATION CHALLENGE CUP (Scotland).

Most appearances in a Scottish Cup winning side were made by J. McMenemy: six with Celtic, 1904-14, and one with Partick Thistle, 1921; and R. McPhail, one with Airdrieonians, 1924, and six with Rangers, 1928-36.

Although he only appeared in two Scottish Cup games during seasons 1947-8 and 1948-9, W. Williamson, centre-forward or inside-forward, gained two Cup winners' medals. The two matches were both Cup Finals with Rangers.

Attendances

See separate section.

Final

In 1879 Vale of Leven were awarded the Cup when Rangers failed to turn up for the Final replay. The first game was drawn 1—1, but Rangers had a goal disallowed for offside. They appealed against the referee's decision, claiming they had won, but the Scottish F.A. decided against them. In protest at this decision, Rangers refused to take part in a replay.

Oddly enough, Vale of Leven were concerned in a similar affair in 1884 when they did not turn up for the Cup Final with Queen's Park who were accordingly awarded the trophy.

In England

Several Scottish Cup ties have been played in England on the Berwick Rangers' ground, Northumberland.

Receipts

The record receipts for a Scottish Cup Final, £42,824, Rangers v. Celtic, Apr. 23, 1966.

Replays

In season 1908-9, Broxburn and Beith met five times in a 1st Round tie. The last three games were played on three consecutive days. Beith finally emerged victorious on a Friday by 4 goals to 2. On the following day, Beith met St. Mirren, their fourth game on successive days.

Results of Finals

1874	Queen's Park	bt.	Clydesdale	2—0
1875	Queen's Park	bt.	Renton	3—0
1876	Queen's Park	bt.	Third Lanark	2—0
	(after draw 1—1)			
1877	Vale of Leven	bt.	Rangers	3—2
	(after draws 0—0 and 1—1)			
1878	Vale of Leven	bt.	Third Lanark	1—0
1879	Vale of Leven awarded Cup after drawn game 1—1 and			
	Rangers declined to replay.			
1880	Queen's Park	bt.	Thornliebank	3—0
1881	Queen's Park	bt.	Dumbarton	3—1
	(after protested game 2—1 for Queen's Park)			
1882	Queen's Park	bt.	Dumbarton	4—1
	(after draw 2—2)			
1883	Dumbarton	bt.	Vale of Leven	2—1
	(after draw 2—2)			
1884	Queen's Park awarded Cup. Vale of Leven failing to appear.			
1885	Renton	bt.	Vale of Leven	3—1
	(after draw 0—0)			
1886	Queen's Park	bt.	Renton	3—1
1887	Hibernian	bt.	Dumbarton	2—1
1888	Renton	bt.	Cambuslang	6—1
1889	Third Lanark	bt.	Celtic	2—1
	(after protested game 3—0 in favour of Third Lanark)			
1890	Queen's Park	bt.	Vale of Leven	2—1
	(after draw 1—1)			
1891	Heart of Midlothian	bt.	Dumbarton	1—0
1892	Celtic	bt.	Queen's Park	5—1
	(after protested game 1—0 for Celtic)			
1893	Queen's Park	bt.	Celtic	2—1
1894	**Rangers**	bt.	Celtic	3—1
1895	St. Bernards	bt.	Renton	2—1
1896	Heart of Midlothian	bt.	Hibernian	3—1
1897	Rangers	bt.	Dumbarton	5—1
1898	Rangers	bt.	Kilmarnock	2—0
1899	Celtic	bt.	Rangers	2—0
1900	Celtic	bt.	Queen's Park	4—3
1901	Heart of Midlothian	bt.	Celtic	4—3
1902	Hibernian	bt.	Celtic	1—0
1903	Rangers	bt.	Heart of Midlothian	2—0
	(after draws 1—1 and 0—0)			
1904	Celtic	bt.	Rangers	3—2
1905	Third Lanark	bt.	Rangers	3—1
	(after draw 0—0)			
1906	Heart of Midlothian	bt.	Third Lanark	1—0
1907	Celtic	bt.	Heart of Midlothian	3—0
1908	Celtic	bt.	St. Mirren	5—1
1909	Cup withheld following riot at replay which ended in a			
	draw Rangers 1, Celtic 1. The teams had previously drawn			
	2—2.			

1910	Dundee	bt.	Clyde	2—1
	(after draws 2—2 and 0—0)			
1911	Celtic	bt.	Hamilton Academicals	2—0
	(after draw 0—0)			
1912	Celtic	bt.	Clyde	2—0
1913	Falkirk	bt.	Raith Rovers	2—0
1914	Celtic	bt.	Hibernian	4—1
	(after draw 0—0)			
1920	Kilmarnock	bt.	Albion Rovers	3—2
1921	Partick Thistle	bt.	Rangers	1—0
1922	Morton	bt.	Rangers	1—0
1923	Celtic	bt.	Hibernian	1—0
1924	Airdrieonians	bt.	Hibernian	2—0
1925	Celtic	bt.	Dundee	2—1
1926	St. Mirren	bt.	Celtic	2—0
1927	Celtic	bt.	East Fife	3—1
1928	Rangers	bt.	Celtic	4—0
1929	Kilmarnock	bt.	Rangers	2—0
1930	Rangers	bt.	Partick Thistle	2—1
	(after draw 0—0)			
1931	Celtic	bt.	Motherwell	4—2
	(after draw 2—2)			
1932	Rangers	bt.	Kilmarnock	3—0
	(after draw 1—1)			
1933	Celtic	bt.	Motherwell	1—0
1934	Rangers	bt.	St. Mirren	5—0
1935	Rangers	bt.	Hamilton Academicals	2—1
1936	Rangers	bt.	Third Lanark	1—0
1937	Celtic	bt.	Aberdeen	2—1
1938	East Fife	bt.	Kilmarnock	4—2
	(after draw 1—1)			
1939	Clyde	bt.	Motherwell	4—0
1947	Aberdeen	bt.	Hibernian	2—1
1948	Rangers	bt.	Morton	1—0
	(after draw 1—1)			
1949	Rangers	bt.	Clyde	4—1
1950	Rangers	bt.	East Fife	3—0
1951	Celtic	bt.	Motherwell	1—0
1952	Motherwell	bt.	Dundee	4—0
1953	Rangers	bt.	Aberdeen	1—0
	(after draw 1—1)			
1954	Celtic	bt.	Aberdeen	2—1
1955	Clyde	bt.	Celtic	1—0
	(after draw 1—1)			
1956	Heart of Midlothian	bt.	Celtic	3—1
1957	Falkirk	bt.	Kilmarnock	2—1
	(after draw 1—1)			
1958	Clyde	bt.	Hibernian	1—0
1959	St. Mirren	bt.	Aberdeen	3—1
1960	Rangers	bt.	Kilmarnock	2—0
1961	Dunfermline	bt.	Celtic	2—0
	(after draw 0—0)			
1962	Rangers	bt.	St. Mirren	2—0
1963	Rangers	bt.	Celtic	3—0
	(after draw 1—1)			
1964	Rangers	bt.	Dundee	3—1
1965	Celtic	bt.	Dunfermline	3—2
1966	Rangers	bt.	Celtic	1—0
1967	Celtic	bt.	Aberdeen	2—0
1968	Dunfermline	bt.	Hearts	3—1
1969	Celtic	bt.	Rangers	4—0
1970	Aberdeen	bt.	Celtic	3—1

Second Division

The only Division II club to win the Scottish Cup is East Fife in 1938.

Withheld

The Cup was withheld in 1909 after the Hampden riot. Rangers and Celtic were the finalists. They drew the first game, 2—2, and at the end of 90 min. in the replay the result was again a draw, 1—1. At that time there was no rule which said that extra time must be played in such circumstances, but a section of the crowd was under the misapprehension that extra time was to be played. When the players were leaving the field and it became apparent that there was to be no more play, the crowd broke loose, tore up the goal-posts, broke down payboxes, and actually started a bonfire at the side of the pitch. Police who tried to intervene were badly manhandled and stoned.

SCOTTISH FOOTBALL ASSOCIATION

The S.F.A. was formed at a meeting attended by the representatives of eight clubs on Mar. 13, 1873. The clubs were Clydesdale, Dumbreck, Eastern, Granville, Queen's Park, Rovers, Third Lanark and Vale of Leven.

Mr. Archibald Rae, the secretary of the Queen's Park Club, was the enthusiast who initiated the move to form an Association and he became the first secretary.

The other men who took office on the first committee were A. Campbell (Clydesdale) President; W. Kerr (Queen's Park) Hon. Treasurer; J. Turnbull (Dumbarton), D. McFarlane (Vale of Leven), E. Hendry (Clydesdale), W. E. Dick (Third Lanark), J. Mackay (Granville), J. McIntyre (Eastern), R. Gardner (Queen's Park), and W. Gibb (Clydesdale).

In the early 1880s the Scottish F.A. threatened to discontinue international games with England because of differences in the interpretation of the Laws of the Game. The English Association suggested a meeting of the four home Associations to draw up a uniform code of rules but at first Scotland re-fused. When a split seemed inevitable, there came a change of feeling in the Scottish F.A. It agreed to a meeting at Manchester on Dec. 6, 1882, and a code of rules acceptable to all four Associations was drawn up. This meeting led to the formation of the International Board (q.v.).

Professionalism was adopted by the Scottish F.A. after prolonged resistance in May 1893.

SCOTTISH FOOTBALL
General

The oldest football club in Scotland is Queen's Park, formed by members of the Glasgow Y.M.C.A. in July 1867.

In season 1929-30 Rangers won the following honours: Scottish Cup, Scottish League Championship, Glasgow Cup, Scottish Second Eleven Cup, and the Glasgow Charity Cup. The Charity Cup was won by the toss of a coin after playing for two hours against Celtic without reaching a definite result (the score was 2—2).

In season 1948-9 and 1963-4 Rangers won the Scottish League Championship, the Scottish Cup and the Scottish League Cup.

Celtic also achieved this treble in 1966-7 and 1968-9.

SCOTTISH INTER-NATIONALS

See INTERNATIONALS (Scotland)

SCOTTISH LEAGUE

The Scottish League was formed after a series of meetings in Glasgow in 1890. Several clubs felt that their existence was threatened if fixtures could not be arranged with some certainty of them being carried out. One or two of the larger clubs were constantly approached with the offers of fixtures, but the lesser-known clubs were finding it increasingly difficult to satisfy their supporters with attractive games.

It was obvious that some regulating body should be formed among the clubs just as it had been done in England two years earlier. Not without some opposition from the Scottish Football Association and certain clubs who feared that the formation of such a League would favour professionalism, an agreement was made between 11 clubs, Abercorn, Celtic, Cowlairs, Cambuslang, Dumbarton, Hearts, Rangers, St. Mirren, Renton, Third Lanark, and Vale of Leven. The Scottish League was in being.

The move to form a League had been largely initiated by Renton who were unable to take full advantage of their enterprise when they were suspended by the Scottish Football Association after playing only five of their League matches. Renton had disobeyed a ban placed on all affiliated clubs restraining them from playing matches with St. Bernards, a club which had been pronounced guilty of a breach of the laws of amateurism. In fact, Renton played a new club called Edinburgh Saints, but the S.F.A. had already ruled them to be one and the same as the banned St. Bernards club. Renton's record in their first five League matches was consequently cancelled. However, they returned to the League the following season.

Division II of the League was formed in 1894. The automatic promotion and relegation plan was introduced in season 1921-2.

In the history of the competition only one club has succeeded in winning all its League matches in any one season. Rangers won all 18 games played in season 1898-9.

Rangers hold the record for the highest number of Championship wins. They have achieved this distinction 34 times (including once as joint holders of the title with Dumbarton in 1891). Celtic have won the Championship on 25 occasions.

There was such a rush of games at the end of season 1915-16 that Celtic actually played two League games in one day—April 15, 1916. They beat Raith Rovers 6—0 at Celtic Park and in the evening beat Motherwell 3—1 at Fir Park.

Entrance fee for clubs joining Scottish League is £10.

Champions

Scottish League: 1890-91 Dumbarton and Rangers; 1891-2 Dumbarton; 1892-3 Celtic.

First Division: 1893-4 Celtic; 1894-5 Hearts; 1895-6 Celtic; 1896-7 Hearts; 1897-8 Celtic; 1898-9 Rangers; 1899-1900 Rangers; 1900-1901 Rangers; 1901-2 Rangers; 1902-3 Hibernian; 1903-4 Third Lanark; 1904-5 Celtic*; 1905-6 Celtic; 1906-7 Celtic; 1907-8 Celtic; 1908-9 Celtic; 1909-10 Celtic; 1910-11 Rangers; 1911-12 Rangers; 1912-13 Rangers; 1913-14 Celtic; 1914-15 Celtic; 1915-16 Celtic; 1916-17 Celtic; 1917-18 Rangers; 1918-19 Celtic; 1919-20 Rangers; 1920-21 Rangers; 1921-2 Celtic; 1922-3 Rangers; 1923-4 Rangers; 1924-5 Rangers; 1925-6 Celtic; 1926-7 Rangers; 1927-8 Rangers; 1928-9 Rangers; 1929-30 Rangers; 1930-31 Rangers; 1931-2 Motherwell; 1932-3 Rangers; 1933-4 Rangers; 1934-5 Rangers; 1935-6 Celtic; 1936-7 Rangers; 1937-8 Celtic; 1938-9 Rangers; 1946-7 Rangers; 1947-8 Hibernian; 1948-9 Rangers; 1949-50 Rangers; 1950-51 Hibernian; 1951-2 Hibernian; 1952-3 Rangers; 1953-4 Celtic; 1954-5 Aberdeen; 1955-6 Rangers; 1956-7 Rangers; 1957-8 Hearts; 1958-9 Rangers; 1959-60 Hearts; 1960-61 Rangers; 1961-2 Dundee; 1962-3 Rangers; 1963-4 Rangers; 1964-5 Kilmarnock; 1965-6 Celtic; 1966-7 Celtic; 1967-8 Celtic; 1968-9 Celtic; 1969-70 Celtic.

Second Division: 1893-4 Hibernian; 1894-5 Hibernian; 1895-6 Abercorn; 1896-7 Partick Thistle; 1897-8 Kilmarnock; 1898-9 Kilmarnock; 1899-1900 Partick Thistle; 1900-1901 St. Bernard; 1901-2 Port Glasgow; 1902-3 Airdrieonians; 1903-4 Hamilton Academicals; 1904-5 Clyde; 1905-6 Leith Athletic; 1906-7 St. Bernard; 1907-8 Raith Rovers; 1908-9 Abercorn; 1909-10; Leith Athletic; 1910-11 Dumbarton; 1911-12 Ayr United; 1912-13 Ayr United; 1913-14 Cowdenbeath; 1914-15 Cowdenbeath; 1916-21 no competition; 1921-2 Alloa Athletic; 1922-3 Queen's Park; 1923-4 St. Johnstone; 1924-5 Dundee United; 1925-6 Dunfermline Athletic; 1926-7 Bo'ness; 1927-8 Ayr United; 1928-9 Dundee United; 1929-30 Leith Athletic; 1930-31 Third Lanark; 1931-2 East Stirlingshire; 1932-3 Hibernian; 1933-4 Albion Rovers; 1934-5 Third Lanark; 1935-6 Falkirk; 1936-7 Ayr United; 1937-8 Raith Rovers; 1938-9 Cowdenbeath; 1940-46 no competition; 1946-7 Dundee; 1947-8 East Fife; 1948-9 Raith Rovers and Stirling Albion joint

* Celtic won deciding match with Rangers.

holders; 1949-50 Morton; 1950-51 Queen of the South; 1951-2 Clyde; 1952-3 Stirling Albion; 1953-4 Motherwell; 1954-5 Airdrieonians; 1955-6 Queen's Park; 1956-7 Clyde; 1957-8 Stirling Albion; 1958-9 Ayr United; 1959-60 St. Johnstone; 1960-61 Stirling Albion; 1961-2 Clyde; 1962-3 St. Johnstone; 1963-4 Morton; 1964-5 Stirling Albion; 1965-6 Ayr United; 1966-7 Morton; 1967-8 St. Mirren; 1968-9 Motherwell; 1969-70 Falkirk.

SCOTTISH PLAYERS IN ENGLAND

Early in the 1955-6 season Accrington Stanley set up a Football League record by fielding a side which included all Scottish-born players. Their all Scottish side made several appearances in the Third Division (N) during that season and, indeed, all but four of the 19 players who appeared for this club during 1955-6 were born in Scotland.

In the First Division the record for fielding a side containing the most Scotsmen goes to Newcastle United in whose team on Oct. 6, 1928, when they defeated Leeds United 3—2, only centre-half, E. Wood, was not Scottish born.

For 30 years, West Bromwich Albion never had a Scottish professional on their books until they signed G. Dudley, a centre-forward from Glasgow who had previously played for Albion Rovers, in Nov. 1937.

See also FOOTBALL ASSOCIATION CHALLENGE CUP (Scotland).

SCOUTS

The demand for first-class players is so great today that the scouting system has reached its peak of efficiency. All the leading clubs employ official salaried representatives whose job it is to watch all classes of football on the look-out for new talent. These men are also sent on specific scouting missions to watch certain players who have been recommended to the club managers.

Obviously, scouting is a job only for the most highly skilled and experienced judges of football. Most of them are former players who can tell at little more than a glance whether a youth has the makings of a first-class footballer.

Not all clubs can afford to employ full-time scouts and many rely on the services of free-lance scouts who move around the country on their own initiative, or rely upon tips from friends outside the game.

It is safe to say that nowadays the competition for new talent is so keen, and the scouting system so thorough and far-reaching, that no junior who is playing consistently good football can be overlooked by all the Football League and Scottish League clubs.

SCUNTHORPE UNITED F.C.

Founded 1904. Amalgamated with Lindsey United 1910 as Scunthorpe and Lindsey United. Dropped name "Lindsey" from title 1951. Elected to Football League, Division III(N), 1950. Honours: Champions, Division III(N), 1957-8. Record attendance: 23,935 v. Bolton Wanderers, F.A. Cup, 3rd Round, Jan. 10, 1959. Address: Old Show Ground, Scunthorpe (Tel. 2954). Colours: All red. Record League goal-scorer: B. Thomas, 31 goals, Division II, 1961-2. Record victory: 9—0 v. Boston United, F.A. Cup, 1st Round, Nov. 21, 1953. Record defeat: 8—0 v. Carlisle United, Division III(N), 1952-3.

SEASON, THE

The duration of the football season according to the rules of the Football Association is from the Saturday next preceding last Saturday in Aug. to the first Saturday in May, but the Council reserves the right to extend this period as they have done in the last four seasons.

The only matches that may be played outside this period are practice matches (during 14 days preceding the season), small side matches (five-a-side, six-a-side, and similar), Charity matches, Army, Navy and R.A.F. and Auxiliary Forces inter-unit matches, and games played while in camp against such organisations as the Boys' Brigade and Scouts. The season may be extended one week for the playing of semi-final and final ties in certain cup or charity competitions.

The season was extended to its present duration for season 1919-20. Im-

THIRD DIVISION. Clubs from this Division win at Wembley. (*Above*) Queen's Park Rangers shooting the first goal of their League Cup win against West Bromwich Albion in 1967. (*Below*) Gould scores for Arsenal in the League Cup Final of 1969, but Swindon Town were the winners.

TRANSFERS. These players were transferred for record fees: Pietro Anastasi (*above left*), Colin Stein (*above right*), Allan Clarke (*below left*) and Martin Chivers.

mediately before that, it began on the first Saturday in Sept. and ended on the last Saturday in April.

The Scottish season begins on the second Saturday in Aug. and finishes at the end of April.

SHEFFIELD UNITED F.C.

Founded 1889, by members of the Yorks County Cricket Club and the Sheffield United C.C.C. One of the original members of the Football League, Division II, 1892. Honours: Champions, Division I, 1897-8. Runners-up, 1896-7, 1899-1900. Champions, Division II, 1952-3. Runners-up, 1892-3, 1938-9, 1960-61. F.A. Cup: Winners, 1899, 1902, 1915, 1925. Runners-up, 1901, 1936. Record attendance: 68,287 v. Leeds United, F.A. Cup, 5th Round, Feb. 15, 1936. Address: Bramall Lane, Sheffield 2 (Tel. 25585). Nickname: Blades. Colours: Red and white striped shirts, black shorts. Record League goal-scorer: J. Dunne, 41 goals, Division I, 1930-31. Record victory: 11—2 v. Cardiff City, Division I, Jan. 1, 1926. Record defeat: 13—0 v. Bolton Wanderers, F.A. Cup 2nd Round, Feb. 1, 1890.

SHEFFIELD WEDNESDAY F.C.

Founded 1867 by the Wednesday Cricket Club, the fourth oldest Football League club. Elected to the Football League, Division I, 1892. Honours: Champions, Division I, 1902-3, 1903-4, 1928-9, 1929-30. Runners-up, 1960-61. Champions, Division II, 1899-1900, 1925-6, 1951-2. 1955-6, 1958-9. Runners-up, 1949-50. F.A. Cup: Winners 1896, 1907, 1935, Runners-up, 1890, 1966. Record attendance: 72,841 v. Manchester City, F.A. Cup, 5th Round, Feb. 17, 1934. Address: Hillsborough, Sheffield 6 (Tel. 343122). Nickname: Owls. Colours: Blue shirts with white sleeves, white shorts. Record League goal-scorer: D. Dooley, 46 goals, Division II, 1951-2. Record victory: 12—0 v. Halliwell, F.A. Cup, 1st Round, Jan. 17, 1891. Record defeat: 10—0 v. Aston Villa, Division I, Oct. 5, 1912.

SHINGUARDS

Shinguards were invented by Samuel W. Widdowson, the Nottingham Forest forward who played for England against Scotland in 1880. It is believed they may have been used in 1874 but were not actually mentioned in the rules of the game until 1880.

SHREWSBURY TOWN F.C.

Founded 1886. Elected to Football League, Division III(N), 1950. Transferred to Division III(S), 1951. Highest in Division III, 3rd, 1959-60. Record attendance: 18,917 v. Walsall, Division III, April 26, 1961. Address: Gay Meadow, Shrewsbury (Tel. 6068). Colours: Blue shirts with amber trim, blue shorts with amber stripe. Record League goal-scorer: A. Rowley, 38 goals, Division IV, 1958-9. Record victory: 7—0 v Swindon Town, Division III(S), 1954-5. Record defeat: 8—1 v. Norwich City, Division III(S), 1952-3, and v. Coventry City, Division III, Oct. 22, 1963.

SOUTH AFRICA

Football has been played in South Africa for more than 80 years but for the greater part of that time it has taken a poor second place to rugby.

The soccer revival which is fast establishing the game as number one favourite ahead of the handling code began soon after World War II and received its biggest boost in 1959 when professionalism was adopted and a National League formed by the leading clubs in the Transvaal and Natal. A second division was added in 1960.

However, South Africa suffered a severe set-back in 1964 when they were suspended from F.I.F.A., a suspension which is still in force.

The oldest Association, the Natal Football Association, was formed in 1882, and the first overseas tour of an English club (outside of Europe) followed in 1897 when the Corinthians visited this part of the world. The famous amateur club revisited South Africa in 1903 and 1907.

The South African F.A. was affiliated to the Football Association of England from 1903 until 1962.

South Africa has never met our full international team. They have, however, played what are known as "Test Matches" against F.A. Touring teams. The results of these matches are as follows:

June 29, 1910	South Africa	0, England 3; Durban.
July 23, 1910	South Africa	2, England 6; Johannesburg.
July 30, 1910	South Africa	3, England 6; Cape Town.
June 26, 1920	South Africa	1, England 3; Johannesburg.
July 17, 1920	South Africa	1, England 9; Cape Town.
July 19, 1920	South Africa	1, England 3; Durban.
June 15, 1929	South Africa	2, England 3; Durban.
July 13, 1929	South Africa	1, England 2; Johannesburg.
July 17, 1929	South Africa	1, England 3; Cape Town.
June 17, 1939	South Africa	0, England 3; Johannesburg.
June 24, 1939	South Africa	1, England 2; Durban.
July 1, 1939	South Africa	1, England 2; Johannesburg.
June 23, 1956	South Africa	3, England 4; Johannesburg.
July 1, 1956	South Africa	2, England 4; Durban.
July 9, 1956	South Africa	0, England 0; Cape Town.
July 14, 1956	South Africa	1, England 4; Salisbury.

The South Africans have made three tours of the United Kingdom. In 1924 they played 26 matches, winning 16 and losing 10. In 1953 they won five and drew four of their 20 matches, and in 1958 they played another 17 games, winning seven, drawing four and losing six.

Many South Africans have appeared in the Football League and they are far too numerous to mention here, but the following have also appeared in full internationals:

G. Hodgson (Liverpool, Aston Villa, Leeds United), England v. Scotland, Ireland, Wales, 1930-31; W. Perry (Blackpool), England v. Ireland, Scotland, and Spain, 1955-6; J. Hewie (Charlton Athletic), Scotland v. England, 1955-6, 1956-7, v. Ireland and Wales, 1956-7, 1959-60, plus eight appearances against foreign countries; P. Kelly (Barnsley), Ireland v. Scotland, 1949-50; F. Osborne (Fulham, Tottenham Hotspur), England v. Ireland and France, 1922-3, v. Belgium, 1924-5, 1925-6.

The address of the governing body: South African F.A., P.O. Box 2694, Johannesburg.

SOUTHAMPTON F.C.

Founded 1885 by the Young Men's Association of St. Mary's Church. Adopted present title, 1897. One of the original members of the Football League, Division III, 1920. Honours: Runners-up, Division II, 1965-6. Champions, Division III(S), 1921-2. Champions, Division III, 1959-60. F.A. Cup: Finalists, 1900, 1902. Record attendance: 31,044 v. Manchester United, Division I, Oct. 8, 1969. Address: The Dell, Southampton (Tel. 23408). Nickname: Saints. Colours: Red and white striped shirts, black shorts. Record League goal-scorer: D. Reeves, 39 goals, Division III, 1959-60. Record victory: 11—0 v. Northampton Town, Southern League, Dec. 28, 1901. Record defeat: 8—0 v. Tottenham Hotspur, Division II, Mar. 28, 1936.

SOUTHEND UNITED F.C.

Founded 1906 from the older Southend Athletic amateur club. One of the original members of the Football League, Division III, 1920. Best in Division III(S), 3rd, 1931-2, 1949-50. Record attendance: 28,059 v. Birmingham City, F.A. Cup, 4th Round, Jan. 26, 1957. Address: Roots Hall, Southend-on-Sea (Tel. 40707). Nickname: Shrimpers. Colours. Royal blue shirts and shorts. Record League goal-scorer: J. Shankly, 31 goals, Division III(S), 1928-9, and S. McGrory, Division III(S), 1957-8. Record victory: 10—1 v. Golders Green, F.A. Cup, 1st Round, Nov. 24, 1934, and 10—1 v. Brentwood, F.A. Cup, 2nd Round, Dec. 7, 1968. Record defeat: 11—1 v. Northampton Town, Southern League, Dec. 30, 1909.

SOUTHERN LEAGUE

This organisation was for many years the principal competition outside the Football and Scottish Leagues. Before the formation of Division III of the Football League in 1920, the Southern League held an important position in the football world.

The formation of this League followed the spread of professionalism to clubs in the London and Home

Counties area. Royal Arsenal was first to suggest such a competition. In 1892 Arsenal circularised several clubs with its proposal and a number of meetings were held. The following year, however, Arsenal secured admission to the newly-formed Division II of the Football League, and abandoned its proposals.

Millwall Athletic was the next club to advocate the formation of such a League, and it was directly due to Millwall's enterprise that a meeting was held at which the Southern League was formed on Jan. 12, 1894. In addition to Millwall, representatives of Ilford, Luton, Clapton, Scots Guards, Reading and Chatham were present at the discussion. Other clubs were circulated and nine clubs—Royal Ordnance and Swindon in addition to the seven at the original meeting—formed the First Division of the new League. Scots Guards dropped out before the first season started and Southampton St. Mary was elected in their place. There was also a Second Division containing seven clubs.

The first three places in the Southern League were held by the same three clubs in the first two seasons, Millwall Athletic, Luton and Southampton. In the next three seasons, Southampton, the outstanding club in the history of the competition, carried off the title.

The most eventful year in the history of the Southern League was 1920 when the First Division members applied en bloc to become members of the Football League. The Football League accepted them in a newly-formed Division III as Associate Members. With all its leading clubs gone, the Southern League lost its status as a major competition. However, it carried on with a First Division of 13 clubs, including 10 who fielded only their reserve teams. A Second Division was formed consisting entirely of Welsh clubs.

In 1923 the Welsh Division was dropped and the League divided into Eastern and Western sections. In 1933 a Central Section was included. The League continued in three sections until 1936 when a single division of 16 clubs was formed. This became 18 in 1937, and 23 in 1938. There was also a mid-week section for two seasons just before World War II.

When the competition was resumed in 1945, there were only 11 clubs, but later the number increased to 24.

For season 1958-9 it was divided into S.E. and N.W. sections totalling 35 clubs, but in 1959 the number of clubs was increased to over 40 and a new formation of a Premier Division and a First Division was established.

The record for the highest number of points registered by any club in a single season in the top division is held by Merthyr Tydfil who collected 71 points in season 1949-50.

The Southern League entered into an agreement with the Football League and the Scottish League in 1909, regarding the transfer of players. This was broken in 1919 following a dispute with West Ham United and the Football League when West Ham United made a last-minute decision to join Division II of the Football League.

Following this dispute the Southern League also discontinued competition with the Football, Scottish and Irish Leagues in inter-League games.

SOUTHPORT F.C.

Founded 1881 as Southport Central. A limited company was formed in 1919 and the club became known as Southport F.C. One of the first members of the Football League, Division III(N), 1921. Honours: Runners-up, Div. IV, 1966-7. Record attendance: 20,010 v. Newcastle United, F.A. Cup, 4th Round (replay), Jan. 26, 1932. Address: Haig Avenue, Southport (Tel. 5353). Nickname: Sandgrounders. Colours: All gold. Record League goal-scorer: A. R. Waterson, 31 goals, Division III(N), 1930-31. Record victory: 8—1 v. Nelson, Division III(N), Jan. 1, 1931. Record defeat: 11—0 v. Oldham Athletic, Division IV, Dec. 26, 1962.

SPAIN

In recent years Spain has developed three or four of the greatest club sides in the history of the game. Outstanding among these, of course, has been Real Madrid, six times European Cup Winners and once unofficial World Champions, and yet, during these glorious post-war years the Spanish international side has never been able to establish itself among the leaders of world soccer, although they did succeed in winning the European Nations' Cup in 1964.

This is the enigma of Spanish soccer. They undoubtedly possess many of the world's finest players in their club sides, but although they have included most of these in their national XI, irrespective of the fact that many are not Spanish-born, they have seldom made the same impression as such clubs as Real Madrid, Barcelona and Atletico Madrid have done in international competitions.

The game is believed to have been first introduced into the country by British mining engineers working around Vizcaya and they formed the first club, Atletico Bilbao, in 1898.

The Spanish Football Federation was founded in 1905 and today it controls over 2,000 clubs.

In 1929, Spain became the first foreign country to defeat England in a full international—(full details are given under INTERNATIONALS (England).

Spain did not enter for the World Cup in either 1930 or 1938. They qualified for the final tournament in 1934, 1950, 1962 and 1966, but failed to qualify in 1954, 1958 and 1970. Their best performance in this competition was their 1—1 draw with Italy, the eventual winners, in 1934. In the replay Italy won by the only goal scored.

Address of the governing body: Real Federación Española de Futbol, Avenida Juan Herrera s/n. Ciudad Universtaria, Apartado pastol 347, Madrid 13. Colours: Red Shirts, blue shorts.

May 15, 1929	Spain 4, England 3; Madrid.
April 26, 1931	Spain 1, Eire 1; Barcelona.
Dec. 9, 1931	England 7, Spain 1; Highbury.
Dec. 13, 1931	Eire 0, Spain 5; Dublin.
June 23, 1946	Spain 0, Eire 1; Madrid.
Mar. 2, 1947	Eire 3, Spain 2; Dublin.
May 30, 1948	Spain 2, Eire 1; Barcelona.
June 12, 1949	Eire 1, Spain 4; Dublin.
July 2, 1950*	Spain 1, England 0; Rio de Janeiro.
June 1, 1952	Spain 6, Eire 0; Madrid
May 18, 1955	Spain 1, England 1; Madrid.
Nov. 27, 1955	Eire 2, Spain 2; Dublin.
Nov. 30, 1955	England 4, Spain 1; Wembley.
May 8, 1957*	Scotland 4, Spain 2; Glasgow.
May 26, 1957*	Spain 4, Scotland 1; Madrid.
Oct. 15, 1958	Spain 6, Ireland 2; Madrid.
May 15, 1960	Spain 3, England 0; Madrid.
Oct. 26, 1960	England 4, Spain 2; Wembley.
April 19, 1961*	Wales 1, Spain 2; Cardiff.
May 18, 1961*	Spain 1, Wales 1; Madrid.
May 30, 1963	Spain 1, Ireland 1; Bilbao.
June 13, 1963	Spain 2, Scotland 6; Madrid.
Oct. 30, 1963	Ireland 0, Spain 1; Belfast.
Mar. 11, 1964	Spain 5, Ireland 1; Seville.
Apl. 8, 1964	Eire 0, Spain 2; Dublin.
May 5, 1964*	Eire 1, Spain 0; Dublin.
May 8, 1965	Scotland 0, Spain 0; Glasgow.
Oct. 27, 1965*	Spain 4, Eire 1; Seville
Nov. 10, 1965*	Eire 0, Spain 1; Paris
Dec. 8, 1965	Spain 0, England 2; Madrid
Oct. 23, 1966†	Eire 0, Spain 0; Dublin
Dec. 7, 1966†	Spain 2, Eire 0; Valencia
May 24, 1967	England 2, Spain 0; Wembley
Apl. 3, 1968†	England 1, Spain 0; Wembley
May 8, 1968†	Spain 1, England 2; Madrid

* World Cup　　† Nations Cup

SPECTACLES (GLASSES)

J. F. Mitchell, an English amateur international and Olympic Games goalkeeper, who played for Manchester University, Manchester City and Preston North End, is believed to be the only player to take part in an F.A. Cup Final wearing glasses when he kept goal for Preston North End against Huddersfield Town in 1922.

Apart from goalkeepers it is believed that there have been only two other bespectacled players to appear regularly in first-class football: H. S. Bourne, West Ham United full-back, 1908-11, and A. Raisbeck, Liverpool and Scotland centre-half of the early 1900s.

At the present time there are a number of first-class players who wear contact lenses.

STIRLING ALBION F.C.

Founded 1945. Elected to Scottish League, Division C, 1946. Honours: Champions, Division C, 1946-7. Champions, Division B, 1952-3. Runners-up, 1948-9, 1950-51. Champions, Division II, 1957-8, 1960-61, 1964-5. Record attendance: 26,400 v. Celtic, Scottish Cup, 4th Round, Mar. 14, 1959. Address: Annfield Park, Stirling (Tel. 3584). Colours: Scarlet shirts with white trim, white shorts with red stripe. Record League goal-scorer: J. Gilmour, 22 goals, Division I, 1958-9. Record victory: 7—0 v. Albion Rovers, 1947-8; Montrose, 1957-8; St. Mirren, 1959-60 and Arbroath, 1960-61, all in the Scottish League. Record defeat: 9—0 v. Dundee United, Division I, Dec. 30, 1967.

STOCKPORT COUNTY F.C.

Founded 1883. Adopted present title 1891 (previously known as Heaton Norris Rovers). Elected to Football League, Division II, 1900. Failed to gain re-election, 1904. Returned when Division II was increased from 18 to 20 clubs, 1905. Honours: Champions, Division III(N), 1921-2, 1936-7. Runners-up, 1928-9, 1929-30. Champions, Division IV, 1966-7. Best in Division II, 10th, 1905-6. Record attendance: 27,833 v. Liverpool, F.A. Cup, 5th Round, Feb. 11, 1950. Address: Edgeley Park, Stockport (Tel 8888). Nickname: Hatters. Colours: Blue shirts with thin white stripes, white shorts. Record League goal-scorer: A. Lythgoe, 46 goals, Division III(N), 1933-4. Record victory: 13—0. v. Halifax Town, Division III(N), Jan. 6, 1934. Record defeat: 8—1 v. Chesterfield, Division II, April 19, 1902.

STOKE CITY F.C.

The second oldest club in the Football League. Founded 1863 by employees of the North Staffordshire Railway. One of the original members of the Football League, 1888. Not re-elected, 1890. Returned after 12 months' absence, 1891. Resigned 1908, returned 1919. Honours: Champions, Division II, 1932-3, 1962-3. Runners-up, 1921-2. Champions, Division III(N), 1926-7. Best in Division I, 4th, 1935-6, 1946-7. F.L. Cup: Finalists, 1964. Record attendance: 51,380 v. Arsenal, Division I, Mar. 29, 1937. Address: Victoria Ground, Stoke-on-Trent (Tel. 44660). Nickname: Potters. Colours: Red and white striped shirts, white shorts. Record League goal-scorer: F. Steele, 33 goals, Division I, 1936-7. Record victory: 10—3 v. West Bromwich Albion, Division I, Feb. 4, 1937. Record defeat: 10—0 v. Preston North End, Division I, Sept. 14, 1889.

SUBSTITUTES

The evolution of the substitute:

1932—International Board decide to allow them in internationals with foreign countries if previously agreed.

1958—Board recommended that in non-competition matches substitute goalkeepers may be brought on at any time and a substitute for any other player before end of first half.

1965—Football League allow one substitute per team in case of injuries. First substitute called on was K. Peacock of Charlton Athletic, at Bolton, Aug. 21, 1965.

1966-67 season—F.A. Cup and Football League Cup allow the one substitute. Scottish F.A. and League follow suit. Substitute goalkeepers allowed in Home Internationals.

June 1967—International Board decides to allow two substitutes per team and not only for injuries, but F.A. and Football League agreed to continue with one substitute.

1968-69—Two substitutes (one to

be goalkeeper) allowed in European Champions and Cup Winners Cups.

SUNDAY FOOTBALL

The popularity of Sunday football has spread so rapidly in recent years that there are more people playing on this day than on any other day of the week. The largest proportion of these are in the London, Birmingham and Liverpool areas, but there are also well established organisations for Sunday football in Manchester and Hampshire as well as other thickly populated areas.

Until 1955 the F.A. did not permit clubs or players under their jurisdiction to take part in Sunday football. In that year, however, it lifted the ban, but also made it clear that they did not intend to organise or control Sunday football. Four years later when the question was considered once again the F.A. at last decided to allow Sunday Football Leagues to become affiliated, and in 1964 they went a step further, actually inaugurating their own Sunday Cup Competition.

However, the F.A. has retained its rule which states that no club, player, official, referee or linesman shall be compelled to take part in football on Sundays, Good Friday or Christmas Day.

The F.A. rules also state that Professional Players' Registration forms signed on a Sunday are not valid. Indeed, it is an offence for a club to induce a player to sign on a Sunday.

The first professional competition match played on Sunday in England —Wisbech v. Dunstable Town, Southern League, Mar. 19, 1967.

SUNDERLAND F.C.

Founded 1879 as Sunderland and District Teachers' A.F.C. Adopted present title 1881. Elected to Football League, Division I, 1890. Honours: Champions, Division I, 1891-2, 1892-3, 1894-5, 1901-2, 1912-13, 1935-6. Runners-up, 1893-4, 1897-8, 1900-1901, 1922-3, 1934-5. Runners-up, Division II, 1963-4. F.A. Cup: Winners, 1937. Finalists, 1913. Record attendance: 75,118 v. Derby County, F.A. Cup, 6th Round (replay), Mar. 8, 1933. Address: Roker Park, Sunderland (Tel. 72077). Nickname: Rokerites. Colours: Red and white striped shirts, white shorts. Record League

goal-scorer: D. Halliday, 43 goals, Division I, 1928-9. Record victory: 11—1, v. Fairfield, F.A. Cup, 1st Round, 1894-5. Record defeat: 8—0 v. West Ham United, Division I, Oct. 19, 1968.

SUPPORTERS' CLUBS
National Federation of Football

" To Help—not Hinder " is the motto of the National Federation of Football Supporters' Clubs. Their members have a proud record of valuable help to their parent clubs over the past three decades.

During this time thousands of pounds have been collected by the sale of programmes, ball tickets, other draw tickets, dances, socials, etc. Many football clubs big and small owe their existence to the hard work and generosity of its Supporters' Club.

The Federation was formed early in 1927. Brentford, Bournemouth, Brighton, Charlton, Northampton and Plymouth were the original members. Today there are over 360 clubs affiliated, associated with both professional and amateur teams. The first amateur club whose supporters' organisation became a member of the Federation was Barking.

SUSPENSION

See also FINES.

Clubs

Crook Town A.F.C. officials and players, were permanently suspended by Durham F.A., Jan. 7, 1928, for alleged breaches of the amateur rules. The club was also suspended from the F.A. Amateur Cup competition, and Bishop Auckland, whom they had defeated, were allowed into the next Round.

Following further investigation into Durham football by the F.A. on June 30, 1928, 342 players and 61 club officials were suspended and fines amounting to nearly £400 were imposed. All the suspended players were declared professionals.

The Council of Durham F.A. also passed a resolution suspending themselves for a year.

Grounds

If a ground is suspended by the F.A., then the club concerned cannot play on any ground within a radius of

12 miles until the suspension is lifted.

When Stockport County's ground was under suspension in 1921, the club played a Division II game with Leicester City at Old Trafford, Manchester.

When their grounds were under suspension in Feb. 1961, Plymouth Argyle played a Division II game with Ipswich Town at Torquay, and Gillingham a Division IV game with Wrexham at Gravesend.

Crystal Palace played a home Division III(S) game with Exeter City at Southampton, Nov. 27, 1920.

Players

In 1915 the F.A. permanently suspended eight of the players who had taken part in a Division I game between Manchester United and Liverpool on April 2. This was the outcome of an investigation during which it was alleged that the match had been "fixed" for betting.

A number of players, including internationals, were suspended for life in 1964-5 following sensational disclosures in the "People" newspaper concerning bribery and match fixing. See also under BETTING.

SWANSEA CITY F.C.

Founded 1911 as Swansea Town. Became Swansea City February 1970. One of the original members of the Football League, Division III, 1920. Honours: Champions, Division III(S), 1924-5, 1948-9. Best in Division II, 5th, 1925-6. Record attendance: 32,796 v. Arsenal, F.A. Cup, 4th Round, Feb. 19, 1968. Address: Vetch Field, Swansea (Tel. 53633). Nickname: Swans. Colours: White shirts, white shorts. Record League goal-scorer: C. Pearce, 35 goals, Division II, 1931-2. Record victory: 8—1 v. Bristol Rovers, Division III(S), April 15, 1922, and v. Bradford City, Division II, Feb. 22, 1936. Record defeat: 8—1 v. Fulham, Division II, Jan. 22, 1938.

SWEDEN

Despite the fact that many of their best players have been lured away to other countries where clubs can afford to pay such attractive wages Sweden has managed to maintain a fairly high rating in World football.

Sweden won the Olympic Soccer title in London in 1948. Two years later they won third place in the World Cup finals in Brazil. Then, in 1952, they gained another third place, this time in the Olympics at Helsinki.

This was a remarkable run of success and although it was broken when they failed to qualify for the World Cup tournament of 1954 in Switzerland and the 1956 Melbourne Olympics, they gave a first-class account of themselves when the 1958 World Cup finals were played in their own country.

They beat Mexico, Hungary, Russia and West Germany, and drew with Wales to reach the final in which they were beaten 5—2 by the brilliant Brazilians.

The early history of the game in Sweden is very sketchy and records contain many contradictions. It is obvious, however, that soccer first became popular in the two principal cities, Stockholm and Gothenburg, where it was introduced in the 1880s by British Embassy officials in the capital and by Scottish textile workers at Gothenburg. The latter formed a soccer section of the Orgryte club which is recognised as the oldest in the country.

A National Championship was established as early as 1896 but this was on a rather limited scale until the formation of the National League in 1924.

The Swedish F.A. was officially founded in 1904, although there had been a similar organisation in existence since 1902. The Corinthians visited Stockholm in 1904 and played three games which they won by an aggregate of 29—1.

Address of the governing body: Svenska Fotbollförbundet, Fotbollstadion, Solna. Colours: Yellow shirts with blue collars and cuffs, blue shorts.

May 21, 1923	Sweden 2, England 4; Stockholm.
May 24, 1923	Sweden 1, England 3; Stockholm.
May 17, 1937	Sweden 0, England 4; Stockholm.
Nov. 19, 1947	England 4, Sweden 2; Highbury.
May 13, 1949	Sweden 3, England 1; Stockholm.
June 2, 1949*	Sweden 3, Eire 1; Stockholm.

Nov. 13, 1949*	Eire 1, Sweden 3; Dublin.
May 30, 1952	Sweden 1, Scotland 1; Stockholm.
May 6, 1953	Scotland 1, Sweden 2; Hampden Park.
May 16, 1956	Sweden 0, England 0; Stockholm.
June 15, 1958*	Sweden 0, Wales 0; Stockholm.
Oct. 28, 1959	England 2, Sweden 3; Wembley.
Nov. 1, 1959	Eire 3, Sweden 2; Dublin.
May 18, 1960	Sweden 4, Eire 1; Malmo.
May 16, 1965	Sweden 1, England 2; Gothenberg
May 22, 1968	England 3, Sweden 1; Wembley.

* World Cup.

SWINDON TOWN F.C.

Founded 1881. Adopted professionalism and joined newly formed Southern League, 1894. Third Division, 1920. Honours: Runners-up, Division III, 1962-3, 1968-9. League Cup: Winners, 1969. Record attendance: 28,898 v. Watford, Division III, Mar. 29, 1969. Address: County Ground, Swindon (Tel. 22118). Nickname: Railwaymen. Colours: Red shirts with white edgings, white shorts. Record league goal-scorer: H. Morris, 47 goals, Division III(S), 1926-7. Record victory: 10—1 v. Farnham United Breweries (A), F.A. Cup, 1st Round, Nov. 28, 1925. Record defeat: 10—1 v. Manchester City, F.A. Cup, 4th Round (replay), Jan. 25, 1930.

SWITZERLAND

Switzerland has post-war victories over all the home countries but her International form over the past decade has been most erratic.

The Swiss qualified for the finals of the World Cup in 1962 and again in 1966 but failed to gain a single point in either tournament.

The Swiss F.A. was founded in 1895 and today it controls about 1,000 clubs including between 400 and 500 part-time professionals.

Address of the governing body: Schweizerischer Fussballverband, BP 24, 3000, Berne 15. Colours: Red shirts, white shorts.

Results of international matches:

May 24, 1931	Switzerland 2, Scotland 3; Geneva.
May 20, 1933	Switzerland 0, England 4; Berne.
May 5, 1935	Switzerland 1, Eire 0; Basle.
Mar. 17, 1936	Eire 1, Switzerland 0; Dublin.
May 17, 1937	Switzerland 0, Eire 1; Berne.
May 21, 1938	Switzerland 2, England 1; Zurich.
Sept. 18, 1938	Eire 4, Switzerland 0; Dublin.
May 11, 1946*	England 4, Switzerland 1; Chelsea.
May 15, 1946*	Scotland 3, Switzerland 1; Hampden Park.
May 18, 1947	Switzerland 1, England 0; Zurich.
May 17, 1948	Switzerland 2, Scotland 1; Berne.
Dec. 1, 1948	England 6, Switzerland 0; Highbury.
Dec. 5, 1948	Eire 0, Switzerland 1; Dublin.
May 26, 1949	Switzerland 4, Wales 0; Berne.
April 26, 1950	Scotland 3, Switzerland 1; Hampden Park.
May 16, 1951	Wales 3, Switzerland 2; Wrexham.
May 28, 1952	Switzerland 0, England 3; Zurich.
June 20, 1954†	Switzerland 0, England 2; Berne.
May 19, 1957†	Switzerland 1, Scotland 2; Basle.
Nov. 6, 1957	Scotland 3, Switzerland 2; Hampden Park.
May 9, 1962	England 3, Switzerland 1; Wembley.
June 5, 1963	Switzerland 1, England 8; Basle.
Oct. 14, 1964†	Ireland 1, Switzerland 0; Belfast.
Nov. 14, 1964†	Switzerland 2, Ireland 1; Lausanne.

* Victory internationals. † World Cup.

T

TACTICS AND TEAM EVOLUTION

See also OFFSIDE.

In its early days football was played between sides of unlimited numbers and without any particular formation. But by 1850 it had become the practice for opposing teams to field between 15 and 20 men each.

These numbers were favoured by several clubs until late in the 1860s, although the famous Queen's Park Club of Glasgow fielded 15 or more players in a team for several years after it had become normal to play with only 11 or 12 men.

Teams of nine forwards and two defenders came into fashion around 1860 and this formation quickly developed into a combination of goalkeeper, one back, two half-backs and seven or eight forwards. The Sheffield Association club seem to have preferred the 12-player team.

An all-round rule of 11 players a side was not adopted until about 1870 when the formation was usually a goalkeeper, one full-back, two half-backs, and seven forwards. The forward line being made up of two right wings, three centres and two left wings.

When England met Scotland for the first official international in 1872, the Scots played with a goalkeeper, two backs, two half-backs and six forwards, while England kept to a goalkeeper, one back (then known as a three-quarter back), one half-back and eight forwards.

As one may gather from the disposition of the players in those days, the emphasis was definitely on attack. Most sides played with virtually nine or ten forwards, for the half-backs were really attackers who paid little attention to defence.

In those early days there was practically no team-work as we know it to-day although there was a system of backing-up players of your own side who were in possession of the ball so as to be able to take it on if one's colleague should over-run it or lose possession. Sides were composed of individual artists who when they got the ball, did their best to beat the opposing side on their own. So were the great dribblers developed. Whatever we may now think of such tactics there must have been real pleasure in watching these football artists weaving their way through the opposition, taking the ball almost from one end of the field to the other before shooting at goal.

Towards the middle of the 1870s it became the practice to line-up with a goalkeeper, two backs, two half-backs and six forwards, the combination first favoured by the Scots. Also about this time the Scots were fast developing stronger teams with the introduction of more unselfish methods. It was in Scotland that it first became the fashion to pass the ball before being tackled.

It was hard to break the English They still preferred to try and dribble through the opposition on their own, of their individualistic type of football. and so remarkable was their ability in this respect that they were not entirely without success.

However, when, after 10 games against Scotland, England had only won two, it became obvious that the passing game must bring greater dividends in the long run. This success of Scotland in international matches not only prompted the adoption of the passing game, but it also encouraged the importation of many Scottish players into England in the 1880s.

In 1882 it also inspired N. L. Jackson, then honorary assistant-secretary of the Football Association, to form the Corinthians, a club which subsequently became noted for the excellent brand of their combined football.

However, even before the advent of the Corinthians the success of the forward combinations who adopted this new style of play made it obvious that some tightening up was necessary in defence. Several teams began to experiment with three half-backs instead of two, but still retained only the one full-back. The Cambridge University team was probably the first to adopt a line-up similar to that of the present day with a goalkeeper, two full-backs, three half-backs and five forwards. This was in 1877. However, most teams continued with six forwards for some time after this.

England first played three half-backs against Scotland in 1884, but the Scots did not adopt this system until 1887 when it became the general practice with all clubs to field three half-backs. Among the first clubs to play regularly with three half-backs was Preston North End. This formation, plus their development of the Scottish passing game, brought them great successes towards the end of the 1880s.

The club which probably did more than any other towards establishing without doubt the real advantages of the passing game was, as already mentioned, the Corinthians. They were the first to show how to draw an opponent and then pass into an open space.

While there may not be as many great individualists in football today, the power of the team as a team is more effective. Indeed, the strength of the modern defensive system is greater than it has ever been. More detailed mention of the " third back " game can be found in this volume under OFFSIDE, but even without considering the " third back ", it can be seen that the excellent positioning, marking and tackling of the defender is the outstanding feature of most teams in recent seasons.

Unfortunately, too many sides nowadays seem to be developing a positive mania for defensive tactics, but because such tactics often breed success, they are difficult to criticise. The partisan spectator cares little about tactics providing his side is winning. The truth is, however, that defensive football cannot possibly be such an attractive spectacle as the better brand of fast, combined, attacking play.

Perhaps the great dribblers of the past were better attackers. But with a few exceptions this type of play meets with disapproval nowadays. The cry is " get rid of it ", and the game has been marred because so many players have taken heed of this cry, booting the ball away before they have found a worthwhile place to put it. This fault may also be part of the modern craze for speed. Unfortunately, too many players cannot think as quickly as this modern game demands.

The claim that the game has declined in recent years is difficult to substantiate. It is true that the modern emphasis on systems such as 4-2-4, 4-3-3 or what have you has almost completely destroyed individualism and enterprise on the part of the players who are now so strictly tied to the system. But despite what the old-timers would have us believe one still doubts whether the Corinthians would prove a match for the so well drilled modern team.

Where the decline has undoubtedly occurred is not in efficiency but in the quality of entertainment provided. Footballers have become too stereotyped and the lact of enterprise shown by some teams, especially when playing away from home, is strongly deplored.

One of the most successful combinations of the post-war era was the Hungarian side of the 1950s. They were an all-out attacking combination in which each man was a brilliant ball-player like the dribblers of old, but each man also knew just where he should be when not in possession of the ball.

The Hungarian defence was perhaps not as good as that of many Football League clubs, but it was difficult to criticise the rearguard as a separate part of the eleven, when in that Hungarian scheme they were an integral part of an all-out attacking team. And is not attack the best form of defence?

What has been said of the Hungarians can also be said of the Brazilians. No one who saw the Brazilians in the World Cup of 1970 would dare to say that football tactics are inferior to those of 60 years ago. They provided an astonishing contrast to the modern concept of the game. To begin with each player is a master of the basic techniques of dribbling, passing, shooting and heading, and they played with flair, imagination and great genius, all the time concentrating on attack.

It is to be hoped that the lesson of Brazil's victory will have a far reaching effect. Starting at the bottom it is obvious that at home we must pay more attention to developing those basic techniques so that we may never again see either one-footed attackers or poor headers in a world class tournament.

TEAM CHANGES

See under PLAYERS for the greatest number and least number to appear for a club in a single season.

The Huddersfield Town defence of W. J. Wheeler; R. Staniforth, L. Kelly; W. H. McGarry, D. W. McEvoy and W. L. Quested, remained unchanged throughout season 1952-3 when they won promotion to Division I.

When Oldham Athletic visited Barrow in Division III(N), Sept. 14, 1957, only outside-left, R. Fawley, retained his position from the previous game.

Derby County also made 10 changes in their League side on one occasion. That was on April 2, 1960, when only centre-half, R. Young, retained his position in the side which defeated Huddersfield Town.

TELEVISION

Whereas the Football Association has agreed to the televising of certain matches played under their immediate jurisdiction, the spread of the new medium since the war has not been met with open arms by the Football League. For some time the League banned live television from their matches, although the ban was reviewed every season.

In 1960, the Football League made a £150,000 agreement with I.T.A. for the screening of a number of matches, but this scheme fell through when a number of the leading clubs refused to take part.

In Aug. 1964 the Football League agreed to allow B.B.C. 2 to screen an edited 55-minute version of one League game per week, to be shown two hours after the game. This was subsequently reduced to 45 minutes following protest by the F.A.

The F.A. always considers the danger of reduced attendances at other games before granting permission for certain games to be televised. More often than not, it is mid-week internationals—when League matches are at a minimum—which appear on the T.V. screens.

The first F.A. Cup Final at which any part of the game was televised was the 1937 Final between Sunderland and Preston North End.

When the B.B.C. resumed television after the war the first game seen on television was Barnet v. Tooting and Mitchum, Oct. 19, 1946, at Barnet.

The first post-war F.A. Cup Final to be televised from start to finish was Charlton Athletic v. Burnley, April 26, 1947.

The first F.A. Cup tie to be televised—other than the Final—was Charlton Athletic v. Blackburn Rovers, 5th Round, Feb. 8. 1947.

The first Football League game to be televised was Blackpool v. Bolton Wanderers, on I.T.V., Sept. 10, 1960.

Closed circuit television of an away game was first seen on the Coventry City ground on Wednesday, October 7, 1965. Four large screens were used to show Coventry's game with Cardiff City as it was played at Ninian Park.

The record attendance for an F.A. Cup tie other than the Final was created on March 11, 1967 when 105,000 saw Everton and Liverpool in their 5th Round tie.

A crowd of 64,851 were present at Goodison Park, but another 40,149 were also watching the game on closed circuit television at Anfield.

TEST MATCHES

See PROMOTION.

" THIRD BACK ", THE

See TACTICS AND TEAM EVOLUTION, and also OFFSIDE.

THIRD DIVISION (Football League)

During season 1919-20, the members of the First Division of the Southern League applied en bloc to be taken into the Football League as a Third Division.

The proposal that this division should be formed and the further proposal that the possibilities of adding a

Northern section in the following season should be investigated, were accepted at the Annual Meeting of the Football League, May 29, 1920.

At that time 22 clubs formed the First Division of the Southern League, but of these, Cardiff City had made application to become a member of the Football League, Division II. The Welsh club was accepted, so Grimsby Town was brought into the newly-formed Division III to make up the 22 clubs.

The members of this new Division were accepted only as Associate Members of the Football League, and, at first, were not entitled to any say in the conduct of the League's affairs. In 1929 the Division III clubs were granted voting power at Football League General Meetings, but were restricted to two votes each section. There are, however, still certain matters upon which they are not permitted to vote.

The 22 clubs forming the original Football League, Division III were: Brentford, Brighton and Hove Albion, Bristol Rovers, Crystal Palace, Exeter City, Gillingham, Grimsby Town, Luton Town, Merthyr Town, Millwall, Newport County, Northampton, Norwich City, Plymouth Argyle, Portsmouth, Queen's Park Rangers, Reading, Southampton, Southend United, Swansea Town, Swindon Town and Watford.

The first champions were Crystal Palace who finished five points ahead of Southampton.

The following 20 clubs took part in the first season of the Northern Section in 1921-2: Accrington Stanley, Ashington, Barrow, Chesterfield, Crewe Alexandra, Darlington, Durham City, Grimsby Town, Halifax Town, Hartlepools United, Lincoln City, Nelson, Rochdale, Southport, Stalybridge Celtic, Stockport County, Tranmere Rovers, Walsall, Wigan Borough and Wrexham.

Stockport County were the first champions of this section, finishing six points ahead of Darlington.

The Northern Section was increased to 22 clubs by the addition of Doncaster Rovers and New Brighton in 1923.

In 1933 the Division III clubs introduced a Cup competition of their own, which was continued until 1939.

These were the winners:

Southern Section

1934—Exeter City
1935—Bristol Rovers
1936—Coventry City
1937—*Watford and Millwall

Northern Section

1934—Darlington
1935—Stockport County
1936—Chester
1937—Chester
1938—Southport

In 1950 both sections of Division III were increased to 24 clubs by the addition of Gillingham and Colchester United to the Southern Section, and Scunthorpe and Lindsey United and Shrewsbury Town to the Northern Section.

The division into Northern and Southern Sections was abandoned at the end of season 1957-8. Then the top 12 teams from each section formed a new Third Division and the bottom 24 teams formed a new Fourth Division.

See also FOOTBALL LEAGUE.

* The final between Watford and Millwall was held over until the 1937-8 season, and then, after playing two drawn games, the clubs were considered to be joint holders.

THROW-IN

The "throw-in" was established by the newly-formed Football Association, 1863.

It had been previously mentioned in the Sheffield Laws of the Game as early as 1858, but in the majority of games before 1863 the ball was kicked back into play after it had crossed the touch-lines. Even in the Cambridge rules published only a couple of months before those of the F.A., the ball was to be kicked into play.

According to the earliest F.A. rules, it was the first player to reach the ball after it had passed out of play who was given the advantage of throwing it in. There was nothing in the rules to prevent a player taking a run-up to the line and throwing it one-handed or two-handed in any fashion he thought best.

The two-handed throw-in was first introduced in 1882, and it was not until 1895 that the rules stated that a player must stand on the touch-line when taking the throw-in.

Of course, players have never been permitted to score direct from a throw-in, but until 1920 they could be given offside when a throw was being taken.

In 1925 the F.A. further improved on the rule that a player must stand on the touch-line when taking a throw-in, by compelling him to have *both* feet on the line. For many years it was the practice to award a free-kick against a player making a foul throw. It was not until 1931 that it became law for the throw-in to revert to the opposing side.

The record distance for a throw-in is claimed by R. Woodruff of Wolverhampton Wanderers. In practice on the Molineux ground in October 1965 he threw the ball 40 yards 2 feet 1 inch, thus beating the previous record of 37 yards 2 feet 6 inches by R. Lunnis (Portsmouth) set up at Fratton Park.

Goal-scoring

There is only one instance on record of a player scoring with a throw-in. It occurred in a 4th Round F.A. Cup tie at Oakwell between Barnsley and Manchester United on Jan. 22, 1938. F. Bokas took a throw-in near a corner flag and threw the ball right into the goalmouth where T. Breen, the Manchester United goalkeeper, deflected it into his own net.

TICKETS

In all F.A. Cup ties before the Semi-final Round the visiting clubs are entitled to claim 25% of all seating accommodation providing they request their share within three days of the draw (in the Scottish Cup 20% of all tickets sold in advance may be claimed.

In the Semi-final the two competing clubs and the club on whose ground the match is being played can each claim one third of the tickets.

Complimentary Tickets

In Football League matches the visiting club can normally claim a total of 37 complimentary tickets—25 for the use of players, manager and trainer, and 12 directors' tickets.

F.A. Cup Final Tickets

The F.A. Cup Final has been an all-ticket game since 1923 when Wembley Stadium was stormed by thousands of fans.

The capacity of Wembley in 1923 was around 127,000 but it is estimated that this figure was exceeded by at least 70,000 on the day. Such was the congestion that the F.A. later had to return £2,797 to ticket holders who had been unable to claim their seats.

Some clubs adopted the practice of issuing Cup Final tickets to "lucky programme number" holders. This system has received the blessing of the F.A. with certain conditions. For instance, the programmes must be sold at their usual price and the club must announce in advance the dates of the matches at which draws will take place and mention the number of tickets to be distributed.

TORQUAY UNITED F.C.

Founded 1898. Elected to Football League, Division III(S), 1927. Honours: Runners-up, Division III(S), 1956-7; 3rd in Div. IV, 1959-60, 1965-6. Record attendance: 21,908 v. Huddersfield, F.A. Cup, 4th Round, Jan. 29, 1955. Address: Plainmoor, Torquay (Tel. 38666). Colours: Gold shirts with blue trim, gold shorts with blue stripe. Record League goal-scorer: R. Collins, 40 goals, Division III(S), 1955-6. Record victory: 9—0 v. Swindon Town, Division III(S), Mar. 8, 1952. Record defeat: 10—2 v. Fulham, Division III(S), Sept. 7, 1931; v. Luton Town, Division III(S), Sept. 2, 1933.

TOTTENHAM HOTSPUR F.C.

Founded 1882. Elected to Football League, Division II, 1908. Honours: Champions, Division I, 1950-51, 1960-61. Runners-up, 1921-2, 1951-2, 1956-7, 1962-3. Champions, Division II, 1919-20, 1949-50. Runners-up, 1908-9, 1932-3. F.A. Cup: Winners, 1901, 1921, 1961, 1962, 1967. Tottenham Hotspur is one of the only three clubs to have completed the "double"— League Championship and F.A. Cup Winners in the same season. They did so in 1960-61. Winners European Cup-winners' Cup, 1963. Record attendance: 75,038 v. Sunderland, F.A. Cup,

6th Round, Mar. 5, 1938. Address:
White Hart Lane, Tottenham, N.17
(Tel. 01-808 1020). Nickname:
Spurs. Colours: White shirts, dark
blue shorts. Record League goal-
scorer: J. Greaves, 37 goals, Division
I, 1962-3. Record victory: 13—2 v.
Crewe Alexandra, F.A. Cup, 4th
Round (replay), Feb. 3, 1960. Record
defeat: 7—2 v. Liverpool, Division I,
Oct. 31, 1914, v. Newcastle United,
Division I, Sept. 1, 1951, and v.
Blackburn Rovers, Division I, Sept. 7,
1963.

TOURS

The first overseas tour by an English
team was that made by Oxford University when they visited Germany in
1875. The second overseas tour of an
English club side did not take place
until 1897 when the Corinthians
visited South Africa.

The first Scottish club to play
abroad was Queen's Park. They
played two games in Copenhagen in
1898, winning 7—0 and 3—0.

The first tour, either at home or
abroad, was made by the Royal Engineers in Dec. 1873. They played Sheffield, Derby and Nottingham, and won
all three games.

Clubs affiliated to the F.A. are obliged to seek permission before playing
anywhere abroad.

The Football League makes a stipulation that clubs on tour abroad must
not pay their players more than £2
per day for out-of-pocket expenses,
further, that the players must not
profit from such payments. Clubs are
entitled to pay the usual £4 (win) and
£2 (draw) bonuses.

The first continental tour to be
made by a representative F.A. team
took place during the 1899-1900
season when a side which included
such famous players as C. W. Alcock,
W. Bassett and C. Wreford-Brown,
visited Berlin, Prague and Karlsruhe.

TRAINERS

The modern football club trainer is
one of the most important men in the
game. He is a specialist in first-aid
and the recuperative treatment of injuries. He must know massage and be
able to make proper use of infra-red
and short-wave electrical treatment.
Some of this equipment could be

dangerous in the hands of a man who
does not understand it, but properly
used, it can return players to physical
fitness far quicker than was ever possible in the old days.

The actual treatment of injuries is
only one side of a trainer's job. As his
title implies he is employed by the club
to train the players not only to a peak
of physical fitness, but in most cases
he is also expected to train them in
the art of football. He must, therefore,
not only be fully conversant with physical culture, but must also have a
first-class knowledge of the game itself.

However, so much importance is
attached to the treatment of injuries
by up-to-date and highly technical
methods, that several of the larger
clubs now have fully qualified physio-
therapists on their staffs. This relieves
the trainer of some of the responsibility which has gradually been over-
burdening him in recent years.

Champions

J. Grierson trained six Football
League Championship winning teams:
Aston Villa in 1894, 1896, 1897, 1899,
1900 and 1910.

F.A. Cup

J. Lewis trained three F.A. Cup
Final teams: Wolverhampton Wan-
derers 1893, Everton 1897 and Bolton
Wanderers 1904.

Long Service

W. Williams was trainer of Sunderland for 32 years during which time
he never missed any of his club's
League or Cup matches. He was
appointed trainer, Feb. 8, 1897, and
retired, April 1929.

Player

G. Lathom (Cardiff City trainer)
played inside-right against Blackburn
Rovers at Ewood Park in a First Division game, Jan. 2, 1922.

TRANMERE ROVERS F.C.

Founded 1883. One of the original
members of the Football League, Division III(N), 1921. Honours: Champions, Division III(N), 1937-8. Relegated after one season in Division II.

Record attendance: 22,217 v. Barnsley, F.A. Cup, 4th Round, Jan. 25, 1936. Address: Prenton Park, Birkenhead (Tel. Mountwood 3677). Colours: White shirts with royal blue edgings, royal blue shorts. Record League goalscorer: R. Bell, 35 goals, Division III(N), 1933-4. Record victory: 13—4 v. Oldham Athletic, Division III(N), Dec. 26, 1935. Record defeat: 9—1 v. Tottenham Hotspur, F.A. Cup, 3rd Round (replay), Jan. 14, 1953.

TRANSFERS

See also REGISTRATION OF PLAYERS.

Transfer fees continue to soar, but the suggestion that transfer fees could be limited by the authorities has long since been proved impracticable. As long ago as 1899 the F.A. made a suggestion to the Football League that there should be a limit of £10. A limit actually came into force nine years later on Jan. 1, 1908 at a much larger figure of £350. But only four months later, at the F.A.'s Annual Meeting, the regulation was expunged.

There were too many easy ways of dodging such a limit. For instance, what was there to stop a club handing over £20,000 for a player, but—to keep within the regulations—signing on a half-dozen other worthless players so as to spread the fee?

Some critics of the present system have gone so far as to label it akin to " white slave trafficking ". But is it not the fairest and only practical system? A club wants a certain player from another club . . . so why should they not pay for him? A transfer fee is the only proper compensation for a club's loss. It also enables the club, if it wishes, to obtain a replacement.

Certainly, if there had never been such a system there would not now be so many first-class clubs in existence. Several of these clubs who are able to bring first-class football home to their local supporters have had to transfer to live.

The paying of transfer fees for players became the practice among the leading clubs even before there was any necessity for them to part with money to obtain a player's services. According to the earliest regulations, a player was bound to his club for a single season only, and at the end of that term he was free to join any other club he wished. Transfers during the season could only be arranged with the special permission of the F.A. Council. Yet fees were paid, and the legislators took very little action, beyond calling it " unsportsmanlike ".

Today, players are not permitted to move from club to club at will. Once a professional is signed by a club he may remain the club's property for so long as it is prepared to exercise the option which is written into his contract and providing the terms offered are not less favourable than those originally agreed. Whether he continues to play for the club is another matter, but he cannot play for any other club affiliated to the Football Association, or indeed, any other Association belonging to the world-wide Federation, as long as the club which originally obtained his signature keep him on their retained list. The player, however, can appeal to the Management Committee if not released by his club by June 30. He *may* then be placed on the transfer list.

At the end of each season, and in other special circumstances, professionals are either offered terms by their respective clubs, placed on the " open to transfer " list, or given a " free transfer ". " Open to transfer " means that a club is willing to receive offers for the player. " Free transfer " means that a club is no longer interested in the player and he is free to go where he pleases.

Clubs are free to approach players on the " open to transfer " list, but no direct approach may be made to any players retained. In these cases any inquiries must be made to the club holding the player's registration. The same applies on the player's side. He must not offer his services to any other club until his existing engagement has ended.

No club can transfer a player without his consent, and players have the right of appeal to the League Management Committee which has the power to overrule clubs in any decision affecting transfers. If, for instance, a player considers that the fee placed on him by his club is so high that it may restrict his chances of obtaining a transfer, he may appeal to have that figure reduced.

The transfer system was upheld in

Law in 1912 when the test case of Lawrence J. Kingaby v. Aston Villa was heard in the King's Bench Division on Mar. 26-7. This was really the Players' Union v. the Football League, for the League undertook to indemnify the club against all costs, and the player was backed by the union. Kingaby claimed damages for loss of employment. The defence submitted that the case was simply a question of law and therefore not one for a jury but for a judge's decision alone. This submission was upheld and the case came before Mr. Justice Lawrence.

The player pleaded that another club had offered him employment but that he was unable to take it because of the transfer fee fixed by his present employers—Aston Villa. He further alleged that his employers had maliciously made their fee excessive.

Judgment was given for the defendants with costs. Mr. Justice Lawrence found no evidence of malice and that the action of the defendants (Aston Villa) was justified by the terms of the employment.

The transfer of players in the Football League after the second Thursday in March in each season is controlled by the Management Committee of the League. Players transferred after this date are not able to play for their new club in League matches unless permission is received. This rule, made in 1911 (originally the deadline was March 16) is designed to prevent clubs engaged in promotion or relegation struggles from strengthening their team at so vital a stage of the season.

The last occasion permission was granted for a club so concerned to include a player signed after deadline, was when Blackburn Rovers were fighting to avoid relegation to Division II at the end of the 1935-6 season. There were special circumstances. They had three goalkeepers out of commission with fractured limbs and permission was obtained to play K. J. Hamill, a goalkeeper signed on April 15.

In 1967 the Football League instituted a system of Temporary Transfers wherein each club is permitted two players on loan.

F.A. Cup

Players transferred cannot play for their new clubs in the F.A. Cup competition if they have already taken part in the competition during the season with another club.

In 1958, because of the Munich disaster, Manchester United was granted special permission to include S. Crowther in their Cup team although he had already appeared for Aston Villa that season.

In season 1945-6 J. Scoular appeared for Gosport in a Preliminary Round of the competition and for Portsmouth in the 3rd Round Proper.

Four-Figure Fees

The first four-figure transfer fee was £1,000, paid by Middlesbrough to Sunderland for the transfer of A. Common, Feb. 1905. Common proved his worth. On Feb. 25, Middlesbrough, who were in a dangerous position near the bottom of Division I, won their first away League game for nearly two years. They defeated Sheffield United with the only goal of the match, scored from the penalty spot by Common. Middlesbrough's previous away win was also against Sheffield United, 3—1, Mar. 7, 1903.

Common's transfer caused such a sensation that a special commission was set up to investigate. They were unable to report anything unlawful or underhand.

The first four-figure transfer between Irish clubs is said to be £1,000, paid by Distillery to Derry City for winghalf G. Bowler, during the last war.

Private and Confidential

Transfer fees as stated in the National Press are usually only estimated. In 1922 the Football League decided that all transfer fees should be treated as private and confidential.

Record Fees

The world record transfer fee is approximately £435,000. This amount is believed to have been paid by the Italian club Juventus to Varese for the transfer of P. Anastasi in 1968.

The record fee in a transfer deal involving only one player with a Football League club is understood to be about £165,000, the amount said to have been paid by Leeds United to Leicester City in June 1969 for the transfer of centre-forward A. Clarke.

WORLD CUP. England's third goal in their World Cup Final victory over West Germany at Wembley, 1966.

WORLD CUP. (*Above*) The vital Brazilian goal in the match with England. Scorer Jairzinho watches the ball enter the net. Martin Peters jumps over Gordon Banks, the England goalkeeper. (*Left*) Pelé heads the ball past Burgnich to score the first goal in Brazil's victory over Italy in the Final at Mexico City, 1970

In March 1970 M. Peters was transferred from West Ham United to Tottenham Hotspur in a deal valued at £180,000, but on that occasion the amount included the value of J. Greaves (said to be £80,000) transferred in part exchange.

The record fee between two Scottish clubs—£100,000 by Rangers to Hibernian for C. Stein, Oct. 1968.

Signing-on Fee

When a player signs for any particular Football League club for the first time (as a professional) then, unless transferred at his own request without good reason he is entitled to a signing-on fee which is 5% of his transfer fee (minimum share £250) or, if given a free transfer then his new club must agree to pay the minimum £250 over the period of the contract.

In many countries abroad players have been known to receive huge signing-on fees and Italian and Spanish clubs have led the world in this respect.

Information concerning these fees is not always reliable for many reports are grossly exaggerated. However, while the accuracy of the following list cannot be guaranteed it is included here as a fair reflection of the degree of inducements currently being offered to the world's top players to sign for some foreign clubs.

L. Suarez, Barcelona to Internazionale (Milan), 1961	£59,000
L. Del Sol, Real Madrid to Juventus (Turin), 1962	£47,500
H. Haller, Bologna to Juventus, 1968	£38,000
T. S. Amarildo, Botafogo to Milan, 1963	£32,000
J. Schiaffino, Penarol (Uruguay) to A. C. Milan, 1954	£23,000
E. O. Sivori, River Plate (Argentine) to Juventus, 1957	£20,000
A. Simonsson, Gothenburg to Real Madrid, 1960	£14,000
E. I. Netto (Vava), Atletico Madrid to Corinthians (Brazil), 1960	£13,000
G. Hitchens, Aston Villa to Internazionale, 1961	£12,000
F. Nielsen, Akademisk Boldklub (Denmark) to Atalanta (Italy), 1961	£10,750
W. J. Charles, Leeds United to Juventus (Turin), 1957	£10,000
J. C. Benitez, Zaragoza (Spain), to Barcelona, 1961	£10,000
H. Nielsen, Frederickshavn (Denmark), to Bologna, 1961	£10,000
D. Law, Manchester City to Torino (Italy), 1961	£10,000
J. Baker, Hibernian to Torino, 1961	£8,000

Special and Unusual Transfers

When Arsenal signed C. Buchan from Sunderland in 1925 they paid a fee of £2,000, and also agreed to pay Sunderland an extra £100 for each goal Buchan scored during his first season. He scored 22 goals.

When Tottenham Hotspur signed W. G. Hall from Notts County in 1932, they agreed to pay an additional fee of £500 if Hall was "capped" as a Tottenham player. Hall got the first of several caps in Dec. 1933, when he played against France.

A. Pape, Clapton Orient's centre forward, travelled with his side to Manchester to play a Division II match against Manchester United on Feb. 7, 1925, but just before the game he was transferred to Manchester United. The Football League sanctioned the transfer when contacted by telephone and Pape helped to defeat his old club 4—2.

F. Laycock, a Barrow forward, was called off the field during a Division III game with Rotherham County in order to sign forms transferring him to Nelson. It was the last day of the season for transfers, Mar. 16, 1925.

There has been at least one player who has played for both sides in the same League match, J. Oakes, a left-back, who captained Charlton Athletic's promotion-winning side of the 1930s, played for Port Vale in a Division II game against Charlton Athletic at The Valley on Boxing Day, 1932. The game was abandoned before the end owing to bad light. When the re-arranged fixture came up, later in the season, Oakes was left-back for Charlton Athletic, having been transferred to the London club in the interim.

Before the Football League altered the rules in 1920 so that players were no longer permitted to receive a share of their transfer fee, the record amount received by a player under the old agreement is believed to have been £1,000, paid to centre-forward J. Lane, transferred from Blackpool to Birmingham for £3,300, season 1919-20.

The list that follows is only intended to show the increase in transfer fees among British clubs over the years:

1893	J. Southworth, Blackburn Rovers to Everton	£400
	J. Settle, Bury to Everton	£400
1902	J. McMahon, Preston North End to Manchester City	£450
1903	G. Dorsett, West Bromwich Albion to Manchester City	£450
1904	A. Common, Sheffield United to Sunderland	£520
1904	A. McCombie, Sunderland to Newcastle United	£700
	A. Common, Sunderland to Middlesbrough	£1,000
1907	G. Wilson, Everton to Newcastle United	£1,600†
1908	A. Brown, Sheffield United to Sunderland	£1,600
1911	J. Simpson, Falkirk to Blackburn Rovers	£1,800
	W. Hibbert, Bury to Newcastle United	£1,950
1912	D. Shea, West Ham United to Blackburn Rovers	£2,000
1913	T. Logan, Falkirk to Chelsea	£2,500
1920	J. Lane, Blackpool to Birmingham	£3,300
	J. Crosbie, Ayr United to Birmingham	£3,500
	S. Fazackerley, Sheffield United to Everton	£4,000
1921	T. Hamilton, Kilmarnock to Preston North End	£4,600
1922	S. Puddefoot, West Ham United to Falkirk	£5,000
	W. Cresswell, South Shields to Sunderland	£5,500
1925	R. Kelly, Burnley to Sunderland	£6,500
1927	J. Gibson, Partick Thistle to Aston Villa	£7,500
1928	D. Jack, Bolton Wanderers to Arsenal	£10,890
1938	B. Jones, Wolverhampton Wanderers to Arsenal	£13,000
1946	A. Stubbins, Newcastle United to Liverpool	£13,500
1947	W. Steel, Morton to Derby County	£15,000
	T. Lawton, Chelsea to Notts County	£20,000
1949	J. Morris, Manchester United to Derby County	£25,000
	E. Quigley, Sheffield Wednesday to Preston North End	£26,000
1950	T. Ford, Aston Villa to Sunderland	£30,000
1951	J. Sewell, Notts County to Sheffield Wednesday	£34,500
1958	C. Jones, Swansea Town to Tottenham Hotspur	£35,000
	A. Quixall, Sheffield Wednesday to Manchester United	£45,000
1959	M. Charles, Swansea Town to Arsenal	£40,000§
1960	D. Law, Huddersfield Town to Manchester City	£55,000
1962	J. Byrne, Crystal Palace to West Ham United	£58,000‡
1962	A. H. Kay, Sheffield Wednesday to Everton	£60,000
1964	F. Pickering, Blackburn Rovers to Everton	£80,000
1965	J. Baxter, Rangers to Sunderland	£85,000
1966	M. England, Blackburn Rovers to Tottenham Hotspur	£95,000
1966	T. Hateley, Aston Villa to Chelsea	£100,000
1966	A. Ball, Blackpool to Everton	£110,000
1968	W. Morgan, Burnley to Manchester United	£118,000
1968	M. Chivers, Southampton to Tottenham Hotspur	£125,000‡
1968	A. Clarke, Fulham to Leicester City	£150,000‡
1969	A. Clarke, Leicester City to Leeds United	£165,000
1970	M. Peters, West Ham United to Tottenham Hotspur	£180,000‡

‡ These deals involved a second player in part exchange.

† Newcastle United was reported to have paid £1,000 to Everton and the remaining £600 to Belfast Distillery.

§ Arsenal also let Swansea Town have two players.

Transfer fees are supposed to be confidential and while it is difficult to establish the precise amounts involved in deals between British clubs it is almost impossible to obtain the precise figure of fees involving foreign clubs.

However, here, for what they are worth, are the estimated amounts of some of the more important transfer deals where one or more foreign clubs have been involved:

1968	P. Anastasi, Varese to Juventus	£435,000
1968	M. Bertini, Fiorentina to Internazionale	£267,000
1968	H. Haller, Bologna to Juventus	£267,000
1963	A. Sormani, Mantua to A.S. Roma	£243,000
1968	R. Benetti, Palermo to Juventus	£233,000
1969	S. Clerici, Atlanta Bergamo to Verona Hellas	£233,000
1966	R. Rosato, Torino to AC Milan	£231,000
1962	L. Del Sol, Real Madrid to Juventus (Turin)	£200,000
1966	V. De Paoli, Brescia to Juventus	£197,000
1962	J. Peiro, Atletico (Madrid) to Torino (Turin)	£170,000
1961	L. Suarez, Barcelona to Internazionale (Milan)*	£150,000
1963	T. S. Amarildo, Botafogo to Milan‡	£142,850
1966	Anquilletti, Atalanta to AC Milan	£132,000
1962	D. Law, Torino (Turin) to Manchester United	£115,000
1957	B. Julinho, Florence to Palmeiras (Brazil)	£111,000
1966	L. Pizabella, Atalanta to A.S. Roma	£109,000
1961	B. Di Giacomo, Napoli to Torino (Turin)	£105,000
1961	D. Law, Manchester City to Torino (Turin)	£100,000
1957	E. Sivori, River Plate (Argentine) to Juventus (Turin)	£100,000
1961	J. Greaves, Milan to Tottenham Hotspur	£98,000
1962	V. Angelillo, Internazionale (Milan) to A. S. Roma	£90,000
1961	J. Umberto, Academica (Portugal) to Internazionale (Milan)	£90,000
1961	J. Greaves, Chelsea to Milan	£85,000
1958	E. Firmani, Sampdoria (Genoa) to Internazionale	£81,000
1961	G. Hitchens, Aston Villa to Internazionale	£80,000
1954	J. Schiaffino, Penarol (Uruguay) to Milan	£72,000
1961	J. Baker, Hibernian to Torino (Turin)	£70,000
1962	U. Maschio, Atalanta (Genoa) to Internazionale†	£68,500
1957	W. J. Charles, Leeds United to Juventus (Turin)§	£65,000
1962	J. Baker, Torino (Turin) to Arsenal	£65,000

* The player received £59,000 of this amount.
† Plus two other players.
§ The player received £10,000 of this amount.
‡The player received £32,000 of this amount.

TRAVELLING

On Good Friday, April 10, 1936, Swansea Town defeated Plymouth Argyle 2—1 in a Division II match at Home Park, Plymouth. The following day Swansea Town met Newcastle United at St. James' Park, Newcastle. Swansea Town lost 2—0.

Between the two games they travelled about 400 miles, a record distance for a League club between matches on successive days.

TROPHIES

Players who have received F.A. Cup medals, League Championship medals and full international honours in the same season are: F. Dewhurst and J. Goodall of Preston North End, 1888-9, C. Athersmith of Aston Villa, 1896-7, D. Blanchflower, D. Mackay, C. Jones, R. Smith and J. White of Tottenham Hotspur, 1960-61.

D. Mackay (Tottenham Hotspur) has a unique distinction. He is the only player to have appeared in both F.A. Cup and Scottish F.A. Cup winning teams (Heart of Midlothian 1956, Tottenham Hotspur 1961, 1962 and 1967); Scottish League and Football League Champions (Heart of Midlothian 1957-8, Tottenham Hotspur 1960-61); Scottish League Cup winners (Heart of Midlothian 1955, 1959); Scot. League v. Football League, Mar. 1957, Oct. 1958; Football League v. Scot. League, Mar. 1960; in addition to Scottish International appearances.

TURKEY

Soccer has been played in Istanbul for more than 60 years and the leading club in Turkey, Fenerbahce, can trace its history back to 1907, or two years after Galatasaray, their first club, was formed.

Turkey first appeared in an international match in 1923 when they drew 2—2 with Rumania in Istanbul and they entered the Olympic tournament in Paris in the following year, but their pre-war matches were very few and far between, and it is in the last decade or so that this country has really begun to make a name in internationals.

In Feb. 1956, they halted the Hungarians' run of successes with a shock 3—1 victory over the Mighty Magyars in Istanbul.

Professionalism was officially adopted by the Turks in 1952 and the Turkish Football Federation which was founded in 1923 now controls about 1,900 clubs.

Address of the governing body: Turkiye Futbol Federasyonu, Fevzi Cakmak Sokak 11, Yenischir-Ankara. Colours: White shirts with one wide horizontal red hoop, white shorts.

Result of international match:

June 8, 1960	Turkey 4, Scotland 2, Ankara.
Nov. 16, 1966†	Eire 2, Turkey 1; Dublin.
Feb. 22, 1967†	Turkey 2, Eire 1; Ankara.
Oct. 23, 1968*	Ireland 4, Turkey 1; Belfast.
Dec. 11, 1968*	Turkey 0, Ireland 3; Istanbul.

* World Cup   † Nations Cup

TWINS

See FAMILIES (Brothers).

U

UNDEFEATED

See DEFENSIVE RECORDS (Undefeated).

UNION OF EUROPEAN FOOTBALL ASSOCIATIONS

This Union of 33 countries is responsible for the European Cup, Cupwinners' Cup, and the Nations Cup.

The Fairs Cup also comes under their control in 1971.

UNITED STATES OF AMERICA

Since World War II soccer has made a big increase in popularity in the United States. This has been due not only to the influx of immigrants from Europe but to the return of American servicemen from countries where they had the opportunity to watch and play football, and catch the enthusiasm for the game from the British, French, Germans, etc.

Soccer, however, is still a poor third to the Americans' most popular games of baseball and American football and although the introduction in 1960 of the U.S. International Soccer League in New York and the inauguration in 1967 of coast to coast professional Leagues added a terrific impetus to the game in the States it still has a long way to go before the average home-born American mentions it in the same breath as either of the two major sports just named.

Football of sorts was played in New England in the middle of the 19th century but this was little more than rough and tumble similar to the old Shrove Tuesday game played on this side of the Atlantic.

However, although early American football subsequently developed into a game resembling rugger rather than soccer, there were many points about the early game as played at some of the colleges in the 1870s that linked it with the latter sport.

Harvard University played a form of soccer as early as 1860 but they subsequently led the field in the development of American football.

The first inter-collegiate match was played between Rutgers and Princetown, at New Brunswick, in Nov. 1869.

Football has been played at Yale since about 1840 but it was not until the 1870s that they began to meet other colleges in regular games. It is interesting to note that at about this time running with the ball was not permitted at Yale although it could be handled and knocked from hand to hand. Goals were scored under and not over the bar and dribbling was also practised.

Twenty-a-side was the normal practice but in 1873 a team of Englishmen, captained by an Old Etonian, met Yale at New Haven and in this game the teams were each composed of 11 men. In fact, 1873 was the first year in which any widely accepted code of rules was adopted in America.

As already indicated the change of direction in development of the American game towards rugger rather than soccer was led by Harvard, in 1875, and they subsequently persuaded Yale to follow suit.

It was not until April 1884 that a meeting was held in New York at which the American Football Association was formed. This subsequently became defunct, but was re-formed in 1911.

The United States first met Canada at Association Football in 1886, clubs sprang up in many parts of the country in the 1890s, and the Californian F.A. (one of the strongholds of soccer in the States) was established in 1902.

Sunderland visited the States in 1894. An Inter-University Association Football League was formed in 1905, the same year in which the Pilgrims F.C. went out from England to play 23 games in America, winning 21 of them. They toured the United States again in 1909, while the famous Corinthians went out in 1906 and 1911.

The United States has suffered several big defeats in the Olympic Games soccer tournament. Their best performance in this competition was probably that in Berlin in 1936 when a side which included several Scots was only beaten 1—0 by Italy.

In 1930 the U.S. reached the semi-finals of the World Cup before being eliminated 6—1 by the Argentine. A 7—1 defeat by Italy put them out in the first round in Italy in 1934, and the only year since then in which they have appeared in the World Cup Finals was 1950. In that year, however, they gained their most shattering victory, beating England 1—0 in Brazil. The teams on that occasion were:

England: Williams; Ramsey, Aston; Wright, Hughes, Dickinson; Finney, Mannion, Bentley, Mortensen, Mullen.

United States: Borghi; Keough, Macca; McIlvenny, Colombo, Bahr; Wallace, Pariani, Gaetjens, J. Sousa, E. Sousa.

Gaetjens scored the only goal of the match.

In 1960 the inaugural tournament of the United States International Soccer League included 12 clubs, each from a different country. The final was won by Bangu (Brazil) who beat Kilmarnock, 2—0. This competition was repeated during the summer months in each succeeding year to 1966.

The first major step to introduce professional soccer into the United States on a national scale was taken during 1966 with the formation of two Leagues, both with considerable financial backing—The National Professional Soccer League and the North American Soccer League (later changing its title to The United Soccer Association).

These two competitions amalgamated in December 1967 and formed a 17-team League which became known as the North American Soccer League, but a considerable amount of money was lost in all-out efforts to indoctrinate a largely disinterested American public, and at the end of only one season the majority of clubs withdrew.

However, despite the comparative failure of the American enthusiasts to promote professional soccer as big-time entertainment for the masses, a great deal of progress has been made since 1966 in introducing the game to the schools, a development which augurs well for the future.

The address of the governing body which now controls something like 3,000 clubs is the United States Soccer Football Association, Inc., Empire State Building, Room 4010, New York 10001. Colours: White shirts, blue shorts, red stockings.

Results of international matches:

June 16, 1924	Eire 3, United States 1; Dublin.
June 28, 1950*	England 0, United States 1; Belo Horizonte, Brazil.
April 30, 1952	Scotland 6, United States 0; Hampden Park.
June 8, 1953†	United States 3, England 6; New York City.
May 8, 1959	United States 1, England 8; Los Angeles.
May 27, 1964	United States 0, England 10; New York City.

* World Cup.
† Under floodlights.

UNIVERSITY FOOTBALL

Although the universities of Oxford and Cambridge have not been able to maintain the strong position they once held in the football world, forced into the background by the keener competitive elements of the professional game, they played a leading role in the game's early development and readers who refer to the index will be able to trace several references to these universities throughout this volume.

Cambridge University men drew up the first code of rules of the game in the middle of the 19th century and Oxford University produced one of the most powerful combinations to enter the F.A. Cup during the earliest years of this competition. Oxford were semi-finalists 1875, 1876, finalists 1873, 1877 and 1880, and winners 1874. Cambridge were semi-finalists in 1877. They dropped out in 1880-81.

The first Oxford v. Cambridge match was played at Kennington Oval in 1874 and was won 1—0 by Oxford. A return match played later in the same year was won 2—0 by Cambridge. This game has been played in every season since with the exception of five seasons 1914-19 and six seasons 1939-45.

During the period before the introduction of professionalism and until the amateurs were no longer able to hold their own with the professional, many university men appeared in full internationals. Indeed, 78 were chosen for England, Ireland and Wales, the last man to receive this honour being C. T. Ashton of Cambridge who actually captained England against Ireland in Oct. 1925.

University Blues who subsequently played as professionals for Football League clubs : G. T. L. Ansell (Oxford University 1928, 1929, 1930) turned professional with Brighton and Hove Albion, 1932. M. King (Oxford University, 1956), Colchester United 1956. A. Smith (Oxford University 1946), Aston Villa 1951, M. Pinner (Cambridge University, 1953), Leyton Orient, 1963, K. Sanderson (Cambridge University), Plymouth Argyle, 1964.

URUGUAY

The footballers of Uruguay have proved themselves to be among the finest in the world and only the loss of so many of their star players to Italy and the Argentine has prevented them from becoming established permanently among the half dozen leading soccer nations.

Uruguay won the football tournament of the 1924 Olympic Games by defeating Switzerland 3—0 in Paris. They retained their Olympic title at Amsterdam four years later when they defeated the Argentine 2—1 after a drawn game. In 1930 they carried off the World Cup on their home ground by beating Argentine, 4—2, and when they next entered this competition, in Brazil in 1950, they again carried off the trophy, this time by beating the host nation, 2—1. In all, a remarkable record in international football.

Since then Uruguay has lost many of their best players. They were beaten in the semi-finals of the World Cup in 1954; failed to qualify in 1958; were eliminated through defeats by Russia and Yugoslavia in the final tournament of 1962, but did better again in 1966 when they won through to the quarter-finals before being eliminated by West Germany. In 1970 they reached the semi-finals, with a hard uncompromising style of defensive football, before losing 3—1 to Brazil.

An English professor at Montevideo University formed the first club in 1882, and Britishers engaged in building the railways established another club in 1891 which subsequently became the famous Penarol club of today.

The leading Uruguayan clubs have been professional since 1932 and the F.A. which was founded in 1900 now controls about 600 clubs including over 1,000 professional players.

The address of the governing body : Associación Uruguaya de Football, Avenida 18 de Julio 1520-28, Montevideo. Colours : Light blue shirts, black shorts.

Results of international matches :

May 31, 1953	Uruguay 2, England 1; Montevideo.
June 19, 1954*	Uruguay 7, Scotland 0; Basle.
June 26, 1954*	Uruguay 4, England 2; Basle.
May 2, 1962	Scotland 2, Uruguay 3; Hampden Park.
Apl. 29, 1964	Ireland 3, Uruguay 0; Belfast.
May 6, 1964	England 2, Uruguay 1; Wembley.
July 11, 1966*	England 0, Uruguay 0; Wembley.
June 8, 1969	Uruguay 1, England 2; Montevideo

* World Cup.

W

WAGES

The early history of players' wages is dealt with in general terms under PROFESSIONALISM. It will be seen there that wages were paid to players before official sanction was given for such payments. In the eyes of the Football Association all Footballers were amateurs. When the first rumours of payments being made to players began to spread, the F.A. made a rule in 1882 that any member of a club would be debarred from football if it was found that he received " remuneration or consideration of any sort above his actual expenses and any wages actually lost ".

Several evasions were adopted to make the payment of wages possible. Duplicate sets of books were often kept : one under the counter and one to be made available for perusal by the F.A. should the occasion arise. In other instances, players were given bogus jobs for which they received payment, the money being refunded to the " employers " by the clubs. Another scheme was to pay players out of the gate money before the total was entered in the books as gross gate receipts.

Preston North End and Blackburn Rovers were among the first clubs to pay wages to players. Another club, Stoke, paid their first professionals 2s. 6d. a week, until one day it leaked out that one of the men was receiving the stupendous sum of 5s. The bulk of the players immediately went on strike until the club eventually agreed to an all-round increase to 5s.

Around 1883, Bolton Wanderers were paying their players 2s. 6d. bonus for winning games and deducting that amount for defeats.

Following the legalisation of profes-sionalism in 1885, there was still no stipulation as to either minimum or maximum wages. One of the greatest players of all times, S. Bloomer, be-came a professional with Derby County in the 1890s at a wage of 7s. 6d. a week. About the same time Sunderland were paying their players as much as 30s. a week. Birmingham's players agreed to receive a share of the gate as their wages when the club turned professional in 1885. Profes-sionals at Fulham were paid 10s. a week and given an " outside job ".

The first move to regulate payment to players concerned the signing-on fee. In 1891 the Football League ruled that this should not exceed £10. (It was not increased until 1958.)

The wages problem came to a head in 1893 when the Football League proposed that players should be limited to £140 per year including a maximum of £1 per week in the close season. But this proposal did not re-ceive the necessary majority and the idea of limiting wages was shelved.

The first maximum wage rule came into force in 1901 when the limit was fixed at £4 per week. Nearly nine years later this figure was raised to £5, providing that the increase was given in two rises of 10s. after two and four years of service.

The Football Association took no further part in the control of weekly wages to players after 1910. This is now left to the respective Leagues and competitions. Until 1966 they re-tained some interest in the actual amounts paid by stipulating the mini-mum which a club must offer any player they wished to retain for a further period of service, but even this has since been erased by the new form of contract.

During World War I there were re-ductions in wages. But in Mar. 1920, following a request by the Players' Union, proposals for an increased maximum came before a Special General Meeting of the Football League. The result was an increase to £9 per week throughout the year (during both the playing season and the close season).

The new wage was not for all players. From a £5 minimum for new players, the rise was to be given in annual increments of £1. It was also decided that players entitled to receive only the £5 maximum (and players receiving less) could sign an agreement with their clubs whereby they would receive £1 extra for each first team appearance. A year later this £1 extra was allowed to all players making first team appearances on a wage of £8 or less.

The Players' Union soon demanded further alterations in the rate of increments and a maximum wage of £10. But 12 months after its demands, the League Management Committee proposed a reduction in the maximum wage. Its proposals were passed by the League on April 12, 1922, and took effect immediately—maximum £8 per week during playing season of 37 weeks, and a maximum £6 per week during the remaining 15 weeks.

Despite the efforts of the Players' Union to secure further alterations in the wage scale, there was no other change until 1945 when the maximum close season wage was increased to £7 per week.

During the war-time seasons special wage rates were in force. From 1939 to 1943 players were paid 30s. per match plus travelling expenses but no bonus. For season 1943-4 this was increased to £2, while players in Championship teams received a bonus of £5, runners-up £3. The rate in 1945-6 was £4 per match.

A most significant wage agreement was made in 1947, thanks largely to the efforts of the Players' Union. For the first time a *minimum* wage level was fixed for all full-time Football League professionals. A National Arbitration Tribunal consisting of Sir Francis Floud and Sir David Ross, under the chairmanship of Lord Terrington, and with Sir Mark Hodgson and Mr. Randall G. Hosking as panel members, were responsible for making the award.

The scale set for the minimum wage was:

Over 17, to 18th birthday £3 and £3.
Over 18, to 19th birthday £4 and £3.
Over 19, to 20th birthday £6 and £4.
Over 20 £7 and £5.

The tribunal also decided that the maximum wage should be raised to £12 in the playing season and £10 in the close season, based on length of service, the maximum wage being reached after five years' service with any club in the Football League, Scottish League, Irish League or Eire League.

Further increases were as follows:

June 1951: Maximum raised to £14.

July 1953: Maximum raised to £15 in the playing season and £12 in the close season. Minimum raised to £3 10s. for a 17-year-old and £7 10s. for a 20-year-old in the playing season and £5 10s. in the close season.

June 1957: Maximum raised to £17 and £14, minimum to £4 10s. at 17, £8 10s. and £6 10s. at 20.

June 1958: Maximum raised to £20 and £17. Minimum to £5 at 17, £8 at 20.

The players made further wage demands in 1960 and when these were backed by a threat to strike on Jan. 21, 1961, the Football League agreed to a number of alterations. The most important of these which concerned wages was the abolition of the maximum.

At the same time it was also decided to raise the minimum wage and graduate from £624 to £780 per annum according to the division of the League in which the player's club is engaged. All these rates are for full-time professionals at age 20 and over in the Football League.

Part-time players of any age must be paid at least £5 per week.

Apprentice professionals must be paid at least £5 per week or up to a maximum of £7 at 15 years of age, £8 at 16, or £10 at 17 years of age.

Wages for the playing season begin on the first Saturday in Aug.

Bonus

In addition to their regular wage, players may receive certain other payments such as match bonuses.

In the Football League the rate of bonus is £4 for a win and £2 for a draw.

The bonus for the various Rounds of the F.A. Cup competition is as follows:

For a win in Rounds 1, 2, 3, 4, 5, 6 respectively, £4, £4, £5, £6, £8, £10.

For a win in the semi-final £20.

For a win in the Final £25.

In the case of drawn games the teams receive half the above amounts.

Where matches are televised each player may receive a payment of up to 10gn. out of the fee paid by the television company, but this payment shall not be made when only short extracts of matches are filmed for transmission.

Fees for Internationals

1886—10s. per match
1887—£1 „   „
1908—£4 „   „
1920—£6 „   „
1937—£8 „   „
1939—£10 „   „
1946—£20 „   „
1952—£30 „   „
1953—£50 „   „
1961—£60 „   „

Players in Under-23 games receive £20.

See also REFEREES AND LINESMEN, CONTINENTAL TOURS, and TRANSFERS (Signing-on fee).

WALES

See under INTERNATIONALS (WALES); WALES, FOOTBALL ASSOCIATION; WELSH CUP; WELSH LEAGUE.

WALES, FOOTBALL ASSOCIATION

In Jan. 1876, a number of Welsh football enthusiasts gathered at the Wynnstay Arms Hotel, Wrexham, to discuss the possibility of arranging an international match with Scotland. They also decided to form the Football Association of Wales. A Committee was elected and final details were agreed at a second meeting on Feb. 2, 1876.

The international match with Scotland took place at Glasgow in Mar.,

and, although Wales was beaten 0—4, the game served to increase Welsh enthusiasm and the Association was definitely established at a meeting at Shrewsbury on May 24, 1876.

Mr. L. Ll Kenrick, of Wynn Hall, Ruabon, a member of the Shropshire Wanderers F.C., who played in the first international match v. Scotland, was the prime mover. He became Chairman and Honorary Secretary.

At this time, most of the football in Wales was played in the North. The earliest club to form was The Druids. They played at Plasmadoc Park, Ruabon, and were soon followed by other clubs at Wrexham, Oswestry and Chirk. It was not until 1890 that the game became sufficiently popular in South Wales to warrant the organisation of an Association League.

This was followed in 1893 by the establishment of the South Wales and Monmouthshire Football Association. But it was not until the early part of the present century that the dribbling code was adopted on a first-class basis. Soccer's growth in Wales was due largely to the efforts of Mr. E. Robbins, Secretary of the Welsh F.A.

The first professional South Wales clubs were Merthyr and Aberdare, followed by Cardiff City in 1910, and Newport County and Swansea Town in 1912.

Address: F.A. of Wales, 3 Fairy Road, Wrexham. Colours: Red shirts with white edging, red shorts.

WALSALL F.C.

Founded 1888 by amalgamation of Walsall Swifts (1877) and Walsall Town (1879). Elected to the Football League Division II, 1892. Failed to gain re-election 1895. Returned 12 months later. In 1901 they dropped out again. Were not seen in the Football League until the formation of Division III(N) in 1921. Best in Division II, 6th, 1898-9. Honours: Champions, Division IV, 1959-60. Runners-up, Division III, 1960-61. Record attendance: 25,453 v. Newcastle United, Division II, Aug. 29, 1961. Address: Fellows Park, Walsall (Tel. 22791). Nickname: Saddlers. Colours: White with red trim, white shorts. Record League goal-scorer: G. Alsop, 39 goals, Division III(N), 1933-4 and 1934-5. Record victory: 10—0 v.

Darwen, Division II, Mar. 4, 1899.
Record defeat: 12—0 v. Small Heath,
Division II, Dec. 17, 1892; v. Darwen,
Division II, Dec. 26, 1896.

WAR-TIME FOOTBALL

During both World Wars the Football League competition was abandoned. One season was played at the
beginning of World War I (season
1914-15), but at the beginning of
World War II the competition was
immediately abandoned with most
clubs having played three games of
the new season.

In World War I the Football
League carried on with two groups,
Lancashire and Midlands, with the exception of five clubs in the South who,
with the Southern League clubs,
played in a London Combination.

The Football League's regional competition was also divided between a
Principal Tournament and a Subsi-
diary Tournament. The latter was run
towards the end of the season when
the Principal Tournament had been
completed.

The London Combination was also
divided between a Principal Tournament and what was known as a Sup-
plementary Tournament.

As the champions of these competitions are not normally included in
most record books, here they are:

League Competition

Principal Tournament
Lancashire Section
1915-16	Manchester City
1916-17	Liverpool
1917-18	Stoke
1918-19	Everton

Midland Section
1915-16	Nottingham Forest
1916-17	Leeds City
1917-18	Leeds City
1918-19	Nottingham Forest

In seasons 1917-18 and 1918-19, the
champions of each section met each
other at home and away, the winner
on the aggregate score being declared
League Champions.

1917-18   Leeds City 2, Stoke 0;
Stoke 1, Leeds City 0;
Leeds City declared Champions.

1918-19   Nottingham Forest 0,
Everton 0;
Everton 0, Nottingham
Forest 1;
Nottingham Forest declared Cham-
pions.

Principal Tournament
London Combination
1915-16	Chelsea
1916-17	West Ham United
1917-18	Chelsea
1918-19	Brentford

In Scotland during World War I,
Division I carried on as usual, but the
Scottish F.A. Cup was abandoned.

During World War I the F.A. made
a rule that no payment or consideration be made to a club or player for
the player's services.

In World War II, however, the
Football League sanctioned a payment
of 30s. per match but no bonus for
either wins or draws. This fee was the
rule for seasons 1939-40, 1940-41,
1941-2 and 1942-3. Fees were increased to £2 per match in 1943-4,
and £4 per match in 1945-6.

A system of Regional League football was adopted during World War
II. The F.A. Cup was abandoned until
1945, when it resumed on a home and
away basis.

The Scottish League, too, played
on a regional basis.

Here are the Champions of the
principal war-time competitions:

1939-40

Regional League:
South " A " Division—Arsenal.
South " B " Division—Queen's Park
Rangers.
South " C "—Division—Tottenham
Hotspur.
South " D " Division—Crystal
Palace.
Western Division—Stoke City.
South-Western Division—Plymouth
Argyle.
Midland Division—Wolverhampton
Wanderers.
East Midland Division—Chester-
field.
North-West Division—Bury.
North-East Division—Huddersfield
Town.
Scottish West and South—Rangers.
Scottish East and North—Falkirk.

North Regional—Preston North End.

1940-41
South Regional—Crystal Palace.
Scottish Southern League—Rangers.

1941-2
North Regional—Blackpool.
South Regional—Leicester City.
Scottish Southern League—Rangers.

1942-3
North Regional—Blackpool
South Regional—Arsenal.
Scottish Southern League—Rangers.

1943-4
North Regional—Blackpool.
South Regional—Tottenham Hotspur.
Scottish Southern League—Rangers.

1944-5
North Regional—Huddersfield Town.
South Regional—Tottenham Hotspur.
Scottish Southern League—Rangers.

1945-6
North Regional—Sheffield United.
South Regional—Birmingham City.

League War Cup Winners:

1939-40—West Ham United
1940-41—Preston North End.
1941-42—Wolverhampton Wanderers.
1942-43—Blackpool (North)
          Arsenal (South).
1943-44—Aston Villa (North)
          Charlton Athletic (South)
1944-45—Bolton Wanderers (North)
          Chelsea (South).

War-time goal-scorers

The aggregate goal-scoring records for World War II are difficult to establish with real accuracy, because of the number of competitions into which the Football League clubs were divided and because many players appeared for so many clubs as " guests ".

However, there can be little doubt that the following three players were top of the aggregate scoring list in war-time Football League Regional matches 1939-46, inclusive. The figures are as accurate as possible :

A. Stubbins (Newcastle United) 226;
E. Dodds (Blackpool) 221; T. Lawton

(Everton, Tranmere Rovers, Aldershot and Chelsea) 212.

The leading Scottish goal-scorers, 1939-46 include: T. Walker (Hearts), D. Wallace (Clyde), G. Smith (Rangers), R. Flavell (Airdrieonians), J. Calder (Morton and Albion Rovers), D. Wilson (Hamilton Academicals), and K. Dawson (Falkirk).

During World War I, principal goal-scorers included such men as S. Puddefoot (West Ham United), H. Barnes (Manchester City), J. McColl (Celtic), W. Davis (Millwall), E. Simms (Luton Town), H. G. Yarnall (Airdrieonians), and R. Thomson (Chelsea).

In the London Combination in season 1916-17, E. Simms scored 40 goals in 29 matches.

In season 1917-18, S. Puddefoot scored 40 of West Ham United's total of 103 goals in the London Combination.

R. Thomson scored 39 goals in 31 London Combination matches for Chelsea, season 1915-16.

War-time Internationals

War-time and Victory internationals did not count as full internationals and no caps were awarded. The following players made the most appearances in War-time and Victory internationals :

England
S. Matthews (Stoke City), 29; J. Mercer (Everton), 27; T. Lawton (Everton), 23; H. Carter (Sunderland), J. Hagan (Sheffield United), and G. Hardwick (Middlesbrough), 17; L. Scott (Arsenal), 16; F. Swift (Manchester City), 14; L. Smith (Brentford and Aston Villa), 13.

Scotland
T. Walker (Hearts), 11; W. Waddell (Rangers), J. Carabine (Third Lanark), J. Caskie (Everton) and J. Dawson (Rangers), 9.

Ireland
(Victory internationals only)
T. Breen (Linfield), W. McMillan (Belfast Celtic), and J. Vernon (Belfast Celtic), 3 each.

Wales
D. Dearson (Birmingham) 15; W. Hughes (Birmingham), 14; C. Sidlow (Liverpool), 11; R. Burgess (Tottenham Hotspur), H. Cumner (Arsenal) and T. G. Jones (Everton), 10.

WATFORD F.C.

Founded 1898 when West Herts and Watford St. Mary's amalgamated. Joined Football League, Division III, 1920. Honours: Champions, Division III, 1968-9. Record attendance: 34,099 v. Manchester United, F.A. Cup, 4th Round (replay), Feb. 3, 1969. Address: Vicarage Road, Watford (Tel. 21759). Nickname: Brewers. Colours: Gold shirts, black shorts. Record League goal-scorer: C. Holton, 42 goals, Division IV, 1959-60. Record victory: 10—1 v. Lowestoft Town, F.A. Cup, 1st Round, Nov. 27, 1926. Record defeat: 10—0 v. Wolverhampton Wanderers, F,A. Cup, 1st Round (replay), Jan. 13, 1912.

WEATHER

All previous records regarding postponements and abandonments due to the weather were broken in the winter of 1962-3.

The severe spell of cold which lasted for about six weeks began to trouble the football clubs just before Christmas and before the thaw had set in over 400 League and Cup games had been postponed or abandoned in England, Scotland and Wales.

The F.A. Cup programme most affected by the weather was on Jan. 5, 1963. Of the 32 3rd Round ties due to be played 29 were postponed. The entire F.A. Cup programme was postponed, Feb. 8, 1969, but that day only eight 5th Round ties were due to be played.

In League Football in England and Scotland the worst day for a full peace-time programme was Saturday, Feb. 9, 1963. Then there were 57 games postponed because of snow and ice. In all only seven Football League games were completed while the Scottish League programme was completely wiped out.

The Football League programme actually suffered worse on Jan. 12, 1963, and again on Feb. 2, 1963, when only four out of 44 and four out of 43 games respectively were completed. But on that first date Scotland managed to get through eight of their League and Cup games (only seven being postponed), while on the other day the total games postponed amounted to 52, including 13 in Scot

land, where four games were played.

During World War II, on Feb. 3, 1940, only one Regional League game was played out of a total of 56 in the whole of England and Scotland. That was between Plymouth Argyle and Bristol City.

Other bad days in the history of the game arranged here according to the total number postponed or abandoned in Football League, F.A. Cup, Scottish League and Scottish Cup:

Jan. 19, 1963—54 games either postponed or abandoned; Feb. 16, 1963—51; Dec. 30, 1961—43; Dec. 29, 1962—42; Jan. 1, 1968—42; Jan. 15, 1955—41; Jan. 26, 1963—41; Feb. 8, 1969—40; Feb. 15, 1958—39; Jan. 17, 1959—39.

The worst season for postponed and abandoned matches in the Football League prior to season 1962-3 was 1946-7 when the total was 146. But the worst day in that season did not produce such alarming figures as those mentioned above. It was Mar. 8, 1947 when only 18 of the 44 Football League games were played.

The hottest day on which a full League programme was carried out is believed to have been Saturday, Sept. 1, 1906, when the temperature in most parts of the country was just under 90deg. Fahrenheit.

WEIGHT

The lightest player ever to appear in the Football League is believed to have been W. Hepworth, a Barnsley inside-right of the 1890s, who weighed around 7st. 5lb.

Next to Hepworth comes outside-right F. Le May who weighed about 7st. 10lb. during his League career with Thames (1930-31), Watford (1931-2), and Clapton Orient (1932-3).

The heaviest Football League player was probably W. Foulke, the Sheffield United, Bradford City and England goalkeeper of the 1890s and early 1900s. With Sheffield United he gradually increased weight from 15st. to over 20st., and later, while playing for Bradford City, he was said to weigh 25st.

WELSH CUP

The Welsh Cup competition was established in 1877 when the F.A. of Wales paid £170 for a trophy to be competed for by clubs in the Principality and the Border counties.

Wrexham were the first winners when they defeated Druids, 1—0, at Acton Park, Wrexham. They have since won the competition 17 times, more times than any other club.

The Welsh F.A. nearly ran out of money in their efforts to establish this competition. So short were they of the necessary capital that more than 12 months elapsed before they could present the first winners with a set of medals.

WELSH INTERNATIONALS

See INTERNATIONALS (WALES).

WELSH LEAGUE

The Welsh Football League was founded in 1902. Today it has a membership of 48 clubs who are divided into three Divisions.

Cardiff City hold the record for the highest number of points in a single season in the Welsh League. They gained 72 in season 1922-3.

Lovells Athletic have a remarkable record in the competition. They won the championship five times in succession in seasons 1937-8, 1938-9, 1945-6, 1946-7, 1947-8.

WEMBLEY, THE EMPIRE STADIUM

The venue of the F.A. Cup Finals since 1923 and the principal home of the England national team, Wembley Stadium is neither a stadium reserved solely for football, nor the property of the Football Association, nor the home of any particular football club.

It is the property of a limited company and is merely hired to the Football Association on certain occasions.

It was in Jan. 1922, that the Duke of York, later to become King George VI, cut the first turf to mark the beginning of the building of this great sports arena. It was completed in under a year at a cost of £750,000. Some 250,000 tons of clay had to be dug out to form the bowl of the stadium and the stands and terraces were built with 25,000 tons of concrete, reinforced with 600 tons of steel rods. The stands were erected with 1,500 tons of steel girders held together with something like 500,000 rivets.

The F.A. Cup Final between Bolton

Wanderers and West Ham United was the first event to take place in the new stadium on April 28, 1923. 126,047 people were officially admitted and the total receipts were £27,776. However, a conservative estimate of the number of people who entered the stadium, including those who broke in, puts the number at 150,000. It may have been nearer 200,000.

The first Wembley international match was between England and Scotland, April 12, 1924.

In 1962-3 £500,000 was spent on transforming Wembley Stadium into a more up-to-date sports arena. Major operation was the erection of a new roof all the way around so as to afford complete protection to all 100,000 spectators. The inner apron of this roof is covered in fibre glass sheeting to allow maximum daylight to the playing pitch.

League Games

Clapton Orient met Brentford and Southend United in Third Division games at Wembley Stadium in season 1930-31. Their ground at Lea Bridge was banned because it did not fulfil official requirements.

See also AMATEURS (FOOTBALL LEAGUE) The Argonauts A.F.C.

" WEMBLEY WIZARDS "

This title was given to the Scottish international XI which gave such a remarkable display of football in defeating England 5—1, at Wembley, Mar. 31, 1928.

It was England's third defeat of the season in the International Championship, the first time they had ever lost all three games.

The Scottish side which so outclassed England on this occasion included eight Anglo-Scots.

The complete line-up was:
England:

Hufton (West Ham United); Goodall (capt.) (Huddersfield Town), Jones (Blackburn Rovers); Edwards (Leeds United), Wilson, T. (Huddersfield Town), Healless (Blackburn Rovers); Hulme (Arsenal), Kelly (Huddersfield Town), Dean (Everton), Bradford (Birmingham), Smith, W. H. (Huddersfield Town).

Scotland:

J. D. Harkness (Queen's Park); Nelson (Cardiff City), Law (Chelsea); Gib-

206

son (Aston Villa), Bradshaw (Bury), McMullan (capt.) (Manchester City); Jackson (Huddersfield Town), Dunn (Hibernian), Gallacher (Newcastle United), James (Preston North End), Morton (Rangers).

Scorers: England—Kelly. Scotland—Jackson (3) and James (2).

Half-time score: 2—0.

Referee: Mr. W. Bell (Scotland).

WEST BROMWICH ALBION F.C.

Founded 1879. Known as West Bromwich Strollers until title changed to West Bromwich Albion in 1880. One of the original members of the Football League, 1888. Honours: Champions, Division I, 1919-20. Runners-up, 1924-5, 1953-4. Champions, Division II, 1901-2, 1910-11. Runners-up, 1930-31, 1948-9. F.A. Cup: Winners, 1888, 1892, 1931, 1954. Finalists, 1886, 1887, 1895, 1912, 1935. League Cup: Winners, 1966. Runners-up, 1967, 1970. Record attendance: 64,815 v. Arsenal, F.A. Cup, 6th Round, Mar. 6, 1937. Address: The Hawthorns, West Bromwich (Tel. 021-553 0095). Nickname: Throstles. Colours: Blue and white striped shirts, white shorts. Record League goal-scorer: W. "G." Richardson, 39 goals, Division I, 1935-6. Record victory: 12—0 v. Darwen, Division I, Mar. 4, 1892. Record defeat: 10—3 v. Stoke City, Division I, Feb. 4, 1937.

WEST HAM UNITED F.C.

Founded 1900 following the disbandment of the five-year-old Thames Ironworks Club. Elected to Division II, 1919. Honours: Champions, Division II, 1957-8. Runners-up, 1922-3. Best in Division I, 6th, 1926-7, 1958-9. F.A. Cup: Winners, 1964. Finalists, 1923. Winners, European Cup Winners Cup, 1965. Record attendance: 41,643 v. Manchester United, Division I, Jan. 17, 1970. Address: Boleyn Ground, Green Street, Upton Park, London, E.13 (Tel. 01-472 0704). Nickname: Hammers. Colours: Claret shirts with blue sleeves, claret and blue trim, white shorts. Record League goal-scorer: V. Watson, 41 goals, Division I, 1929-30. Record victory: 8—0 v. Rotherham United, Division II, 1957-8 and v. Sunderland, Division I, Oct. 19, 1968. Record defeat: 10—0 v. Tottenham Hotspur, Southern League, 1904-05.

WINNING RUNS

See also AWAY WINS, HOME WINS, DEFENSIVE RECORDS.

In season 1905-06 Bristol City won 14 consecutive League matches and set up a Football League record which was not equalled until 1950-51 when Preston North End recorded the same number. Both clubs were in Division II.

From the start of season 1963-4 Morton gained 23 consecutive victories in Scottish League, Division II. They did not drop a single point until losing 3—1 at East Fife.

In season 1898-99 Rangers (Glasgow) won all 18 of their Scottish League, Division I games. They won the first four games of the following season but then their run of victories was halted with a 1—1 draw against Heart of Midlothian at Tynecastle.

Celtic also had a run of 23 victories (including League, League Cup and European Cup games) to Nov. 5, 1966 when they were held to a 1—1 draw by St. Mirren.

Tottenham Hotspur began season 1960-61 with 11 consecutive victories in Division I. This is a Football League record for the beginning of a season.

WINS, MOST IN A SEASON

Football League

		Wins	Games	
Division I	Tottenham Hotspur	31	42	1960-61
Division II	Tottenham Hotspur	32	42	1919-20
		Wins	Games	
Division III(S)	Millwall	30	42	1927-28
	Plymouth Argyle	30	42	1929-30
	Cardiff City	30	42	1946-47
	Nottingham Forest	30	46	1950-51
	Bristol City	30	46	1954-55

Division III(N)	Doncaster Rovers	33	42	1946-47
Division III	Hull City	31	46	1965-66
Division IV	Crystal Palace	29	46	1960-61
Scottish League				
Division I	Rangers	35	42	1920-21
Division II	Morton	33	38	1966-67

WITHOUT A WIN

The longest run without a win in the Football League was made by Crewe Alexandra during 1956-7. After beating Scunthorpe United, 2—1, Sept. 19, 1956, they did not win again until April 13, 1957, when they defeated Bradford City 1—0—a run of 30 games in Division III(N) without a victory.

Merthyr Town created a Football League record with a run of 61 away games without a win in Division III(S), September 1922 to September 1925.

See also DEFEATS.

WOLVERHAMPTON WANDERERS F.C.

Founded 1877. One of the original members of the Football League, 1888. Honours: Champions, Division I, 1953-4, 1957-8, 1958-9. Runners-up, 1937-8, 1938-9, 1949-50, 1954-5, 1959-60. Champions, Division II, 1931-2. Runners-up, 1966-7. Champions, Division III(N), 1923-4, F.A. Cup: Winners, 1893, 1908, 1949, 1960. Finalists, 1889, 1896, 1921, 1939. Record attendance: 61,315 v. Liverpool, F.A. Cup, 5th Round, Feb. 11, 1939. Address: Molineux Grounds, Wolverhampton (Tel. 24053). Nickname: Wolves. Colours: All gold. Record League goal-scorer: D. Westcott, 37 goals, Division I, 1946-7. Record victory: 14—0 v. Crosswell's Brewery, F.A. Cup, 2nd Round, 1886-7. Record defeat: 10—1 v. Newton Heath, Division I, Oct. 15, 1892.

WORKINGTON F.C.

Founded 1884. Re-formed 1921. Elected to Football League, Division III(N), 1951. Record attendance: 21,000 v. Manchester United, F.A. Cup, 3rd Round, Jan. 4, 1958. Address: Borough Park, Workington (Tel. 2871). Nickname: The Reds. Colours: Red shirts, white shorts. Record League goal-scorer: J. Dailey, 26 goals, Division III(N), 1956-7. Record victory: 9—1 v. Barrow, League Cup, 1st Round, Sept. 2, 1964. Record defeat: 8—0 v. Wrexham, Division III(N), Oct. 24, 1953.

WORLD CHAMPION CLUB

The unofficial championship of the world is contested each year between the winners of the European Cup (League Champion Clubs' Competition) and the South American Clubs' Cup. It is decided on a two leg home and away basis. Originally points decided the winner, but since 1968 it has been decided on goal aggregate.

1960	Real Madrid Champions:
	Penarol (Uruguay) 0, Real Madrid (Spain) 0; Montevideo.
	Real Madrid 5, Penarol 1; Madrid.
1961	Penarol Champions:
	Benfica (Portugal) 1, Penarol (Uruguay) 0; Lisbon.
	Penarol 5, Benfica 0; Montevideo.
	Decider:
	Penarol 2, Benfica 1; Montevideo.
1962	Santos Champions:
	Santos (Brazil) 3, Benfica (Portugal) 2; Rio de Janeiro.
	Benfica 2, Santos 5; Lisbon.
1963	Santos Champions:
	Milan 4, Santos 2; Milan.

Santos 4, Milan 2; Rio de Janeiro.
Santos 1, Milan 0; Rio de Janeiro.

1964   Internazionale Champions:
Independiente (Argentine) 1, Internazionale (Italy) 0; Buenos Aires.
Internazionale 2, Independiente 0; Milan.
Internazionale 1, Independiente 0 (after extra time); Madrid.

1965   Internazionale Champions:
Internazionale 3, Independiente 0; Milan.
Independiente 0, Internazionale 0; Buenos Aires.

1966   Penarol Champions:
Penarol 2, Real Madrid 0; at Montevideo.
Real Madrid 0, Penarol 2; Madrid.

1967   Racing Club Champions:
Glasgow Celtic 1, Racing Club (Argentine) 0; Hampden Park.
Racing Club 2, Glasgow Celtic 1; Buenos Aires.
Racing Club 1, Glasgow Celtic 0; Montevideo.

1968   Estudiantes Champions:
Estudiantes (Argentine) 1, Manchester United 0; Buenos Aires.
Manchester United 1, Estudiantes 1; Old Trafford.

1969   A. C. Milan Champions:
A. C. Milan 3, Estudiantes 0; Milan.
Estudiantes 2, A. C. Milan 1; Buenos Aires.

WORLD CUP

Since World War II the World Cup has developed into one of the most important international sporting competitions and the interest created in almost every part of the globe has had far reaching effects which are felt well outside the limited sphere of football.

The trophy originally presented to the World Cup winners was a gold cup known as the Jules Rimet Cup, after the late Monsieur Jules Rimet, who was Honorary President of F.I.F.A. from 1921 to 1954. This trophy was won outright by Brazil with their victories in 1958, 1962 and 1970.

F.I.F.A. inaugurated the World Congress of 1928 when it was decided to hold a World Championship every fourth year.

Uruguay requested the opportunity of organising the first of these competitions in 1930, but when it took place it was only a pale imitation of a World Cup series, and certainly nothing like as universal as the more recent tournaments. Only 13 countries entered and the competition was won by the hosts.

Italy were hosts of the next World Cup in 1934 and again the host nation emerged as winners. 29 countries took part.

In 1938 the tournament was held in France and from an entry of 25, Italy retained the title.

Because of the war the next competition did not take place until 1950. This was the first time that the home Associations were included among the entries. England, Scotland, Ireland and Wales were not members of F.I.F.A. from 1928 to 1946. (See FEDERATION INTERNATIONALE DE FOOTBALL ASSOCIATION.)

In 1950 the home International Championship was made part of the qualifying competition for the World Cup tournament, the finals of which took place in Brazil. The two top countries in the International Championship qualified for the finals, but while England (winners) went to Brazil, Scotland (runners-up) declined the invitation.

It is now a matter of football history that this was the most disastrous year ever for English football prestige abroad.

On June 25, 1950, at the giant new Rio Stadium, England won her first game against Chile, 2—0. Four days later, however, came the shock: England lost 0—1 at Belo Horizonte, beaten by the rank outsiders—United States of America.

England's final elimination from the competition with a defeat by Spain (0—1) was not so much a surprise, but it proved conclusively that England was no longer at the top of the soccer ladder.

In the Final of this 1950 World Cup the record crowd for a football match, 199,850, assembled at the Rio Stadium to see Uruguay win the trophy for the second time, beating Brazil, 2—1.

In 1954, 35 countries entered. The final tournament took place in Switzerland, and this time, Scotland, as well as England, were among the 14 nations who emerged from the qualifying competition. Added to these were Uruguay and Switzerland, exempted from the qualifying rounds as Champions and hosts respectively.

England's elimination from the competition this year was not as sudden as it had been in 1950. She won through the first round with a 2—0 victory over Switzerland and a 4—4 draw with Belgium. But in the quarter finals, against the Cup holders, Uruguay, England went down 2—4 fighting all the way.

Scotland's display was probably as disastrous a debut for them as the 1950 tournament had been for England. The Scots could not score a goal in their two games and were eliminated in the first round with a 0—1 defeat by Austria and a 0—7 defeat by the Cup holders, Uruguay. Like England, Scotland had fallen from the high pedestal of the soccer masters.

The 1954 tournament will always be notorious because it not only produced one of the finest games ever seen, but also one of the toughest and roughest of international matches. The rough game was the quarter-final between Hungary and Brazil. Hungary won, 4—2, but not before English referee, A. Ellis, of Halifax, had sent off two Brazilian players and one Hungarian, as well as awarding a penalty to either side. Scenes at the end of the game, both on and off the field, were unforgettable as well as unforgivable. Several players, officials and policemen were injured.

Some critics suggested that after this exhibition the World Cup should be abandoned, but all relented when soon afterwards it was seen what good football this tournament could produce. No one can expect to see a finer exhibition of football than the semi-final match between Hungary and Uruguay played at Lausanne on June 30, 1954, and refereed by B. M. Griffiths of Newport (Mon.), Hungary won 4—2.

There is little doubt that the great Hungarian team was still feeling the strain of that game when they met Germany in the Final, four days later. They were well below form and lost 3—2 after being two goals up. The Germans had an outstanding forward line and were deserving winners on the day's play, for they were faster on the rain-soaked pitch. This final was refereed by W. Ling (Cambridgeshire).

The entry for the 1958 World Cup increased to 51 countries. Four of these withdrew without playing a game.

England, N. Ireland and Scotland qualified for the final tournament, while Wales, though eliminated with a defeat by Czechoslovakia, subsequently got through after being appointed to meet Israel when Egypt and Sudan had withdrawn. Wales then beat Israel to qualify.

In the final tournament which took place in Sweden, England and Scotland were eliminated in the first round, but both Wales and Ireland got through to the quarter-finals by dint of some surprisingly good performances. For instance, Wales shook the soccer world by holding Hungary to a draw and later by defeating that same country when they met again in a play-off. Ireland had two victories over Czechoslovakia. The second being a particularly gallant effort achieved despite injuries and in a strenuous game which went into extra time.

It was no surprise when Ireland's valiant effort was brought to a close with a 4—0 defeat by France, while Wales, resorting largely to negative football, were beaten 1—0 by Brazil.

Brazil, who had not made a very convincing show in getting to the Final, then produced their real form in that match to beat Sweden 5—2.

England was the only representative of the British Isles to reach the final tournament of 1962 in Chile. 56 countries had entered for this competition and England went as far as the quarter-finals before losing 3—1 to Brazil who carried off the trophy by beating Czechoslovakia 3—1 in the final played in Santiago.

53 countries competed for the 1966 World Cup in which England as the

host country was automatically seeded to the final tournament and then went on to win the coveted trophy with some determined football and a particularly well organised defence.

England finished top of her group and then beat Argentine in a dramatic quarter-final, Portugal in a so entertaining semi-final, and West Germany in a final which proved to be a real test of endurance, the game going into extra time before England emerged the winners by 4 goals to 2.

England's team in the Final tie: Banks; Cohen, Wilson; Stiles, Charlton, (J.), Moore; Ball, Hurst, Hunt, Charlton (R.), Peters.

Automatically seeded to the Finals in 1970 England were eliminated by West Germany in the Quarter Finals, the Germans fighting back from 2—0 to win 3—2 in extra time.

Although highly organised and particularly strong in defence this series served to highlight the weakness of England's attackers in the art of shooting and heading as compared with the Brazilians.

Results of World Cup Finals (the name of the "host" and the number of National Associations who actually took part in each competition are given in parentheses):

1930	Uruguay 4, Argentine 2. (Uruguay) (13). 90,000
1934	Italy 2, Czechoslovakia 1† (Italy) (29). 50,000
1938	Italy 4, Hungary 2. (France) (25). 45,000
1950	Uruguay 2, Brazil 1. (Brazil (29). 199,850.
1954	West Germany 3, Hungary 2 (Switzerland) (35). 60,000
1958	Brazil 5, Sweden 2. (Sweden) (47). 49,737.
1962	Brazil 3, Czechoslovakia 1. (Chile) (53). 68,679.
1966	England 4, West Germany 2† (England) (53). 96,924
1970	Brazil 4, Italy 1 (Mexico) (69). 107,000.

† After extra time

The record individual scoring feat for a single game in the World Cup Final tournament is four goals. Eight players have scored this number as follows:

G. Wetterstroem, Sweden v. Cuba, 1938; Leonidas da Silva, Brazil v. Poland, 1938; E. Willimowski, Poland v. Brazil, 1938; Ademir, Brazil v. Sweden, 1950; S. Kocsis, Hungary v. W. Germany, 1954; J. Schiaffino, Uruguay v. Bolivia, 1950; J. Fontaine, France v. West Germany, 1958; Eusebio, Portugal v. N. Korea, 1966.

Best individual aggregates for Final tournaments (six or more goals)—13, Fontaine (France), 1958; 11, Kocsis (Hungary), 1954; 10, Muller (W. Germany), 1970; 9, Eusebio (Portugal), 1966; 8, Stabile (Argentine), 1930, Leonidas (Brazil), 1938; 7, Szengeller (Hungary), 1938, Ademir (Brazil), 1950, Jairsinho (Brazil), 1970; 6, Morlock (W. Germany), 1954, Pelé (Brazil), and Rahn (W. Germany), 1958.

The leading goal-scorer in each tournament can be seen in the above list except the 1934 finals when top place was shared by Schiavio (Italy), Nejedly (Czechoslovakia), and Conen (Germany), each with four goals, and the 1962 finals when top scorer was Jerkovic (Yugoslavia) with five.

Brazil created a record by playing through 13 games undefeated (P. 13, W. 11, D 2) in the Final Tournaments of 1958, and 1962, and until beaten 3—1 by Hungary in their second game in England in 1966.

WREXHAM F.C.

The oldest Association Football club in Wales, founded 1873. One of the original members of Division III(N), 1921. Honours: Runners-up, Division III(N), 1932-3. Runners-up, Division IV, 1969-70. Record attendance: 34,445 v. Manchester United, F.A. Cup, 4th Round, Jan. 26, 1957. Address: Racecourse Ground, Mold Road, Wrexham (Tel. 2414). Colours: Red shirts with white trim, white shorts with red stripe. Record League goal-scorer: T. Bamford, 44 goals, Division III(N), 1933-4. Record victory: 10—1 v. Hartlepools United, Division IV, Mar. 3, 1962. Record defeat: 9—0 v. Brentford, Division III, Oct. 15, 1963.

Y

YORK CITY F.C.

Founded 1903. Adopted profession-alism, 1912. Club re-constituted 1921 as a limited company. Elected to Foot-ball League, Division III(N), 1929. Re-cord attendance: 28,123 v. Hudders-field Town, F.A. Cup, 5th Round, Mar. 5, 1938. Address: Bootham Cres-cent, York (Tel. 24447). Colours: White shirts with red trim, white shorts. Record League goal-scorer: W. Fenton, Division III(N), 1951-2, and A. Bottom, Division III(N), 1955-6, 31 goals. Record victory: 9—1 v. Southport, Division III(N), Feb. 2, 1957. Record defeat: 12—0 v. Chester, Division III(N), Feb. 1, 1936,

YOUTH FOOTBALL

Since World War II a number of national and international competitions catering for players under the age of 18 (usually they are between 16 and 18) have been created.

The principal competitions in what is known as " Youth Football " are as follows:

International Youth Championship: Representative teams of each of the four British Associations, namely, the F.A., the Scottish F.A., the F.A. of Wales and the Irish F.A. meet each other once during each season, the championship being decided on a points basis. Only players who are under 18 years of age on the 1st Sept. of the current season and are members of an " Amateur " club under the jurisdiction of one of the four National Associations are eligible to take part.

This competition was inaugurated in season 1947-8.

International Youth Tournament: This is another amateur competition for youths of the same age as the above but this under the auspices of

F.I.F.A., includes several European countries. The tournament is played over a period of four or five days, usually at Easter, at a different centre each year.

The inaugural tournament took place in England in season 1947-8 and included teams from eight different countries.

Internationals: Youth internationals other than the above competitions are also played each season between the home Associations and foreign Associa-tions, but these games include profes-sionals. All players are under the age of 18 at the start of the then current season.

F.A. County Youth Challenge Cup Competition: A knock-out cup com-petition for amateurs under the age of 18 (on Sept. 1). Each team being re-presentative of one of the County F.A.s in England affiliated to the Football Association.

This competition was inaugurated in 1944-5 when it was won by Staf-fordshire F.A.

F.A. Youth Challenge Cup: This competition is also played on a knock-out basis but it differs from the above in that it is played between club sides and professionals may be included. All players must be under the age of 18 on the *commencing day of the current season.* Professionals must have been registered with their clubs as profes-sionals for at least 14 days before the match, unless already qualified as amateurs, and the latter must have been a recognised playing member of his club for the same minimum period.

This competition was inaugurated in season 1953-4 with the trophy being donated by the Football League, which was appropriate enough as most of the Football League clubs enter their youth sides.

YUGOSLAVIA

Yugoslavia was the first Continental side to escape defeat in England in a ful international. That was in November 1950 when they forced a 2—2 draw at Highbury.

Yugoslavia's record in international matches since the war places her well to the fore among the leading football powers in the world. The country's record in major international competitions speaks for itself:

World Cup: 1930—Semi-finalists. 1934—Failed to qualify. 1938—Failed to qualify. 1950—Eliminated in first round of final tournament. 1954—Quarter-finalists. 1958—Quarter-finalists. 1962—Semi-finalists. 1966 and 1970—failed to qualify.

Olympic Games: 1920—1st round. 1924—1st round. 1928—1st round. 1936—Did not enter. 1948—Runners-up. 1952—Runners-up. 1956—Runners-up. 1960—Winners. 1964—Quarter-finalists. 1968—Did not enter.

Yugoslavia, as a country whose boundaries resemble those in existence today, did not come into being until 1918, and their Football Association was founded in the following year, but it is known that football was played in Belgrade at least 20 years earlier. The oldest of the senior League clubs is Hajduk (Split) formed in 1911.

After four or five years of part-time or severely restricted semi-professionalism the Government lifted their ban and full-time professionalism was adopted in 1966.

There are 4,090 registered clubs, but the First Division of the National League numbers only 18.

Address of the governing body: Futbalski Savez Jugoslavije, 35, Terazije, Belgrade. Colours: Blue shirts, white shorts, red stockings.

Results of international matches:

May 18, 1939	Yugoslavia 2, England 1; Belgrade.
Nov. 22, 1950	England 2, Yugoslavia 2; Highbury.
May 21, 1953	Yugoslavia 5, Wales 2; Belgrade.
May 16, 1954	Yugoslavia 1, England 0; Belgrade.
Sept. 22, 1954	Wales 1, Yugoslavia 3; Cardiff.
May 15, 1955	Yugoslavia 2, Scotland 2; Belgrade
Oct. 19, 1955	Eire 1, Yugoslavia 4; Dublin.
Nov. 21, 1956	Scotland 2, Yugoslavia 0; Glasgow.
Nov. 28, 1956	England 3, Yugoslavia 0; Wembley.
May 11, 1958	Yugoslavia 5, England 0; Belgrade.
June 8, 1958*	Scotland 1, Yugoslavia 1; Sweden.
May 11, 1960	England 3, Yugoslavia 3; Wembley.
May 9, 1965	Yugoslavia 1, England 1; Belgrade.
May 4, 1966	England 2, Yugoslavia 0; Wembley
June 5, 1968†	England 0, Yugoslavia 1; Florence.

* World Cup   † Nations Cup

INDEX

216

217

222